Atlantic

Cousins

ALSO BY JACK FRUCHTMAN JR.

AUTHOR:

Thomas Paine: Apostle of Freedom

Thomas Paine and the Religion of Nature

*The Apocalyptic Politics of Richard Price and Joseph Priestley:
A Study in Late-Eighteenth-Century English Republican
Millennialism*

EDITOR:

*Common Sense, Rights of Man, and Other Essential Writings of
Thomas Paine* (with an introduction by Sidney Hook)

A Life in Jewish Education: Essays in Honor of Louis L. Kaplan

Britain in the Hanoverian Age, 1714–1830: An Encyclopedia
(associate editor for politics, history, and religion)

*An Eye-Witness Account of the French Revolution by Helen Maria
Williams: Letters Containing a Sketch of the Politics of France*

Atlantic
Cousins

BENJAMIN FRANKLIN AND
HIS VISIONARY FRIENDS

Jack Fruchtman Jr.

THUNDER'S MOUTH PRESS
NEW YORK

ATLANTIC COUSINS
BENJAMIN FRANKLIN AND HIS VISIONARY FRIENDS

Published by
Thunder's Mouth Press
An Imprint of Avalon Publishing Group Inc.
245 West 17th St., 11th Floor
New York, NY 10011

AVALON
publishing group incorporated

Library of Congress Cataloging-in-Publication Data is available.

ISBN 1-56025-668-0

9 8 7 6 5 4 3 2 1

Book design by Jamie McNeely
Printed in the United States of America
Distributed by Publishers Group West

To Jane K. Schapiro

Contents

Illustrations

The Rev. George Whitefield by John Wollaston, 1742
National Portrait Gallery, London

Anthony Benezet Instructing Colored Children
From John Warner Barber, *Historical, Poetical and Pictorial
American Scenes.* (New Haven: Published for J. H. Bradley, 1850).

Granville Sharp by G. Dance, engraved by Henry Meyer, 1820
The Library of Congress, Washington, D.C.

Dr. Benjamin Rush by Charles Willson Peale, 1783
Courtesy of the Winterthur Museum
Gift of Mrs. Julia B. Henry

Thomas Paine by James Watson, 1783
National Portrait Gallery, Smithsonian Institution,
Washington, D.C.

The Rev. Joseph Priestley by Rembrandt Peale, 1801
Collection of The New York Historical Society

The Rev. Richard Price, engraving after Benjamin West, 1793
National Portrait Gallery, London

Jean-Paul Marat by H. Grévedon after J. Boze, 1793
Wellcome Library, London

Franz-Anton Mesmer, 1766
Wellcome Library, London

The Marquis de Condorcet by François Bonneville
Photo Courtesy of The Newberry Library, Chicago

Jacques-Pierre Brissot by N. F. Maviez after François Bonneville
National Portrait Gallery, London

Prologue

Franklin's Atlantic Cousins

L iberal eighteenth-century writer-activists in England, America, and France created a remarkable archipelago of ideas and visions of the future. Exchanged in an atmosphere of steady transatlantic communication, their published and private correspondence, which numbers into the thousands of letters, were two ways they transmitted social and political views, sometimes to their own hazard. Governmental authorities, always on the lookout for subversive material, often opened and read letters between private citizens. Published correspondence frequently exposed them to arrest and imprisonment. Some were often in danger of execution and even eventually suffered death for their views. Many held views that we would regard as incomprehensible in the twenty-first century: how the universe works, how to cure disease, what the meaning of madness is, how best to achieve political and social goals.

Still, they were earnest in their efforts even when they faced

1

immovable barriers held up against them or, worse, failure. They exchanged books, pamphlets, and essays that either they or others had written, and they sent each other articles from newspapers and journals that caught their attention. They told one another stories they had read or heard about. They met in coffeehouses and in salons to continue the discussions, much of which criticized the foibles of their governments. All this was in an effort to carry on an international exchange of ideas at a level the world had never before seen. In a way, these writer-activists were conspirators because of their passionate dedication to transform the world in accordance with their liberal values. Even if they were only loosely organized, many of them—the Americans especially, but also the French—brought about the changes that became the keystone for the founding of the modern democratic state.

For a long time I considered how best to identify these writer-activists appropriately, and as the reader may tell from the very first word, I chose the term "liberal" rather than "progressive," "reformist," or even "radical." I rejected the last three mainly because I thought they did not quite fit in with the thoughts and dreams of Benjamin Franklin and his Atlantic cousins, his "visionary" friends. "Progressive" has become encumbered by that period in late nineteenth-/early twentieth-century American history that we call the Progressive Era. "Radical" was a term not commonly used in the sense of a political strategy until the early nineteenth century. While the *Oxford English Dictionary* reports the earliest usage by the Dissenting minister and reformer John Jebb in 1786, it was not until after 1798 that it referred to thorough and complete change in English politics. Finally, "reformist" is ambiguous because it may mean change in any direction: toward the past, to recapture an earlier set of political and social relationships (Edmund Burke argued that the English Revolution was reformist), or toward the future, to restructure government in ways that may or may not be in the common interest, but only in the interest of the few.

I have settled on calling them "liberals" because that is precisely what they were. Eighteenth-century "liberals" wanted to achieve the end of tyranny, rank, and privilege. They wanted to see a new society and a new politics based on representative government, constitutional protections that guaranteed a free press, free speech, and religious liberty, and ultimately a sense of fair play, justice, and equity in the legal system. For them, the American Revolution and the new American government that came into being in 1789 were models for all European nations that were still ensnared by the iron rule of kings and aristocrats. Franklin himself decried the Society of the Cincinnati when he heard of its existence while he was the American minister in France. The society, formed by veteran army officers and financiers after the Revolution, was nominally a charitable organization, but its members were often accused of desiring to create a hereditary aristocracy in the new United States. Its bylaws allowed for only eldest sons to become members. George Washington served as its president-general. Franklin thought the society was the dangerous beginning of nobility in America. Rights and privileges by heredity were not only "groundless and absurd," he wrote, but also "hurtful." Besides, he said, after nine generations, some three hundred years, the blood of the founding ancestors will be so diluted that descendants will possess only 1/512 of the original blood flowing in their veins.

Just who were these Atlantic cousins of Franklin, and what was their vision of a better future? In this study, we will examine the life and work of several men who considered Franklin their friend, men who shared many of his values about politics and society, science and technology, and civic education. They all shared a common vision of the possibilities of what they could do to improve the world, through political action (by war and revolution, if necessary), through societal change (such as the abolition of slavery and the slave trade), or through scientific and technological invention. They valued enlightenment, progress, and improvement. Optimism reigned.

They believed human beings possessed the potential to achieve all of their earthly goals and, in some cases, even otherworldly ones. In society this meant the spread of greater freedom and fewer taxes; and in politics, it meant the establishment of the republic, where citizens participated in making the decisions that affected everyone. Vigorous political campaigns, open public debate, and free and contested elections were the hallmarks of the democratic republic, where virtuous representatives worked hard to help their constituents and to contribute to the common good of society.

Their story follows three major countries where Franklin resided throughout his extraordinary career. First, we find him among his friends in America, where Franklin was born in 1706 and worked, except for a very early two-year stay in England, until 1757, when he became the Pennsylvania colonial agent to London. Dr. Benjamin Rush, regarded as a founder of modern medicine, was also a prominent political and social activist. Rush's older friend, the pamphleteer Thomas Paine, played a pivotal role in the American cause and then went off to France to continue the battle there for justice and freedom. George Whitefield, an English Methodist minister, became famous up and down the American East Coast for his outdoor preaching. His liberal ideas were blemished by an unfortunate reliance on slavery, while he continually advocated the humane treatment of all creatures, including slaves (today, one wonders how this would work). Unlike Whitefield, Anthony Benezet was one of the great Philadelphia abolitionists of his time. He opened schools for black children because he understood better than anyone that all children, no matter their race or previous condition of servitude, had the same intellectual and social abilities. Finally, Granville Sharp, a leading London advocate for abolition, acts as a transitional figure for Franklin from America to England. Sharp never knew Franklin in Philadelphia as did Rush, Paine, Whitefield, and Benezet, but he had a profound impact on his older American friend in turning him against slavery in the mid-1770s.

Franklin lived in London on two long occasions, from 1757 to 1762, and then again from 1764 to 1775. There he enjoyed convivial relations with two important liberal activists. Richard Price and Joseph Priestley were both Unitarian ministers, but they were also passionate political commentators and scientists. Price is today regarded as a founder of actuarial science (the science of the life insurance industry), and Priestley is best known as the discoverer of the chemical element of oxygen. Both were deeply religious—in fact, both were trained Presbyterian ministers who adopted a Unitarian faith (Priestley today is regarded as a founder of modern Unitarianism). They argued that the transforming events in their time, such as the American and French Revolutions, were manifestations of an unfolding divine plan. Priestley even went further and argued that the spirit of God dwelled in all things throughout the entire universe, so much so that, for him, the universe was mainly composed of spirit, not matter.

In 1776, just after the publication of the Declaration of Independence, Franklin was named the first American minister to France in an effort to secure French aid and support during America's Revolutionary War against Britain. He served in that position until his "retirement" in 1785, when he returned to Philadelphia. Almost as soon as he set foot in Philadelphia, he was not only elected to the Pennsylvania Supreme Executive Council but also served as its president, and within two years he became a delegate to the American constitutional convention at the remarkable age of eighty-one. During his years in Paris, Franklin met a wide array of fascinating, even eccentric, people. Perhaps Jean-Paul Marat and Franz-Anton Mesmer were among the most intriguing. Marat is probably best known for his rabid actions and murderous talk during the French Revolution and his eventual murder in his bathtub in the summer of 1793. Before that notorious time, however, he was a respected physician and scientist, who politely asked Franklin to endorse his many scientific discoveries. Mesmer, also trained as a physician, developed what some historians of science say was an early form of hypnosis and psychiatry. Others, however, believe he was merely a quack. But he, too, like Marat, asked Franklin to witness his experiments and hoped the great scientist would endorse them. (Both men were sorely disappointed.) Finally, two prominent political writers, who themselves believed they were friends of Franklin, developed views of political and social change during the French Revolution and paid the ultimate sacrifice for advocating their ideas: the Marquis de Condorcet, a mathematician and the permanent secretary of the *Académie royale des sciences,* the Royal Academy of Sciences, and Jacques-Pierre Brissot, the leader of the Girondin faction that actually headed the French government in 1792 and 1793.

Some of these men were experimenters in science like Priestley and Marat, in architecture and engineering like Paine, in medicine like Rush and Mesmer, or in actuarial science like Price. Many of them held idealistic views of a political future, like Paine, Rush, Priestley, and Price or Condorcet and Brissot. Some argued for their vision of the central importance of education, such as Rush's founding of Dickinson and Franklin Colleges or Price and Priestley in their lifelong work in the English Dissenting academies (the institutions of higher education for those young men who were not admitted to Oxford or Cambridge because they chose not to be members of the Church of England). Condorcet practically stood alone as an advocate of women's education on the same scale as that for men. In addition, many of them were convinced that inevitable human social progress would ameliorate the evil conditions of poverty or landlessness, something Paine was deeply concerned about when he drafted a social welfare plan, or when we understand the vision of a godly future held by those like Priestley and Rush, who believed in the coming Millennium.

All were liberal, intellectual men of action who devoted their lives to doing practical things to bring about their vision of a better future; in short, they were men of the Enlightenment or men of many "enlightenments." They were what the eighteenth century called philosophes, not philosophers such as David Hume or Immanuel Kant. Their concerns led them to develop concrete political and social programs rather than "intricate philosophical stories." Surely they were intellectuals, because they were deeply engaged in formulating and discussing new ideas, but they were also men who actively tried to implement these ideas into practice. They fought long and hard for their principles, opposing everything from slavery and torture to injustice and tyranny.

They all wanted to perform good deeds, as they called them. Franklin, too, believed that a person's highest calling in life was to do good, to improve life in practical ways. As a young Philadelphia printer in 1727, he formed a group of similarly minded young men who often met to discuss the issues of the day—usually seeking ways to improve Philadelphia life. Based on ideas that Franklin drew from Cotton Mather in Boston, who argued that the best thing a person could do in life was to contribute to the improvement of society, these Leather Apron Men became Franklin's Junto, as he called it, his friends in the trades who met weekly to discuss the issues of the day or any subject that fancied their imaginations. As he bluntly told the orthodox Christian Joseph Huey in 1753, even the God of the most pious believers, like Huey, would prefer "the Doers of the Word to the meer [*sic*] Hearers. . . . Those who gave Food to the Hungry, Drink to the Thirsty, Raiment to the Naked, Entertainment to the Stranger, and Relief to the Sick, &c. tho' they never heard of his Name, he declares shall in the last Day be accepted, when those who cry Lord, Lord; who value themselves on their Faith tho' great enough to perform Miracles but have neglected good Works shall be rejected." (Church ministers in the eighteenth-century Church of England as Latitudinarianism had expressed these same ideas with an emphasis on salvation through good works, not faith alone.)

From that time onward, Franklin developed friendships and

associations with many people—not all of whom were visionary in the sense described here. Franklin and his Atlantic cousins were dreamers, but they were also doers, bound by the bonds of friendship to varying degrees. All of them wholly encompassed Washington's adage that "true friendship is a plant of slow growth; to be sincere, there must be a congeniality of temper and pursuits."

In the three venues of America, England, and France, we find Franklin's visionary friends working tirelessly to perform good works to bring an end to heredity, rank, and privilege; to end slavery and the slave trade; to spread freedom throughout the world; and to bring about improvements in the daily lives of the ordinary citizen. Never once did these men hesitate to submit their work to the public for comment and criticism, to air their views to convince those who were straggling behind them, and to argue with those who disagreed with them.

While they all shared a boundless curiosity about life, no figure had an impact on them as enormously as Benjamin Franklin. If we can say he was the hub in the intellectual wheel, then they were its spokes and often its sparks. Because Franklin lived almost through the entire century, he knew scores of people, and even more knew of him, respected or perhaps even hated him, the vast majority of which will not appear here. Those selected for this study are writers and activists who have not only interested me for many years, but who, as major thinkers, illustrate the power of Franklin's influence. The reader will immediately note that no women appear in this group. While Franklin knew many women (and flirted with scores of them, even wanting to marry at least one of them in France in his later years), he did not know well those who fit into the category of what I call "visionary." Mary Wollstonecraft was too young; and Madame Helvétius, even as the wealthy widow of a great philosopher and Encyclopedist, offers us only her life as a salonnière. Historian Daniel Royot said of her: "a coquette with the airs of Molière's Célimène, Madame Helvétius entertained young abbots in her home, flirting with Tout-Paris and throwing parties night and day." Nor is there any evidence that Franklin knew the work of botanist Jane Colden, whose work was not discovered until the middle of the nineteenth century (he did know and correspond with her father, Franklin's longtime correspondent Cadwallader Colden).

While Franklin's long life was not always a straight line of achievement and goodwill, he comes across the pages of history as someone who, though flawed, wore his mistakes and indiscretions with character, humor, and charm. Even late in life, when he was in his seventies and lived in Paris as the American minister famously flirting with the ladies of the court, he seems to us not as an old crackpot out of his element, but as someone in control of a situation that he—and they—clearly enjoyed. History presents him as having had few blemishes—until two recent studies concentrated on the darker side to his personality. Now we know more clearly than ever that he made enemies, held grudges, and often schemed against those whom he could not tolerate. Nor can we always believe him when he told someone something—and this included his wife, Deborah: his motives were often self-serving. Everyone knows that no matter how much of a charmer he was, he had a Brobdingnagian ego. He was many things throughout his long life—a printer, an editor, a publisher, an essayist, a scientist, an inventor, a diplomat, a statesman, a philanderer—but he was always, above all else, the consummate and wildly practical and successful entrepreneur and a most effective one at that, especially when it came to making money and selling himself. But even with bad publicity, we still regard Franklin, more than two hundred years after his death, as the best of the best among those in America's founding generation. As a model of the good citizen and statesman, he virtually personified George Washington's call in his *Farewell Address* that "virtue or morality is a necessary spring of popular government." His many achievements magnetize us still.

A short list of some of Franklin's visionary achievements hardly does him justice, but it gives us a sense of the range of his interests and successes. In politics he was an elected official in Philadelphia, first to the city's Common Council in 1748 and then later the Pennsylvania Assembly in 1751, becoming its speaker in 1764. In 1753, by royal appointment, he became deputy postmaster general of America. He negotiated treaties with the American Indians, and he advocated American colonial union under the aborted Albany Plan as early as 1754—which was eventually rejected by both the British government and the colonies. He served in the Second Continental Congress in 1775 (the Congress that eventually resolved to break with England), and at the end of his life he served as the president (as the office of governor was then called) of the Commonwealth of Pennsylvania. But as his inclination was always to be a man on the move, a doer, he served as the agent of Pennsylvania (and later for Georgia, New Jersey, and Massachusetts) in England on two occasions, in 1757–1762 and 1764–1775, and then as the American minister to France from 1776 until his "retirement" in 1785, only to return to America to serve in the constitutional convention two years later.

He was influential in founding voluntary associations, pulling together groups of citizens to improve the conditions of their city and to enhance the intellectual and creative powers of the individual. He developed the first lending library, the Library Company of Philadelphia, in 1731 and organized the first fire department in America four years later. In 1749 he developed the plan for the Philadelphia Academy, later the College of Philadelphia, which opened two years later and by the end of the century became the University of Pennsylvania. In 1743 he founded the first true learned society in America, the American Philosophical Society. Eight years later he argued for and won passage of a bill to create the Pennsylvania Hospital. Both Mozart and Beethoven composed music for his glass armonica, an instrument he improved upon that produces sounds of unusual beauty and which is still played today (contemporary musicians compose orchestral pieces for it as a solo instrument). His bill providing for Philadelphia night watchmen and street-lights passed the Pennsylvania Assembly in 1756. His numerous inventions include "the 'long arm' (grandfather of the gadget used by grocers to take small boxes down from shelves), a stool that opened up into a ladder, a rocking-chair that fanned the reader while he rocked, a letter press . . . bifocal glasses (badge of many a library scholar) . . . and an improved form of stove which posterity has named in honor of the inventor, the 'Franklin stove,' but which he called the 'Pennsylvanian fire-place.'"

Most Americans know Franklin as the scientist who har-nessed electricity from the sky with his lightning experiments (though one recent scholar has raised questions about whether he ever really flew the kite), leading to his lightning rod in 1750 that proved to be controversial on both sides of the Atlantic. He attached one of these for the first time to his own house in 1752. Awarded the Royal Society of London's Copley Medal in 1753 for his work on electricity, three years later he was unan-imously elected a member of the society itself. Three years after that, he received an honorary Doctor of Laws from the Univer-sity of St. Andrews in Scotland, and thereafter he was known as Dr. Franklin, though he never referred to himself with the hon-orific. Oxford followed up three years later with an honorary Doctor of Civil Law. He became a foreign member of the German Royal Society in 1766, and six years later, a foreign associate (*associé étranger*) of the *Académie royale des sciences*.

As a prolific writer as well as a very successful printer, Franklin earned enough money to "retire" from the printing business at forty-two when he turned the day-to-day operations over to his partner, David Hall, while receiving half the profits. *Poor Richard's Almanack,* written between 1732 and 1757, his essays in the *Pennsylvania Gazette,* which he bought in 1728, his auto-biography, and hundreds of other works, including his corre-spondence, demonstrate his amazing productivity in the letters.

There was hardly a subject that did not attract his imagination and attention. From politics and science to the very light subjects in his hoaxes and bagatelles, Franklin's interests were enormously wide-ranging—and he did them all well.

Some commentators have accused him of bigotry and deception. Some claim he embellished his autobiography or simply failed to tell the truth, trying to convince his readers that he was "a model American hero." Moreover, like many men of means in Philadelphia, he owned black slaves as early as 1748. But in just three years we find him writing about the economic weaknesses of slavery, and he eventually became a staunch abolitionist and made arrangements to free his slaves as early as 1757.

Franklin also had a vindictive and bitter side. He spent a great deal of time fighting with and even hating the Penns, the absentee Pennsylvania proprietors, trying to force them to pay a share of the colony's defense against French and Indian attacks. When they refused, in the 1760s he led the Pennsylvania Assembly's fight to have them removed, by asking the king and Parliament to transform Pennsylvania into a royal colony under the jurisdiction of the Crown. Perhaps his obsession with the Penns skewed his vision of what America was and what it could be. He became a fawning admirer of George III and his chief advisor, Lord Bute, and might well have temporarily lost his perspective of asserting American interests to the ministry.

Still others, such as John Adams, did not like Franklin. When Adams arrived in France, he immediately thought that the minister was an old, lazy bon vivant—and Adams was not all wrong.

Nonetheless, one thing is certain: the America, England, and France of the eighteenth century were undergoing rapid transformation. Invention and experimentation were major watchwords of the moment in politics and society, science and technology, and even religion and faith. Franklin himself once noted that "this is the Age of Experiments," while his young protégé Thomas Paine insisted that "we live to improve, or we live in vain." It was a time of innovation, from trying to develop new ways to improve the daily lives of the common people and to develop new forms of government. Americans especially, in their quest for progress, were engaged in a struggle to overcome tyranny and superstition of all kinds: from the old, wrong-headed theories of science to the physical enslavement of men by other men. Alexis de Tocqueville could have been thinking of Franklin himself when he described how Americans in particular took seriously the great French philosopher René Descartes's emphasis on the application of scientific principles to practical, everyday use: "America is therefore one of the countries where the precepts of Descartes are best studied, and are best applied."

But the same was true of England and France. If the Americans by the end of the century achieved independence and a nascent republican state, the French were wrapped in the throes of revolution and ultimately the Reign of Terror that forever changed the landscape of their nation. Britain, too, was changing: though it suffered under the challenge that the French Revolution posed to all monarchical regimes, it was gradually entering into the age we now call the Industrial Revolution just as it was on the verge of extending the vote to a larger (though still male) electorate. These changes were not the direct result of any particular action taken by Franklin or his visionary friends—men like Rush and Paine in America, Price and Priestley in England, or Condorcet and Brissot in France—but all of them contributed to these manifest transformations.

Like Franklin, they were curious about the nature of man and the universe in which he lived; how he might live better; and what technological, medical, scientific, and even social and political transformations were necessary to make life better, easier, and fulfilling. Some of these men believed they were doing God's work on earth revealing the mysteries of His creation, whereas others thought they were doing what they thought best for everyone. In a very real sense, human liberation meant destroying the intellectual and physical shackles that were constricting mind and body. For many, especially Franklin himself and Rush later in life, but also Condorcet and Brissot, this meant advocating the end of slavery and the slave trade. They were not always successful in promoting a new life of dynamic social, political, and religious freedom (where engagement meant dedicating one's entire career to laying the foundations for a fair and just society); many of them died trying to succeed, notably Condorcet and Brissot.

In short, Franklin's visionary friends, like the great polymath himself, envisioned a world in an ineluctable state of political and social improvement, making them participants in the Enlightenment optimism that human progress and achievement were inevitable. The eighteenth century, particularly its last three decades, produced major transformations in politics: new experimental governments, first in America and then France, provided new political forms very different from the corrupt states from which they emerged. It was an age that worshipped reason, progress, and human rights.

The central political aspiration of most of these men was to create the republic where citizens, however they were defined, participated in decision making in an ongoing search for the best way to preserve human rights and liberty. Liberal writers in America and England saw that America's war against England and the creation of the American republic provided the foundation and model for future betterment, an archetypal political framework that was transferable to the English-speaking world in general. With the revolution in France, these ideas became even more radicalized in the argument that revolution was a worldwide phenomenon applicable to every geographical area of civilization.

Moreover, their world was one that marveled at new scientific and technological discoveries and experiments. Franklin was well known not only as the man who did everything, but who did everything well: he served as a supreme model for those younger men who came not only to know him, but also to admire and respect him. Some of their ideas were very strange and wondrous indeed. Benjamin Rush, trained as a physician, was deeply concerned with the welfare of his patients and never hesitated to try to develop new skills and new remedies to cure them (many seem controversial and oddball to our—and even his own—generation). His copious use of bleeding and vomiting to cure the body sent many of his fellow physicians into paroxysms of anger and hysteria. For Price and Priestley, unlocking the mysteries of God's universe through scientific and mathematical inquiry would lead them to learn how to set all people free from tyrannical scientific ideas and political policies. Meantime, Priestley developed very strange ideas about the nutshell theory of matter (all of the matter in the universe could fit into a nutshell). He left many of his readers for a time wondering what that was all about. Condorcet denied the role of God in everyday affairs while he passionately argued that his analytical inquiry into mathematics, statistics, and probability could be directly applied to make politics truly rational. Jean-Paul Marat and Franz-Anton Mesmer, who were, like Rush, trained physicians, dedicated their lives to improving physics and medicine—though the scientific establishment soundly, almost angrily, rejected them and their work. It is no wonder that the French Revolution transformed Marat into a manic revolutionary, the persona we most recall in history. But Marat and Mesmer were serious and curious scholars whose contacts with Franklin were imperative to them if they were to have their work accepted by the scientific establishment in France.

In the eighteenth century, the practical application of ideas to everyday life and politics was embodied in several organizations. In Franklin's America we see it in the spirit of cooperation and enterprise he promoted when he organized his fellow leather-apron workers into the Junto. More significant still was the intellectual outgrowth of the Junto, the American Philosophical Society, which he formed in 1743, the western hemisphere's counterpart to the learned societies of most major European countries. Here men of learning gathered to discuss the major issues of the day. Franklin was its first secretary, and served as its president until his death (his immediate successors were astronomer and instrument maker David Rittenhouse and Thomas Jefferson).

In England two groups in particular, the Royal Society of London and the Club of Honest Whigs, were focal points for Franklin and his English friends. These groups prove the principle that contexts clearly conditioned thought. The Royal Society of London was the most prestigious scientific association in the world. Founded in 1660, the society, which included Isaac Newton among its early presidents, was designed to promote scientific and intellectual discussion in the physical sciences and to advise the government on these matters. Unlike its French counterpart, the *Académie royale des sciences,* which included only the most accomplished scientists in France (and only eight foreign associate members), the membership of the Royal Society was not limited to professional scientists such as the botanist Sir Joseph Banks or the physicist Sir Humphry Davy (both of whom served as its president in the late-eighteenth and early-nineteenth centuries). By 1780 nearly three-quarters of the society's members were nonscientists. The glue holding them together was a vast and endless curiosity about the nature of the universe. They read papers to one another, corresponded in a continual flow of letters, traded essays about their experiments, and published two of the most important scientific journals of their (and our) time, the *Philosophical Transactions,* dating from 1771, and its *Proceedings.* For his world-famous work on electricity, Franklin was unanimously elected a member in 1756, the year before he arrived in London as the Pennsylvania agent.

A social and political counterpart to the Royal Society was Franklin's group of visionary thinkers and doers who met every other Thursday evening to discuss everything from scientific discoveries to issues of political controversy—similar to the Algonquin Roundtable in the 1930s in New York. Franklin called it his Club of Honest Whigs. The club met during the winter, first at St. Paul's Coffeehouse, and then, in 1772, at the London Coffeehouse, where the members permanently set up shop. It included among its members Peter Collinson, who sent books and other material to Franklin from London for the new Library Company of Philadelphia. There you would also find the political writer and historian James Burgh; physicians John Pringle and John Fothergill; the Dissenting ministers Andrew Kippis, Richard Price, and Joseph Priestley; and Franklin's closest London friend until the Revolutionary War, the printer William Strahan. Brissot visited there, and James Boswell, Samuel Johnson's companion and biographer, was a member— though he scarcely ever attended. Once, Boswell noted that on one evening "much was said against the Parliament." It was, he went on, a collegial group where they talked "pretty formally, sometimes sensibly, and sometimes furiously." They began the evening by drinking and smoking and then dined at nine. Franklin did not smoke; Benjamin Rush later reported that Franklin told him "he had never snuffed, chewed, or smoked," though, to Rush's consternation, he was no teetotaler. The club provided these men with the perfect venue to discuss what was on their minds, to argue how new inventions and technologies and new directions in society and politics, and religion, too, could lead to a better world for everyone.

Finally, in France, the *Académie royale des sciences* was a rigorously constructed organization whose members were very fussy about who may or may not join their ranks. As one of the rare foreign members of the *Académie*, Franklin knew its permanent secretary, the Marquis de Condorcet, when he first attended its meetings while serving as minister to France from 1776 until 1785. Although Franklin was initially impressed with the work of Marat and Mesmer (or shall we say, he found their experiments and practices curiously and oddly interesting—he served on official *Académie* commissions that reviewed their work), once it became clear that Condorcet and other officials viewed their ideas as heretical or just plain silly, he consented to deny them admission. They never forgave the French scientific leadership—although they seemed not to begrudge Franklin his role in their rejection—and railed against it for the rest of their lives.

Just as political reform and transformation and scientific and technological discovery were an intrinsic part of Franklin and his visionary friends' lives and work, so was the involvement of many of them in seeking the abolition of slavery and the slave trade.

One of the most fascinating aspects of Franklin's life and personality in the fifty-year period from the 1730s to the late 1780s was the evolution of his views about the slave trade and slavery; he evolved from slave owner to abolitionist. No matter how brilliant or creative Franklin was, he was a fairly conventional man. His changing views about slavery illustrate this point. It is not enough to say we should not ascribe to eighteenth-century men and women political and social positions that are appropriate for the twenty-first century; certainly, Franklin knew many Philadelphia and English abolitionists. Nonetheless, he also knew that many people in his world accepted slavery and understood that one way to increase the slave population was to transport them from Africa to America. For forty years he condoned the slave trade and the institution of slavery—and he even owned slaves himself. In time, however, he gradually became aware of the inherent evil of both the institution and the trade.

Perhaps his evolving consciousness resulted from his association with very strong and articulate abolitionists on both sides of the Atlantic. By the mid-eighteenth century, as the international trade began to slow, an active internal trade remained on the Continent. Attitudes began to change, too, when for religious and moral reasons the Pennsylvania Quakers began to advocate emancipation. According to David Brion Davis, the preeminent historian of slavery, "partly because of the Friends' testimony against war, slaveholding occasioned moral tensions that were less common among other denominations." The anti-slavery movement generated even greater momentum after the Seven Years' War, which ended in 1763. But Quaker efforts were uneven. George Fox, the founder of the Society of Friends, had taught a century before that all human beings were equal in the sight of God. Although he condemned the practice of slavery in 1671, he never advocated abolition; his main purpose was to advocate the education of slaves. It took another hundred years before the Philadelphia Meeting voted to prohibit Quakers from owning slaves. While many Quakers, among them Anthony Benezet, finally convinced their co-religionists to advocate a ban on the trade and an end to the institution, they were far slower in persuading others. We do, however, find that a number of Anglicans like Granville Sharp in England and Presbyterians like Benjamin Rush in America supported their efforts and worked with them. The abolitionist societies in America and England were mirrored in France with the creation of the *Société des Amis des Noirs,* the Society of the Friends of the Blacks, a creation of Condorcet and Brissot in 1788.

As the international slave trade declined, abolitionists increased their pressure to end the institution itself. Franklin's longtime English friend, the Dissenting minister Richard Price (a member of Franklin's Whig Club and an early supporter of American independence), wrote a small advice book for the Americans in which he included all the reform ideas of his era: a warning against standing armies, against a national debt, the dangers of paper money, the separation of church and state, and the need for public education. He did not fail to include his desire that the Americans should end slavery immediately—not only because slavery was not economically viable or because it was morally wrong, but because the Americans themselves might wind up as slaves if they persisted in hanging on to the practice. "For it is self-evident, that if there are any men whom

19

they have a right to hold in slavery, there may be *others* who have had a right to hold *them* in slavery." Needless to say, Price's advice was not taken. That abolition of slavery did not take place until after the American Civil War with the ratification of the Thirteenth Amendment in 1865 is a testament to the tragedy of the abolitionists' failure, but not to their aspirations and advocacy.

At the center of all these movements was Benjamin Franklin, who worked tirelessly to ensure that the world would be better when he left it than when he entered it. Though no single métier ever defined him (printer, scientist, inventor, writer, journalist, editor, publisher, statesman, diplomat . . . individually, each is insufficient), a common denominator is clear: politics was always in Franklin's lifeblood, because he understood at an early age that change would most likely be successful if the political establishment supported it. His achievements in Philadelphia before he left for London in 1757 demonstrate what a single individual can do to improve the lot of ordinary people. His actions, especially late in life, serving as president of Philadelphia's abolitionist society, indicate that almost until his death he was willing to fight for what he believed to be right and just.

These same qualities, as we shall see, permeate the vision of his younger friends and admirers who dedicated their lives, just as he did, to civic improvements and political change—even to the point of revolution and death. This study, then, is designed to illuminate the work of these extraordinary late-eighteenth-century visionary men whose liberal ideas and ideals have carried into our own time. And in the front line of their ranks stood the towering figure of Benjamin Franklin, certainly one of the most extraordinary and remarkable of Americans in the past two centuries.

America

1

Three Men and the Horrors of Slavery: Whitefield, Benezet, and Sharp

Three men—George Whitefield, Anthony Benezet, and Granville Sharp—had profound influences on Benjamin Franklin's thinking about black slavery. Each in his own way impressed upon Franklin the growing importance of the abolition movement, and although he himself owned slaves and advertised them for sale in his *Pennsylvania Gazette,* he was finally persuaded that not only were blacks as intelligent and educable as whites, but that for them to reach their greatest potential they had to be freed from the shackles of slavery and, worse, the horrors of the slave trade.

Again, it is too facile an argument to say we cannot ascribe contemporary ideals to an earlier era; many people in the eighteenth century, educated and uneducated alike, found slavery abhorrent. To Franklin's credit, over time, he too saw the reason for the abolitionists' argument.

The great outdoor English Methodist evangelist George

Whitefield and Franklin enjoyed "an uncommon friendship." Perhaps more than any other man in the 1730s and 1740s, Whitefield influenced Franklin's thinking about the humane treatment of slaves. Born in England in 1714, Whitefield came from a middle-class family; his father was a wine merchant, and he thought he, too, was destined for the wine trade. But as an undergraduate at Oxford, it became clear to him he could combine his love of acting and public speaking in a pious life. He fell under the spell of the Wesley brothers, John and Charles, the cofounders of Methodism, and joined their religious society, derisively called the "Holy Club" by students who did not attend its meetings. Ordained into the Anglican Church at age twenty-two, Whitefield became a Methodist—a movement that all three young men believed would cleanse and purify the Church. They fervently remained Anglican churchmen, whose goals were to reform the Church from within to generate a new spiritual awakening among its members. Dedicating themselves to an ascetic way of life, "they lived by an exact method that regulated everything they did: how they spent each hour and each penny;" for long hours they studied scripture methodically (hence, "Methodism") to find its true meaning.

Whitefield came to Georgia in 1738, and the following year he arrived in Philadelphia. A thunderous and charismatic speaker, he was "one of the first modern celebrities," a revivalist from the same mold as modern evangelists such as Billy Sunday, Billy Graham, and Robert Schuller. As his fame grew, he drew thousands to hear his message stressing the evils of original sin. Franklin was impressed. He found that Whitefield held an amazing sway over those who heard him and later recalled that "the multitudes of all sects and denominations that attended his sermons were enormous, and it was matter of speculation to me, who was one of the number, to observe the extraordinary influence of his oratory on his hearers. . . . From being thoughtless or indifferent about religion, it seem'd as if all the world were growing religious, so that one could not walk

The Reverend George Whitefield (1714–1770) preaching, by John Wollaston, 1742. (The female figure in the front is most likely Mrs. Whitefield.) Courtesy of the National Portrait Gallery, London.

thro' the town in an evening without hearing psalms sung in different families of every street."

Of medium height and well proportioned, Whitefield's "complexion was very fair, his features regular, and his dark blue eyes small and lively. In recovering from the measles he had contracted a squint with one of them; but this peculiarity rather rendered the expression of his countenance more remarkable, than in any degree lessened the effect of its uncommon sweetness." It is said that Whitefield's severe comportment and dignity made most people ignore or forget about his eyes, although Horace Walpole once noted that he seemed to have one eye on heaven, the other on earth. His appearances were fervently anticipated. Said one Connecticut follower in 1740 as he witnessed the twenty-six-year-old Whitefield, "When I see Mr. Whitefield come upon the Scaffold, he looked almost angelicall [*sic*]—a young, slim, slender youth before some thousands of people, and with a bold, undaunted countenance. And my hearing how God was with him everywhere as he came along, it . . . put me in a trembling fear before he began to preach, for he looked as if he was Cloathed with authority with the great God." Here we see the origins of a truly American civil religion, where faith and politics combined to proclaim that God's work could be achieved in this life through political and social action.

Whitefield was blessed with a remarkably powerful voice. David Garrick, the great actor, was said to have observed that he would give a hundred guineas to be able to say "Oh" like Whitefield. According to a contemporary of Whitefield's, Sir George Beaumont, Whitefield did not roar, but his "voice could be heard at an immense distance; but that was owing to its fulness [sic], roundness, and clearness. It was a perfectly sound voice. It is an odd description, but I can hit upon no better; there was neither crack nor flaw. To describe him as a bellowing, roaring field preacher, is to describe a mountebank, not Whitefield." A friend of his once claimed that the preacher had addressed upward of eighty thousand people at one time, and he never denied it. As incredible as that sounds in an age before voice amplification, Franklin described how he determined the number of people who could reasonably hear Whitefield at any one time. While Whitefield was speaking from the top of the courthouse steps on Market Street, Franklin walked backward as far as he could, until he got to the Schuylkill River—where noises from the water and traffic along Front Street obscured Whitefield's voice. From this distance, Franklin measured the area taken up by a semicircle around which Whitefield had been speaking, and concluded that "he might well be heard by more than Thirty-Thousand. This reconcil'd me to the Newspaper Accounts of his having preach'd to 25000 People in the Fields, and to the antient Histories of Generals haranguing whole Armies, of which I had sometimes doubted." It is, needless to say, both an amusing and edifying image to picture Franklin in mental-wrapped calculations while around him thousands stood in rapt reverence.

Whitefield not only preached the gospel in America, he also helped the Wesley brothers and James Oglethorpe settle the colony of Georgia. Whitefield's goal was to establish an orphanage—which he called "Orphan House"—for children whose parents had died while establishing settlements there. His main purpose, of course, was religious; namely, to instruct the children in his religious teachings and influence them to join the clergy. He used his magnificent voice and powers of persuasion to raise money throughout America for this purpose. In Philadelphia his words not only had the great effect of motivating people to sing psalms, they also prompted the city fathers to close the concert and dancing hall and the assembly room. Such things, he thought, were inconsistent with the teachings of the gospels. On hearing him preach, Franklin later said that Whitefield often became so riled that he called his listeners *"half Beasts and half Devils."*

Although Whitefield never wanted to separate from the Church of England, the Anglican clergy eventually barred him from their pulpits for that very reason. He was far too zealous and filled with religious enthusiasm, and, to the horror of his colleagues, he often criticized the clergy for being insufficiently religious. He once wrote that he "was much carried out in bearing my testimony against the unchristian principles and practices of our clergy." In any case, because he could not preach in the churches, Whitefield preached wherever he could draw a crowd. On his first trip to Philadelphia, in 1739, the young preacher's reputation was such that Franklin and others made plans to build a large indoor auditorium for him. Completed in 1740, it was named the New-Building. Franklin thought it should be open to all people, no matter their religious background or beliefs—but Whitefield objected. He said that if the building were designed for him to preach in, only the "converted" (perhaps what we would call today "Born Again Christians") would be allowed to attend. The building was also to house a charity school for children. Ten years later, in 1750, this structure—this school, in fact—became the location of Franklin's Philadelphia Academy, the institution that eventually became the University of Pennsylvania. Whitefield immediately signed on as a trustee of the academy at its creation.

His power as a preacher aside, by all accounts Whitefield seems to have been a genuinely affectionate man, who inspired friendship in those around him. Franklin found his own respect shifting into something more personal. Writing in 1747, he said, Whitefield "is a good man and I love him." Franklin was hardly alone. In 1765 the young Benjamin Rush, then studying to be a physician, poured out his heart to a friend after he saw Whitefield preach, exclaiming, "O, sir, it was a sight that no doubt pleased and astonished angels, to see such a number of faithful zealous ministers convened in one place and eating and drinking around the Lord's table." One woman remarked that she found him so cheerful in his disposition, "It tempted her to be a Christian." Not so Franklin, at least not a Whitefield Christian: "He us'd indeed sometimes to pray for my Conversion, but never had the Satisfaction of believing that his Prayers were heard. . . . Ours was a mere civil Friendship, sincere on both Sides, and lasted to his Death." Or, as one of Whitefield's biographers puts it, "In the end, Franklin became Whitefield's best American friend and, reciprocally, Whitefield was Franklin's only evangelical friend. . . . Such was their mutual affection that Franklin forever encouraged Whitefield to look after the state of his badly deteriorating health, while Whitefield continually encouraged Franklin to look after the state of his badly deteriorating soul." Apparently neither one was successful in his task: Whitefield suffered terribly from asthma (ironic, considering his strong lung power), which eventually killed him in 1770, and Franklin died never having achieved—or, for that matter sought—the piety that Whitefield desired for him.

Still, the two men were together whenever Whitefield was in Philadelphia, as their collaboration on the construction of the

New-Building demonstrated. In fact, the preacher often stayed at the Franklin home, and in 1756 Franklin even proposed that they join together to establish a colony in the western lands. In the *Pennsylvania Gazette,* Franklin continually reported White-field's travels throughout America and England in his pursuit of establishing his Orphan House—which he would later name Bethesda ("house of mercy"), and would end up being built out-side of Savannah.

Franklin began to publish Whitefield's works soon after they met. Whitefield himself reported in November 1739 that Franklin "told me he has taken above two hundred subscriptions for printing my *Sermons and Journals*"; and Whitefield told Franklin he wanted him to print his autobiography. Franklin soon adver-tised that he would be selling the sermons and journal in two volumes for two shillings each. By May of 1740 he announced in the *Gazette* that the print run was already oversubscribed. As Frank Lambert has stated, for Franklin especially, but for all colonial printers, "Whitefield was a hot commodity representing profits in the print markets. Franklin's ledgers reveal the evan-gelist as fast-moving inventory."

In addition to the sermons, Franklin began printing White-field's writings on slavery. One of these was a hard-hitting tract that Franklin released as a pamphlet in 1740. In it, Whitefield attacked the manner in which masters treated their slaves, using words that could have been drawn from the Hebrew prophets:

> *Your dogs are caressed and fondled at your tables; but your slaves who are frequently styled dogs or beasts, have not an equal privilege. They are scarce permitted to pick up the crumbs which fall from their masters' tables. Nay, some, as I have been informed by an eye-witness, have been, upon the most trifling provocation, cut with knives, and have had forks thrown into their flesh: not to mention what numbers have been given up to the inhuman usage of cruel task-masters, who by their unrelenting scourges, have*

*ploughed upon their backs, and made long furrows, and at
length brought them even to death itself.*

He called the perpetrators of such acts "monsters of barbarity,"
and suggested that if slaves should "get the upper hand" by
Providence's will, "all good men must acknowledge the judgment would be just."

That Whitefield used an image of a master and his dog is not
surprising. Slaves often wore padlocked collars. The collars
were sometimes decorated with pieces of silver, depending on
the wealth of the owner. However decorative they may have
appeared, they were certainly not jewelry nor were they intended
to dress up a horrible human condition. They were degrading
emblems of slavery. But even more so, they were handy devices
with which the masters could hold the slaves or tie them up like
animals. (We could, of course, spend pages enumerating the
degradations of slavery: slaves were muzzled, shackled, and
chained or forced to wear thumb screws, and they were, of
course, sold at auction.)

Franklin never commented on whether these aspects of
slavery bothered him. We do have, however, his 1751 comments about slavery, which appeared in his essay, "Observations
Concerning the Increase of Mankind, Peopling of Countries,
&c.," a plan for America to become a stronger nation. Included
in the essay were ideas Franklin thought American leaders
ought to consider, from food and animal production to ways to
increase the marriage rates. He could not ignore slavery. Nor
did he endorse it. However, he made it clear that his interest
was only in how well America's white population would fare in
the future. Slavery, he argued, stunted the progress of a nation
because of its bad effect on white people. He feared whites
would rely so heavily on slaves that they would become idle and
lazy. "The Whites who have Slaves . . . are enfeebled," he said,
and slavery's impact on their children was even worse: "The
white Children become proud, disgusted with Labour, and

being educated in Idleness, are rendered unfit to get a Living by Industry." Franklin could not help noting the slaves' obvious misfortune: "The Slaves being work'd too hard, and ill fed, their Constitutions are broken, and the Deaths among them are more than the Births."

But Franklin concluded his essay with some strong observations on race. He noted that most of the world's population was nonwhite, either black or "tawny" or "swarthy," and that only two races belonged in America: the indigenous people, who, he said, included the red man and the white newcomer. His definition of a "good" versus an "inferior" race was skewed in favor of the English and Anglo-Americans—and clearly against the continental Europeans. So we have the swarthy races, which included "Spaniards, Italians, French, Russians, and Swedes . . . as are the Germans." Only the English (and he included the Saxons) were truly a white people (unless Franklin knew swarthy Germans or Swedes, he was doubly mistaken about them). And then in a kind of reverie, he suggested that if there were people residing on distant planets, he hoped that "their [the white's] Numbers were increased."

Franklin's solution was simple: keep the Africans out of America: "Why increase the Sons of *Africa,* by Planting them in *America,* where we have so fair an Opportunity, by excluding all Blacks and Tawneys, of increasing the lovely White and Red? But perhaps I am partial to the Complexion of my Country, for such Kind of Partiality is natural to Mankind." Franklin's only redeeming words were embodied in Whitefield's warning that blacks ought not be mistreated, especially when they lived in a far-off country, like Africa. Of course, he did not advocate the end of slavery or the slave trade. He merely argued that America was for whites and reds only.

What changed Franklin's mind was his later encounter with an effort led by the Associates of Dr. Bray, an English organization that was originally part of the Society for the Propagation of the Gospel in Foreign Parts. Founded in 1701, as its name suggests, the society was the missionary branch of yet another religious organization, the Society for Promoting Christian Knowledge. Its organizer, Thomas Bray, the vicar of St. Botolph, Aldgate, was also a missionary active in Maryland who wanted to convert as many people as possible in North America and the West Indies to Anglicanism. In 1723 an offshoot organization developed, called Dr. Bray's Associates for Founding Clerical Libraries and Supporting Negro Schools. After Bray died, seven years later, the group continued to work according to the principle that black children should be educated because they were as capable as white children.

While in London in 1759, Franklin was invited to join the Associates of Dr. Bray as an American member (by this time, thanks to his relationship with Anthony Benezet, Franklin was convinced that black children could at least be educated). A year later he was elected its chairman. Samuel Johnson (often referred to as Dr. Johnson) was also a member, and it was there that Franklin met the celebrated essayist. The first schools for black children in the colonies opened in Philadelphia, but soon others were established in New York, Rhode Island, and Virginia. Deborah Franklin, Benjamin's wife, was so impressed with the Philadelphia school that she enrolled her "Negrow boy," Othello, in it. Franklin visited these schools when he went on tour as deputy postmaster in 1763, after his return from England. Like Whitefield, he found the "Negro" children "to have made considerable Progress in Reading for the Time they had respectively been in the School, and most of them answer'd readily and well the Questions of the Catechism; they behav'd very orderly, showd a proper Respect and ready Obedience to the Mistress. . . . I was on the whole much pleas'd, and from what I then saw, have conceiv'd a higher Opinion of the natural Capacities of the black Race." Remarkably, he really did not see any intellectual difference between black and white children, especially "Their Apprehension," which was "as quick, their Memory as Strong and their Docility in every Respect equal to that of the White Children."

Whitefield was never to go this far. When Bethesda, Whitefield's orphanage near Savannah, Georgia, tottered on shaky financial grounds, he supported slavery as a means to make the orphanage profitable. Whitefield "held out the possibility that the institution might bring spiritual benefit to the slaves themselves," and besides, "the legality of slavery posed no problem for Whitefield." As Whitefield himself noted, "Whether it be lawful for christians to buy slaves, and thereby encourage the nations from whence they are bought to be at perpetual war with each other, I shall not take upon me to determine; but sure I am it is sinful, when bought, to use them as bad as, nay worse than brutes." He searched the scriptures and claimed he never once found there a prohibition against slavery. Worse, he himself owned slaves, and at his death in 1770 he willed them along with Bethesda and all of his possessions to the Countess of Huntingdon. Three years after Whitefield's death, in an event redolent of sweet irony and pointing toward the potential existence of divine intervention, Bethesda burned to the ground.

Franklin's connections with Whitefield's attack on the mistreatment (if not the institution) of slavery and his later relationship with the Bray Associates gave Franklin pause when he considered slavery, even as early as 1740. Franklin might have thought that Whitefield's criticism of the mistreatment of slaves did not apply to him directly, since he most likely did not own slaves in 1739 and perhaps not until he retired in 1748—and there have never been reports that he physically abused them. He likely treated them with humanity and kindness (though they were still slaves, of course). Now with Whitefield's admonitions before him, he had to consider how others abused their human property. His association with Whitefield had clearly planted in his mind the seeds of reservations about the future of slavery in America. An even greater influence was his friend, the Philadelphia Quaker abolitionist Anthony Benezet.

Anthony Benezet (1713–1784) instructing colored children. From John Warner Barber, *Historical, Poetical and Pictorial American Scenes.* (New Haven: Published for J. H. Bradley, 1850).

A near contemporary of Franklin's, the Huguenot Benezet had fled France with his family and become a Quaker in England before he immigrated to America. In Philadelphia he became a lifelong schoolmaster in the Friends' English school. He later founded two schools—one for white children, the other for free black children—and he even taught black children in the evenings in his home for many years. In 1770 he convinced the Quakers to open an "Africans' School in Philadelphia, and the first class included an equal number of boys and girls, some twenty-two in all." They learned the usual basics of reading, writing, and arithmetic, but the girls also learned practical skills such as how to sew and knit, while the boys studied more advanced academic subjects. Between 1770 and 1775, some 250 blacks, including some adults, attended the school.

A mild man, Benezet believed in a simple, modest life. He was nearly always frail in health, a man who possessed a "quiet, calm disposition, combined with an urbanity of manners—truly a French trait." He is also said to have been "an ugly man, with courtly manners and a warm human charm." Benezet believed in temperance, and he influenced Benjamin Rush's views against alcohol consumption. As an early follower of holistic medicine, Benezet loved to garden as a hobby and grew herbs for medicinal purposes. He was widely admired and respected: J. Hector St. John de Crèvecoeur, the author of the famous *Letters from an American Farmer*, once said that Benezet was "a man whom I have loved for twenty years." Benezet's wife, Joyce, was said to be "a simple, wise, and sweet damsel." She was just twenty-two when they married. A lovely young Quaker of "piety, ready sympathy, and open-handed hospitality," she was the perfect match for the man she married.

Rush, a devout Presbyterian with deep learning in scripture, once characterized Benezet as a "holy man." In 1774 he told Granville Sharp, the great English abolitionist, that Benezet

> *is not only a good man, but a great man in the full import of those words. He appears in every thing to be free from prejudices of all kinds, and talks and acts as if he believed all mankind however diversified by color—nation—or religion to be members of one grand family. His benevolence and liberality are unbounded—I believe he has not spent an idle hour for these forty years. In a word—he seems to have lived as if he always had in his eye, and upon his heart the words of our Saviour "Wist ye not that I must be about my Father's business."*

Benezet's epitaph, Rush later commented, would simply say, "'He went about doing good.'"

Years later, when Jacques-Pierre Brissot traveled to America, he stopped in to see Benezet. He said he was deeply impressed with Benezet's school for black children: he was amazed to find "a land where these poor Negroes are believed to have souls and intelligence, where there is felt obligation to shape their character to virtue and to give them instruction." The pupils were truly learning to read, write, and calculate, just as white children had done for ages. "America owes this useful establishment to Benezet," he went on, and he asked, if blacks can learn whatever

Benezet taught them, then why were they not free? As far as Brissot was concerned, slaves were "property acquired by theft." Who then could work on their behalf if not men like Benezet?

Benezet was a self-effacing man with high principles. According to Rush, "few men, since the days of the Apostles, ever lived a more disinterested life;" and the Chevalier de Chastellux, who fought alongside Lafayette during the American Revolution and was a member of the French Academy, said that Benezet was always "wholly occupied with the welfare of mankind." Indeed, perhaps they all thought as Brissot did. Benezet was so impressive that Brissot rhetorically asked, "Where is the man in all Europe, of whatever rank or birth, who is equal to Benezet?" In all, Benezet wrote nine tracts against slavery between the 1750s and his death in 1784.

Franklin first came to know Benezet perhaps as early as 1735 when Benezet became a customer at Franklin's printing office. He was also an early financial contributor to Franklin's newly established Philadelphia Hospital (his name is listed among the subscribers). A year later, when local Indians attacked the Moravian community in Bethlehem, Pennsylvania, and the town needed guns, ammunition, and other supplies, Benezet suggested that Franklin was the man the town should appeal to, and the supplies were sent.

At the time Franklin was drafting his "Observations concerning the Increase of Mankind," long before Benezet opened his schools, Benezet began a writing campaign attacking slavery and the slave trade. After some experience with blacks in the classroom, Benezet wrote that he could "with truth and sincerity declare, that I have found amongst the negroes as great variety of talents, as among a like number of whites; and I am bold to assert, that the notion entertained by some, that the blacks are inferior in their capacities, is a vulgar prejudice, founded on the pride or ignorance of their lordly masters; who have kept their slaves at such a distance, as to be unable to form a right judgment of them." These were just the views that

Franklin would express when he visited the black charity schools a few years later on his tour as deputy postmaster.

Benezet was among the first to try to change the minds of most of his non-Quaker friends, including Whitefield, and he even wrote to the Archbishop of Canterbury, Thomas Secker, asking him to intervene on behalf of poor black slaves. He told Secker that their masters had subjected "them to a state of perpetual bondage, the most cruel and oppressive, in which the English nation is so deeply engaged." He apprised Secker of "the great inhumanity and wickedness which this trade gives life to, whereby hundreds of thousands of our fellow creatures, equally with us the objects of Christ's redeeming grace, and as free as we are by nature, are kept under the worst oppression, and many of them yearly brought to a miserable and untimely end." Although Benezet failed to change the minds of either Whitefield or Secker, he was successful in persuading many of his co-religionists to oppose the slave trade. He even succeeded in convincing some of them to join him in asking Parliament to end the practice. More important, he also had an impact on Franklin, who soon began to consider how he could help blacks. Franklin knew that those who were free still had little hope of a manageable life, because they had no education and therefore few prospects of advancing themselves. As he was to learn with the Associates of Dr. Bray, schools could be established on their behalf, as Benezet had done in Philadelphia.

Benezet's first major contribution against the slave trade and slavery appeared in 1766, a book with a title that encompassed his views: *A Caution to Great Britain and her Colonies in a Short Representation of the Calamitous State of the Enslaved Negroes in the British Dominions.* Here he hoped to convince Parliament to abolish both aspects of slavery. He based his argument on religion and morality. First, the trade and slavery denied the truths of the gospels and the inner-light spirituality that the Quakers promoted. Slaves, he said, are undoubtedly the brothers of the slave owner: "his neighbors, the children of the same

Father, and some of those for whom Christ died, as truly as for the planter himself." Indeed, because Christ had died for the sins of all the people, the inherent equality in his life and death made blacks the equal to whites. After all, God had "imposed no involuntary subject of one man to another."

Moreover, it was not only against the gospels but also philosophically unethical for one person to claim ownership over another, because under natural law, all men were born free and equal. Benezet cited several legal and moral authorities to bolster his case. The most well known were the works of the French philosopher, the Baron de Montesquieu, and the Scottish philosopher, Francis Hutcheson. Slavery was simply unjust and shocking to humanity. Benezet also noted that the Scottish jurist George Wallace had argued that "no man has a [legal] right to acquire or purchase" another man; "men and their Liberty are not either saleable or purchaseable," so "every one of those unfortunate men, who are pretended to be slaves, has a right to be declared free." In a later work, *Historical Account of Guinea,* published five years later, Benezet argued that the people of Africa had been mostly happy and prosperous until the English slave traders arrived. The British and the Americans would now experience God's just retribution, which they had always hoped to avoid, for "the blood of *one* man unjustly shed calls loudly for vengeance."

By 1772 Benezet persuaded John Wesley that slavery was theologically and ethically wrong. Had Whitefield lived long enough (he died two years before), perhaps Benezet could have convinced him as well. In 1774 Wesley published his *Thoughts on Slavery,* in part a plagiarism of Benezet, sounding the tocsin to devote the last twenty years of his life to the abolitionist movement. Franklin, too, was rapidly changing his mind. We can see clear evidence of his transformation in a piece he wrote in 1770 for *The Public Advertiser* while he was in England. In "A Conversation on Slavery," he reported a dialogue that allegedly took place between an Englishman, a Scot, and an American, all unnamed, though Franklin was undoubtedly the American: the Englishman accused all Americans of hypocrisy. As the great English reformer and abolitionist Granville Sharp argued, the Americans claimed they wanted to promote liberty, but as slave-holders they could not say they favored freedom. The American [Franklin] responded he thought that Sharp was "too severe upon the Americans, and passes over with too partial an Eye the Faults of his own Country."

But thanks to Anthony Benezet, Franklin was soon to meet Sharp himself and change his views of the man, and of slavery. When he finally came round to advocating the end of slavery and the slave trade, Franklin argued that the principal duty of white society was to educate the freedmen. "To instruct, advise, to qualify those, who have been restored to freedom, for the exercise and enjoyment of civil liberty, to promote in them habits of industry, to furnish them with employments suited to their age, sex, talents, and other circumstances, and to procure their children an education calculated for their future situation in life." These goals promoted the public good not only for the white citizens of Pennsylvania but for the blacks too. They led to "the happiness of these our hitherto too much neglected fellow-creatures."

Two years after Franklin wrote these words, the case of James Somerset was one of the most important legal English proceedings of the century. Somerset, a slave from Virginia, had taken his freedom by fleeing his master once he set foot on English soil, and Lord Chief Justice Mansfield eventually ruled in Somerset's favor. Benjamin Franklin, then in London, immediately wrote to Anthony Benezet to tell him he was delighted to hear that as a result of the court's decision, opposition to slavery was growing in America. "I am glad to hear that the Disposition against keeping Negroes grows more general in North America," Franklin said. "Several Pieces have been lately printed here against the Practice, and I hope in time it will be taken into Consideration and suppress'd by the Legislature. Your Labours have already been attended with great Effects. I hope therefore you and your Friends will be encouraged to proceed [to advocate the end of slavery generally]."

Franklin was of course wrong. While there may have been some increased opposition to American slavery, it was mainly directed against the trade, not the institution. Benezet reminded Franklin of the appalling numbers of slaves involved in the trade: "By a late computation there is now eight hundred and fifty thousand negroes in the English Islands and Colonies; and an hundred thousand more yearly imported, by our Nation; about a third of this number is said to perish in the passage."

These staggering figures were as horrifying to Franklin as they were to Granville Sharp, the great English (and Anglican) abolitionist. By the time Sharp took Somerset's case to court, he had already spent half a lifetime advocating the end of slavery and seeing to it that British courts freed individual slaves, even if they did not end the practice itself. In May of 1772 Benezet wrote to Sharp that he thought he should meet Franklin, because the American scientist and diplomat "has a due sense of [slavery's] iniquity and evil consequences, and would, I am persuaded, use his influence that an end should be put to the trade." He then made the introduction through correspondence. By February of the next year, Franklin wrote to Benezet that "I have commenc'd an Acquaintance with Mr. Granville Sharp, and we shall act in Concert in the Affair of Slavery." Benezet immediately wrote to Sharp, using almost the same language, that he was "glad to understand from my friend Benjamin Franklin, that you have commenced an acquaintance, and that he expects in future to act in concert with thee in the affair of slavery." Franklin had already indicated in his 1770 "Conversation on Slavery" that he was familiar with Sharp and his work.

A curious fact is that had Sharp stuck to his professional career, which was working as a clerk in the state ordnance office, neither Franklin nor we would ever have heard of him. Few people today recall Sharp as the single most important voice for humanitarian reform in England at a time when children and the poor were regularly beaten or imprisoned for light offenses. For the English slave, life presented a horrid existence. Often called "personal servants" by their masters, most arrived from the West Indies having worked on the plantations, sometimes in the houses, but mainly in the fields. Granville Sharp, if only by accident, was on the leading edge of the movement to change all of that.

Granville Sharp (1735–1813) by G. Dance, engraved by Henry Meyer, 1820. Courtesy of the Library of Congress, Washington, D.C.

Born in 1735 in the county of Durham in England, Granville Sharp came from a family with deep roots in the Anglican Church. There were several mainstream Britons in the Church of England, like Sharp, who were not among the liberal Dissenters and Quakers, but nevertheless strongly advocated emancipation. Unlike his older brothers, young Granville did not have the advantage of a formal education, except for a few years at the Durham grammar school. With so many children, his father simply could not afford for him to attend school and then the university. One of his oldest brothers, John, followed his father as Archdeacon of Northumberland; his brother William became a surgeon; and James, an ironmonger and engineer. Like Franklin's family, they were close knit and enjoyed a settled middle-class life. This was fortunate for Granville, given that William and James supported him while he engaged in his many causes. He also tried to create a colony in Sierra Leone in Guinea for freed slaves, a project that, like Whitefield's Bethesda, dismally failed.

Sharp's main objective in life was to work on behalf of several humanitarian causes in addition to abolition: as a conscientious objector, he objected to war (though ironically, he worked in the state ordnance office), and he also opposed the practice of dueling and fought against the impressment of seamen. He wrote on religious matters, and, coming from a highly musical family, he wrote about music as well and played the flute and hautboy (the predecessor to the modern oboe). The family played concerts together for family and friends, including author Frances Burney, actor David Garrick, and writer Oliver Goldsmith. The family more than once played for Lord North and even for George III himself. We should also remember that Sharp believed an Anglican episcopacy should be established in America, which jibed with the official position of the Archbishop of Canterbury, Thomas Secker. Sharp's American friend Benjamin Rush vehemently opposed the idea in 1774 but changed his mind after the Revolution, as long as the bishops never possessed "civil revenue or jurisdiction."

Sharp was deeply devout, and like Benezet he was "the kindest and mildest of men." Physically unimpressive, he presented a "neat stooping little figure" with a "mild gentle face," which possessed "inflexible courage and determination." He primarily traveled in Anglican circles, often conferring with Samuel Johnson about matters close to his heart, such as the impressment matter. He might even have asked Johnson about slavery and the slave trade, because Johnson was a well-known opponent of both. In *Taxation No Tyranny*, Johnson posed a now-famous rhetorical question after he learned the Americans opposed paying English taxes. "We are told, that the subjection of Americans may tend to the diminution of our own liberties: an event, which none but very perspicacious politicians are able to foresee. If slavery be thus fatally contagious, how is it we hear the loudest yelps for liberty among the drivers of negroes?" While he probably did not have Franklin in mind, he was certainly thinking of Thomas Jefferson and other Southern plantation owners with large numbers of slaves.

In 1750 Granville's father apprenticed his young son, whom everyone called Greeny, to a Quaker linen draper in London. When the Quaker died, Sharp apprenticed successively, he tells us, for a Presbyterian and then a Catholic master draper. He argued with all of them about theological matters, an experience he called "extraordinary" and one that "has taught me to make a proper distinction between the opinions of men and their persons. The former I can freely condemn, without presuming to judge the individuals themselves." His interest in linen making was slim, but he found the shop to be an outlet for his many intellectual and theological interests. He often argued about biblical texts with one of his fellow apprentices, who, as it turned out, insisted on looking only at the New Testament in the original Greek. To keep up, Greeny learned to read Greek. Later, the same situation occurred again when he worked with a young Jewish apprentice who insisted that to understand the prophecies properly, they had to be read in their original Hebrew. So

Greeny learned to read Hebrew. Perhaps the theological profession of his grandfather, father, and oldest brother stimulated these interests, or perhaps he was just interested in a variety of matters. In any case, his intellectual and theological interests never outshone his practical ones: although he learned the linen-making trade, he soon tired of it and went to work in the ordnance office, sending supplies and materiel to the armed forces.

In the mornings before work, Greeny's habit was always to stop by his brother's surgery. One morning, he encountered or, rather, he bumped into, a black man named Jonathan Strong. William Sharp's medical appointments in the morning were always reserved for poor patients, whom he treated for free. Strong had gone to the office for emergency treatment: he had been a slave to David Lisle, a lawyer in Barbados, who had so badly beaten Strong that the black man was lame and, even worse, nearly blind from repeated blows to his head. Finding him totally useless, Lisle had thrown him into the streets to fend for himself.

Until that moment, young Granville Sharp had never thought about slavery and had little interest in helping someone like Strong. And yet, as he was leaving his brother's office, perhaps with his head down in a reverie, he ran smack into Strong. He and William were so taken by the man's grisly condition that for four months they nursed him back to health and even saved his sight. The younger Sharp found Strong a job at an apothecary shop, and the brothers were certain they would never see him again. They were wrong.

Two years later, by chance, Strong ran into his former master, Lisle, on a London street corner. When Lisle saw that his former slave was whole again, he had him incarcerated and went about finding a buyer. From jail, Strong sent a frantic note to Granville Sharp, who stopped the proceedings by demanding proof that Strong had been arrested on criminal charges. When it became clear that Strong had disobeyed no law, the magistrate released him.

But now, Lisle had him physically seized as his personal property (in fact, Lisle had already sold him for 30 pounds to a plantation owner in Jamaica). Sharp threatened to press charges for assault; in turn, Lisle pressed his own charges against Sharp, for having robbed him, "the original master, David Lisle, the lawyer, of a Negro slave."

Sharp's lawyer told him his case would be lost because of a legal precedent in British law: in 1729 attorney general Philip York and solicitor general Charles Talbot had informally held (at dinner, no less) that no slave became free simply because he stepped foot on free English soil. It now appeared that this opinion was the precedent that Lord Chief Justice Mansfield (William Murray), who heard the case, would follow. Though undeterred, Sharp knew the odds were against Strong: "Those gentlemen of the law, whose contrary doctrines I am unfortunately obliged to oppose, are numerous, eminent, and learned," he wrote. He had his lawyer meet with the current solicitor general, the Recorder of London, and even Sir William Blackstone, the great commentator on English law. Blackstone's opinion was directly opposite to the precedent. He had written that "a slave or a Negro, the moment he lands in England, falls under the protection of the laws, and with regard to all natural rights becomes *eo instanti* a freeman." But in stating the law, Blackstone muddied the waters when he added that even if English law protected the slave, then as the property of his master, the slave should be regarded as a permanent apprentice. It was a step forward, though a small one.

So the prospects were dim that Mansfield would overturn the York and Talbot precedent. An extremely conservative, even cautious man, Mansfield is known as the founder of English commercial law. He served as chief justice as long as John Marshall later did in America. Just as Marshall (the fourth chief justice of the United States) today still holds the record for the longest service, thirty-five years, from 1801 to 1835, Mansfield served for thirty-two years from 1756 to 1788. In addition to reforming commercial law, he is known as one of the greatest jurists in matters of contract, tort, and maritime law. For our purposes, his rulings in several spectacular cases have made his name synonymous with the use of the law to improve society—though he himself by no means possessed a liberal political philosophy. Catherine Macaulay called him "the father of modern Toryism," for example. Even so, in 1768 he found a legal technicality to free the radical statesman John Wilkes from prison, and two years later he ruled that judges, not juries, had the final say in libel cases. More spectacularly, he freed George Gordon in 1781 after the Gordon Riots of the year before—a weeklong rampage of plunder and arson stimulated by the anti-Catholic demonstrations in London, and led by Lord Gordon.

A Scot by birth, Mansfield was born William Murray into a family of Jacobites (those who followed the now discredited Stuart family of kings). Although his father was a peer, by fourteen young Will had left Scotland, never to return. He was regarded as a magnificent orator, but apparently he never lost his Scottish accent, as he had wanted to, and thus "pronounced words oddly in a studied effort not to mispronounce them." An Oxford graduate who studied law at Lincoln's Inn, Murray quickly advanced in the legal profession, ultimately taking a seat in the House of Commons under the Duke of Newcastle's patronage. He was appointed solicitor general in 1742, then attorney general, and by 1776 he was made the first Earl of Mansfield. A powerful and wealthy jurist by this time, he enjoyed the company of James Boswell, Richard Cumberland, and other notables of the day.

Curiously, his nephew's daughter, Dido, whose mother was black, seriously complicated his view of slavery. Dido adored her great-uncle, and he apparently loved her (if we are to believe what visitors said about their relationship—he apparently never commented on it). She often served as his secretary: "One wonders how as a judge he distinguished between the theoretical and the particular; whether he looked at Dido as she wrote his letters and saw a connection between her privileged and manumitted state and that of the young black men and women tied to masts on the Thames, dragged screaming from their English homes to ships bound for Jamaica, or running errands in the streets of London, hoping not to be spied by their former masters." It was a curious and fascinating whirl of events to contemplate, even from the perspective of more than two centuries later. Perhaps this is ultimately why James Oldham notes that Mansfield "was genuinely ambivalent about the subject of slavery": he suspected the slave trade was good for the English economy, yet he had deep doubts about the theoretical and legal grounds for slavery and hated to see slaves mistreated by their masters.

Unmoved by Mansfield's stubborn adherence to precedent, Sharp deeply immersed himself in English law and wrote a tract that argued against the legal theory of slavery, which he later published in 1769 as a pamphlet titled *A Representation of the Injustice and Dangerous Tendency of Tolerating Slavery.* The work received wide distribution in America and moved Franklin. Sharp tried to limit the ways a man might legally bind himself to another. He focused primarily on the right of a person to make a contract: if, in fact, a person agreed to enter into a position of servitude with another, then it was lawful only if a legally binding, written contract confirmed it. As he put it, "There have been many instances of persons being freed from Slavery by the laws of England; but (God be thanked) there is neither law nor even a precedent (at least I have not been able to find one) of a legal determination, to justify a master in claiming or detaining any person whatsoever as a Slave in England, who has not voluntarily bound himself as such by a contract in writing." He argued that slavery was an antiquated, miserable system of bondage that had no place in modern Britain, and the court should recognize that fact immediately. It was rooted in the system of serfdom from the medieval world, a remnant of "Feudal tyranny," he called it, a result of "the violent and unchristian usurpation of the uncivilized barons in an age of darkness."

The power of his argument convinced Lisle to withdraw his case. Strong had certainly never signed a contract with Lisle to become his or anyone else's slave, so he was the exception to the York and Talbot precedent. Slaves, like all men, had certain natural rights and privileges that other men could not willy-nilly take away.

Just as the Strong case was developing, another case came to Sharp's attention. John Hylas, an African slave in England who had been freed by his master, married another slave, who was not free. When the owner of Hylas's wife seized her and sent her back to Barbados with neither her husband's nor her consent, Hylas argued, on the basis of a memorandum that Sharp prepared, that his wife became free when she married Hylas, because he was already a free man. When the court unexpectedly agreed, Sharp began a campaign to bring his case against slavery to all quarters in England. Like Benezet, he lobbied whomever he could: he wrote to the Archbishop of Canterbury, and he entered into a lengthy correspondence with the physician and Quaker abolitionist, John Fothergill, Franklin's friend and personal physician when he was in London. He soon entered another case in the matter of Thomas Lewis, a former slave who had been seized by men who wanted to sell him to a Jamaica plantation owner. Lord Mansfield, who heard the case, dismissed it on technical grounds: when Lewis showed up in court, the jury determined he was not the property of his owner; there had been a break in his ownership when Lewis served a Spanish captain in Havana for a short time.

Mansfield never had to rule directly on the case after the work of the jury was done. And yet the issue of slavery on English soil was far from settled, and Sharp was not yet finished with Mansfield. Sharp had never intended to be a leader in emancipation, and he certainly had no legal preparation for it. All he had was his own informal legal training and an open-mindedness he had derived from his Anglican father; namely, that opinions could be fought, but not the person who argued them. He continued to help as many blacks as he could, sometimes offering his "legal" and sometimes material assistance, although he himself was not a wealthy man. In this atmosphere of legal ambiguity, the case of James Somerset suddenly reared up, a case during which Sharp was to make his most fundamental argument: a slave is free once he sets foot on English soil. His goal was to show that the 1729 opinion by the attorney and solicitor generals was wrong and should be overturned by the court.

Despite his inconsistent rulings, Mansfield believed precedent bound him even if York and Talbot had only informally set it out. There were also practical problems, because Mansfield worried about the negative impact that the sudden freedom of some fourteen thousand English slaves (the exact figure is disputed) would have on the national economy in general—and the individual finances of slave owners in particular. He estimated that each slave was worth about 50 pounds and determined that 700,000 pounds sterling would be lost if the slaves were freed at once. He also wondered what would happen if the newly freed slaves sued their masters for damages—punitive damages, no less—or sued them for past wages. The costs could be enormous.

If Mansfield's attitude was ambivalent, there is some evidence that he might have worked with Sharp to select the example of James Somerset to determine the case's final outcome. Somerset's former owner, Charles Stewart, was a Scottish merchant residing in Virginia. He most likely dealt in trading wine, rum, tobacco, molasses, corn, shingles, and probably several other commodities. As historian Mark Weiner points out, Stewart also enjoyed a lively commerce in slaves, "large numbers of them." It is not surprising, therefore, that having seized Somerset in England, Stewart wanted to return him to Jamaica for sale. In urging Somerset to file a complaint against Stewart to demand the court to recognize him as a free man, Sharp was convinced that the time was right for this case to go to court, because he thought Mansfield had an open mind. In a note to the Lord Chief Justice, Sharp remarked that Mansfield had begun to soften, because he "went so far as to drop some hints of favorable wishes for the cause of the Negro."

In the meantime the lead counsel in Somerset's case was Serjeant William Davy ("serjeant" was the title given to leading barristers), soon to be joined by Francis Hargrave and two other barristers. Hargrave was a perfect addition to the legal team, because he believed "the state of slavery in which a Negro may be before his arrival in England gives no title whatever to service *here*, either on the ground of property or on presumption of a contract. This opinion I shall be zealous to support." In all, five lawyers represented Somerset, all of whom agreed to forego the costs of their services. Sharp himself did not attend the sessions: he was afraid his presence would antagonize the chief justice.

One of the first things Sharp did was to send Davy a muzzle that masters or slave hunters often placed over the faces of their captives. It was "a Brief against Slavery" because it was so evidently inhuman and inhumane. "It is, indeed an *Iron Argument,* which must at once convince all those whose hearts are not a harder metal, that MEN are not to be entrusted with an absolute authority over their brethren." Whether Davy ever had any doubts about the proceedings is not known, but he certainly was emboldened when he received this little gift from Sharp.

When the trial opened in February 1772, much was made of Somerset's Virginia origins. Davy immediately pressed his strongest argument that a man is free whenever he is on English soil, no matter his previous condition of servitude. Would England allow a bashaw with several women slaves to come into the country when he treated them for his own sexual amusement? Would England allow a ship full of galley slaves into the country, permitting the owner to keep them "in the most wretched state"? When Lord Mansfield postponed further arguments until the spring, Sharp took advantage of the hiatus to ask Lord North to convince Parliament to halt all slavery in the empire. At almost the same time, he was delighted to receive from John Fothergill a copy of his own tract as abridged by Anthony Benezet and published in America.

In May the trial resumed. The legal issue was now simply whether Somerset was a slave in England just because he had been a slave in America. The slave himself might answer, "I am now in a country where the laws of liberty are known and regarded; and can you tell me the reason why I am not to be protected by those laws, but to be carried away again to be sold?" Hargrave argued that if a slave were still a slave when he entered England, then slavery would inevitably forever remain in that nation: "It will come, not only from our own colonies, but from those of the other European nations; from Poland, Russia, Spain, and Turkey; from the Coast of Barbary, from the Western and Eastern Coasts of Africa, from every part of the world where it still continues to torment and dishonor the human species." He reviewed how the people of the western world came to enslave the African peoples. Echoing Sharp's pamphlet, Hargrave cited the ancient laws of *villeinage* (serfdom) in England that permitted a form of slavery but also restrained the lord from having the authority to force the *villein* out of the country. Finally, Somerset's attorneys argued that a former slave from Virginia might well enjoy natural and civil rights in England: "It appears, that by the laws of Virginia this man is a slave; but I submit that the laws of Virginia extend to Virginia alone. In this country, how does this man stand as a slave, where the meanest have a title to enjoy the rights of freedom? This man is *here*; he owes submission to the laws of England, and he claims the protection of those laws; and as he ceases to be a citizen of Virginia, and stands in no such relation *now* to Mr. Stewart, so he is certainly not bound to him." With that remark, Somerset's lawyers rested their case.

The defense argued the legal theory in reverse, namely that Stewart did indeed own Somerset, because the laws of Virginia as a colony of the British Empire were binding on England. A man could not be divested of his lawful property, even if it is property in a human being. In addition, counsel contended that chaos would result should all of England's slaves be freed, and besides, it would upset the fragile balance between master and slave, a balance that was "unchangeable."

Throughout the trial, Mansfield often suggested a way out. (Was he thinking of his niece Dido, to whom he left a very comfortable legacy of five hundred pounds with an additional one hundred pounds per year for life, and specifically freed her?) All Stewart had to do, he said, was free Somerset, thus making the issue at trial moot. But Stewart refused. Within a month, Mansfield handed down his historic decision: he overturned the opinion that York and Talbot had set forth in 1729 that had supported the planters and their ownership of slaves. While he argued that the laws of England, not the laws of Virginia or anywhere else, applied to this case, his was a memorable, though narrow, decision and relied only on the *villeinage* argument that Hargrave had made. It applied only to Somerset and no others. "Tracing the subject to natural principles, the claim of slavery never can be supported," wrote Mansfield. "The power claimed never was in use here, or acknowledged by the law. Upon the whole, we cannot say the cause returned is sufficient by the law; and therefore the man must be discharged." In short, Stewart could not forcibly remove James Somerset from England "to be sold abroad . . . for any . . . reason whatsoever," unless statutory (positive) law specifically required it.

Somerset was now a free man, and while Franklin seemed pleased for the man, he was appalled that only Somerset alone was emancipated. He complained to Benezet "of the Hypocrisy of this Country, which encourages such a detestable Commerce by Laws for promoting the Guinea Trade; while it piqu'd itself on its Virtue, Love of Liberty, and the Equity of its Courts, in setting free a single Negro." The slave trade would not end until 1807, and full American emancipation was not to come for another fifty-six years. Mansfield's ruling in effect meant only that a slave, once brought to England, could not be forced out of England by his master (or former master) against his will. Nor did it mean that all (now former) slaves had to be paid as if they were hired servants. They were not—and Mansfield time and again ruled that way. He even went so far as to say that an out of work former slave was not entitled to the benefits of pauper legislation because those laws did not encompass slaves. Still, his ruling, despite its extreme narrowness, was a step forward for England—a small liberty that was still far larger than the Americans, and the Pennsylvanians in particular, were willing to grant at the moment.

Franklin indicated his pleasure with the outcome of the Somerset case when he wrote a piece that he fired off to the *London Chronicle* in June of 1772. In "The Somerset Case and the Slave Trade," Franklin blasted not only the slave trade, but also slavery itself. He hoped "that the same humanity may extend itself among numbers; if not to the procuring liberty for those that remain in our Colonies, at least to obtain a law for abolishing the African commerce in slaves, and declaring the children of present Slaves free after they become of age." He noted that the trip from Africa usually led to the deaths of huge numbers of people. Using the figures he had earlier received from Benezet, he stated that at least eight hundred fifty thousand slaves already resided in America, and that this number would grow because the import rate stood at an additional one hundred thousand each year, "of which number about one third perish by the gaol distemper on the passage, and in the sickness called *seasoning* before they are set to labour."

Even more, he argued, slavery did not lead to that happy, fulfilled life that many supporters claimed. Many slaves became sick and died while working in "excessive labour, bad nourishment, uncomfortable accommodation, and broken spirits." Britain may have thought it performed a wondrous deed by setting James Somerset free. "*Pharisaical Britain!*" he exclaimed, "To pride thyself in setting free *a single Slave* that happens to land on thy coasts, while thy Merchants in all thy ports are encouraged to continue a commerce whereby so many *hundreds of thousands* are dragged into slavery that can scarce be said to end with their lives, since it is entailed on their posterity." He did not ignore the miserable slave trade either. Once again, thanks to Whitefield, Benezet, and Sharp, Franklin joined the ranks of those who advocated the end of the slave trade and slavery. In his last years, he and Benjamin Rush led the Pennsylvania Society for Promoting the Abolition of Slavery and wrote the first request to Congress to end the institution in America.

2

Benjamin Rush, Revolution, Religion, and Medicine

Benjamin Rush, like Franklin, was not an early supporter of American independence, but also like his older friend and mentor, he became one of the most fervent advocates after he was converted to the idea. Again, like Franklin, he was not always a believer in republican government; but by 1776 he was unmatched when he finally adopted republicanism. He, too, took time to come to grips with the horrors of slavery and the slave trade; but by the 1770s Rush came to believe that slavery and the slave trade should be ended for moral and practical reasons. But even then, make no mistake, he modulated his abolitionism by advocating the gradual end of slavery—slaves had to be readied for their freedom. In any case, in 1787 he, along with Franklin, helped revitalize the Pennsylvania antislavery society (Franklin was its first president; Rush followed years later in 1803). A physician and scientist, he was never a pure rationalist. Philosophically, he differed with Franklin on fundamentals: underlying his ideas—political, social, scientific, medical—was an intense, unshakable religious fervor that he acquired while in school and remained with him all of his life. Earth-shaking events like the American Revolution inspired in him images of the return of Christ and the onslaught of the Millennium. Franklin never indulged in such religious enthusiasm.

Rush once summed up his overall outlook when mixing his political and religious sensibilities (something we rarely find in Franklin, whose sole acknowledgement of religion would be to mildly invoke the name of God). Here Rush included much of what he advocated throughout his political life and even highlighted his final break with the Presbyterian Church when he found that it, too, had become corrupted with infighting and politics.

> Yes . . . I anticipate with a joy which I cannot describe the speedy end of the misery of the Africans, of the tyranny of kings, of the pride of ecclesiastical institutions, whether founded in the absurd ideas of apostolic succession or in the aristocracy of Presbyterianism. Connected with the same events, I anticipate the end of war and such a superlative tenderness for human life as will exterminate capital punishments from all our systems of legislation. In the meanwhile let us now be idle with such prospects before our eyes. Heaven works by instruments, and even supernatural prophecies are fulfilled by natural means. It is possible we may not live to witness the approaching regeneration of our world, but the more active we are in bringing it about, the more fitted we shall be for that world where justice and benevolence eternally prevail.

But Rush took time to come to these conclusions. At first, he endorsed slavery, only to reject it; at first, he embraced the British Empire, only to reject that too.

Dr. Benjamin Rush (1746–1813) by Charles Willson Peale, 1783.
Courtesy of the Winterthur Museum, gift of Mrs. Julia B. Henry.

Above average height for his time, about five feet, nine inches tall, Rush was a handsome man with a long curving nose, high cheekbones, highly animated blue eyes, and an expressive face. He apparently had an unusually large head, giving the impression of a man of strength and intellect, and he had the gift of gab. Certainly Rush was an intense man. He loved to converse on all subjects, from medicine, to politics, to social issues like temperance and slavery. An admirer late in life recalled that he was a man with "great powers of conversation," but it was also clear that those who hated his nonstop talking and know-it-all attitude detested him.

As a man with a mind of his own, Rush also had some rather intriguing and outlandish ideas. First, he added the term "phrenology" to the English language; and second, he developed quasi-medical/quasi-spiritual theories that are truly bizarre by today's standards. In considering why monks were prone to baldness more than the average man, his answer was founded in "an empirical-spiritual explanation." He suspected that the French had whiter teeth than the English because they wore nightcaps to bed. Surely one of his greatest contributions took place in 1811 when he single-handedly reconciled John Adams and Thomas Jefferson, who had not spoken or corresponded for years.

Outspoken nearly all of the time and articulate on every issue that came before him, Rush demonstrated through his autobiography and letters that he never feared to comment on any subject and problem that the new nation faced. At times, he was downright cantankerous. His writings attacked "strong drink, slavery, war, capital punishment, public punishments, test laws, tobacco, [and] oaths," while at the same time he deeply supported "beer and cider, free schools, education for women, a college of Pennsylvania Germans, a national university, the study of science rather than Greek and Latin, free postage for newspapers, churches for Negroes, and the cultivation of the sugar-maple tree." He was convinced that a lack of exercise and the consumption of alcoholic beverages contributed to the deterioration of man's moral sense, and thus blunted a person's sense of the difference between right and wrong. His outspokenness often got him into trouble, especially when it affected his medical practice, which sometimes declined when he attacked his fellow physicians' ideas of treating disease or when he advocated emancipation.

As contentious, bullying, and self-confident as he was, Rush was also a man with a strong moral sense. Rush thought that humans possessed "a moral sense," "a conscience," and "a sense of the Deity"—which for him meant that we had to be fully educated. Rush was a prime mover, founding many educational institutions in Pennsylvania, and he wrote several essays on education to promote the spread of his ideas. With knowledge, he said, men in the republic enacted good and wise laws, for everyone to follow, so that the goals of society were virtuous and tended toward the achievement of the common good. This was why he later argued for a balanced government with dispersed authority—in a constitution much like that of the new American Constitution of 1787, with its representative system, its checks and balances, and its frequent, though divided, elections among the executive and legislative branches. As for a bill of rights, he initially claimed it was immaterial, since the constitution itself was a bundle of rights; then again, James Madison initially opposed a bill of rights until Thomas Jefferson, then in Paris, convinced him to advocate one in the first Federal Congress.

As a lifelong Philadelphian and a signer of the Declaration of Independence, Rush counted among his friends the entire constellation of the American founding, especially Franklin, forty years his senior, who thought of him as a son, as well as English friends and correspondents like Richard Price, Joseph Priestley, and physician John Coakley Lettsom, with whom he had earlier attended medical school in Edinburgh. Rush said even the politically conservative Noah Webster was among those he most admired. Rush was proud of his generation. He told his friend John Adams that their work in science, medicine, moral thought, political action, and social reform inculcated in the people of the United States "all those great national, social, domestic, and religious virtues which alone can make a people free, great, and happy."

Moreover, as the quintessential physician, Rush sought only the best treatment for his patients, no matter how controversial the procedures might be. He visited them when they were ill and tended to their needs until their death. For his time, he was highly trained, unlike most physicians of the age, who were often self-taught or, even worse, simply practicing with no background at all. As Benjamin Franklin once told him, "Quacks," whom Franklin despised, "were the greatest liars in the world, except their patients." The most notorious treatment he prescribed was a combination of bleeding and purging. While many physicians thought this was extreme and useless, Rush disagreed. Still, he was the preeminent American physician of his day. Other doctors sought his advice, and his influence reverberated long after his death in 1813. "He was idolized by the doctors of his own period, who called him the Fothergill, the Sydenham, the Hippocrates, of American medicine. So deeply did Rush plant in the minds of American doctors his theory of the unity of fevers and their cure by depletion, that long after his death it was the dominant American practice."

Eighteenth-century American medicine was very primitive by twenty-first-century standards. Many patients simply treated themselves with home remedies sometimes handed down by tradition, sometimes by what they heard might work, sometimes what they learned from native practices of the American Indians. Others relied on medical practitioners who lacked formal training. While some doctors and surgeons like Rush did undergo medical training, there was no real surgery as we know it, although army surgeons practiced amputation and sewed up wounds. Body cavities were rarely touched, and anesthesia and thermometers to measure body temperature did not appear until the mid-nineteenth century. There was no concept of the antibiotic or the hypodermic syringe. Nor was there any idea of the relationship between disease and germs and the use of disinfectants. The stethoscope as a medical device did not exist before 1819.

Nor did everyone accept a crude form of vaccination, then called inoculation. Modern vaccination had to wait until 1798 when it was first discovered to prevent smallpox. Only then did the science of immunization truly begin. Eighteenth-century inoculation was a technique a physician used to try to ward off smallpox. He first scratched smallpox from an infected patient, then rubbed it into the healthy person's skin with a quill or other sharp object. Some doctors complained it caused more illness than it prevented, because smallpox occasionally would result, sometimes with fatal results. In 1736, Franklin's four-year-old son, Franky, died of smallpox. Because Franklin was positive his little boy would have survived had he been inoculated, from that time on he urged everyone to be inoculated. Sixty years later, however, the procedure was vastly different—when the science of immunization really began with Edward Jenner's discovery that rubbing cowpox virus on the skin did not actually cause the disease: when he vaccinated an eight-year-old boy, he found that the vaccine created antibodies that prevented the disease.

Just as Franklin promoted inoculation, Rush, too, highly favored it. In 1768 he told John Morgan, a founder of and professor of medicine at the College of Philadelphia, it was "the 'ne plus ultra' in this kingdom." Moreover, antidotes for other illnesses and diseases were wildly popular in the eighteenth century, and Rush followed them as well. When bloodletting or blistering (blisters were raised on the skin with a patch of cloth or leather soaked in some caustic material) was not used as a remedy, the main therapeutic treatments consisted of large doses of cathartics, emetics, opium, and barks to stimulate vomiting. Patients generally expected to receive these "heroic" treatments of their ailments. It was called heroic "because of its dramatic and severely debilitating effects, caused by intensive bleeding and purging." In these techniques we may find the way Rush was trained as a physician.

First apprenticed to Dr. John Redman, a physician at the Philadelphia Hospital and also a founder and first president of the College of Physicians there (now part of the University of Pennsylvania), young Rush actually resided with his mentor for five and a half years. Eighteenth-century medical practitioners like Redman believed the body consisted of four humors: blood, phlegm, yellow bile (sometimes called "choler") and black bile (or wonderfully termed "melancholy"). As Aristotle had taught, the universe consisted of the four elements of earth, air, fire, and water. The four bodily humors matched each of these: the air could be hot and wet like blood; water was cold and wet like phlegm; fire was hot and dry like choler; and finally, the earth was cold and dry like melancholy. The doctor's duty was to keep these humors in balance, lest the patient sicken and die.

In the early eighteenth century the Dutch physician Hermann Boerhaave refined this theory of medicine by suggesting that health was a matter of balancing bodily solids and fluids. For example, when solids were out of kilter, such as in their size, placement, or number, illness resulted. By the same token, the fluids had to be kept from becoming sour or salty, aromatic, fatty, or alkaline. In many respects Boerhaave newly interpreted the theory of humors: because disease occurred when the blood was too thick, he developed ways to thin the blood through purges or vomits, some bloodletting, and sweats, or through any technique he could think of to rid the body of its morbid humors. Bloodletting, of course, had been around since the days of the second-century Greek practitioner Galen, the physician to Marcus Aurelius. Galen was said to cut off tails of leeches so they would not become so engorged that they stopped sucking blood. Redman, who had studied in Holland, was thus thoroughly imbued with Boerhaavian and Galenic ideas.

Another of Rush's early mentors, William Shippen Jr., gave his first medical lectures on anatomy in 1762. (The two would enter into a long and bitter rivalry during the American Revolution and ultimately hated each other personally over their deep disagreements about appropriate medical care and procedures.) Initially, though, Rush and ten other students regularly attended Shippen's lectures. One controversial subject in which Shippen was engaged was dissection. While Galen, too, had practiced dissection, it was often regarded as barbaric or even immoral when the physician dismembered a human body. Its very existence in Philadelphia sometimes caused riots outside the laboratories where it took place. Shippen persevered and mainly used corpses exhumed from the graves of slaves and paupers. He also taught at the medical school of the College of Philadelphia when it opened in 1765.

But it was Redman above all who prodded the young Rush to continue his medical studies in Edinburgh, where one of Europe's best schools was located.

In 1766, at twenty-five, Rush left Philadelphia for London, where he introduced himself to Benjamin Franklin. The relationship between the older statesman Franklin and the younger, budding, know-it-all physician Rush had begun in 1765 with a rather bumpy start. Parliament had just passed the Stamp Act, which imposed a tax without the consent of the local American assemblies; most Americans regarded it as a burden and a symbol of their inferior status in the empire. Some Philadelphians thought Franklin did not object strongly enough to the act. Some actually thought he intended to use his "support" of the act, so that once the Penns were ousted as proprietors, he would be named governor of Pennsylvania.

But Franklin knew that passage of the Stamp Act was inevitable; his "support" was merely the politically expedient thing to do, a means of limiting the bad effects of a bad law. Still, when he had his friend John Hughes appointed as the Stamp Act agent in Pennsylvania, figuring it was better to have a friend than an enemy in the office, Franklin's standing in the colonies deteriorated. (Hughes, by the way, once appointed, feared for the safety of his life, his family, and his property and soon resigned.) Deborah was writing to Franklin she was afraid their house would be burned to the ground and that both her and Sally's life were in danger (she moved Sally to an aunt's house in New Jersey).

Young Rush thought Franklin was a traitor to Pennsylvania and America. He wrote to his boyhood friend, Ebenezer Hazard: "*O Franklin, Franklin,* thou curse to Pennsylvania and America, may the most accumulated vengeance burst speedily on thy guilty head!" Shortly afterward, Franklin appeared before the House of Commons to answer questions about why

Pennsylvanians opposed the act. Pitt clearly wanted it repealed, and the Commons finally went along, followed by the House of Lords, in 1766.

In Edinburgh, Rush worked long hours with Dr. William Cullen, professor of medicine at the Edinburgh Medical School, whose many American students founded and then staffed the Philadelphia Medical School. Rush learned from Cullen (whom Rush called "my master") that contrary to Boerhaave's ideas, medical ailments were not rooted in the solids or fluids of the body, but implanted in the body's nervous system. Illness occurred when the body's nerves were either overstimulated or understimulated. Cullen claimed that fever, for example, was caused when the "sedative powers" of the brain took over. The remedy was to activate the brain and other organs. If the nervous system was too active or working too powerfully, the nerves went into what he called spasms. If they were too weak or motionless, the result was something called atony. He identified both as illnesses, and he prescribed drugs as cures for these problems. Cullen worked up a classification system of illness and disease, so that from his perspective the physician need only determine the symptoms of his patient and then look up Cullen's classification chart for the diagnosis. Depressants worked well to relieve spasms, whereas stimulants were the best for atony.

Rush now agreed that the Boerhaavian system was simplistic, inaccurate, and unsound. This turned out to be one of the major disputes he would later have with Shippen. He wrote to a Philadelphia friend that "the present era will be famous for a revolution in physic. The old [Boerhaavian] doctrines of the blood, nerves, &c., are now exploded, and much more rational ones substituted in their room. . . . The theory of physic is like our dress, always changing, and we are always best pleased with that which is most fashionable." With his newfound medical knowledge, Rush was awarded his medical degree in June of 1768 after completing a thesis on digestion: he had experimented on himself by taking an emetic to discover what happened to the ingested food.

After completing medical school in Edinburgh, but before returning home, Rush stayed in London for nearly six months, where he and the elderly diplomat became good friends (he had met Franklin two years earlier when he had the gall to ask him to write letters of introduction for him to several Edinburgh luminaries, including Cullen). Franklin introduced the young physician to his friends and acquaintances, including Richard Price, and the prominent bookselling and publishing brothers, Edward and Charles Dilly, who later published Franklin's pamphlets and books in England. Rush later recalled that it was his "peculiar happiness to be domesticated in [Franklin's] family." Franklin took him "to Court with him and pointed out to me many of the most distinguished public characters of the nation. I never visited him without learning something." So impressed was the young Rush with Franklin's generosity and friendship, that he eventually dedicated his medical thesis to him, calling him the "worthy delegate to the Britannic Court, known far and wide." When he returned home the following year, thanks to his medical thesis, he was promptly elected to the American Philosophical Society.

Rush's problems started almost immediately when he publicly challenged the well-established Boerhaavian medical treatment, which was so popular in Philadelphia. His adherence to the Cullen medical theory made him the enemy of his erstwhile mentor William Shippen, who was quite conservative in dispensing medications. Rush thought he achieved the best cures through diet and heavy sweating. For the first seven years of his practice, Rush did not receive a single referral from any Philadelphia physician. Still, because of his background and training and thanks to his earlier association with John Morgan, Rush managed to win an appointment as professor of chemistry at the Medical School of the College of Philadelphia, where he continued to advocate his new ideas about the nervous system. He was the first person to hold this position in America.

Soon, anonymous articles appeared in the newspapers attacking him and his practice, and he responded in kind. His strong response, always intemperate, shows his intolerant, self-righteous attitude. These exchanges, which often focused on small points of medical practice, took their toll on his reputation and were enough to make him an unwelcome member of the Philadelphia medical community. Because none of his colleagues sent him patients, he ministered mainly to the poor. He searched through Philadelphia alleys and walked out to the countryside (he could not afford a horse) to visit the impoverished sick. He sat on their beds when there were no chairs and climbed ladders to the upper floors when there were no steps. His cures were prescriptions of his own making. Sometimes he bled his patients, or sometimes he gave them enemas or induced vomiting. He did anything to restore the nervous system to its proper balance. He never forgot the poor, and years later he helped set up the Philadelphia Dispensary, the first free medical clinic in the United States. (He had gotten the idea from his long-time London friend and colleague John Coakley Lettsom; Lettsom had created such a dispensary fifteen years earlier in London.)

With all of his patients, rich or poor, Rush practiced what today would be called preventive medicine. He advocated a balanced diet and lots of exercise, including walking, running, dancing, fencing, swimming, skating, jumping, and golf. His emphasis on exercise may have come from his student days at the Nottingham Academy in Maryland, where all boys were required to engage in agriculture, specifically in the harvest and haying. When he lived with the Redmans, he learned exercise was part of the Redman family's daily life. He later recalled that "these exercises were both pleasant and useful. They begat health, and helped to implant more deeply in our minds the native passion for rural life." In the 1770s Rush wrote several papers on exercise that he published in America and sent to friends in London, including Lettsom and Franklin, with the hope they would have them published in England. He also wrote on the evils of the gout, overeating, and hives. His essay on intestinal worms, which he thought could be killed by an ingestion of a combination of sugar, salt, honey, and fruit, was the one he hoped would lead to his election to the Royal Society of London—but many physicians and scientists in the society rejected his views. To his deep disappointment and lasting sorrow, he was never admitted to the Royal Society.

At the same time, after some urging by his friend Anthony Benezet, Rush wrote an antislavery tract, the first by a Philadelphian Presbyterian. Like Franklin, Rush must have had some ambivalent feelings, because he was also a slave owner. He did not accept manumission until almost fifteen years after he published his famous antislavery essay. In a way, Benezet hornswoggled him into writing it, because while Rush condemned slavery in theory, as a practical matter he was reluctant to give it up. Still, he was obviously proud of the essay. He almost immediately sent a copy to Granville Sharp, in 1773, along with a letter that introduced himself to the great abolitionist:

> *From the amiable character which I have received of you from my worthy friend Mr Anth: Benezet I have taken the liberty of introducing myself to your correspondence by sending you a pamphlet entitled 'An Address to the Inhabitants of the British Settlements in America.' It is a hasty production, and was written amidst many interruptions from a business which admits of but little leisure for studies or pursuits of that nature, I meant the profession of physic. Few of the arguments are new, and yet I have endeavoured by their conciseness &c to give them new force. A spirit of humanity and religion begins to awaken in several of the colonies in favor of the poor Negroes. . . . Anthony Benezet*

stood alone a few years ago in opposing Negro slavery in Philadelphia and now ¾ of the province as well as the city cry out against it. I sometimes please myself with the hopes of living to see it abolished or put upon another footing in America.

Published anonymously in 1773, the address was signed only "By a Pennsylvanian"—Rush did not want his name associated with it, because he feared it would hurt his medical practice. Soon, however, he was revealed to be its author, and almost immediately, just as Rush had feared, many of his antiabolitionist patients stopped coming to see him. "It did me harm," he recalled, "by exciting the resentment of many slaveholders against me. It injured me in another way, by giving rise to an opinion that I had meddled with a controversy that was foreign to my business." Rush was neither embarrassed nor deterred. He believed, theoretically at least, in what he had written, and he was confident his practice would pick up, and it did. Within two years, he was doing so well financially that his practice "was worth about 900 pounds a year, Pennsylvania currency."

In the address, Rush argued, as had Benezet, that slavery's impact on human beings was so "foreign" that "the moral faculties, as well as those of the understanding are debased, and rendered torpid by it," and that white people grew to think they were naturally superior to those of the black race. The problem was not the black man; it was slavery: "All the vices which are charged upon the Negroes in the southern colonies and the West-Indies, such as Idleness, Treachery, Theft, and the like, are the genuine offspring of slavery, and serve as an argument to prove that they were not intended, by Providence for it."

Rush further argued that the economy, especially in the South, with its emphasis on the production of rice, sugar, and indigo, would flourish without slaves if plantation owners gave up tobacco and cotton growing. Slaveholders disingenuously claimed that blacks were actually happy as chattel, because they were provided with a home and a job. This was absurd: "Slavery and vice are connected together, and the latter is always a source of misery. Besides, by the greatest humanity, we can show them, we only lessen, but do not remove the crime, for the injustice of it continues the same."

Again like Benezet, Rush believed the first step was to abolish the slave trade. This, he thought, could be achieved if all anti-slavery proponents boycotted those who imported slaves and all the ships that brought them to America. With Franklin's endorsement, a petition campaign led by Benezet and Rush urged the Pennsylvania Assembly to double the import tax on the trade from seven to fourteen pounds per slave. They hoped the cost would become hopelessly prohibitive, and the trade would end. Rush also believed the king and the Parliament could be convinced "to dissolve the African Company. It is by this incorporated band of robbers that the trade has been chiefly carried on to America."

The main issue was not the slave trade, however, but slavery itself and its permanent abolition. In words reminiscent of the Quaker abolitionist, Rush asked his readers to bear testimony "against a vice which degrades human nature. . . . The plant of liberty is of so tender a nature that it cannot thrive long in the neighborhood of slavery. Remember, the eyes of all Europe are fixed upon you, to preserve an asylum of freedom in this country after the last pillars of it are fallen in every other quarter of the globe." After slaves were freed, which he believed had to take place over a long period of time, society's duty was to educate them: "Let the young Negroes be educated in the principles of virtue and religion, he wrote in his address, let them be taught to read and write—and afterwards instructed in some business, whereby they may be able to maintain themselves."

Benezet and Franklin could not have agreed more: Benezet of course had been teaching "young Negroes" in his own home and running a school for black children; and Franklin, as a member of the Bray Associates, argued for the education of black children. In addition, Rush deplored the breakup of families in Africa that occurred when the blacks were seized, and he especially decried the separation of families on the auction block in America. He appealed to the clergy that "slavery is a Hydra sin, and includes in it every violation of the precepts of the Law and the Gospel." In vain, "will you command your flocks to offer up the incense of faith and charity, while they continue to mingle the sweat and blood of Negro slaves with their sacrifices." If the Americans did not act and act immediately, God would punish America until slavery was ended. "Remember that national crimes require national punishments, and without declaring what punishment awaits this evil, you may venture to assure them, that it cannot pass with impunity, unless God shall cease to be just or merciful." Rush's was a message filled with passion, if not urgency. And yet, not until a decade and a half later, in 1788, did Rush finally free his own slave, William Grubber.

As might be expected, his pamphlet drew an angry response from many, such as one Richard Nisbet, a British subject living in Nevis in the Caribbean. His argument against Rush was summed up in the title of his work: *Slavery not Forbidden by Scripture.* Rush immediately answered it in a response he also sent to Sharp. Here, he argued that despite Nisbet's title, the scriptures deplored slavery. (It is worth noting he asked Sharp to keep his name off either pamphlet, should Sharp republish them in England; he was afraid his opposition to slavery would harm his medical practice.) Nisbet eventually went insane and, ironically, became a psychiatric patient of Rush's in the Pennsylvania Hospital.

In May, Rush sent Franklin, then in London, a copy of his pamphlet, telling him he had written it "at the request of Anth: Benezet." The upshot was that the Pennsylvania Assembly doubled the import tax—but the Privy Council in London overruled the increase and formally canceled it the next year. Still, Franklin had high hopes that the tax would stick. In July 1773 he wrote Benezet, "There is Reason to hope Our Colonies may in time get clear of a Practice [the slave trade] that disgraces them, and without producing any equivalent Benefit, is dangerous to their very Existence." On the same day, he wrote Rush that he hoped slavery would end, and end soon: "I hope in time that the Friends to Liberty and Humanity will get the better of a Practice that has so long disgrac'd our Nation and Religion." Rush predicted that attitudes were so changed in America that slavery would no longer exist in forty years—that is, by the second decade of the nineteenth century. He was, of course, wrong.

With all this public dialogue and debate on the subject, the time was therefore ripe for the creation of antislavery societies. In 1775 James Pemberton, a Quaker merchant and philanthropist who was a member of one of Philadelphia's most powerful families, Benezet, and others founded the first such abolitionist society in America. Perhaps still stinging from his lost patients as a result of his antislavery tracts, Rush chose not to join. Nor did he lobby the Pennsylvania Assembly to end slavery, which it formally did on March 1, 1780, though the legislature also passed a sojourner law: it allowed travelers from slave states to keep slaves in Pennsylvania for up to six months (out-of-state, slave-owning federal officials residing in Philadelphia had no such time limit). Pennsylvania did not repeal its sojourner law until 1857.

In the meantime, events that eventually led to America's final break with Britain were increasingly occupying Rush's attention. Though termed a "revolutionary gadfly" by his biographer David Freeman Hawke as a vigorous supporter of the American cause and a signer of the Declaration of Independence, Rush, like Franklin, initially believed that negotiations between Britain and America could resolve their problems. He told Granville Sharp in July 1774 he hoped the First Continental Congress would send a petition to England restoring "the wished for harmony between Britain and the colonies. . . . There is not a *man* in America who wishes for the independence of the colonies. We glory in our connection with your country, and we wish it to be perpetual." Hardly the *cri de coeur* of a revolutionary.

However, he also told Sharp there was a rather important qualification to his (and all Americans') loyalty—and this made him mirror Franklin's English patriotism and imperialism even more: "We wish [the connection between Britain and the colonies] only upon the firm basis of the English constitution," which guaranteed the rights of all Englishmen, particularly the right to consent to those taxes that Parliament wished the Americans to pay. In his letter to Sharp, Rush added this warning: "If this cannot be obtained we are ready to welcome all of the inconveniences of a cessation of our trade, and what is more— all the horrors of a civil war." Still, he hoped that a civil war could be avoided, and revealed to Sharp he had prayed for God to "avert these calamities from both countries!" We must note that he uses the phrase "two countries" here to describe England and America—a distinction that Sharp would no doubt pick up on. Just a year later Rush was urging his new friend, Thomas Paine, to write the pamphlet that eventually carried the title Rush himself suggested, *Common Sense,* which never once recommends that the English and Americans reestablish friendship and harmony. Seven months later, along with Franklin and the others, Rush signed the Declaration of Independence.

Rush's change of heart resulted from the unwarranted and unnecessary attack on unsuspecting American militiamen standing on the Lexington Green in April 1775. Rush was far more introspective than his older friend Paine. "The battle of Lexington," he wrote with simple eloquence, "gave a new tone to my feelings." He decided to participate in the activities of the Continental Congress to help the Americans prepare for war against England. "I considered the seperation [*sic*] of the colonies from Great Britain as inevitable," he wrote. "The first gun that was fired at an American cut the cord that had tied the two countries together. It was the signal for the commencement of our independance [*sic*] and from this time all my publications were calculated to prepare the public mind to adopt that important and necessary measure." Rush was now ready for the civil war he had told Sharp he hoped could be avoided.

Even as Rush psychologically prepared for war, he was still a relatively late convert to republican government. He recalled later in life that he had once met a young medical student by the name of John Bostock in Edinburgh when he was there studying medicine. As a staunch republican, Bostock instructed Rush in new ways of thinking about politics. "Never before had I heard the authority of Kings called in question. I had been taught to consider them nearly as essential to political order as the Sun is to the order of our Solar System. . . . [F]rom that time to the present all my reading, observations and reflexions have tended more and more to shew the absurdity of hereditary power, and to prove that no form of government can be rational but that which is derived from the Suffrage of the people who are the subjects of it." Rush had earlier opposed the Stamp Act for denying the rights of Americans as Englishmen, but now he gradually began to oppose England herself and began to think of separation as the only reasonable course.

We cannot separate Rush's political ideas from his deep religious faith. While political progress might be inevitable, he thought, it did not take place by human agency alone. After all, the eighteenth century was a time in American history known as the Great Awakening, when a series of religious revivals spread throughout the colonies with the ministry of Gilbert Tennent and the outdoor preaching of George Whitefield in Philadelphia (a northern equivalent was led by Jonathan Edwards in Massachusetts). Though baptized in the Episcopal Church, Rush became a Presbyterian when his mother took him to Tennent's Presbyterian congregation, after his father died in 1751. As Rush grew older, the Awakening to him meant that progress was a manifestation of God's will made known on earth. When he was writing about America's future, he punctuated his determination that America would soon be independent from Britain by drawing on his religious and spiritual beliefs. Above all stood his hope for a redemptive future for all mankind, which he saw as the true goal of politics.

In the fourth decade of the century, a historic schism was dividing Presbyterianism: on the one hand, the purists, styled the Old Sides, wanted the Church to remain the same way it was founded and administered in Scotland from the time of Oliver Cromwell and the Westminster Confession; on the other hand, the New Sides consisted of preachers who wanted to create a singularly *American* Presbyterian church. It was a time of great optimism quite unlike Calvinist pessimism about sin and the salvation of the Elect Few—it was also a time of deep religious faith that Christ's imminent return would redeem mankind. In this spirit, Rush's fervent religious views intersected with his revolutionary politics.

Americans who, like Rush, followed the New Sides belief, dreamed of achieving a new spiritual awakening, giving them the certainty that this virtuous country contrasted sharply with corrupt European nations. This idea, that virtuous America was different from corrupt Europe, was a commonly held and growing view (and vestiges of it may still be sensed today in the cynicism with which Americans occasionally view European politics). It is best reflected in a letter Franklin wrote from London to Joseph Galloway in 1775, at a time when Franklin had given up on America's reconciliation with England:

> [W]hen I consider the extream Corruption prevalent among all Orders of Men in this old rotten State, and the glorious publick Virtue so predominant in our rising Country, I cannot but apprehend more Mischief than Benefit from a closer Union. I fear they will drag us after them in all their plundering Wars, which their desperate Circumstances, Injustice and Rapacity, may prompt them to undertake; and their wide-wasting Prodigality and Profusion is a Gulph

that will swallow up every aid we may distress ourselves to afford them. Here Numberless and needless Places, enormous Salaries, Pensions, Perquisites, Bribes, groundless Quarrels, foolish Expeditions, false Accounpts and no Accounpts, Contracts and Jobbs, devour all Revenue, and produce continual Necessity in the Midst of natural Plenty.

Of course, Franklin's political views were devoid of all religious coloration; but Rush's certainly were not.

As matters between Britain and America heated up in the early 1770s, Rush held the struggle would move quickly toward a final settlement only God Himself controlled. In the fall of 1773 he wrote a piece, published anonymously in the *Pennsylvania Journal*, concerning the absolute need for patriotism, which he said was "as much a virtue as justice, and is as necessary for the support of societies as natural affection is for the support of families." He advocated a peculiar sort of patriotism to sweep the colonies at this critical time. Certainly, he could have argued that as British subjects, the Americans should direct their patriotic attitudes and love of country to the Mother Country. But he did not. Instead, he strongly suggested that the Americans' country was on these shores, far from the towers of Westminster.

Although Rush did not favor separation quite yet, he held that love of America was the same as one's faith in the Bible and an afterlife. While he used several secular examples of past patriots, most of his examples were religious figures, including his neat idealization of Jesus as a patriot: "Even our Saviour himself gives a sanction to this virtue. He confined his miracles and gospel at first to his own country. He wept at the prospect of her speedy desolation, and even after she had imbrued her hands in his blood, he commands his Apostles to begin the promulgation of his gospel at Jerusalem. I might go on further and show that this benevolent virtue sometimes goes beyond humanity and extends itself to the very soil that gives us birth."

For patriotism to go "beyond humanity" meant that it played a cosmic role in America's inevitable future of greatness and salvation, and in the coming Millennium, the end of time itself.

When the First Continental Congress met in Philadelphia in the fall of 1774, Rush met most of the delegates. They either became his patients, or he regularly invited them to his house for dinner. He especially wanted to meet the famous members of the Massachusetts delegation. He went out to meet them as they approached the city, and John Adams invited him to ride into Philadelphia in his carriage. Rush had always admired and respected Adams, but on this occasion, he noted that his conversation was "cold and reserved." This first meeting of the Continental Congress was a new experience for the Americans, this gathering of a congress, and it was dangerous as well; the British government always looked suspiciously upon, even feared, "extra-parliamentary" conventions, associations, or in this case a congress, unless Parliament itself had permitted it. Begun on their own, they directly challenged the authority of the established order. Still, George Washington, the very young Thomas Jefferson (he was just thirty-one), John Adams, his second cousin Samuel Adams, Patrick Henry, and all the others impressed the doctor with their fluid talk of "liberty and Republicanism," and their collective solidarity allayed their fears that the Crown would later bring the charge of treason against them all.

One way we may see how revolutionary Rush's ideas had become is to look at the correspondence between him and Thomas Ruston at the end of 1775. Rush and Ruston had been classmates at the College of New Jersey, and they had also traveled together to Edinburgh to study medicine. By 1775, with Ruston living in England, Rush, despite the treasonous tone of his letters, hoped that Ruston would have them printed in the London papers to show the English reading public, if not the government, how deep was American resolve to separate from the empire. Here he did not hold back. He struck a tone of absolute certainty that the Americans were right, the British dead wrong, and if they wanted war, then the Americans were pre-pared to whip them and whip them badly. One solution to the British-American dispute that Rush immediately dismissed was reconciliation. Things had gone too far. British troops in America "execrate us, for they *hate* us." And we in turn "laugh at them, for we *despise* them." As war was now inevitable, the American troops were to be led by Colonel Washington, who "has aston-ished his most intimate friends with a display of the most won-derful talents for the government of an army." He was a man of "zeal," "disinterestedness," "politeness," "manly behavior," the perfect officer to lead the Continental Army. He possessed "so much martial dignity in his deportment that you would distin-guish him to be a general and a soldier from among ten thou-sand people."

If his remarkable tribute to Washington were not enough to get him into trouble with British authorities, he went even fur-ther, laying down the final trump card: Washington was so great, he exclaimed, that "there is not a king in Europe that would not look like a valet de chambre by his side." Surely Rush included George III in this large category of European royalty, and he was not merely addressing Washington's height and size. He was talking about how a mere commoner, an American planter and surveyor from Virginia, outsized a king. Even more, Rush went on to tell Ruston that the Americans were preparing both an army and a navy for the coming war and were already in the midst of producing ammunition and other munitions. And all this was a year before Paine's *Common Sense* appeared in print.

As a growing number of Americans accepted independence, especially after the Battle of Lexington, Rush wrote to his young wife, Julia, in the spring of 1776 with words that echoed Paine's in *Common Sense* a few months earlier—"America's cause is the cause of all mankind." However, Rush added his religious beliefs that "the hand of heaven is with us. Did I not think so, I would not have embarked in it. You have everything to hope, and nothing to fear from the part which duty to God, to my country, to my conscience have led me to take in our affairs." Then, in words that Paine later wrote in the *Rights of Man* bearing witness to the cosmic role that God had given to him, Rush proclaimed that he was "*constrained* to believe I act under the direction of Providence. God knows I seek his honor and the best interests of my fellow creatures supremely in all I am doing for my country." He told Julia that he knew how things would turn out. He knew that "happy days" would arrive if he "contributed even a mite to hasten or complete them." That would be to "rise above all the Caesars and Alexanders of the world." And just in case Julia did not get the message, he told her a month later, "I trust the spirit of God himself moves me to declare that I will never desert the cause I am [embar]ked in, till I see the monster tyranny gnash [his] impotent teeth in the dust in the Province of Pennsylvania." Elected to the Second Continental Congress, the one that edited and approved Jefferson's draft of the Declaration of Independence, Benjamin Rush was ready to do his duty to God and country.

Positive that he was right—he was always positive that he was right—Rush developed a theory of personal morality based on God's gift to all human beings of an innate moral sense. Every person automatically knows the difference between right and wrong, though at times bad people refuse or simply fail to recognize it. (This was not akin to Richard Price's ethical intuitionism or the Scottish Common Sense philosophers, because Rush thought they strayed too dangerously close to deism, the doctrine, which was manifested in many forms, that asserted that while God exists, Christ was not part of His substance.) Rush liked to think of this moral faculty as being the same as one's memory or imagination. A person could therefore develop it just as he could improve those other faculties. It was also potentially at some risk, because it could be damaged in an accident (as memory loss occurs when a person is struck in the head). As he told Granville Sharp, the moral sense "is equally innate—equally capable of cultivation and equally liable to injuries from causes of a *physical* nature." That said, the moral faculty, so natural to man that it was like our appetite for bread and water (his examples), leads us to know the difference between good and evil, right and wrong. "Its operation is instinctive—and hence we are often led *at once* to avoid evil, and pursue good in cases where the slow inductions of reason would remonstrate to no purpose."

In other words, we do not have use of our reason to see whether the actions of the British Empire were good or bad for America. God has implanted a moral faculty in us, and all we need is to use it, and not reason about things, to make good decisions, the right decisions. It was clear that "Lord North seems bent upon the destruction of the British constitution," at least in America, and that was wrong. Because "liberty seldom dies a natural death in any country," the Americans might soon have to take up the sword, unless British policies toward America changed. Americans were carrying out God's will just as He wished them to.

Despite his initial admiration and support of General Washington, once the war began to go badly, as it did in its first years, Rush had a change of heart. He now thought Washington was no longer under God's superintendence, and he vigorously advocated his replacement. He was pained to see how rapidly American losses were growing and how inept American officers under Washington's leadership were. Elected to Congress under the Articles of Confederation, Rush believed he could run the war better than the commander in chief; while he did not want to take the office himself, he was extremely critical of the general's abilities. In fact, so was John Adams. An attempt was made to replace Washington with General Horatio Gates, whose troops had won the Battle of Saratoga under his command.

Later in life, Rush was far too shameless when he brazenly denounced any accusation that placed him in an anti-Washington camp. He might well have torn page after page from his commonplace book that snorted of anything hostile about Washington. In one of the few surviving comments, Rush told John Adams that while General Gates's army might be compared with "a well-regulated family," General Washington's "imitation army" was nothing more than "an unformed mob." The general should be dismissed, because he was "unequal to the discipline and decision necessary to win a war." Rush was particularly concerned about the disgraceful mess in which the military hospitals had fallen, and he blamed both Dr. Shippen (Director General of the Army Medical Corps) and General Washington for being lax and negligent. As he told John Adams during the height of the controversy over Washington's leadership, "God alone I know must save us at last, but I wish for the future honor and safety of our country he may do it through the *instrumentality* of human wisdom and human virtue."

Rush retired from Congress when his term expired in March 1777 largely because of his open opposition to the Pennsylvania constitution, with its single-house legislature, a document he had originally supported while he was a member of the constitutional convention in Pennsylvania. He told a friend, Anthony Wayne, an officer in the American Continental Army, "Our people . . . have formed a government that is absurd in its principles," and that it "substituted a mob government to one of the happiest governments in the world." As president of that convention, Franklin had led the battle in the summer of 1776 to craft what turned out to be most radical of the new constitutions in America. He believed a unicameral legislature was best, because the people would work together to resolve petty political differences and only for the good of the people, whereas a bicameral legislature created a recipe for inaction; in short, the two simply cancel each other out. The lower house demands one thing, the upper another, and the two might never agree. It was Franklin's faith in the people's ability to govern themselves that convinced him a single-house legislature was superior to a bicameral one.

But Rush was of a different mind. He argued that only a bicameral assembly could achieve the checks and balances so necessary in law making. Writing in opposition to a single legislature, he said, "The supreme, absolute, and uncontrolled power of the whole State is lodged in the hands of *one body* of men. Had it been lodged in the hands of one man, it would have been less dangerous to the safety and liberties of the community. . . . The Supreme Being alone is qualified to possess supreme power over his creatures. It requires the wisdom and goodness of a Deity to control, and direct it properly." In the end, Rush's view proved correct and Franklin's wrong when the constitution was revised in 1790 to reflect his, not Franklin's views, and a two-house legislature came into being. (And Franklin changed his mind at the 1787 Constitutional Convention.)

In the meantime he returned to the army to help run the hospital department. During the American Revolution, Rush served as the physician general in charge of the Middle Department (or the mid-Atlantic states). Diseases were rampant, especially among American troops, because of poor hygiene and the lack of care. British soldiers had far better and more medical care and thus suffered less, and their hygiene was far better than that of the Americans. British forces brought with them so many trained physicians and surgeons that at any sign of illness or disease, they were immediately cared for. It is said that for every American soldier killed in combat, nine died of some illness. Besides smallpox, typical diseases included dysentery, venereal disease in its most virulent form, and something called "camp fever," which was probably typhoid fever or typhus. Rush treated camp fever with Peruvian bark, tartar emetic, laxative salts, opium, blisters, and bloodletting. Wine, too, was a highly valued treatment, though Rush generally opposed alcohol use under any circumstances.

Rush's major concern was to prevent smallpox by using live pox from the men who had contracted a mild case of the disease. Patients were first given a cathartic to make them vomit: he usually used calomel, jalap (a purgative root from a Mexican plant, something like a morning glory), nitre (or saltpeter), Peruvian bark (cinchona and other crystalline alkaloids), and snakeroot (plants thought to cure snake bites, among them Virginia snakeroot, senega snakeroot, white snakeroot, or button snakeroot). Dysentery and pleurisy (rheumatism) were also problems: dysentery often led to death, and Rush thought pleurisy led to typhus, which was often fatal. He noticed that blacks were infected with pleurisy more often than whites, and he also noticed that when troops slept outside rather than in tents, they were healthier than those who did not. Moreover, soldiers on the march (and thus always outside) were healthier than those who were mostly indoors. Fresh air, he thought, seemed to have salubrious effects in the prevention of smallpox, typhus, rheumatism, and other diseases.

Rush wrote to Franklin to tell him that he firmly believed disease was often transferred from a sick person to someone else simply by the "putrid" breath of the patient (or "the frowzy corrupt Air"). Franklin replied that "after having discover'd the Benefit of fresh and cool Air apply'd to the *Sick,* People will begin to suspect that it may do no Harm to the *Well.*" For Franklin, fresh air had obvious and immediate health benefits. He once wrote of how he sat naked for up to an hour before he got dressed in the mornings because he was convinced that it was "agreeable to my constitution. . . . This practice is not in the least painful, but on the contrary, agreeable." He was able to read or write during this time and even found that if he wanted, he could go back to bed for "the most pleasing sleep that can be imagined." He called this his "bracing or tonic bath." In other words, cold air did not make a person sick; only air with germs did. "Travelling in our severe Winters, I have suffered Cold sometimes to an Extremity only short of Freezing, but this did not make me *catch Cold.*"

Franklin later argued that sleeping with the windows open so fresh air could come in, even in cold weather, was the best way to stave off illness. "Another means of preserving health . . . is the having a constant supply of fresh air in your bed-chamber," he wrote. "It has been a great mistake, the sleeping in rooms exactly closed, and in beds surrounded by curtains. No outward air that may come in to you is so unwholesome as the unchanged air, often breathed, of a closed chamber. As boiling water does not grow hotter by longer boiling, if the particles that receive greater heat can escape; so living bodies do not putrefy, if the particles, so fast as they become putrid, can be thrown off." But Rush never went so far. He spent his nights with the windows tightly shut, with the covers over his head, and secure with his head in a nightcap.

During the war, Rush became disgusted with the wretched conditions in the hospitals. He described them as "the sinks of human life in an army. They robbed the United States of more citizens than the sword. Humanity, economy, and philosophy, all concur in giving preference to the conveniences and wholesome air of private houses; and should war continue to be the absurd and unchristian mode of deciding national disputes, it is to be hoped that the progress of science will so far mitigate its greatest calamities, as to produce an abolition of hospitals for acute diseases." Rush publicly attacked Shippen, who was now the director general of the medical corps in charge of hospitals. He thought Shippen was corrupt, ignorant, and incompetent: he was convinced Shippen collected graft when he ordered supplies, and he thought Shippen was speculating on the price of those supplies, purchasing them at a discount but then submitting invoices that were in higher amounts. In addition, Rush thought Shippen deflated the number of dead and wounded he reported to Congress to make it appear the medical corps was more efficient and competent than it really was. In response, Shippen thought Rush wanted to be director general, but Rush claimed he would never accept the position. In any case, he had decided to resign from his position as physician general of the Middle Department. "I was crushed at the ruins of the fabric of corruption which I had demolished. The friends of the Director [Shippen] partook of his resentments. . . . I therefore resigned my commission, on the 30th of January, 1778. The Director continued in office."

Rush's medical practice flourished after the war. Indefatigable, he put in long hours all day and into the evening, and he was especially well known for providing high-quality medical care to his patients. In 1783 he was made a staff physician at the Pennsylvania Hospital, which Franklin had founded. It was a position that paid nothing, but proved to be a powerful testimony to the esteem his colleagues had of his medical competence and personal integrity. "The hospital's physicians were automatically considered among the city's most distinguished members of the medical profession." Precise in his diagnosis, Rush was always forthright in conveying it. For about ten years, he was among the most sought-after physicians in America, giving him little time to concentrate on those political and social issues that moved him, including slavery.

In 1780 Pennsylvania passed a law that prescribed the gradual elimination of slavery in Pennsylvania, which was exactly what Rush had advocated—possibly because he himself owned a slave, William Grubber. Rush learned that Nathanael Greene, one of Washington's top generals during the Revolution, had been given a large tract of land in South Carolina, including hundreds of slaves, because of his contributions in the war. Slavery, Rush told Greene, "is to make war on nature"; still Rush said, Greene need not free them all at once, but only over a long period of time.

Meantime, the Pennsylvania abolition law stated that the children of slaves would be freed only when they reached the age of twenty-eight. Until then, these children would enjoy the same rights as indentured servants and apprentices. Other states hesitated, leading Benezet to tell Franklin he found it "sorrowfully astonishing that after the declaration so strongly and clearly made of the value & right of liberty on this continent, no state but that of Pennsylvania & that imperfectly, have yet taken a step towards the total abolition of slavery." (New York and New Jersey followed suit in 1799 and 1804, respectively. Rhode Island, New Hampshire, and Massachusetts soon added their names to the roster.)

The Revolution had disrupted the meetings of the Philadelphia abolition society, essentially dissolving it until it was finally reorganized after the Treaty of Paris in 1784. Rush, still a slave owner, now became a member. It was now called the Pennsylvania Society for Promoting the Abolition of Slavery, the Relief of Free Negroes Unlawfully Held in Bondage, and for Improving the Condition of the African Race (the inclusion of the words "abolition of slavery" reflected the new emancipation law, which had set forth *gradual* emancipation). When Franklin returned to America in 1785, he became its president; Rush became its secretary. Pemberton succeeded Franklin as president, and Rush became president in 1803 and remained in that office until his death in 1813.

The society distributed several pieces of important literature throughout the new state: copies of its own constitution; the Pennsylvania Emancipation Act; an essay on the slave trade by the young London abolitionist Thomas Clarkson, who helped create a London abolitionist society; and one by the French liberal Jacques-Pierre Brissot, who advocated the creation of a parallel society in Paris. Benezet, too, had influenced Clarkson in his antislavery views, especially after he read Benezet's history of Guinea. When Clarkson wrote his *History of the Abolition of the Slave Trade,* he stated, "Benezet's account of Guinea became instrumental beyond any other book ever before published, in disseminating a proper knowledge of the slave trade." Moreover, like the correspondence societies that were becoming popular in England (the Society for Constitutional Information, for example, and also the soon-to-be created London Corresponding Society), the abolition society communicated with sister associations in other states (all states had abolition societies by the late 1780s) and in London and Paris.

The Pennsylvania society opened a letter-writing campaign to representatives and governors, including the federal convention that began to meet in Philadelphia in May 1787. Its advocacy of the immediate end to the slave trade and slavery failed when the new United States constitution contained a compromise empowering Congress to end the slave trade only twenty years later (that is, after 1808). Nothing in the document mentioned slavery, given the precarious presence of the Southern delegations to the Philadelphia convention. Had an antislavery provision been added (or even attempted), the entire South, from Maryland to Georgia, would have walked out of the convention well in advance of the constitution's final draft and declined to ratify the new document.

Rush was heartened when he saw what freed blacks could do once they were prepared—that is, once they were educated. Five years after the passage of the Pennsylvania abolition law, he told Richard Price, "We perceive already the good effects of the abolition of Negro slavery in Pennsylvania. The slaves who have been emancipated are in general among the more industrious and orderly than the lowest class of white people." He noted that Benezet's school for black children was thriving, thanks in large measure to the legacy he had left it after his death the year before. "We have the pleasure of seeing them improve in religion and morals under their instruction, as well as in English literature."

With these beliefs fully binding his heart, in 1788 he finally freed Grubber. He claimed at long last he was "fully satisfied that it is contrary to reason and religion to detain the said slave in bondage beyond such a time as will be a just compensation for my having paid for him the full price of a slave for life." But, curiously, Grubber was not to go free immediately, but only six years hence. "I do hereby declare that the said William shall be free from me and from all persons claiming under me, on the twenty-fifth day of February on the year of our Lord one thousand seven hundred and ninety four." Rush obviously wanted to give

William some time to prepare himself before he was actually free, a policy he reserved for all slaves. He addressed many meetings held by blacks, and he visited every black organization in Philadelphia. He wondered why whites never attended blacks' funerals; for he himself did. Four years after freeing Grubber, he went to the funeral of a Mrs. William Gray. He noted that at least fifty whites were there as well. "The sight was a new one in Philadelphia, for hitherto, a few cases excepted, the negroes alone attended each other's funerals. By this event it is to be hoped the partition wall which divided the blacks from the whites will be still further broken down and a way prepared for their union as brethren and members of one great family."

In addition to the rapidly changing political climate with the Constitutional Convention and the new constitution itself, Rush might also well have been motivated to release Grubber after Rush rejected the Calvinist doctrine of predestination (he had been raised to adhere to the Westminster Confession with its emphasis on the role of the Elect Few). After he read the work of the English minister John William Fletcher, who believed in universal salvation, Rush was transformed. As he later told Richard Price, "These principles, my dear friend, have bound me to the whole human race; these are the principles which animate me in all my labors for the interests of my fellow creatures. No particle of benevolence, no wish for the liberty of a slave or the reformation of a criminal, will be lost. They must all be finally made effectual, for they all flow from the great Author of goodness, who implants no principles of action in man in vain." As he noted in his autobiography, after he read Fletcher and listened to the Reverend Elhanan Winchester, a Baptist minister who had recently arrived in Philadelphia, he said, "From that time I have never doubted upon the subject of the salvation of all men." Rush reconciled his Christian beliefs with liberal enlightenment ideas of reason and progress into what he hoped would be the "kingdom of Christ" and an "empire of reason." Whatever the ultimate causes of his belief in emancipation and his eventual decision to free Grubber, Rush was now a confirmed abolitionist.

Another law that irked him was the Pennsylvania Test Act, which required all voters and officeholders to espouse a belief in God and to subscribe to the divine authority of both the Old and New Testaments. It disenfranchised the Jews, the Quakers, the deists, and most of the Germans who refused to take oaths. While the new constitution of the state was among the most radical, it kept about two-fifths of the residents from voting or holding office, including all of the Quakers and many of the German immigrants. In arguing against the Test Act, Rush used the arguments that the English opposition had been using since the days of John Wilkes, for greater freedom and the right of the people to govern themselves. Reformers wanted frequent elections, no standing armies, low taxes, and the end to corruption through influence and patronage. The Pennsylvanians thought they had gotten it right in the new document. But the Test Act was anathema to all those who believed in religious liberty, including Rush.

He was particularly annoyed when he saw that the main supporters of the constitution and the test law were his co-religionists, the Presbyterians, and he soon broke ranks with them. As early as 1783, just as the Treaty of Paris was settling relations between Britain and America, he began to advocate changes in the constitution through a new convention. He especially advocated for the revocation of the Test Act. He told John Bayard, a Philadelphia merchant and like-minded constitutional reformer, "The opposition of our society to a convention I find adds fresh vigor to the prejudices against us. I lament it!" he exclaimed, "because I am sure that event must take place sooner or later. Pensylvania [sic] cannot be happy or united under its present form of government." He was unsuccessful in convincing the assembly to call a new convention, but continued to work to eliminate the Test Act. In 1784–1785 he widely distributed his pamphlet, *Considerations upon the Present Test-Law of Pennsylvania,* though it was published anonymously. At the same time, he began to organize a statewide repeal campaign. He sent a copy of his pamphlet to Price, who was shocked to learn Pennsylvania had such a repulsive law. "That is a miserable legislature," Price told him, "which relies much on the use of tests; for in general they bind only honest men."

Rush thought Price's condemnation was so good he reprinted it. He was delighted when the new governor, Benjamin Franklin himself, who had just returned from Paris, was surprised to learn the law was still in effect. Rush knew Franklin would work to maneuver an end to it. Just before Franklin got back to Philadelphia, Rush wrote to Price, saying, "While Spain boasts of her Ximenes, France of her Fleury, and Britain of her Mansfield, all of whom sustained the burden of government after they passed their eightieth year of their lives, America claims a Franklin, inferior to none of them in activity of mind and clearness of perception on the great affairs of government. We expect, on his arrival, a revolution in favor of reason, justice, and humanity in our country. He has already begun to point out abuses and to propose schemes that are full of wisdom and benevolence." And Rush was right. In April 1786 he wrote to Price that the assembly had finally repealed the despicable law so "as to confer equal privileges upon every citizen of the state." He was positive a new day was dawning for the state and for the nation. And in fact, it was: the American Constitutional Convention met that next May to draft the new document, and the new Pennsylvania constitution with its bicameral legislature was drafted in 1790. "Republics are slow in discovering their interest," Rush lamented to Price, "but when once they find it out, they pursue it with vigor and perseverance." He was right again—though at the time he could not have known how right. Only five states were represented at the September 1786 Annapolis Convention, which was why those few delegates advocated a larger meeting to take place in Philadelphia the following year.

Rush's optimism actually panned out when he reported to Price that by June 1787 eleven states had shown up to take part in the convention. He was particularly amazed at Franklin, who, despite his age, was always punctual when the meetings were held and took an active role in the deliberations. Franklin told him, "It was the most August and respectable Assembly he ever was in in his life." John Dickinson, who was Franklin's immediate predecessor as governor, was very optimistic about the unity the delegations displayed. But we know through James Madison's notes and the records of the convention that many times the convention almost broke up with the ongoing disputes between the large and small states, between the Northern and Southern states, over the fractious debates over election terms, over whether a bill of rights should be added, and on and on. Rush was delighted when a new document was finally sent to Congress and promptly forwarded to the states for ratification. A bill of rights would not be necessary, because the republican nature of the new document was so perfectly contrived, there was no reason for one (Rush changed his mind by 1789, when the Federalists were elected to office; the states ratified the Bill of Rights two years later). Once everything was in place, he told John Adams that his own republican views had been consistent since the Revolution. He wanted him to know, "I am as much a republican as I was in 1775 and 6, that I consider *hereditary* monarchy and aristocracy as rebellion against nature, that I abhor titles and everything that belongs to the *pageantry* of government, that I love the *people.*"

These views neatly fitted into his religious faith in universal salvation. He told Granville Sharp that "we err in politicks, as in other things, by not knowing, or by not properly understanding the Scriptures." He was convinced that reform in government came about only when men believed, as he did, in the Gospels, which "renders *viable and real* all their projects of universal peace and order." Every step human beings took to improve the world, to improve even their individual lives, was a step toward bringing the kingdom of God to this one. "This kingdom I believe will be administered in person by our Saviour upon our globe." Rush was absolutely certain Jesus' return was imminent but he dared not say when: "How long it be before he will revisit our earth for that purpose I know not." The upheavals in the world were a natural part of how God was working out his plan, which was precisely why Rush decided to remove himself from politics after 1790. Let others fight the political battles; he wanted to retire from politics and return to his medical practice. "Tyranny, anarchy, war, debt, standing armies &c are the natural consequences of liberty and power uncontrouled by the spirit of Christianity [*sic*]. They must therefore exist,—perhaps to furnish an opportunity of a display of divine power in destroying them."

His sensibilities of the innate goodness that could be found in the soul of all people led him, in 1787, to take over supervision of the insane at the Philadelphia Hospital. This was a most difficult job, since most physicians believed insanity was either incurable or the result of the wrath of God directed against unbelievers or evildoers—and therefore, likewise, incurable. Rush argued that even if no cure were available, the patients could be made more comfortable living elsewhere than in the hospital's perpetually wet and drafty basement: "These apartments are damp in winter and too warm in summer. They are moreover so constituted as not to admit readily of a change in air; hence the smell of them is both offensive and unwholesome. . . . [S]everal have died of consumption in consequence of this cold." Just as he prescribed fresh air for his yellow fever patients, so he demanded the same for the insane. It was to no avail. The hospital directors refused to let them leave the basement. Still, he tried to cure his patients by treating them with warm and cold baths: "I direct the cold to succeed the use of the warm bath while the patient is in the lowest state of debility [the term was from Cullen] and the highest state of irritability from the action of the warm water."

With the election of the new president and the first sessions of the First Federal Congress, Rush left politics for good. Rush wrote he was finally satisfied that the forward march of progress was ineluctable. Soon, all of his dreams would be achieved, not merely by men, but also through the grace of a benevolent and all-powerful God. His last years were punctuated by new efforts to bring people together in moral voluntary associations. Franklin had done the same when he first brought his friends together in the Junto. Rush now sought an alternative mechanism to make changes, the changes he believed were still possible. Active participation in civic and church affairs became the hallmark of his renewed sense of the way that the public spirit of each citizen could best function in the new republic.

Working with members of all Protestant denominations, he became an active member and leader of the abolition society and, with the realization of the First-Day (or Sunday School) Society, a founder of the Sunday School movement. With them, he helped form organizations that brought medical care to the poor in the Philadelphia Dispensary, better and humane treatment to the deranged and insane, and an end to the death penalty. He worked to improve prisoners' conditions in jails through the mechanism of the Philadelphia Society for Alleviating the Miseries of Public Prisons. And in the early 1790s he supported the efforts to establish a church for freed blacks in Philadelphia.

In 1791 Rush helped start a movement to create a black church in Philadelphia. He asked Granville Sharp to collect funds in England for this purpose, and Sharp sent fourteen pounds, fourteen shillings from six Londoners, and another five pounds from the Duke of Grafton. The African Church was finally erected on August 22, 1793, and the guest of honor was Rush himself, who attended the dinner to celebrate the completion of the church roof. About one hundred white people were there: "Never did I see people more happy, some of them shed tears of joy." Still, working on behalf of the abolitionist cause was not foremost in Rush's mind. His main focus remained his medical practice and the contributions he could make to the progress of modern medicine.

Despite the phenomenal success of his medical practice in the ten years after the Treaty of Paris formally ended the Revolution, his prosperity was not to last. It badly stagnated during the dreadful Philadelphia yellow fever epidemics of the 1790s. By then, he had totally abandoned Cullen's theory of fevers to develop his own "unitary" theory based on the idea that sick people actually contract a single disease in their arteries; what we think of as different fevers, he said, are therefore really only many different phases of a single fever. This new concept of disease led him to decide upon his remedy for yellow fever, and with it, his reputation as a bleeder became the only thing people talked about when they mentioned his name. As he put it, "From the year 1793 'till 1797 my business was stationary in Philadelphia. After 1797 it sensibly declined. I had no new families, except foreigners . . . My name was mentioned with horror in some companies."

Philadelphians had experienced several yellow fever outbreaks in the past: 1699, 1741, 1762, and 1780. But the worst was to come in the 1790s. In his 1811 *Picture of Philadelphia*, James Mease, a former Rush medical student, reported that the worst outbreak occurred in 1793 when an estimated four thousand people died. Four years later some thirteen hundred fell victim to the disease, and one year later, in 1798, more than thirty-six hundred people died. In the final serious outbreak of the century, over one thousand victims died the following year. These were years of a terrible plague in Philadelphia, and Rush worked tirelessly to defeat it with his heroic methods—though he again failed ignominiously.

Rush long suspected yellow fever was rooted in environmental causes, and, to a certain extent, he was right. As we now know, yellow fever is a virus transmitted by the bite of a female mosquito (the *Aedes aegypti*) that flourishes in stagnant water near human habitation. Its name is derived from the jaundice that appears on the second or third day. Although Rush could not have known about the mosquito, he was right about the environment, and he developed what we may call today "a green theory," which fitted perfectly into his general environmentalism.

Disease of this kind, he said, broke out because of man-made problems when dams were erected for millponds and when forests were cut down. The result was that marshes filled with stagnant water, which expelled a smelly, disease-ridden "marsh effluvia" (a perfect attraction for the deadly mosquito). The problem worsened after spring rains, when the wet ground produced "the generation and exhalation of febrile miasmata." To overcome these problems, Rush recommended the city plant trees around millponds as a shelter from the sun. He understood that the natural action of the trees removed the bad air ("mal-aria"), absorbing the carbon dioxide and giving off oxygen.

Rush had even more ideas about the etiology of yellow fever. He said that men should immediately cultivate the soil after the clearing of forests so that the cut areas were drained of the bad effluvia. And he went even further: he thought that smoke and fire were good antidotes to the disease. He apparently did not understand (nor could he have been expected to) the consequences of air pollution, and he clearly did not make the connection between smoke and lung disease. He simply preferred to believe that chimney smoke destroyed the effects of the marsh miasmas.

In the late summer and early fall of 1793, when yellow fever hit Philadelphia in its worst outbreak, Rush initially tried several remedies, all of which failed. He first tried gentle purges, then bark with wine, brandy, and aromatics. He applied blisters to the limbs, neck, and head, and then wrapped the body in clothing doused in warm vinegar while rubbing the sides with mercurial ointment to stimulate the body through the liver. He even tried throwing several buckets of cold water on his patients. Three of four of his patients died of this treatment. Then he returned to a manuscript written in 1741 by John Mitchell, which Franklin had given him just before his death in 1790. Rush soon discovered the ultimate remedy for yellow fever, or so he thought. The illness, he now concluded, was caused by overstimulation. Not only did he have to bleed his patients, he also had to purge them to bring the nerves back into balance. In short, he had to stop the overstimulation to calm down the excited blood vessels. The result was his classic purge and bleed treatment.

Bloodletting was a controversial remedy. Perhaps the best-known case of excessive bleeding was the fate of George Washington in 1799. After diagnosing the former president's sore throat, the physicians removed nine pints of his blood within twenty-four hours, a procedure that likely contributed to his death, if not killed him outright. Physicians, including Washington's, believed the body contained some twelve pints of blood, when it was in fact closer to six (obviously Washington's body was working hard to restore the lost blood over the period he was bled). Publicist William Cobbett quipped that because of Rush's fervent use of bloodletting, his major contribution to medical science was his discovery of how to depopulate the world. He called him "Dr. Sangrado," the physician in Alain-René Le Sage's *Gil Blas*, who bled his patients to death in order to "save" them. Because of Cobbett's incessant attacks on Rush and his reputation, Rush successfully sued the journalist and won a judgment for five hundred dollars against him. Cobbett fled to New York to avoid paying it.

Rush's methods were widely condemned. His critics claimed he killed more people than he cured. Rush responded by placing an open letter to the College of Physicians in the *Federal Gazette* defending his methods. "I have bled twice in many, and in one acute case, four times, with the happiest effects. I consider intrepidity in the use of the lancet at present to be necessary, as it is in the use of mercury and jalap, in this insidious and ferocious disease." But the matter did not end there. The high point of the disease was reached when 720 people died during the second week of October. Even Rush himself was sick mid-month for several days. When the disease finally ended with the coming of the November frosts, Rush claimed about 6,000 people were saved when they took his purge and bleed method. Of course he had no way of ever proving this claim.

New disputes centered on how the fever began and what to do to prevent it in the future. Because Rush was convinced that yellow fever was caused by bad air, he insisted the most recent recurrence was due to rotten coffee thrown into the Delaware River, which polluted the water and the air around it. Several doctors disagreed, saying the disease emanated from people from the West Indies or elsewhere. Dr. Isaac Cathrall claimed, for example, it came from infected sailors on a ship from Denmark. The attacks on Rush became so fierce that on November 5, 1793, he resigned from the College of Physicians, an organization he had helped found.

The following summer, just as he was writing his analysis and defense of his treatment of the disease, *An Account of the Bilious Remitting Yellow Fever, As It Appeared in the City of Philadelphia, in the Year 1793,* yellow fever unexpectedly reappeared. Rush continued to follow the same treatment, this time believing the filth in the gutters and the stagnant water in the neighborhoods were responsible. When the city's Committee of Health denied that the disease was present in Philadelphia, Rush was infuriated. His adversaries in this new battle were Dr. Adam Kuhn and his followers, whom Rush called the "Kuhneans." They attacked Rush incessantly for creating a panic by calling the epidemic yellow fever and by treating it with bleeding and purging.

By now, Rush's full complement of treatment consisted of bleeding, purging, cool air, cold drinks, and cold water applied to the body, all followed by the consumption of all sorts of tonics, including fresh fruits, bread, milk, chicken broth, white meats, eggs, oysters, and malt liquors, in an effort to restore health and vigor to the depleted body. Most important, he was now drawing from 50 to 150 ounces of blood a day from each patient.

Social consequences followed Rush's medical practices. Philadelphia merchants complained that his statements that the disease was in the city and was due to poor air and water quality hurt their businesses. They charged that people were abandoning the city in droves, and that the blame lay with him. Undaunted, he continued his work: he saw about two hundred patients in the 1794 epidemic, and remarkably only four of them died. He argued that one of his physician enemies, William Currie, who did not use the bleed and purge method, saw twenty-three patients, and seventeen died. After 1794 Rush was convinced the disease was contagious and a citywide quarantine needed to stop its spread. The disease only sporadically returned in 1795 and 1796.

During the 1797 epidemic, of the thirteen hundred people who died, nine were physicians. After Governor Thomas Mifflin asked for a report reviewing the course of the disease, the College of Physicians again concluded it had been imported from the West Indies after ships from that part of the world docked in Philadelphia. Rush was livid. "I was opposed by nearly the whole College of Physicians, who derived it from a foreign country, and who believed it to be a specific disease. They were followed by nearly all the citizens of Philadelphia." In the meantime the University of Pennsylvania medical faculty blamed it on the gutters and marshes and asked that the gutters be cleaned and the marshes drained. Out of his disagreement with the university faculty, a new medical society, the Academy of Medicine of Philadelphia, came into being, which he helped organized.

The attacks on Rush were always on his treatments, and not on his ideas concerning the origins of the disease. Philip Syng Physick, a former apprentice to Kuhn who later became a professor of surgery at the University of Pennsylvania, supported Rush with a letter to the *Gazette of the United States*. Physick (a perfect pen name for an eighteenth-century physician) said he had cured a man with the fever by successfully bleeding 176 ounces of blood from him in twenty-two bleedings in ten days. He also said he cleared the patient's bowels and salivary glands. Rush was delighted to have this support, but he did not have much more. He remained obstinate and dogmatic about his treatments for the rest of his life.

In September 1797 Rush contemplated abandoning Philadelphia altogether because of the attacks on him, which he likened to the Tory criticism of him during the Revolutionary War. He wrote his friend John R. B. Rodgers of Columbia College in New York that his medical practice "for several years past has been upon decline in this city since the year 1793, and were I not employed by strangers I could not maintain my family by my Philadelphia patients." He contemplated joining the medical faculty at Columbia, if Rodgers could convince the board of regents to hire him—of course, the board would have to allow him to teach medicine, as he understood it. "If you think there is any chance of the above proposition succeeding, you are at liberty to commend it in confidence to some of the regents of the University. If not, you will please to burn this letter." Rodgers did not burn it.

On October 20 Rush was invited to Columbia by the medical faculty, but his appointment still needed the acquiescence of the board, which included Alexander Hamilton, a Federalist and an inveterate Rush enemy (Rush was a known member of the Democratic-Republican Party, which made him a follower of Thomas Jefferson). Hamilton managed to get the vote postponed at the November meeting, because he did not want a republican on the faculty (not that it would matter from a medical perspective). With that, Rush withdrew his nomination. He instructed Rodgers to "stop the business in its present stage, and assure the trustees of the University that I shall not accept of the appointment should it be offered to me after the obstacles that have been thrown in the way of it by Mr. Hamilton."

With his practice in decline at the end of 1797, Rush continued to practice medicine, but only haphazardly. He now wanted to become the treasurer of the United States Mint. He had intermittently been offered the directorship during Washington's administration, but declined because his practice was so strong, and he was still developing new medical ideas; besides, Alexander Hamilton, the secretary of the treasury, opposed his nomination. Two years later, despite opposition to him as "a French Democrat," his friend John Adams appointed him to the post at an annual salary of $1,200. The two men respected each other, although Rush had outwardly supported Jefferson in the election of 1796. Adams wrote he "had known, esteemed, and loved [Rush] these three and twenty years," and therefore thought he was just the man for the job. Long after Adams had left office, Rush wrote to thank him, telling Adams he had lost approximately $30,000 during the yellow fever epidemics between 1797 and 1807. "Had it not been for the emoluments of the office you gave me. . . . I must have retired from the city and ended my days upon a farm upon the little capital I had saved from the labors of former years."

It was a position in which Rush remained until his death in 1813, but it never interfered with his medical practice or his teaching. Of course, he stubbornly kept to his original medical principles. Later in life, he remarked he was probably too blunt in his criticism of others and in defense of his practices. "In reviewing my conduct upon this occasion, I have examined its motives with leisure and severity, and have not been able to encriminate [*sic*] myself. I condemn myself only for some harsh expressions which I made use of in speaking of their conduct and practice. . . . The most offensive thing I did to my brethren was refusing to consult with them." In the end, Benjamin Rush's vision of America's future had a powerful influence on politics, society, and the practice of modern medicine.

3

∽

Paine, Revolutionary Zeal, and Engineering

More than any liberal eighteenth-century political figure, Thomas Paine defies categorization. A believing/nonbelieving, nonpacifist Quaker, Paine has been condemned in history as an unreconstructed atheist revolutionary on two continents. Just who was Thomas Paine, this younger friend and protégé of Benjamin Franklin? John Adams thought he knew. In an 1805 letter to his friend Dr. Benjamin Waterhouse, Adams wrote he was deeply wounded that the era he himself had tried to shape was now called the Age of Reason because a wretched book by Paine (that "disastrous meteor") carried that name. Adams went on to tell Waterhouse that:

> I am willing you should call this the Age of Frivolity as you do, and would not object if you had named it the Age of Folly, Vice, Frenzy, Brutality, Daemons, Buonaparte, Tom

Paine, or the Age of the Burning Brand from the Bottom-less Pitt, or anything but the Age of Reason. I know not whether any Man in the World had more influence on its inhabitants or affairs for the last thirty years than Tom Paine. There can be no severer Satyr on the Age. For such a mongrel between Pigg and Puppy, begotten by a wild Boar on a Bitch Wolf, never before in any Age of the World was suffered by the Poltroonery of mankind, to run through such a Career of Mischief. Call it then the Age of Paine.

Whether it was the age of Paine or the age of reason, Paine was a fascinating iconoclast. He was convinced, like Prince Metternich, that he was always right and that anyone who disagreed with him was plainly wrong and, most likely, stupid. Franklin's story about the French woman in a dispute with her sister applies to Paine. She apparently remarked, "I don't know how it happens, Sister, but I meet with no body but myself that's *always* in the right. *Il n'y a que moi qui a toujours raison.*"

Born in Thetford, England, about ninety miles northeast of London, to a lower-middle-class family (his father was a maker of stays for women's corsets), Paine did not immigrate to America until 1774, when he was thirty-seven years old. By that time he was a tall man for his time, standing nearly five feet, ten inches, with broad shoulders and a strong jaw. He had a long nose that seemed to protrude more and more over time as he aged, and he had penetrating gray eyes. A garrulous man of the people, he loved to engage in debate over all kinds of issues or just sing songs or recite poetry (some of it his own bad poems). He quickly grew to enjoy nearly everything about America—the company, the political debates, the oysters, the ale, the brandy, if not in that order. His ideas of government and society had developed during his earliest years in several small towns and hamlets in the Midlands and southern England, where he worked at odd jobs variously as a staymaker himself, a schoolmaster, a collector of excise taxes (twice dismissed), and a

Thomas Paine (1737–1809), mistakenly identified as "Edward Payne Esq.," mezzotint by James Watson, 1783, after a portrait by Charles Willson Peale. Courtesy of the National Portrait Gallery, Smithsonian Institution, Washington, D.C.

retailer. He changed jobs almost as fast as contemporary office workers change their shirts—failing miserably at all of these occupations.

Paine's decision to visit London in 1757 to listen to scientific lectures led to his introduction to Benjamin Franklin. Despite a lack of formal education, he always had a wide array of interests, and, as for science, he once wrote, "The human mind has a natural disposition to scientific knowledge and to the things connected with it." This was, he said, because "the natural bent of my mind was to science." In London he bought a pair of globes and attended scientific lectures, when he met James Ferguson, a respected itinerant lecturer from Scotland with a specialty in astronomy. Ferguson was Franklin's friend, and he introduced Paine to Franklin, who immediately took a liking to the young man. While there is no record of their meeting, it is safe to guess their conversation was spirited and animated. They almost certainly would have talked about the colonies' problems with England, especially their desire to remain loyal in light of the disagreement over taxes. Franklin had written in 1768, in an essay that was republished just as Paine arrived in town, that historically taxes were a voluntary gift to the Crown. Whenever money was raised from the people, their assemblies must first give their consent, just "as the money raised in Britain is first granted by the House of Commons." But now an "unhappy new system of politics" has arisen that is undermining American loyalty and destroying "those bands of union" that might well "sever us forever." Paine was moved because this encounter did not comprise his introduction to politics.

The first appearance of Paine's interest in social and political issues came in 1768 when he moved to the town of Lewes as an excise tax collector for the second time (he had been dismissed once for allowing goods to move through without being taxed, but was now reinstated). Lewes boasted a coffeehouse for discussion and debate, a theater that played comic opera and Shakespeare, a lending library, a large Dissenting community, and, most important for Paine's political education (and relaxation), a large tavern called the White Hart Inn, with oak-paneled walls and a huge fireplace. As the center of the town's social life, it was a drinking establishment and a hotel for travelers (its stables could house about one hundred horses). The town, with a population of around four thousand inhabitants, lay just ten miles from Brighthelmston, which was within Paine's service area as a tax collector.

Moreover, Lewes had a long tradition of self-government. Its townspeople had supported the Puritans during the English Revolution (one of its two members of Parliament, Colonel Anthony Shapley, had signed Charles I's death warrant in 1649), and it was a leading center of Cromwellian politics. This background translated into a town with distinct republican sympathies that were not quashed in 1660 when the monarchy was restored. While its local self-governing council, known as the Society of Twelve, was declared illegal in 1663, it was reestablished immediately following the death of the Duke of Newcastle (Thomas Pelham-Holles)—fortuitously, the same year Paine arrived in Lewes. The duty of the society was simple: run the town; make sure the streets were kept clean; capture stray dogs, cats, pigs, and cows; and appoint various town officials, such as the clerks of the market and, more importantly, the two constables. Well connected, Paine met Samuel Ollive, who was one of the constables, and soon, Paine himself, most likely through Ollive's influence, became a member of the Society of Twelve.

Here was where Paine's political education seriously took shape. In the Society of Twelve and at the White Hart Inn, everything converged: while the society often met in the town hall, more often than not it met at the tavern, where the Twelve discussed the financial and political matters of the moment, such as taxes, mortgages, and other town questions. The society was accountable to no one (it was not an elected body, but a self-perpetuating "oligarchy" of the most prominent citizens). Paine's participation in it gave him a sense of belonging, no doubt, but also a sense that he was no longer the craftsman whose career had been shabby and unspectacular. It also taught him the crucial importance of having local voices involved in political decision making (even if unelected). Moreover, as a member of the Society of Twelve and as a frequent visitor to the White Hart, Paine was introduced to, for the lack of a better name, a social club (or drinking club, perhaps), known locally as the Headstrong Club. It comprised some of the most prominent local men, who gathered weekly to partake of plates of oysters and jugs of ale and lager, port, brandy, and Madeira while they discussed the local, national, and international issues.

Paine was in the perfect environment. For six years, from 1768 to 1774, he discussed and argued with his friends about

Britain's deteriorating relationship with her American cousins. We do not know the details of these discussions and arguments, because no records of the club survive. Nor do we know for certain how much they talked about John Wilkes and his troubles with Parliament. (Wilkes, a Member of Parliament [MP], was engaged in political behavior so outrageous to the Crown that the government attempted to oust him from the Commons and put him in jail. He charged that the king's minister, Lord Bute, bribed MPs in order to secure the treaty ending the Seven Years' War in 1763 and then accused Bute of being the lover of the king's mother.) We do know that in 1770 Wilkes passed through Lewes; again, it is safe to guess Wilkes stopped in at the White Hart, and very likely Paine met him. The townspeople surely knew that Wilkes had been elected three times to Parliament and three times rejected (when Parliament itself refused to recognize his election), despite the fact that he had soundly defeated his opponent, Colonel Henry Lawes Luttrell. They understood that this was not merely a local issue for Middlesex, but one that raised important national questions about the rights of Englishmen, freedom of speech, and the right to vote. When Wilkes entered the town, he was greeted with the ringing of church bells. The local newspaper, the *Sussex Weekly Advertiser,* was known as a republican sheet that made no bones about its support for Wilkes. Its publisher, William Lee, was Paine's close friend.

In 1772 Paine's colleagues in the excise service asked him to represent them before both houses of Parliament, with the hope that the Lords and Commons would increase their salaries or at least make their working conditions better. From their annual salary of 50 pounds, the men could not afford to pay for the basic necessities of life: everything from grooming, feeding, and housing their horses to lodging and feeding their families, to paying the expenses of clothing and charitable contributions to the costs of moving when orders came through requiring them to relocate to another borough.

Even the collectors in urban areas, who had no need of a horse (the "footwalks" vs. the "outrides"), could not meet their living expenses, because the cost of living in the cities was higher than that in rural areas. Paine calculated that the actual wage was really 32 pounds a year after these basic expenses, or, as he put it, "One shilling and ninepence farthing a day." No wonder corruption, collusion, and neglect resulted: some tax men accepted tips or bribes, others let batches of goods like tea, tobacco, or brandy pass through without payment or perhaps only a partial one. Fraud, Paine acknowledged, was part of the men's empowerment, a result of "the temptations of downright poverty." Outriders relied on their friends and family to "keep their children from nakedness, supply them occasionally with perhaps half a hog, a load of wood, a chaldron of coals, or something or other which abates the severity of their distress."

In the meantime the English excise collected five million pounds a year for the Crown, surely enough to allow for a modest increase in wages. The men deserved a living wage—an outrageous thought to those who believed that the differences between rich and poor were as natural as the sunrise and sunset.

Aside from collecting taxes, the job itself was inherently dangerous, because the exciseman was also charged with looking out for smugglers. Armed only with his writing instruments and paper, he rode alone through the countryside on lonely roads in all kinds of weather and sometimes into the night. Smugglers knew the penalty for being caught was hanging, and so they were always armed. They were fearless and sometimes ferocious if they came upon an exciseman who demanded either the tax or the goods.

Paine's appeal to Parliament on behalf of the excisemen was his first foray into social reform and the first public display of his writing. His words were extraordinary for their time: he called for the organization of men to demand both wage increases and better working conditions; moreover, he was challenging the established political order on its own turf, in Parliament itself.

Paine's was an extreme statement; nonetheless, this work was not published for the general public until more than twenty years after Paine wrote it.

While his argument was extreme, it was not particularly revolutionary. Paine did not directly challenge British authority, its structure, or hierarchy. Instead, he couched his language in uncharacteristically soft, pleading, and polite terms. His friend William Lee, who might well have helped him draft it, printed all four thousand copies of his essay to take with him to London. Paine and others distributed it to Members of Parliament, the electors, excisemen themselves, and their supporters. The expenses of printing and Paine's trip were paid for by subscription: almost every exciseman in England, some three thousand of them, chipped in three shillings. But it was to no avail. The petition failed. Paine returned to Lewes and learned he had been dismissed from the excise service a second time; he had left his post without permission.

In 1774 Paine left Lewes for London to look up Franklin, whom he had met eight years earlier when he was first dismissed from the excise service. He had gone there to teach reading and writing in a school for artisans' children, but he also had an interest in scientific matters, and it was this connection that drew him to Franklin. His years of wandering from town to town, from career to career, must have seemed exhausting: he likely appeared to himself like the carpenter bee that went from window to window smacking up against the glass until it finally found the wood into which it could bore its hole. Franklin agreed to write him a generous letter of introduction to his son-in-law, Richard Bache, in Philadelphia (Franklin later referred to Paine as his "adopted political son"):

The bearer, Mr. Thomas Pain, is very well recommended to me as an ingenious worthy young man. He goes to Pennsylvania with a view of settling there. I request you to give him your best advice and countenance, as he is quite a

> *stranger there. If you can put him in a way of obtaining employment as a clerk, or assistant tutor in a school, or assistant surveyor (all of which I think him very capable) so that he may procure a subsistence at least, till he can make acquaintance and obtain a knowledge of the country, you will do well, and much oblige your affectionate father.*

Within a short time, Paine left England.

With virtually no formal education (like Franklin, he was self-educated), and with no writing experience (with the exception of his failed appeal to Parliament), Paine shortly became involved in the literary and political milieu of Philadelphia. Bache was a good person for Paine to know. He was an underwriter of marine insurance in Philadelphia and was soon to organize (and head) that city's Republican Society (with the support of his father-in-law).

Finding a residence on the corner of Market and Front Streets directly across from the slave market, Paine soon frequented the Library Company, founded by Franklin in 1731, and a variety of bookshops, where he browsed through the stacks and bought a few books, including Joseph Priestley's new work on different kinds of air. Next door to his residence was the bookshop and printing company of Joseph Aitken, who was beginning a new enterprise, *The Pennsylvania Magazine.* Paine was soon writing for it and became its editor. From this moment, Paine's name would become a familiar one to David Rittenhouse, Benjamin Rush, John and Sam Adams, Thomas Jefferson, as well as Franklin (now back in Philadelphia from his first tour of duty in London). By 1775 all of them, including Paine, were talking about America's potential separation from England, just as Franklin had done seven years earlier. They were meeting in Philadelphia in an illegal session of a Continental Congress. Soon Paine would explode onto the world, with his first major, downright revolutionary publication.

Paine was not one to run from a fight. He demonstrated that

whenever he went to the White Hart—and certainly when he agreed to go to Parliament to fight on behalf of himself and his colleagues. Still, he said he came to America to live a private life out of the public view. He sought no political office and hoped to live in peace. But as he later remarked, "All the plans or prospects of private life (for I am not by nature fond of, or fitted for a public one and feel all occasions of it where I must act personally, a burden) all these plans, I say, were immediately disconcerted, and I was at once involved in all the troubles of the country."

He would claim he did not fully comprehend the extent of the problems the Americans had with the British. Later, on reflection, he made some useful distinctions about this early period, that is, the period before he really joined the battle. When he arrived in America, he "found the disposition of the people such, that they might have been led by a thread and governed by a reed. Their suspicion was quick and penetrating, but their attachment to Britain was obstinate, and it was at that time a kind of treason to speak against it. They disliked the ministry, but they esteemed the nation. Their idea of grievance operated without resentment, and their single object was reconciliation." Or, at least, he, like so many others, thought reconciliation was possible and was what most colonists wanted. And then came the Battle of Lexington in the spring of 1775: British troops, under Major John Pitcairn, had approached the Lexington Green, searching for stores of weapons and powder that General Thomas Gage believed the rebels were hoarding in the event of a full-blown war with Britain. Pitcairn found only a small group of some forty militiamen milling about the green. When they refused to disperse, someone—no one knows for certain whether it was a militiaman or a frightened British redcoat—fired; within seconds, eight Americans lay dead, ten were wounded, and one British soldier suffered a slight wound when a ball grazed his leg. From this moment, Paine came to believe Britain was uninterested in reconciliation.

She was interested only in conquest. And so, when Rush came to him in the fall of 1775 and suggested Paine compose a short pamphlet on American separation from Britain, he jumped at the chance; the spectacle of Lexington—as well as the Battle of Concord—primed the cannon of Paine's first major American pamphlet.

The result was his remarkable 1776 pamphlet *Common Sense*. It was a tour de force and the first time anyone had, in print, called for American separation from Britain. Its rhetoric was matched on only two occasions afterward: the opening lines of his famous first essay in the *American Crisis* series ("These are the times that try men's souls") and his later defense of the French Revolution in the two-part work titled the *Rights of Man*. *Common Sense* was more than just one of the first printed arguments for American separation from Britain. It was a sparkling and treasonous call to action, for sure, and it is true that most of its focus fell on the American continent and the particular problems caused there by a vigorous attempt by the British government to ensure an uninterrupted stream of revenue from its colonies; still, its ringing arguments can be interpreted universally, even though Paine was careful to ensure that the core of his argument was, so to speak, local not international. Mostly in the section titled "Thoughts on the Present State of American Affairs," we find the most quotable phrases, which are still cited today: "Now is the seed time of continental union, faith and honor"; "This new world hath been the asylum for the persecuted lovers of civil and religious liberty from *every part* of Europe"; "The blood of the slain, the weeping voice of nature cries, 'TIS TIME TO PART"; and "in America THE LAW IS KING."

Finally, and perhaps the most famous phrase of all, is one that American presidents, among others, have enjoyed quoting ever since Paine first wrote it: namely, "We have every opportunity and every encouragement to form the noblest, purest constitution on the face of the earth. We have it in our power to begin the world over again. A situation, similar to the present, hath not happened since the days of Noah until now. The birth-day of a new world is at hand." To *form a constitution*, he said, as if to say that America had no constitution, and indeed, in his mind it did not; and neither did Britain (a charge he later used against Burke in responding to the statesman's harsh attack on the French Revolution). As early as 1776, just a few months after the appearance of *Common Sense*, we find Paine writing that there was no such thing in Britain as a constitution: "If you ask an Englishman what he means when he speaks of the English constitution, he is unable to give you any answer. The truth is, the English have no fixed constitution."

Surely, the pamphlet was about America's inevitable separation from Britain, about her independence and freedom. But we must not reduce its underlying purpose: although he was sometimes oblique in his argument, Paine was calling for revolution, not just for separation, but an end to the British monarchy, a fact that placed him leagues ahead of his Philadelphia, Boston, and Virginia compatriots. Paine's words, for all their simplicity, straightforwardness, wonderful imagery, and quotability, were designed to appeal to a worldwide audience and help create democratic republics everywhere. He hated kings and nobility, and he made no bones about this; kings were useless scum who preyed only on the weak and did virtually nothing save wreak havoc on people. Note his universal assault on monarchy as he condemned the British monarch: "In England a king hath little more to do than to make war and give away places; which in plain terms is to impoverish a nation and set it together by the ears. A pretty business indeed for a man to be allowed eight hundred thousand sterling a year for, and worshiped into the bargain! Of more worth is one honest man to society, and in the sight of God, than *all the crowned ruffians that ever lived*" (emphasis added).

There can be no doubt that Paine saw no use whatsoever for the English Crown—indeed, it was not merely a matter that the crown was useless; it was dangerous and perfidious. The only thing worthwhile in the world of politics was that "one honest man," the virtuous citizen, a public-spirited everyman, who must be allowed to run his own affairs without the threats of brutish kings. In fact, Paine referred to George III many times as the "Pharaoh," "Savage," or "the brute of Britain." And he was no different from all of the other "crowned ruffians that ever lived."

In other words, Paine's vision was more expansive than America. "The cause of America is in very great measure the cause of all mankind," he proclaimed. "The laying a Country desolate with Fire and Sword, declaring War against the natural rights of all Mankind, and extirpating the defenders thereof from the Face of the Earth, is the Concern of every Man to whom Nature hath given the Power of feeling." Paine rejected the polite, civil style of his excise petition for a hard-hitting, direct and blistering assault on monarchy. Revolution was the game to be played here, not merely separation, even if the ensuing war left the British monarchy intact (which he dearly hoped it would not).

For Paine, however, this revolution was the cause of "all" mankind for "all" lovers of freedom, not just Americans. Most Americans who despised the manner in which the British ruled the colonies, who declared that they were deprived of the rights of Englishmen, and who demanded a say in local colonial affairs far more than the ministry allowed, discussed and debated on the street, in the taverns, in the coffeehouses, and even in their businesses and shops what future action the colonies ought to take, including the demand that the colonies break all political, military, and economic ties with the Empire. And most who advocated such a step knew the consequences would likely include war, in this case a civil war, since combat would be between brothers and cousins (figuratively if not literally) on the battlefield of America. But this was not Paine's purpose.

Preceding the Declaration of Independence by six months, *Common Sense* surely demanded separation, but it went even further: a more careful reading shows that Paine demanded nothing less than the end of the British monarchy. Comparing the rhetorical effects, Jefferson's cerebral style in the declaration justified separation, while Paine's visceral style was to get the muskets into the field. Before the work was published, Paine asked Franklin, Rush, and Sam Adams to review his draft. Did they understand the nature of Paine's enterprise? Rush assured Paine they all believed in separation by that time, and he even secured the services of a printer, the Scot Robert Bell, who had the same sympathies. They approved it and let him send it off. But it is difficult to say they understood the extremism of the pamphlet the way Paine did. Because if they did, they may not have endorsed its message.

The only salvation for the Americans was to create a republic. "Common sense will tell us" that there can be no other conclusion. His argument was what Winthrop D. Jordan has rightly called "the killing of the king." Paine's rhetoric was so strong, perhaps as a leftover pain from his ill treatment in England, or perhaps because, as is so often the case, as a convert to republicanism he was particularly revolutionary. Had he had it in his power, he himself might have killed the king (or, better, kings)—just as his political ancestor, the Lewes parliamentarian in 1649, had signed Charles I's death warrant. Later, in an open letter to Lord Richard Howe, commander in chief of British naval forces (and the brother of Lord William Howe, the ground forces commander in chief), which appeared as the second *Crisis* paper, Paine said, "If I have any where expressed myself over-warmly, 'tis from a fixed, immovable hatred I have to cruel men and cruel measures. I have likewise an aversion to monarchy, as being debasing to the dignity of man."

In making his argument, Paine appealed to the deepest religious beliefs of his audience, and at the same time he was using religion for his own political (and ultimately, he hoped, the country's military) purposes. He was very careful to make sure he personalized his words. This was not simply a political treatise; like the Bible's Old and New Testaments, it was his own political testament, his bearing witness to the tyrannies of the past and what the Americans (himself included) must do to end them. George III and his minions (including all of the ministry and most of Parliament) he now demonized as godless, devilish, crazed, and deserving of defeat. Their downfall, thanks to God's help, was inevitable.

> *I have as little superstition in me as any man living, but my secret opinion has ever been, and still is, that God Almighty will not give up a people to military destruction, or leave them unsupportedly to perish, who have so earnestly and so repeatedly sought to avoid the calamities of war, by every decent method which wisdom could invent. Neither have I so much of the infidel in me, as to suppose that He has relinquished the government of the world, and given us up to the care of devils; and as I do not, I cannot see on what grounds the king of Britain can look up to heaven for help against us; a common murderer, a highwayman, or a house-breaker, has as good a pretence as he.*

After the war, if he could only return to France (he had served there for the new United States in 1781), he would work on behalf of these principles, leading a revolution there, which would eventually result in a French democratic republic and the beginnings of an international civil society. As a product of the Enlightenment, Paine believed that the progress in commerce, literature, and the sciences gave evidence that the world was improving. With vast alterations in the political wind, as witnessed by the first step taken in the American Revolution, global revolutionary action would wipe out tyranny everywhere.

When Paine finally returned to France in 1787, his immediate purpose was not to foment revolution. He had bridge engineering and construction on his mind. After the Revolutionary War, he had found the time to design a new bridge. He was convinced his design, once implemented, would be a great improvement:

his bridge would never be in danger of falling, like wooden bridges with piers in ice water during the winter months. For his writing services for the new United States during the war, he collected enough money to devote time to perfecting his design. New York State awarded him a farm in New Rochelle, the former home of a Loyalist; Pennsylvania awarded him five hundred pounds; and Congress gave him a stipend of three thousand dollars. He even bought a farm in Bordentown, New Jersey, so he would be closer to Philadelphia. When he was not working on his bridge, he wrote as a government propagandist (though he claimed he never wrote anything he did not believe in), especially in favor of the new national bank.

His main focus once the war ended was his immersion "in his project to the exclusion of everything else: indeed, he virtually retired from the political scene to press his bridge scheme, enlisting the services of a man by the name of John Hall, a middle-aged mechanic from Leicestershire who had settled in Philadelphia in 1785." He hoped to erect his first bridge across the Schuylkill River. "The river Schuylkill, at Philadelphia . . . requires a single arch of four hundred feet span. The vast quantities of ice render it impossible to erect a bridge on piers, and is the reason why no bridge has been attempted. But great schemes inspire great ideas. The natural mightiness of America expands the mind, and it partakes of the greatness it contemplates."

Paine's 1781 trip to France, when he accompanied American commissioners trying to arrange French loans and military supplies to help the war effort, first stimulated his interest in bridge construction. Paine wanted to do what he could to help secure French loans and grants, but also with an eye to determining whether any other country, England or France in particular, might be prepared for a democratic revolution. While there, he had time to observe a long-span iron bridge in Paris that had been designed and built by the French engineer Vincent Montpetit, whose structural models Paine found very impressive.

"With such circumstantial evidence one speculates that there was in Montpetit's design the germ of Paine's idea for long span iron bridges." Less than four years later he was engaged in building his first model, with John Hall as his mechanic. At first, his friend Col. Lewis Morris of Morrisania asked him to construct a bridge spanning the Harlem River, but when Morris was unable to fund the project, it was shelved.

Paine sent Franklin two models of this bridge: one made of wood, the other of cast iron that he and Hall had constructed in Bordentown. He asked Franklin to comment on them— favorably, he hoped. Though the structure, made of cherry wood, had held the weight of four men, Paine was uncertain how many more it could bear before splitting, and he didn't want to try: "What weight it will bear, as it cannot be ascertained without breaking it, I am unwilling to put to an experiment." Meantime, his main concern seemed to be not only the strength of the wooden model, but also the "compressibility and perishableness of the material. The ends of the timber by continually pressing against each other will in time diminish something in their length either by splitting up or wearing away." On the other hand, the iron model, given its greater strength and pliability, avoided these problems.

He was convinced that with the length reaching some 420 feet, the arch itself should be no more than "twenty feet in the center." With the plan for a bridge across the Harlem now pretty well scrapped, he told Franklin he hoped it could be constructed across the Schuylkill. "Could a bridge be erected on the plan of the iron model, it would exceedingly benefit the city and county, and besides its usefulness would, I believe, be the most extensive arch in the world, and the longest bridge without piers. I should therefore wish to see it undertaken and performed during your Presidency [of Pennsylvania], as any share I might have therein would be greatly heightened by that circumstance." Hall arrived with the models and soon had them set in Franklin's garden, where crowds of people could see. A little while later Paine and Hall dismantled the larger model and erected it inside the assembly building, where members could examine it and even walk over it.

Paine hoped that with Franklin's endorsement he could sell the model to the Commonwealth of Pennsylvania, and it would eventually span the river. He was surprised to learn that a competitor had already approached the Agricultural Society with an alternative; and, to his greater misfortune, it was becoming clearer that not only were the funds unavailable, but no one knew where so much iron could be cast to build a bridge so large. Paine, however, was undeterred. He wrote to George Clymer, a friend, a signer of the Declaration of Independence, and now a member of Congress, that he hoped "this business will not be gone into too hastily. A bridge on piers will never answer for that river, they may sink money but they never will sink piers that will stand." Working furiously to finish a larger model, this one of wrought iron, Paine managed to have it ready by January 1, 1787; he and Hall had it erected on the State House grounds.

Paine estimated that the cost of construction across the river would run to about $330,000, a substantial amount of money at a time when Pennsylvania was still paying its war debts. Paine asked Franklin what he should do, and the great scientist/diplomat responded that maybe he ought to take the model to England and France—because if he could secure the endorsements of the Royal Society of London and the *Académie royale des sciences,* he might have a better chance in persuading the Pennsylvania Assembly to build it. Paine thought this was an excellent idea. (And, after all, if he could not build it in America, perhaps a span over the Thames or the Seine would be just as satisfying.)

In 1787 Paine returned to France, this time with yet another letter of introduction from Franklin, writing to his old friends in Paris: La Rochefoucauld d'Enville, who had translated into French each of the state constitutions of the United States; Jean

Baptiste Le Roy, of the *Académie royale;* Louis Le Veillard, Franklin's Passy neighbor; and the Marquis de Chastellux, who had accompanied Lafayette to America during the war. The letters were all pretty much the same:

> *The bearer of this is Mr. Paine, the author of a famous piece entitled* Common Sense, *published here with great effect on the minds of the people at the beginning of the Revolution. He is an ingenious, honest man, and as such I beg leave to recommend him to your civilities. He carries with him the model of a bridge of a new construction, his own invention, concerning which I intended to have recommended him to M. Peyronnet [sic], but I hear he is no more. You can easily procure Mr. Paine a sight of the models and drawing of the collection appertaining to the* Ponts et Chausées. *They must afford him useful lights on the subject. We want a bridge over our river Schuylkill, and have no artist here regularly bred to that kind of architecture.*

Franklin also alerted Jefferson to Paine's arrival and hoped he would "introduce him where it may be proper and of advantage to him." Once in Paris, Paine wrote to Franklin to tell him he was delighted to learn that Jean Peronnet, the great French bridge architect, "is yet living. I was introduced to him by M. Le Roy. He has taken a residence in the Elysian Fields for the purpose of being near the works. He has invited me to see his house at Paris where all his drawings and models are."

Franklin's letters gained Paine access to the brightest scientific, engineering, and mechanical minds in France. Frequently dining with Lafayette, Le Roy, and Le Veillard, he soon secured an audience with a commission from the *Académie royale,* consisting of Jean Charles de Borda, the Abbé Charles Bossut, and Le Roy. Without a single reservation, they approved the design: "That Mr. Paine's plan of an iron bridge is ingeniously imagined, that the construction of it is simple, solid and proper . . . and that it is deserving of a trial." While the report did not go so far as to say the bridge should or could be built across, say, the Seine, it was sufficiently encouraging for Paine to send it to Sir Joseph Banks, then president of the Royal Society of London, with the hope of an endorsement. (He soon discovered he had a better prospect of building the bridge in England than in France when he received word that a rival had come forward in Paris, the shady Caron de Beaumarchais, who had been involved with Silas Deane's corrupt dealings during the American Revolution. Deane, sent by the Congress in 1776 to acquire war materiel from France, made a fortune, which he soon lost, through speculation.) Paine obtained patents for his bridge in England, Scotland, and Ireland and began to make plans to purchase enough iron to build a model.

Thanks to his contacts with Banks, Jefferson, and Franklin, he met Edmund Burke (his later adversary in the debate over the French Revolution). Together, the two of them in 1788 traveled throughout the Midlands, seeking iron for a model. Paine decided to first visit the Shropshire Ironworks owned by Isaac Wilkinson, and the Yorkshire Ironworks near Sheffield, which the Walker family had owned since 1749. He was more inclined to rely on the Yorkshire works. As he told Jefferson, "The Iron Works in Yorkshire belonging to the Walkers near to Sheffield are the most eminent in England in point of establishment and property. The proprietors are reputed to be worth two hundred thousand pounds and consequently capable of giving energy to any great undertaking." He had already spoken to them about his project, and apparently impressed, they had come to London to inspect the model.

While Paine eventually concluded an agreement in early 1789 with the Walkers to build a bridge, it would not be over the Thames: he began work on a much smaller one of some ninety feet in length. A local squire, identified only as Mr. Foljambe, wanted to build a bridge across the River Don that ran past his property. Paine described Mr. Foljambe as a nephew of the late George Savile, a Member of Parliament. The construction took place in Rotherham under Paine's supervision. He soon heard from Foljambe: "I saw the Rib of your Bridge. In point of elegance and beauty it far exceeded my expectations and is certainly beyond any thing I ever saw." Again Paine went to London, to seek a site where he could erect the larger model of the bridge, and left the work on the Don under the supervision of his foreman, William Yates, whom he called, no doubt as a joke, "the president of the Board of Works." He hoped by April Foljambe's bridge would span the river.

Meantime, he located a place in London to store his model. He was still certain it would someday traverse the Thames, and he began to seek out sites for it. He also knew he had to learn additional engineering techniques. He found that the arch, weighing three tons, held a dead weight of six tons, and that the compression and expansion possibilities of the bridge were so great it could hold enormous weight.

By July of 1789 he lost interest in the smaller bridge for Foljambe, and he told Jefferson he intended to work out a deal with the Walkers to build the bridge of his dreams across the Thames. "The Walkers are to find all the materials, and fit and frame them ready for erecting, put them on board a vessel and send them to London. I am to undertake all expense from that time and to complete the erecting. We intend first to exhibit it and afterwards put it up to sale, or dispose of by private contact." A scant two months later he again wrote Jefferson to tell him that "my bridge goes excellently on and my Partners (the Walkers) who are at all the expense except the erecting it in London, which is my part, have full as much confidence in the work as myself. About three fourths of it are already finished." He hoped to erect the bridge, he said, in Soho Square, where Joseph Banks lived. He thought he could persuade the Marquis of Lansdowne (formerly Priestley's patron, the Earl of Shelburne) to fund it, but if not, as an alternative, he would transport it to France, where he might find a financial backer to erect it across the Seine.

But Paine's attention in these months began to be drawn in opposing directions. In July the Bastille had fallen after crowds of people in the streets of Paris had demanded the release of its prisoners (all two of them), thus sparking the fires of the French Revolution. Paine was most interested in seeing a democratic republic rise from the ruins of the French monarchy, though he had to wait another three years for that to happen. He wrote to Walker in September from London that the weather was so beautiful that he "took a walk to see Dr. Price at Hackney who was all gay and happiness at the Progress of Freedom in France." At the same time, Paine longed to return to America, and he envied Jefferson, who was about to return as Washington's Secretary of State in the new federal government. "Remember me to overflowing affection to my dear America," he told Jefferson, "The people and the place. Be so kind to shake hands with them for me, and tell our beloved General Washington, and my old friend Dr. Franklin how much I long to see them."

What he did not realize was his backers and partners were in serious financial trouble. Paine had funded his part of the bargain with the Walkers by an agreement with Peter Whiteside, a businessman who helped him when he first returned to England in settling his mother's accounts (he wanted her to be comfortable in her last years). Paine had not known his father had died while he was in America; when he learned, he arranged, through Whiteside, for his mother to receive nine shillings a month for the rest of her life. Now, he got Whiteside to fund his side of the bargain with the Walkers—but Whiteside shortly thereafter filed for bankruptcy. When the creditors learned that Paine owed Whiteside some 620 pounds, they came after him. Paine refused to pay and was arrested at the London Tavern, where he was attending a meeting of the reform-minded Society for Constitutional Information. He was hauled off to jail in King's Head. Though humiliated, he was soon released and never faced trial.

By the spring of the following year, Paine was still trying to get his large bridge model down to London. He wrote to Thomas Walker, saying he hoped he could spare a workman to help him, since it was clear that Walker was not going to spare Billy Yates, the "president of the Board of Public Works," to do the job. He also told Walker he was furious at his friend Burke, who had made it clear that he was writing an attack of the French Revolution ("I am so out of humour with Mr. Burke with respect to the French Revolution"). Finally, in May, when the bridge arrived in London, Paine hoped it would attract sufficient attention to get built, and he would be done with it. He wanted desperately, he told Washington, to return to America: "My bridge is arrived and I have engaged a place to erect it in. A little time will determine its fate, but I yet see no cause to doubt of it success. . . . With much affection to all my friends, and many wishes to see them again," and he closed the letter. The model was erected on Leasing Green near Paddington.

Despite Paine's optimism, the prospects of the bridge ever being built under his direction were growing increasingly remote. By the fall, Paine built a fence around it—not only to protect to it, but so he could charge the public a shilling merely to look at it. While it stayed up for a year, by the time it was dismantled (it was actually owned by the Walkers, who returned with it to Rotherham), Paine left England permanently, having replied to Burke's famous attack on the French Revolution and having busily engaged himself in the events in Paris. As he later told Jefferson, "The French Revolution and Mr. Burke's attack upon it, drew me off from any pontifical works."

A few years later, in 1802, Paine returned to America. He brought models of his bridge back with him, but he never saw it built. In fact, a bridge that he was convinced was of his design had been built in England: "Since my coming from England in '92, an Iron Bridge of a single arch 236 feet span, versed sine 34 feet, has been cast at the Iron Works of the Walkers where my Model was, and erected over the river Wear at Sunderland in the county of Durham in England." Paine's friend James Monroe asked one of the Walkers whether it was Paine's design; if it *were*, perhaps he was due some compensation. The response to Monroe was disappointing: "I have good grounds for saying that the first idea was taken from Mr. Paine's bridge exhibited at Paddington. But with respect to any compensation to Mr. Paine, however desirous of rewarding the labors of an ingenious man, I see not how it is in my power, having had nothing to do with the bridge after the payment of my subscription." Paine never received anything for the Sunderland Bridge.

That the Sunderland Bridge was not based on Paine's design, or that he never did see his design actually used, does not diminish his creativity and energy. He took the initiative to develop his ideas and to put them into practice and repeatedly came up with better ideas and then built several scale models of the bridge—in wood, in cast iron, and in wrought iron. Certainly, Paine's bridge, designed at a time when there were but few made of iron, was an inspiration and a contribution to eighteenth-century engineering. This man of little formal education would arouse the thinking of many later engineers who constructed bridges based on his design.

Meanwhile, in 1790 the French Revolution was foremost on Paine's mind. He had not forgotten that he possessed a peculiarly, even God-given, individual role to unleash the power of what it meant to be free and to enjoy human rights, and he intended to undertake that role with all the force and power he could muster within him:

> *Why may we not suppose, that the great Father of all is pleased with variety of devotion; and that the great offence we can act, is that by which we seek to torment and render each other miserable. For my part, I am fully satisfied that what I am now doing, with an endeavor to conciliate*

mankind, to render their condition happy, to unite nations that have hitherto been enemies, and to extirpate the horrid practice of war, and break the chains of slavery and oppression, is acceptable in his sight, *and being the best service I can perform, I act it cheerfully.*

He was ready, and he was willing. Whether he could actually spark world revolution the way he envisioned was another story that nearly killed him.

In the first part of the *Rights of Man,* Paine's 1791 response to Burke's great work *The Reflections on the Revolution in France,* monarchy, rank, and privilege come off even worse than they do in *Common Sense.* We would be hard-pressed to find a more severe critique of these three evils. Now that Paine had established he was God's chosen instrument to lead the global revolution, he had to make certain that his reasoning would be followed, and that his leadership not ignored. Burke and Paine were actually good friends from the time they first met in 1787 and remained so until their clamorous disagreement over the French Revolution; eleven years earlier, Burke had supported the American cause before Parliament, but he began to feel queasy about the events in France after the fall of the Bastille. During this time, he never told Paine about his true feelings. At the same time, Paine kept Burke up to date on French events and thus became an unwitting supplier of factual fodder for Burke's coming assault.

In September of 1789, just as Thomas Jefferson was readying to leave Paris as the American minister, he told Paine he was jubilant over the progress of French politics. "These are the materials of a superb edifice," he said in commenting on the declaration of rights of man that the Constituent Assembly had drafted. "The hands which have prepared them are perfectly capable of putting them together, and of filling up the work of which these are only the outlines. While there are some men among them of very superior abilities, the mass possess such a degree of good sense as enables them to decide well." Paine passed this letter on to Burke and became Burke's inadvertent accomplice in his rapidly growing skepticism about the Revolution. A few months later Paine was back in France, sending Burke more information on events there: how well things were going with the drafting of the new constitution, how good the government's finances seemed to be, and how "tranquil" the king was with the new political arrangements. He even told Burke the events in France, like those in America thirteen years earlier, heralded a new day. So watch out, Britain, he seemed to be saying, because "the Revolution in France is certainly a forerunner to other revolutions in Europe." Burke's *Reflections* appeared on November 1, 1790, and Paine's answer, the *Rights of Man,* part one, appeared almost immediately, on February 22, 1791, and part two, almost exactly one year later.

For Paine, revolution and the rights of man were handmaidens in man's striving for political and social progress. Interestingly, in his mind, Louis XVI was no George III. Both were kings, but Louis was never the "brute of France" as George was the "brute of Britain," as Paine had called him in *Common Sense.* In September of 1792 Paine was elected to the French National Convention, whose primary duty was to prepare a new democratic-republican constitution for France. A committee led by the Marquis de Condorcet included Paine, and the men began their work, only to be interrupted by holding a trial for Louis XVI in January 1793. As a member of the convention (and hence the king's "jury"), Paine found one "palliative" measure that should spare the king's life: he argued in the convention that the king's support of the new United States "enabled [the Americans] to shake off the unjust and tyrannical yoke of Britain." Although "a monarchical organ ruled France," it was an organ that "certainly performed a good, a great action." Besides, Louis had gone along (no doubt he thought he had to) with the sweeping changes brought on by the events of July 14, 1789.

In Paine's mind, George III never would have agreed to these changes. Yes, Paine said, Louis Capet (he was calling him by his given name to reduce him to a man who was no longer king), the king should definitely be tried. After all, he had committed what appeared to be conspiracy with the "crowned brigands" of Europe when in June 1791 he and the queen fled Paris to join French royalist forces and Austrian troops in an effort to reestablish absolute rule in France. "There was formed among the crowned brigands of Europe a conspiracy which threatened not only French liberty, but likewise that of all nations. Everything tends to the belief that Louis XVI was the partner of this horde of conspirators." Paine claimed the fault lay not with Louis Capet, but with the institution of monarchy itself. While Louis Capet was in the dock, monarchy itself was really on trial. "I voted that Louis should be tried," he told the convention at the trial, "because it was necessary to afford proofs to the world of the perfidy, corruption and abomination of the monarchical system."

But there was a world of difference between the man and his office: "I am inclined to believe that if Louis Capet had been born in obscure condition, had he lived within the circle of an amiable and respectable neighborhood, at liberty to practise the duties of domestic life, had he been thus situated, I cannot believe that he would have shown himself destitute of social virtues." The question was simply not what should be done with the *king,* whom Paine considered to have abdicated his throne when in April 1791 he and the queen attempted to flee Paris and were caught in Varennes; the question was "what is to be done with this *man?*" Paine argued he should be banished forever to America.

So Paine distinguished between George III and Louis Capet, a distinction that had no impact on his view of revolution or on his goal to destroy monarchy everywhere and to create a world federation of nations to ensure everlasting peace. France had shown it could change through revolutionary action, whereas England was still stuck under a tyranny of the worst sort, one that demanded the people to act against their government. Monarchy, whether under the Stuarts or the Prince of Orange and his English queen, was still monarchy; and, besides, for one generation to bind another was absurd and inhuman (something Burke had long advocated). After all, "it requires but a very small glance of thought to perceive, that although laws made in one generation often continue in force through succeeding generations, yet that they continue to derive their force form the consent of the living." This was Paine's famous reiteration of Jefferson's principle that the earth belonged to the living, and any attempt by one generation to bind the next—even from the grave—was the moral and political equivalent of despotism.

In one generation, as Paine noted, the world was moving quickly. It had witnessed two revolutions—one in America, the other in France—and soon revolution would spread to the rest of the world, because this was a worldwide and universal phenomenon. "The objects that now press on the public attention, are the French Revolution, and the prospect of a general revolution in all governments," he proclaimed toward the end of the second part of the *Rights of Man*. In this utopian vision of the near future, peace, liberty, and prosperity would reign everywhere. And here Paine offered his readers what has become perhaps one of the most well-known and delightful images in the work. "It is now towards the middle of February," he mused at the end of the second part.

> Were I to take a turn into the country, the trees would present a leafless winterly appearance. As people are apt to pluck the twigs as they walk along, I perhaps might do the same, and by chance might observe, that a single bud on that twig had begun to swell. I should reason never unnaturally, or rather not reason at all, to suppose this was the only bud in England which had this appearance. Instead of deciding thus, I should instantly conclude, that the same appearance was beginning, or about to begin, everywhere;

and though the vegetable sleep will continue longer on some trees and plants than on others, and though some of them may not blossom for two or three years, all will be in leaf in the summer, except those which are rotten. What pace the political summer may keep with the natural, no human foresight can determine. It is, however, not difficult to per-ceive that the spring is begun.

Paine was determined that the time had come for action, and he was convinced of his own role in the coming cosmic events (until he ran into the buzz saw of the Terror just eighteen months later—Paine did not see it coming). In the meantime he crafted his fourth great work, the second part of the *Rights of Man*, which continued to condemn monarchy and aristocracy but now also unveiled a social welfare program, something so revolutionary for the time that the ideas of only one or two others matched his.

While Paine truly wanted to see the end of monarchical gov-ernment everywhere, he also wanted this new world to end poverty. This meant governments had to do more than merely tax their citizens; they had to provide their citizens with the kinds of social services that developed only in the twentieth cen-tury. He knew poverty: he had seen it in his hometown, in the Midlands, in London, and now in America. He had experienced it himself firsthand and had tried, and failed, to persuade Par-liament to alleviate the horrible financial conditions of the excisemen. But he did not give up.

Paine's social welfare program, which he outlined in great detail in 1792, consisted of several parts, all of which were geared toward helping the working poor. First were programs for younger people and families. Until they were fourteen, children would receive an automatic payment from the govern-ment of four pounds per year (about twelve hundred contem-porary dollars), so their parents could provide them with an education; and the parents themselves were to receive ten shillings per child every year for this purpose. Moreover, the government should set up a system of public education to ensure children had the basic knowledge they needed when they finally left their parents. (He was soon to work on a public education system with his friend and colleague the Marquis de Condorcet.) Finally, since newlyweds often had difficulty setting up households, they should be assisted financially at the beginning of their marriage, which meant that the government should give them a stipend of twenty shillings when they married.

Paine did not neglect the unemployed. He advocated a public employment program in which workers would go to "employment buildings," where every able-bodied man and woman would find work. The government would pay them based on their production (something that Karl Marx argued nearly half a century later), and it would house and feed them too. Paine wrote, "The only condition to be, that for so much, or so many hours work, each person shall receive so many meals of wholesome food, and a warm lodging, at least as good as a barrack. That a certain portion of what each person's work shall be worth shall be reserved and given to him, or her, on their going away; and that each person shall stay as long, or as short time, to come as often as he choose, on these conditions."

Paine also had a rudimentary social security program for the elderly, who, when they reached fifty, would have their annual income supplemented by the government by six pounds per year. He believed people at this age were slowing down and did not earn on a daily basis what they had when they were younger (after all, craftsmen were paid by the piece produced, not by the hour or day). After age sixty, when retirement began, these annual payments increased to ten pounds. For those who died a long distance from their families, the government would cover funeral costs. Such support was "not the nature of a charity," he said, "but of a right."

While other writers also wrote about the responsibility of

governments to care for their less fortunate citizens, Paine was among the most influential, if only through the sheer sales of his writings. The idea here is clear: he was not advocating the "rights of man" as political rights only, such as the vote, free speech, a free press, and the like. He went further, saying the "rights of man" included the right to be free from ignorance and poverty, and that if certain people were unable to obtain an education and a reasonable income on their own, it was the government's duty to provide them.

Even as he was crafting these ideas, however, he had no idea how dangerous life in Paris was becoming. After the execution of Louis XVI on January 21, 1793, he could not have known that from the end of May to the beginning of June, the second Girondin ministry would be thrown from office, all of the Girondin deputies expelled from the convention, and all of them pursued, most of them soon arrested, and executed. The mistake in practice, as it affected Paine, was that his close association with the Girondin faction got him into deep trouble. Many of his friends, within a very short period, were executed or committed suicide. Two years earlier, he had written a letter to three of them, the Marquis de Condorcet, Nicolas de Bonneville (with whom Paine lived in Paris), and François-Xavier Lanthenas (Paine's later translator), who had just founded a new republican society and a new journal (*Le Républicain*) that he hoped to write for. Paine alerted them to the reverberations of the highly unstable period: "During the early period of a revolution mistakes are likely enough to be committed—mistakes in principle or in practise; or perhaps, mistakes both in principle and practise."

In December 1793 he was arrested and for the next eleven months confined to the Luxembourg Prison, where he suffered not only the abject fear that his own execution was imminent, but also from a grave illness (a horrid abscess in his side and a high fever, akin to pneumonia) that he feared would kill him even if the guillotine did not. But he survived, and when he was released from prison, he stood for and won reelection to

France's new National Convention, which was charged with writing yet another constitution for the country (the previous convention had approved what was to be the Constitution of 1793—written largely by Condorcet and Paine—but Maximilien Robespierre set it aside when the Terror began). Once seated in the new body, Paine now pulled back from world revolution and sang a new tune of reform and the virtues of voting.

In 1795 he no longer argued that revolution was the sole means people had to end monarchy, privilege, and rank; but he also never admitted Burke had been right or that the Revolution in France was doomed to end in horrible consequences for its citizens and, ultimately, in dictatorship (though the latter was still a few years off). He was a hurt man, physically and intellectually, and he reevaluated positions he had firmly and consistently held since 1775.

The shift in his thinking may be seen in the following terms. *Common Sense* had opened with the classical eighteenth-century idea that limited government was the best form of government (which, "even in its best state" was "a necessary evil"). Now, just about twenty years later, he argued, "there is no subject more interesting to every man than the subject of government. His security, be he rich or poor, and in a great measure his prosperity, are connected therewith; it is therefore his interest as well as his duty to make himself acquainted with its principles, and what the practise ought to be." Government was to take on the new responsibility to provide for the needs of its citizens. The practice of government was rooted in its origins: did citizens have a hand in its formation through the promulgation of a constitution or were they merely subjects of a king? Hereditary government, by which he meant all governments claiming power by usurpation, never had the right to begin. "The right which any man or any family had to set itself up at first to govern a nation, and to establish itself as hereditarily, was no other than the right which Robespierre had to do the same thing in France." So how were changes to be made? Severely burned by the Terror, Paine now saw that revolution was not the ultimate panacea to all political and social ills.

He argued in 1795 that the grounds on which the people should undertake revolutionary action were the same for all radical transformations. Oppression and monarchy alone were insufficient for revolution. Under a constitution, "nothing, therefore, can justify an insurrection, neither can it ever be necessary where rights are equal and opinions free." Good constitutions obviated the need for revolution. Without a constitution, however, revolution might still well be necessary, but only with a great caution. Insurrection was the alternative *only when people faced despotism,* because despotism could not change by itself. Once the Revolution rid the country of its despots and their cohorts, the new rulers, to preserve liberty, must "permit to themselves a *discretionary exercise of power* regulated more by circumstances than by principle, which, were the practice to continue, liberty would never be established." Once begun, the revolution must cease as soon as possible. The people, then, must never take revolutions lightly. Revolutions were unnecessary in democratic republics that had sufficient channels to rectify oppression. Even in republics, some dangers arose when revolutions lasted too long. Revolutionaries must avoid becoming like those whom they had overthrown.

This was one of France's problems during the Terror. Revolutionary France had failed to establish a strong democratic constitution, even though one had been drafted and sent to the convention for approval. If it had been implemented, as Paine thought it should have been, "the violences that have since desolated France and injured the character of the Revolution, would, in my opinion, have been prevented." Rather than creating a democratic republic, the first National Convention failed in its task. It allowed France to transform itself into "a revolutionary government, a thing without either principle or authority. . . . [V]iolences . . . and crime . . . followed from the want of a constitution; for it is the nature and intention of a constitution to *prevent governing by party,* by establishing a common principle that shall limit and controul the power and impulse of party, and that says to all parties, *thus far shalt thou go and no further."* Instead of revolution, men must turn to the vote, "a species of property of the most sacred kind."

The vote had to be universal—all men (he did not include women) over the age of twenty-one must be eligible to vote, and not just the propertied few. It was as ridiculous as it was unjust to make property the qualification for voting: "Wealth is no proof of moral character; nor poverty of the want of it." Indeed, he went on, wealth could often be a sign of moral depravity and dishonesty whereas poverty a sign of innocence and a pure spirit. (Paine's enormous ego would have led him to believe he was addressing himself here.) Besides, the consequences would be disastrous when those who were excluded from voting united against the government, because they had no say in its decision making. A government was not a true republic if it forced some of its citizens to be disenfranchised, if it forced them to remain outside the pale of public spiritedness. Such a government was no different, really, than one based on the hereditary principle, because it turned the people into slaves: "To take away this right is to reduce a man to slavery. . . . The proposal therefore to disenfranchise any class of men is as criminal as the proposal to take away property."

Paine's ideas continued to focus, therefore, on the plight of the common man, the everyday person who struggled to maintain a basic daily subsistence. We see this again in his 1797 *Agrarian Justice,* his last major work, where he argued that private property was the cause of ignorance and poverty. While he did not advocate a redistribution of property, he believed those who had earned great profits from their property owed part of those profits to those who owned no property.

His reason was that God had originally given human beings the earth to own in common and that some people had unjustly seized large parts of it to call their own, to create their estates.

They now passed this seized property on to their children and children's children. "There could be no such thing as landed property originally," he said. "Man did not make the earth, and, though he had a natural right to *occupy* it, he had no right to *locate as his property* in perpetuity any part of it." And just in case the reader did not get the point, he added, in the jocular manner so characteristic of him, "Neither did the Creator of the earth open a land-office, from when the first title-deeds should issue." Paine was never one to mince words—and he was never one to allow a good joke to pass unsaid.

Paine's plan was decidedly not an agrarian law, which calls for all land to be seized by the government and redistributed equally to all its citizens. It was agrarian justice. His ideas make him a liberal in our contemporary sense, where social welfare is a right, not a gift, and the government has the responsibility to care for the less fortunate. His program was rather simple and in many ways quite thoughtful and serious. He wanted the government to reimburse those who had been disinherited from the land, and therefore he created the legal fiction that those who owned the land actually owed a debt to the poor. Before civil society, when men and women lived in a state of nature, poverty did not exist, because the earth was rich and bountiful. Now that some men had seized the land or bought it or stolen it outright, the solution had to be both right and just. The only opportunity was "to remedy the evils and preserve the benefits that have arisen to society by passing from the natural to that which is called the civilized state." This remedy had to be based on the proposition that "the condition of every person born in to the world, after a state of civilization commences, ought not be worse than if he had been born before that period."

The solution: government had to fund a payback through the payment of a "ground rent" to each and every individual who did not own land. This "rent" was to be paid in the form of an inheritance tax worth one-tenth the value of a parcel of land being passed from decedent to beneficiary. No one lost land; no one was disinherited from the lands of ancestors. He had only to pay a premium to pass it on to the next generation. In words echoing *Rights of Man,* he wrote it was "a right not a charity that I am pleading for." The principle underlying how this fund worked was simple: whenever people reached the age of twenty-one, rich or poor, the government would give them a stipend of fifteen pounds sterling to compensate for the loss of their "natural inheritance, by the introduction of private property." Paine often spoke of the "loss of his or her inheritance"—so men and women were both eligible. Nor was it based on need, since all people, no matter their income, received the same amount from the government. Paine claimed that he did not want to see "invidious distinctions" made between people.

The good this would do was, in his mind, enormous: "The plan here proposed will reach the whole. It will immediately relieve and take out of view three classes of wretchedness—the blind, the lame, and the aged poor; and it will furnish the rising generation with means to prevent their becoming poor; and it will do this without deranging or interfering with any national measures." Eager that the program might begin, he offered to contribute one hundred pounds of his own money into the fund in 1797 to get it started in France. No one took him up on the offer. Still, it displayed his passionate desire to help the poor and less unfortunate. Paine clearly was a man ahead of his time, whose ideas prefigured twentieth-century social welfare.

In 1802 he finally returned to America. Among the things he was anxious to see was how the new Constitution had operated during the first electoral crisis, which eventually led to the Federalists being voted out of office (though barely) in Congress and the presidency. In 1800 the Jeffersonians were in ascendancy and would remain so long after Paine's death—until the election of John Quincy Adams in 1824. This stability would have demonstrated to Paine that a vigilant citizenry protected its rights by means of a good constitution, one that kept party, faction, and corruption in check. It also proved that in a true democratic republic, power could pass peacefully from one political party or faction, without revolution or civil war. The American Constitution allowed citizens to have a high awareness of the day's public issues. For only when they were fully acquainted with the issues could they confront and resolve them. The people's natural political character forced them always to employ their inventive powers. As long as the Constitution protected their natural and fundamental civil and political rights, they would use them to undertake the necessary changes as the conditions of life changed. As a leading spokesman for social and political progress, Thomas Paine was a spiritual cousin of Benjamin Franklin.

England

4

Price and Priestley, Religious Dissent and Revolution

Richard Price and Joseph Priestley were linked by a mutual friendship with Benjamin Franklin, an endearing relationship with each other, and a shared ideology concerning political reform and religious sensibilities. Presbyterian preachers by trade, they were nearly as prolific in their political writings as they were in their theological and scientific work. Though they lived in different parts of England (Priestley was a constant mover to different parts of the country—mainly in the Midlands—while Price stayed put in Stoke Newington just outside of London), the prolific correspondence between them took up a great deal of their time. Whenever Priestley visited London, he invariably met Price for a meal at Franklin's Club of Honest Whigs, a supper club of liberals and Dissenters. It was a convivial world for the two of them. And yet, as close as they were, when Price and Priestley came to write a book together, they took very different sides of

141

a philosophical discussion about free will (Price) and determinism (Priestley).

Together, they devoted an enormous amount of time and energy to the late-eighteenth-century English parliamentary reform movement. This largely took the form of their fight to end the political disabilities that all Dissenters and Catholics suffered under the Clarendon Code, named for Charles II's chief minister, which barred non-Anglicans from the universities at Oxford and Cambridge and denied them the right to vote or hold public office. The code passed Parliament between 1661 and 1665. It included the Corporation Act, which required all public officers to accept the liturgy of the Church and the Act of Uniformity, which required all ministers to use the Book of Common Prayer and to subscribe to its teachings and beliefs. The Conventicle Act prohibited the assembly of any more than five non-Anglican people in any one place. In 1673, when the Test Act became law, Dissenters and Catholics were excluded from public service because they refused to accept the liturgy of the official Church, refused to take the oath of allegiance and supremacy, and declined to take communion in accordance with the rituals of the Anglican Church.

Priestley and Price came from Dissenting religious backgrounds, so named because Dissenters (or nonconformists) refused to adhere to the tenets of the officially established Church of England. Most Dissenters had Calvinist backgrounds, but the Dissenting movement itself included the non-Anglican Protestant religions, historically identified as Presbyterians, Baptists, and Independents (Congregationalists). It also included the Quakers, and, of course, the Unitarians. Catholics, Jews, and people of other non-Protestant religions were not counted among the Dissenters. As Presbyterians-turned-Unitarians (though of different stripes), Priestley and Price, like all Dissenters, practiced and preached a creed that was technically illegal—until, that is, Lord Chief Justice Mansfield declared Dissenting sects legal in 1767.

Price and Priestley, as had many Dissenters before them, fought for the repeal of the Test and Corporation Acts in order to end the monopoly of the Church of England. In fact, religious disestablishment in England did not take place until 1832. Thanks to the exemption Dissenters received in the 1689 Act of Toleration, they could practice their religion if they were members of one of the Dissenting faiths. The act rewarded Dissenters who supported the Restoration and allowed non-Anglicans to worship as they pleased—provided they believed in the Trinity (which neither Price nor Priestley did), abided by the oaths of allegiance and supremacy, and denounced the doctrine of transubstantiation (Price and Priestley agreed with the last two). With the passage in 1727 of the Indemnity Acts, Dissenters were freed from the harsher punishments of the Test and Corporation Acts, but penalties still remained. Meanwhile, the Toleration Act also allowed those who qualified to set up their own Dissenting academies and teach there. Both Price and Priestley flourished in the academies they joined as faculty members. Despite the limited freedom that Dissenters enjoyed, Price and Priestley devoted much of their political activism to the repeal of the Test and Corporation Acts in order for Dissenters to become full-fledged, first-class English citizens.

There was also a secular side to their liberal views. English boroughs and counties were notoriously corrupt. In fact, "corruption" was the buzzword among liberal political reformers of the eighteenth century. Its opposite was "virtue," a characteristic they hoped to generate in men who led the government. Ultimately, corruption meant the absence of independence, autonomy, and freedom: Members of Parliament from a particular county or shire were most likely paid puppets of some wealthy landed magnate who virtually owned the district (and himself was a toady to the king and his court). Many districts were in fact bought and paid for, so that the landed gentry always knew who from their district served in the Commons and who fulfilled his wishes. Often, the local patron simply reserved a seat for his eldest son or someone he trusted. These rotten boroughs were regarded as property to be passed from father to son like the rest of the landed estates. But not all boroughs were like that. Some, where the landed elites were not as powerful, actually had contested elections. Until the Reform Act of 1832, probably only a quarter of the elections had more than one candidate.

Franklin, always skeptical that England would ever reform itself, once told Price:

> *When I think of your present crazy Constitution [at least Franklin thought England had a constitution, even if Paine did not], and its Diseases, I imagine the enormous Emoluments of Place to be among the greatest, and while they exist I doubt whether even the Reform of your Representation will cure the Evils constantly arising from your perpetual Factions. As it seems to be a settled point at present that the Minister [William Pitt the Younger] must govern the Parliament, who are to do everything he would have done; and he is to bribe them to do this, and the people are to furnish the Money to pay these bribes, such a Parliament appears to me a very expensive machine for Government.*

To reduce this expense, he suggested in his usual irascible, jocular way that maybe Parliament just ought to be done away with, and Pitt could then run the entire government by himself. It would save everybody money.

Liberal reformers like Price and Priestley wanted to expand the franchise, or the right to vote, which was so limited, and they wanted to reform the borough system, making all elections free and open to all candidates. They also advocated frequent elections, because they believed that once a Member of Parliament took his seat in the Commons, he was almost immediately tempted to accept the offer of a place in the court; such MPs were known as "placemen," the mosquito-like office seekers perennially humming around the court. For this reason, Price and Priestley also lobbied for paid salaries for MPs. Most importantly, they wanted to transform England from a monarchy to a republic and thus end the entire process of office seeking. They hoped a representative government in England with a freely elected executive, even if he were a king, and legislative branches elected by a broad constituency would lead to good (at least better) political decision making.

What distinguished their views from, say, those of Tom Paine or Benjamin Rush, was their conviction that with England's long history as a monarchy, it was pointless to transform the executive office into an elected president like America's. For England, there should be an elected king, and he would be treated as an ordinary citizen and subordinate to the law; and Parliament would still be sovereign, according to the settlement after 1688. This was not a rare concept among eighteenth-century liberal Dissenters like Price and Priestley.

Born in 1733, Joseph Priestley was a man of average height, striking if not exactly handsome, with straight brown hair, very thin lips, a long nose, and a weak chin. Perhaps the strangest thing about his face was that it was notoriously lopsided: his right and left profiles made him look like two different people. Early in life, he had a speech impediment, probably a stutter; he claimed it came on him during his early Calvinist upbringing when he became fearful that he was not one of the Elect Few. He also claimed he overcame the worst of the impediment in his early twenties by breathing exercises and by reading "very loud and very slow," techniques he learned from a London physician. Throughout his life, he played the flute in his leisure time for pleasure. His friends commented that he was "an amiable person of an open and benevolent disposition, and a man of great accomplishments, real piety, and outstanding industry."

The Reverend Joseph Priestley (1733–1804) by Rembrandt
Peale, 1801. Collection of the New York Historical Society.

By profession a Presbyterian minister, Priestley eventually
moved to the extreme end of Unitarianism. He adopted the
Socinian version of Unitarianism that held Jesus to be a mere
man, though an extraordinary man with an extraordinary message, but not divine. Combining a philosophy of natural goodness with human rationality, Socinianism also included a strong
respect for and belief in the Scriptures. As a Dissenting preacher,
Priestley spent a lifetime determined to demonstrate Jesus'
humanness (he once wrote that Jesus was "a man like ourselves"),
a subject with revolutionary overtones that led to a bitter
exchange with the grand historian of the Roman Empire,
Edward Gibbon. In addition, by training and inclination,
Priestley was a schoolteacher and a writer on many subjects. At
one point he opened his own school, but for most of his life he
worked as a preacher and schoolmaster in various Dissenting
academies in and around the Midlands.

In 1769 he founded the first truly liberal religion magazine, the *Theological Repository,* and three years later demanded the repeal of the Test and Corporation Acts (the petition failed). These progressive views marked him throughout his career. He favored the separation of church and state and for all English male citizens the right to vote, no matter their religion, social status, or wealth. He fervently believed in American independence from England, and he was an immediate supporter of the French Revolution, hoping that the end of monarchy there would spread throughout Europe—including, of course, England. For Priestley, progress, especially as human reason directed men to do what was right, was guided by Divine Providence: "the widespread demonstration of the facts of natural providence was to lead to the emancipation of reason and the displacement of illegitimate and corrupt authority in church and State."

As a historian and an expert in ancient and modern languages (Hebrew, Latin, Greek, French, German, and Italian) and rhetoric, he was incredibly prolific (his printed nonscientific works run to twenty-six volumes); as a Wesleyan preacher, he was methodical and careful. In fact, he was so prolific and methodical at once (two traits that don't always go hand in hand), he produced several books at the same time—which led some wit to remark Priestley wrote books faster than people could read them.

Richard Price, in the meantime, spent most of his career preaching at several Presbyterian chapels and teaching in Dissenting academies. The young Mary Wollstonecraft was one of his congregants when he was the minister at the Chapel on the Green in Stoke Newington, where he and his wife lived for almost thirty-five years. One of their steady visitors was the Scottish philosopher and historian David Hume, with whom Price sustained a long and warm friendship, though the two rarely agreed on any philosophical or theological question. Price's first philosophical work, which appeared when he was thirty-five, was a tract on moral philosophy challenging Hume's philosophical skepticism. This tract immediately established Price's reputation as an original and major writer on ethics and morality. Like everything he said or wrote, it was deeply rooted in his religious faith.

The Reverend Richard Price (1723–1791), engraving after Benjamin West, 1793. National Portrait Gallery, London.

Price is known in the history of philosophy as an ethical intuitionist. He claimed we know right from wrong because all humans possess a moral sense telling us the difference. Whereas Hume's skepticism drew the Scot to conclude we can never have certainty over right and wrong, Price claimed to know better: "The power within us that perceives the distinctions of right and wrong is the understanding. . . . Price holds that right is irresolvable; it is a simple and ultimate idea that cannot be analysed into anything else. It is perceived by the intuitive reason." It is our way of knowing when to act with the assurance that what we do is right, and right all of the time. The moral law, which we intu-itively know, demands us to act morally. It is obligatory, and we disobey God when we fail to do good deeds. This insight was what made Price's contribution so distinctive for eighteenth-century moral philosophy. Morality was not directly tied to our reason, he said, but to the conscience that God had given to us; we are guided by divine authority. Price's work would always be based on his deep faith in God and His providential care of the world.

Price's first major work in theology, his *Four Dissertations,* appeared in 1767. It was an attempt to prove the reality of mira-cles; once again he challenged Hume, who had argued that mir-acles were impossible. Price's book was well received, and he was awarded an honorary Doctor of Divinity degree from Marischal College, University of Aberdeen. The work also caught the attention of the Earl of Shelburne (later the Marquis of Lans-downe), who wanted to meet the young preacher. Lady Elizabeth Montagu, whose salon, the Bluestockings, was famous for attracting the leading literati of London, introduced them; they became lifelong friends. Shelburne promised Price he would work to repeal the hated Test and Corporation Acts. After the fall of the ministry of Lord North in 1782, he tried to do so, though he failed.

Price also kept up a lively correspondence with Benjamin Rush during the 1780s. They sent each other copies of their political, scientific, and theological writings, and they discussed a wide array of issues, chief among them American independ-ence. In 1784 Price wrote a pamphlet extolling the success of the American Revolution, and in October of that year he sent Rush several copies for distribution in Pennsylvania. Price was so enthralled by the Americans' victory, he exclaimed, "Perhaps, I do not go too far when I say that, next to the introduction of Christianity among mankind, the American Revolution may prove the most important step in the progressive course of human improvement." He particularly wanted the Pennsylvania governor, John Dickinson, to receive a copy. Price highly respected Dickinson, the author of the 1768 *Letters from a Farmer in Pennsylvania to the Inhabitants of the British Colonies,* and it was in Price's honor that Rush later worked to found a college named for Dickinson in the western part of the state.

Price would later retract his lavish praise of the American Revolution, after Rush told him that several states, including Pennsylvania, still had test acts: to be considered full-fledged citizens as voters and public officials, people first had to swear they believed in the divine inspiration of the Old and New Testaments.

Price is best known for delivering a famous sermon called *A Discourse on the Love of Our Country* as the keynote speech in November 1789 to the Revolution Society. The society met annually to commemorate the anniversary of the 1688 English Revolution. The speech strikingly affirmed the goals of the French Revolution that had begun just four months earlier. Price was so lavish in his praise of the Revolution and in his profound hope that England would soon follow France's example that philosopher and statesman Edmund Burke was provoked the next year to write his even more famous and most antirevolutionary *Reflections on the Revolution in France.*

Born in Wales in 1723, Price was a half a generation younger than Franklin. Price is said to have been a small, thin, gentle man of fundamental humility and deep piety. Samuel Rogers, his neighbor in Stoke Newington, said Price "would often drop in, to spend the evening with us, in his dressing-gown; he would take and read the Bible to us till he sent us to bed in a frame of mind as heavenly as his own. He lived much in the society of Lord Lansdowne and other people of rank; and his manners were extremely polished. In the pulpit he was great indeed,—making his hearers forget the *preacher* and think only of the *subject.*" Benjamin West, the artist, painted Price's portrait twenty years later, when he was sixty-one, showing Price in a quiet repose. Surrounded by his books, he appears to be just looking up from a paper he has been reading or writing. He grasps his spectacles in his right hand and wears a powdered wig. It may be that he is readying himself to preach and is holding the sermon that he has been working on. His face displays a slight smile, dark eyebrows, a long broad nose, and a thin upper lip. As a Unitarian minister, he had a deep faith in both God and the moral duty that all humans have to remake the world as a better place. But he held with the Arians that Jesus himself was not divine, and thus neither coeternal nor consubstantial with God. In any case, his faith imbued his social and political ideas with certainty and soundness.

Activities to reform English politics began in earnest in the late 1760s, with the controversy over the contested election of John Wilkes, a member of the House of Commons from Middlesex. The owner and editor of *The North Briton* newspaper, Wilkes had outrageously attacked the king, Parliament, and anything he found hypocritical or worthy of censure. He once suggested that the king's first minister and confidant, Lord Bute, was receiving bribes and was possibly a lover of the king's mother. Arrested on a general warrant, but freed because he had parliamentary immunity, Wilkes was charged with seditious libel. He fled to France. When he returned, he stood for reelection to the Commons and won, but he was expelled by the membership and rearrested. Sentenced to twenty-two months in jail, he enjoyed public outcries in his support and some financial assistance too, and he won reelection votes three times, in February, March, and April 1769. Each time the government denied his victory and gave it to the losing opponent.

Wilkes's case set off a series of riots, public disturbances, and petitions with cries of "Wilkes and Liberty!"—all to the consternation of Franklin (and the Tory Samuel Johnson as well). Wilkes was elected a London alderman later in 1769, then sheriff the following year, and finally Lord Mayor in 1774. That same year, he was again elected to Parliament and finally took his seat. By then, the Commons agreed that the electorate would have the right to have its winning candidate seated, but the Commons would still have the right to expel whomever it thought unfit to serve. Nonetheless, it was an important victory for the reformists' cause, because it generated the formation of new organizations devoted to the reform of English government.

This is the environment in which Price and Priestley flourished during the 1770s and 1780s as they, too, took on the most corrupt aspects of the government. They demanded governmental reform, they wanted to see the transformation of corruption to virtue, and they argued for the end of the inseparable relationship between the Church and the government. Along the way, they supported the American and French Revolutions—Price to the day he died in 1791, and Priestley with dire consequences that threatened his life and the life of his family. Living in England under a monarchy, they agreed that a republic with a king was possible—but only with a right-thinking king, one who avoided the pitfalls of corruption, patronage, and influence. A true republic consisted of three divisions of authority, all separated by the powers allotted to each one: it was based on the Aristotelian principle of the one, the few, and the many.

In Aristotle's great work *Politics,* which was well known to an eighteenth-century educated public, the most practicable government was not a monarchy, an aristocracy (or oligarchy), or a democracy. It was the mixed regime of the one, the few, and the many, where political forms reflected the social realities of a community. In the ancient world (as in that of Price and Priestley), *the one* represented the royal authority embodied in the single person who wore the crown; *the few* reflected the elite class of aristocrats who possessed the wealth, education, and leisure to serve for long periods in an upper legislative house; and *the many* were the common people whose representatives made laws on their behalf in a lower house. No single authority, if the constitutional structure was properly and efficiently created, infringed on the powers of the others. No two of them could gang up on a third. They were to be kept separate and distinct.

Supporters of the "happy constitution" in England boasted about English freedom because of the balanced or mixed regime, while Tory trust in the king was routine. Oliver Goldsmith has the Vicar of Wakefield exclaim at one point: "I am then for, and would die for, monarchy, sacred monarchy; for if there be any thing sacred amongst men, it must be the anointed sovereign of the people, and every diminution of his power in war, or in peace, is an infringement upon the real liberties of the subject." For liberals like Price and Priestley, this was nonsense. English government had become corrupt largely by the overweening power of the king (the one) working in collusion with the court, though sometimes with the Lords (the few) against the people, or sometimes against the Commons (the many). The greatest commentator on the laws of England, William Blackstone, confirmed this view in his monumental four-volume compendium of Oxford lectures that appeared between 1765 and 1769. Liberals always emphasized the primacy of the Commons, the house that was the true representative of the people (and thus the United States Constitution in 1787 gave primacy to the Congress by according it first place, that is, in Article I of the document). The Crown and court, they argued, corrupted it by subverting its members with tantalizingly ugly financial rewards and downright bribery.

Once corruption appeared, the people, said Priestley, had no choice but to uproot the government, a traitorous idea that could get him into terrible trouble. The people must "do what Englishmen are renowned for having formerly done" when the government subverted the House of Commons: get rid of those responsible for the subversion. Priestley was advocating nothing less than revolution, because those who debased English liberty were usually unelected, so it was impossible simply to vote them out of office. Corrupt kings and aristocrats had to be deposed "in those cases" when governmental power "must be very extensive and arbitrary."

Price, too, no less than Priestley, advocated the same. When a powerful court under a corrupt king and miserable Lords, spiritual and temporal, subverted the Commons, English liberty was in dire danger, because the representatives of the people no longer performed their sacred duty as independent, autonomous citizens. "If there is any higher will which directs their resolutions," he said, "and on which they are dependent, they become the instruments of that will; and it is that will alone that in reality governs the state." The English government and others like it were "ill-modeled" and had to be transformed to "constitute a wise form of government."

It is a wonder Price and Priestley were not immediately charged with treason, but the ministry had bigger fish to fry. The chief problem in the 1770s was the Americans, not two Dissenting preachers whose audiences, it was assumed, were limited to their paltry congregations.

The authorities were wrong. Not only did Price and Priestley enjoy corresponding with each other about these matters, but in the spirit of transatlantic friendship, they also wrote to Benjamin Rush and their other American friends and sent each other articles, pamphlets, and essays. They talked about legal, penal, and university reform; manhood suffrage; equal election districts; and annual Parliaments with their like-minded liberal friends in various venues, such as Franklin's Whig Club, with Franklin and men like the Reverend John Jebb, a Dissenter, and John Cartwright, a writer. Throughout the 1770s and 1780s, Jebb and Cartwright constantly advocated reform. When they found they made little impact, they joined together with others in 1780 to form one of the first truly reformist organizations that demanded changes in parliamentary representation.

As its name suggests, the Society for Promoting Constitutional Information was designed to disseminate news and information about the demise of liberty throughout England (though many Europeans and Englishmen, too, universally regarded England as a beacon of liberty with its mixed constitution and the lip service its supporters gave to English liberty). The society's very existence provoked serious consternation and real fear in Westminster, because the authorities now realized these people were not merely quirky or loud-mouthed blokes like Wilkes. They were actually talking to each other about taking revolutionary action against the government. The authorities saw how dangerous they all were, especially in light of the recently concluded American war. With the outbreak of the French Revolution in 1789, an event even more radical than what had happened in America—when no king was threatened—even more deeply radical organizations emerged. One of these, the London Corresponding Society (LCS), openly indicated that it was "corresponding" not only with its own members, but also with sister organizations all over England, Scotland, Ireland, and America. Dissidents like Price and Priestley were responsible for these developments, the ministry thought, even though by the time the LCS was formed in 1792, Price had been dead for a year, and Priestley was already contemplating a move to America.

To refine their thoughts about these matters, Price and Priestley both wrote books on civil rights and civil liberty: Priestley in 1768 during the Wilkes controversy and again in 1774; Price just as the American Revolution was about to explode. Both authors analyzed the appropriate definitions and categories of liberty, although their approach differed. In 1776 Price's *Observations on the Nature of Civil Liberty, the Principles of Government, and the Justice and Policy of the War with America* appeared almost simultaneously with Paine's *Common Sense* in America. While it did not sell nearly as well as Paine's pamphlet, the first American best seller, it had sales the first year of some sixty thousand copies (it cost two shillings). With Price's consent, an inexpensive version was soon off the press. For producing this work, he was honored by the city council of

London with the Freedom of the City award, although not all people were happy with him or the work. Edmund Burke, in a forecast of his later 1789 attack on Price's Revolution Society sermon in praise of the French Revolution, disliked it. It was eventually reprinted in America with editions in Boston, New York, and Philadelphia.

Still, the work was well received by anyone unconnected to the king or court, the landed gentry (except for a few renegade liberal lords), and the ministry. Price divided liberty into four categories: physical, moral, religious, and civil. Physical liberty was most obvious: it encompassed the right of locomotion or mobility, the right of a person to move from one place to another without hindrance as long as the move neither bothered nor harmed anyone. Physical liberty encompassed Price's idea of moral liberty. As we have seen earlier, he believed that humans possess an inherent (and God-given) ability to distinguish right from wrong. This was the basis of his ethical intuitionism. When you take this idea from the moral sphere, however, as he had first placed it in his *Review of the Principal Question of Morals,* and put it in the political sphere, it becomes a far more radical statement. It holds, as Franklin believed, that humans have the ability and the right to make their own moral judgments, and that they do not need anyone else telling them what to believe and when to believe it. If they decided that monarchy is evil, that is, morally wrong, they have the perfect (again Price would say God-given) right to say so.

Price went even further, arguing in favor of religious liberty, in what amounted to a direct attack on the Test and Corporation Acts and the unusual (or, as Price would say, the ungodly) relationship between the English government and the Anglican Church. The attempt by the government and its church to impose their will over religious faith conflicted with God's desire for human beings to believe as they wished. Faith was a matter of individual, not state, choice. Thus Price denied the religious settlement from 1660.

Coupled closely with this view of religious liberty was Price's concept of civil liberty. If we have the right to believe what we want and to worship however we feel, then we also possess the same authority to participate in governmental decision making. This does not mean we are to have some sort of direct democracy, a New England town meeting where all citizens gather in town hall to discuss various articles and then vote on them. England was too big for direct democracy, but it was just right for representative democracy (he did not use the term "democracy," a term most people avoided in the eighteenth century, except the most radical self-styled democrats like Paine). Civil liberty was "the power of a *Civil Society* or *State* to govern itself by its own discretion, or by laws of its own making, without being subject to the impositions of *any* power, in appointing and directing which the collective body of the people have no concern, and over which they have no controul."

In other words, because the people have the power and authority to make their own moral decisions, they also should be able to make their own political decisions—if not directly, then through voting for the representative of their choice. In this way, all of the laws their government makes will be laws of the people's choosing, because they had a hand in the choice of representatives. A truly free government is conducted, therefore, under the direction of the people. "In every free state every man is his own legislator." Price's work on civil liberty was so influential that he began a correspondence with liberal French writers and government officials, such as the Marquis de Condorcet, the Physiocrat Anne-Robert-Jacques Turgot, and other luminaries of the French Enlightenment (the Physiocrats were followers of the Louis XV's physician, François Quesnay, who upheld the agrarian ideal as the way to national wealth).

Like Price, Priestley also categorizes liberty; though instead of four, he uses two: political and civil. Taken together, they are a natural part of a person's very being. Just as Price said, we can discern right from wrong without any outside instruction, so for

Priestley, the natural form of government is free government, and again it is the republic. A government has no right to exist if it opposes the will of the people through their duly elected legislators or if it violates the public trust. To go against the people is the same as enslaving them. Political liberty, then, "consists in the power which the members of the state reserve to themselves, of arriving at the public offices, or . . . of having votes in the nomination of those who fill them." It is the people who exercise political authority when they elect candidates to public office. In other words, it defines who is to vote and who is to serve in office. In some countries only one person, the king or tyrant, exercises political liberty. In others only a small group, like an oligarchy, possesses it. But in a nation like England, the people themselves must have the opportunity to exercise their liberty.

Priestley's other category, civil liberty, is directly linked to political liberty. It absorbs Price's concept of physical, moral, and religious liberty. In a free society there should never be restraints on these liberties, because they encompass "the power" the people have "over their own actions, which the members of the state reserve to themselves, and which their officers must not infringe."

Both Dissenters shared an understanding of what it meant for a citizen to be free. They disagreed, however, over how a person comes to know the difference between right and wrong. Priestley thought Price's ethical intuitionism to be silly and messy. He argued instead that we come to know the difference between right and wrong through our life experiences, beginning with our earliest years. As we grow older, the contrast between right and wrong becomes clear to us. For Price, it is our intuition that guides our lives; for Priestley, our experiences. Despite their differences, they both unequivocally held that good government is the only one that promotes the health and happiness, the prosperity and good of the people. If it does not achieve these things, it is a bad government and needs to be changed. Franklin would never have engaged in such an ethereal argument (except for his youthful attempt in 1725, when he wrote his *Dissertation on Liberty and Necessity* while he was in London); in any case, he would have agreed with them about good government.

Both Price and Priestley, therefore, fervently opposed the Test and Corporation Acts and favored the separation of church and state. As Dissenters, they also wanted to be regarded as full citizens. With those two acts in force, the people who were not accorded full civil and political rights, said Priestley, were as good as slaves. Price agreed, saying that before the end of time, God had decreed that religion "must lose that connection with civil power which has debased it, and which now in almost every Christian country turns it into a scheme of worldly emolument and policy, and supports error and superstition under the name of it."

As they were writing and thinking about these matters, events were moving quickly in America toward war with England, a fact of life now that reinforced reformists' claims of English tyranny. In 1776 Price and Priestley's radical friend John Cartwright published his antigovernment tract about the disgusting consequences of the English political system. His title said it all: *Take Your Choice! Representation and Respect; Imposition and Contempt. Annual Parliaments and Liberty. Long Parliaments and Slavery.* Within weeks, Price and Cartwright were exchanging pamphlets. A man of few words, Price got right to the point: he thought "it fitted to do good" and hoped it would have an impact. He also told Cartwright his own follow-up work, his *Additional Observations on Civil Liberty,* which was to be printed shortly, made him "full of fears," because he was "sensible to the caprice of the public." Once published, it did as well in sales as his first book on civil liberty with editions in America, Holland, and France. These works made "the good Dr. Price" well known in England, America, and throughout much of Europe.

When Price said he was "sensible to the caprice of the public," he meant he was afraid the British public was still uncertain about the Revolutionary War. Unlike that public, Price was undeniably positive about America's separation from England, as was his liberal friend and confidant Lord Shelburne, who believed America should be free, but who feared for England. In September 1777 Shelburne wrote to Price, "America is safe, my Dear Friend, but what will become of England?" Many of Price's friends, Priestley included, since he was then also a confidant to Shelburne, thought only Shelburne, a liberal Whig grandee, could reconcile Britain and America and that he should be prime minister.

But Lord North was still in power, and few liberals knew what to do about reconciliation. (North, first minister to the king, led the ministry before and during the American Revolution; he was largely responsible for Parliament's passage of the Stamp Act and other taxes levied on the colonies; he resigned in 1782.) While no single event brought down the North ministry, one 1780 pamphlet with the simple title of *Facts!* may have helped. Coauthored by Price and John Horne Tooke, the radical agitator and one of the original founders of the Society for Promoting Constitutional Information, the pamphlet railed against the North ministry, which soon collapsed under its own weight of failures. When Shelburne succeeded North, he became a key voice in opening negotiations with the Americans. Unfortunately, his ministry did not last. It fell at the end of the year, and the talks ended. In the meantime, Price's work on civil rights and civil liberties was excoriated by his English compatriots for its openly hostile stance against the North policy of pursuing war against the Americans. The government paid a number of writers to attack it, but that tactic backfired, because the attacks actually increased sales of Price's *Observations* and the *Additional Observations* to such an extent that Price published the two of them in a single volume in 1778.

When the war ended three years later Price was exuberant

about America's victory. He told Benjamin Rush, "From a regard to the general rights of mankind and a conviction that all dominion of one country over another is usurpation and tyranny, I have allways [*sic*] defended, as far as I have been able, the cause of America and opposed the late wicked war; and in doing this, I have gone thro' much abuse and some danger in this country." He hoped that now with peace, the Americans would create a model form of government, where liberty reigned supreme and where war was ended. One way for them to do this, he told Rush in repeating one of his constant refrains, was to make certain that religion and government were kept separate.

While he lived to hear of the 1787 constitution, he did not live to see the addition of the First Amendment that established in law the principle of separation of church and state (even if the states did not immediately implement the practice). Even so, in 1784, his *Observations on the Importance of the American Revolution* repeated his statement that the Americans must guarantee there would be no established church in the new United States. As mentioned, he believed the American Revolution rivaled the introduction of Christianity in importance.

After reading this work, Rush told Price he must continue to offer advice to the Americans. Price responded, "I am by no means a *Franklin,* who at 80 preserves so wonderfully his abilities and vigour; but a poor weak creature, who at 63 finds himself under the necessity of considering the working time of his life almost over." But his life was hardly over: Price wrote these words when he was about to embark on the next phase of his political engagement; namely, the revolution in France.

Once Price finished his book on the American Revolution, he sent a copy to Franklin, then in Paris, who was delighted with the gift. He told Price, "I think with you, that our Revolution is an important Event for the advantage of Mankind in general. It is to be hoped that the Lights we enjoy, which the ancient Governments in their first Establishment could not have, may preserve us from their Errors. In this the Advise [*sic*]

161

of wise Friends may do us much Good." When Jefferson arrived in Paris to relieve Franklin, he, too, told Price he had read Price's observations "with great pleasure. . . . The spirit which it breathes is as affectionate as the observations themselves are wise and just."

Meantime, Priestley, too, believed that the liberal ideas underlying the American Revolution would soon spread throughout the world. In 1774 Franklin and Priestley's friend John Fothergill encouraged Priestley to write about American affairs. "No part of America, Africa, or Asia, will be held in subject to any part of Europe," Priestley wrote, "and all the intercourse that will be kept up among them, will be for their mutual advantage." It was too bad England did not simply let the Americans go free, Priestley felt, because the enormous sums of money spent on the war effort could have gone to where it was most needed: "The expence of the late American war only would have converted all the waste grounds of this country into gardens. What canals, bridges, and noble roads, &c. &c. would it not have made for us? If the pride of nations must be gratified, let it be spent in such things as these."

But these expressions of support for America that Price and Priestley were publishing did not have a completely favorable reception in England. They were not arrested, but they were subjected to severe criticism for their outspokenness. Price's views on liberty caused the ministry to go into a tizzy. In one case, Lord Sandwich, the First Lord of the Admiralty, was convinced an agitator who wanted to subvert the government should be arrested, because a copy of Price's pamphlet was found in his room. Price's wife was so alarmed at her husband's bluntness that she had every package she and her husband received delivered to a friend's house in case theirs was searched. Worse yet, disregarding their own safety, when Price and Priestley advocated humane treatment and even the return of the American prisoners of war in England, they were viewed as giving the enemy aid and comfort.

Undeterred by public criticism, both Dissenters had even more to say about the French Revolution, which was turning into a world-transforming event with far more consequences than the American War. Now corruption, slavery, and tyranny would inevitably end. Sermonizing at the annual meeting of the Revolution Society in November 1789, Price urged his audience to seize control of the government by getting rid of those who debased English liberty and English rights. Yes, he said, we should love our country, but we must never forget that the most dangerous people were its *internal* enemies—by which he meant the ministry. Although he and his fellow citizens were all Englishmen by birth and by choice, they also had a higher responsibility to make the entire world a better place. "We should love [our country] ardently, but not exclusively. We ought to seek its good, by all the means that our different circumstances and abilities will allow; but, at the same time, we ought to consider ourselves as citizens of the world, and take care to maintain a just regard to the rights of other countries." The rights of Englishmen must never be compromised. France was a truly enlightened country and England must become one too, and soon. "Ignorance is the parent of bigotry, intolerance, persecution and slavery," he proclaimed, and if a government insisted on keeping its subjects in darkness, there was only one solution: revolution.

When he offered an action plan, he prompted Burke's pen. When Price wrote that the English had "the right to resist power when abused" and "the right to chuse [*sic*] our own governors, to cashier them for misconduct, and to frame a government for ourselves," his intentions could not have been clearer. The image of a king, whom he called an "arbitrary monarch," being forced to march before his triumphant people was one that Burke and the authorities deeply feared. Priestley, in attendance at the meeting, later said Price's sermon "moved him to tears." When copies of the sermon were printed, some were sent to France, and several French constitutional societies sent congratulatory notes of appreciation to Price. He had become a true world champion of human rights.

But Edmund Burke was unhappy. His attack on "political theologians" and "theological politicians" in his great 1790 work, the *Reflections on the Revolution in France,* only underscored his total repugnance of the strangulation of the French monarchy. Price hardly had time to comment on Burke's attack. Only in the preface to the fourth edition of his *Discourse* did Price say how deeply disappointed he was that his friend Burke had misunderstood his Revolution Society sermon. He also did not know why Burke had misrepresented the actual events in France, especially when liberty had undoubtedly expanded. Price asked what Burke really knew about the French situation: "What candour or what moderation can be expected in a person so frantic with zeal for hereditary claims and aristocratical distinctions as to be capable of decrying popular rights and the aid of philosophy in forming governments; of lamenting that the age of Chivalry is gone; and of believing that the insults offered by a mob to the Queen of France have extinguished for ever the glory of EUROPE?"

But soon the British government cracked down on the authors of such seditious words. Price was unaffected by the power unleashed on the people, because after a lingering illness, he died on April 19, 1791. He had fallen sick with what was probably influenza while officiating in the cold rain at a funeral. He never recovered. His wife, Sally, who had been ill most of their life together, had died just five years earlier. It would be left to others to continue the battle against tyranny.

Meantime, Priestley, who was always late getting information about French events while living in Birmingham, was devastated by the loss of his political soul partner. He managed to arrive in time for his friend's funeral on April 26 and served as a pallbearer. Tributes came in from all over England and France at the loss of this great man who argued so forcefully against despotism. The Revolution Society received condolences from constitutional societies throughout France, calling him "this implacable enemy of tyrants," "this generous defender of liberty," "the benefactor of mankind," "the apostle of liberty," "the apostle of humanity." Five days later, at the Gravel-Pit Meeting House, Price's last congregation, Priestley gave a funeral oration for his friend, saying "in real candor, I question whether Dr. Price ever had a superior."

Priestley's views of the French Revolution echoed those Price had expressed in his Revolution Society sermon. Only Priestley placed the events in France on a higher cosmic level, because he thought human progress was always linked to God's plan to save human souls. His writings after 1789 shared Benjamin Rush's millenarian longing for the inauguration of a future state of paradise on earth. Price never went quite that far, but Priestley was nearly certain with the global expansion of liberty and human rights—the end of days was fast coming. First, revolution, as Paine said, was spreading to the far corners of the world. In a 1790 letter to Price on his sermon before the Revolution Society, Priestley congratulated his friend on the success of the French Revolution "and especially on the share that is, with so much justice, ascribed to you, with respect to the liberty of that country and America, of course all those other countries that, it is hoped, will follow their example." All the kings and courtiers of the world were clearly frightened by the spectacle of what happened when the people rose up. "The time is approaching when an end will be put to all usurpation, in things civil and religious, first in Europe, and then in other countries."

Convinced that these events were bringing on the imminent return of Jesus, Priestley delivered sermons to the Old Jewry and the Gravel-Pit Meeting House, laying out his interpretation of how the French Revolution was part of God's larger plan to save the world. When war broke out all over Europe as the Old Regime states attempted to restore the French monarchy, Priestley wrote to his old friend, the Reverend Theophilus

Lindsey, to say that "some important prophecies, I believe, are about to be fulfilled." The Reverend Thomas Belsham, a tutor at the New College in Hackney, where Price had also taught, and a young friend and protégé of Priestley, wrote this about his older friend some years later in his collection of Lindsey's papers: "Upon one occasion the topic of discussion was the second advent of Christ; and Dr. Priestley, who had studied the Apocalypse with great attention, inferred, from the state of the world, compared with the language of prophecy, that the second personal appearance of Christ was very near at hand. 'You,' says he, 'may probably live to see it; I shall not. It cannot, I think be more than twenty years.'"

In a 1794 fast sermon Priestley repeated that the time for Christ's return could not be far off. He told Lindsey, "The late events, and my continued attention to the prophecies, make me see this in a stronger light than when I wrote my Fast sermon. Many more of the prophecies that I was then aware of indicate the great destruction that will be made of mankind before the restoration of the Jews" to Palestine (one of the events to precede Christ's return). The time to come would be glorious, with the creation of a perfect society for the good of all people. These ideas went beyond what even Benjamin Rush could accept. He later commented just after Priestley's death in 1804, "I never was a believer in his peculiar religious principles, but I am forced to own they produced in him in his last sickness uncommon resignation, peace, and composure of mind. He died in a full belief of a happy immortality."

Such a strong and enduring religious faith was never part of Franklin's worldview, especially after the 1734 Hemphill affair. The Reverend Samuel Hemphill, a young Irish Presbyterian preacher in Philadelphia, gave sermons he had pilfered from other ministers (a common practice of the time, in fact), but also sermons Franklin had ghostwritten for him. These stressed Franklin's emphasis on good deeds rather than salvation. When Presbyterian Old Sides led by the Reverend Jedediah Andrews, who was schooled in the strict Calvinism of New England, attacked Hemphill for deemphasizing salvation, Franklin openly supported Hemphill with articles in *The Pennsylvania Gazette*. In the end, Hemphill was disgraced and forced to leave town—to Franklin, an unjust, ill-timed, and unnecessary action. He never returned to the Presbyterian Meeting. From that time onward, Franklin kept his deist views to himself and emphasized the importance of diligence and good works rather than relying on a belief in the plan of an all-powerful deity who rules humanity from afar.

Price died two years before the English government turned extremely reactionary as a result of Louis XVI's execution on January 21, 1793. At that time, Priestley became a target of those who thought he was caught up in a French conspiracy. The government regarded him as a subversive whose true goal was to end the English monarchy and establish a democratic government. This was hardly the case, since Price and Priestley thought that a democracy brought only chaos and anarchy. Even so, the ministry criminalized all subversive writing and activity, including the publication of political tracts that attacked the Crown or Parliament or that were judged too friendly to revolutionary France. Several well-publicized state trials of radical writers and activists were held in England, primarily in 1794. Some men were convicted, a few jailed, a few others transported to Botany Bay, but most were acquitted. Thomas Paine was among those tried and convicted, though it was in absentia, since he was then residing in France during his trial. From that moment on, Paine knew if he ever tried to return to America, an English warship might pick him up on the high seas and send him to England to jail—or worse. Instead, he remained in France until 1802, when President Thomas Jefferson finally sent a ship to bring him home.

While Priestley was never tried, he unfortunately became the victim of a wildly conservative backlash. The government spread the word that "Gunpowder Priestley" (the reference was to the infamous Gunpowder Plot of 1605 to blow up Parliament) wanted to bring down the monarchy. In 1791 rioters in Birmingham burned down his house and laboratory, destroying all of his scientific papers and experiments, Priestley hastily relocated to London. There he took over the pulpit that Price had occupied until his death that same year, and taught for a while at New College in Hackney. But Priestley was never again comfortable, if even safe, in England. Within three years, he immigrated to America and set up his home along the banks of the Susquehanna River in Northumberland, Pennsylvania. Today, his house and laboratory there are museums.

It makes sense that these men admired the new American republic: its constitutional design was based on a true balance of the one (the president), the few (the Senate), and the many (the House of Representatives). It specifically, at least after the 1791 addition of the First Amendment, prohibited an established church and set forth the guarantee of free speech and a free press and the right to a free assembly. In many respects the new American government was the model of what they had been fighting for all along. Little wonder, then, that Priestley left England forever.

Price and Priestley were among the most optimistic souls when it came to their faith in human progress, the eventual success of the American republic, and the coming political reformation of England. For Franklin, they were the best of friends even long after Franklin had left England forever. In 1788, at the end of his long life, he asked Benjamin Vaughn to "remember me affectionately to good Dr. Price and the honest heretic, Dr. Priestly [*sic*]. I do not call him *honest* by way of distinction; for I think all the heretics I know have been virtuous men. . . . Do not mistake me. It is not my good friend's heresy that I impute his honesty. On the contrary, it is his honesty that has brought upon him the character of heretic."

5

∽∾

Price, Priestley, and Scientific Inquiry

J
ust as they were actively engaged in liberal reform advocacy, Price and Priestley also achieved fame and notoriety in two major scientific realms: Priestley in chemistry, Price in mathematics and actuarial science. Priestley is known in history primarily as the discoverer of the chemical element of oxygen. His scientific and political interests melded together because he yearned to see the human mind (and body) freed from both intellectual and physical tyranny and mindless superstition.

Price and Priestley were barred from attending Oxford and Cambridge because of their religious nonconformity. In many ways this was just as well, because the curriculum at those institutions had barely changed in 150 years. It was still heavily grounded in classical education, and its graduates typically trained for the clergy or the law. In contrast, the newer Dissenting Academies, where Price and Priestley studied and later taught, focused on the education of the "whole man," with an emphasis on history, literature, science, modern languages, and all varieties of practical knowledge. They provided the true grounding of the modern liberal arts colleges in England and America.

The eighteenth century's pervasive interest in air, like that of electricity, was a curious phenomenon. It touched everyone—Americans, English, French. Everyone understood that air was necessary to life, but inquiring into its properties and its nature opened the door to so many ways of looking at the world that it appeared there was no end to the investigation. Balloon launches into the heavens conclusively demonstrated that heavy objects with human beings on board could soar upward; such spectacles never ceased to fascinate. Benjamin Rush captured the moment in 1793 when he witnessed an "aerial voyage," which he called "a truly sublime sight." And sublime it was in more ways than merely being a lasting achievement of the human mind and spirit: for Rush, as it was for Priestley, such unusual, delightful, and bewildering devices had practical uses, such as weather forecasting and military reconnaissance.

Priestley's interest in science, particularly in electricity, air, and gases, began at an early age and stemmed from a curiosity about the natural world, the mysteries of the universe, God's plan for human history, and his own role in it. Education was for him a liberating affair. It opened young minds to knowledge of all sorts and ultimately was the basis of his democratic outlook: the more a person knew, the greater intellectual weapons he would possess to combat tyranny, whether in science or government. Priestley's younger brother tells the story of how curious young Joseph was at age eleven: he enclosed spiders in a bottle to see how long they lived without air. Modern readers know Priestley best for his discoveries in chemistry, especially his work on air and gases. He was a lifelong believer in the phlogiston theory (discussed below) and refused to recognize his own discovery of oxygen. But his use of the theory shows us the profound fertility of his mind and how he believed that the theory, even if later disproved, gave us a true picture of God's universe.

Early modern scientists like Priestley believed that all inflammable materials possessed a colorless, odorless, weightless, and imperceptible substance called phlogiston (from the Greek, meaning "burnt up"). When paper was burned, for example, the ash that remained was the real substance, the true material, not the paper. The result is the release of phlogiston. In a 1774 experiment Priestley revealed the true nature of combustion and discovered the element of oxygen: he noted that oxygen, as we now know, was necessary for burning the paper, and the result is the release of carbon dioxide. But Priestley was so infatuated with the phlogiston theory, he refused to believe the results of his own experiment—and it was left to the French chemist and Priestley's intellectual rival, Antoine Lavoisier, to recognize the existence of oxygen.

Even so, Priestley is generally credited today with discovering, in addition to oxygen, a very long list of gases, including nitrogen, nitrous oxide (laughing gas), nitrogen dioxide, ammonia, hydrogen chloride, sulphur dioxide, and carbon monoxide. He also developed, in 1767, the principle of carbonation when he injected "fixed air" into water—creating, for the first time in history, carbonated or soda water. "Fixed air" was carbon dioxide, a term coined by Joseph Black (who taught Benjamin Rush medicine in Edinburgh). Black actually thought carbon dioxide had marvelous medicinal qualities and argued it would prevent scurvy in sailors. He mentioned this to the statesman Sir George Savile, who in turn informed Lord Sandwich, then the head of the Board of Admiralty. The board invited Priestley to demonstrate his carbonation experiment to the College of Physicians on April 1, 1772, an experiment witnessed by Franklin, as well as Sir Joseph Banks, past president of the Royal Society, and Daniel Solander, a botanist working for Banks. They were all profoundly impressed and accepted soda water as a medication. Three weeks later the college instructed Captains James Cook and Tobias Furneaux to use it on their voyages to prevent scurvy. Priestley thought this was perfectly reasonable: "My method of impregnating water with fixed air, was considered at a meeting of the College of Physicians, before whom I made the experiments, and by them it was recommended to the Lords of the Admiralty, (by whom they had been summoned for the purpose) as likely to be of use in the sea scurvy."

When Cook sailed for more than three years on his second voyage, only one man died of disease, and the cause was not scurvy—but then again he never really bothered to carry out Priestley's experiment. Priestley's theory was based on the principle that when the body loses fixed air, scurvy sets in, and the cure was simply to restore carbon dioxide to the body (scurvy, of course, develops as a result of a lack of vitamin C, not because of a carbon dioxide deficiency). Priestley published his theory in a 1772 publication titled *Directions for Impregnating Water with Fixed Air.* In large part for this work, the Royal Society awarded Priestley its Copley Medal in 1773, exactly twenty years after Franklin had received the medal for his work on electricity. Nine years later, again like Franklin before him, he was elected as an *associé étranger* of the *Académie royale des sciences*. Because only a total of eight such foreign associates at any one time could be members, it was "a rare honor."

Finally, Priestley described a process in nature that later came to be termed photosynthesis, that is, the way in which green plants in the sunlight release oxygen after they have absorbed carbon dioxide. He told Franklin of his experiments with sprigs of mint in a closed jar of what he called putrid air (air that had released carbon dioxide) and how it became purified after he inserted the mint. As Franklin told him in the summer of 1772, "The strong thriving state of your mint in the putrid air seems to shew that the air is mended by taking something from it, and not by adding to it." And then in a note that indicates his hope that air pollution could possibly be solved by the use of vegetation, Franklin added, "This will give some check to the rage of destroying trees that grow near houses, which has accompanied our late improvements in gardening, from an opinion of their being unwholesome."

Priestley pursued his studies at the Daventry Academy, a Dissenting undergraduate institution specially designed for young men who held nonconforming beliefs. Priestley was argumentative and unusually pugnacious in his writings (he loved nothing more than to go after those who disagreed with him). He soon secured a teaching position at the Warrington Academy. The founder of the academy, the Reverend John Seddon, was the pastor at one of the two large Dissenting chapels in town and a founder of the local lending subscription library. At Warrington, Seddon and Priestley quickly became friends (when he arrived, Priestley was twenty-eight, Seddon thirty-five). Seddon had long known John Canton, the first Englishman to independently confirm Franklin's experiments in electricity, especially the identical nature of lightning and electricity. Priestley really wanted to meet Canton, and he knew it was not easy to get to London, because it took him about three days to travel by coach from Warrington to London.

Before he left, Seddon gave him a letter of introduction to Canton with a postscript that while he was there, Canton should also introduce Priestley to Benjamin Franklin, who was twenty-seven years his senior. In 1765 Priestley went off to London, where he met both Canton and Franklin, and he was soon attending the meetings of the Club of Honest Whigs. He also saw several other Dissenters and scientists there, such as Richard Price and Franklin's friend William Watson, the physician and experimenter on electricity who had commented on Franklin's theories for the Royal Society. Soon Price and Priestley became the closest of friends, sharing and exchanging ideas about science, theology, and politics. Priestley later recalled, "For the most amiable simplicity of character . . . a truly

Christian spirit, disinterested patriotism, and true candor, no man in my opinion ever exceeded Dr. Price."

The Whig Club proved an important intellectual outlet for Priestley and his scientific interests. For one thing, Franklin's influence was enormous. As Priestley told him when he left London for the last time in 1775, "The club of *honest whigs,* as you justly call them, think themselves much honoured by your having been one of them, and also by your kind remembrance of them. Our zeal in the good cause is not abated. You are often the subject of our conversation." Indeed, it is no exaggeration to say Priestley loved Franklin almost as a son would a father. He called Franklin's discoveries and experiments "the greatest, perhaps, since the time of Sir Isaac Newton." But, like Whitefield, he failed to convince Franklin to become a believer. In his memoirs, Priestley noted, "It is to be lamented, that a man of Dr. Franklin's general good character, and great influence, should have been an unbeliever in Christianity, and also have done so much as he did to make others unbelievers." When Franklin returned to America, he asked Priestley to send him some good theological treatises on the evidence of Christianity, so the two could correspond about them. Priestley recommended his own work on natural religion and the philosopher David Hartley's on Christianity, but as Priestley noted, the American Revolution soon broke out, and "I do not believe that he ever found himself sufficiently at leisure for the discussion."

In any case, Priestley told the club members that though he was a schoolmaster in literature and languages, he wanted to write a history of electricity. All of them encouraged him and supplied him with books and materials for his research. Franklin suggested to Priestley that he carry out his own electrical experiments to confirm what he learned through the work of others. In the meantime, while he was working on the history, Priestley corresponded with Franklin, because he could not easily get to London from Warrington. In describing his own electrical experiments, he told Franklin his "great ambition would be to act under your auspices in the business of electricity." In Priestley's mind, Franklin's stature as a natural philosopher and experimenter was unequaled.

When Priestley's history was finally published in 1767, he gratefully acknowledged the help, support, and advice of his Whig Club friends, especially Franklin. In all, five English editions of this history were published during Priestley's lifetime: 1767, 1769, 1775 in two volumes octavo, 1775, and 1795 with translations in French and German. It was last reprinted in 1966. The work was a monumental achievement. Priestley had written the first comprehensive history of electricity and included in it accounts of his own discoveries, as he studiously repeated many of the experiments that he wrote about.

Franklin was so taken with the young scientist's fluency with experimentation that he nominated Priestley for the Royal Society's Copley Medal (he failed to win it then, but managed to do so five years later, for his work on carbonation). In his nomination letter, Franklin cited Priestley's discovery of the "electrical wind" (the blast of air that occurs with an electrical charge), an important discovery especially to Franklin, because he had once doubted it ever existed at all. It is a phenomenon still studied today. In addition, Priestley later investigated something he called "lateral force" in electrical explosions (such as lightning) to determine why there was an electrical shock near, but not at, the point of impact. And yet, while he performed many electrical experiments successfully and described their effects, he could not always explain them. He also discovered the so-called Priestley Rings—though apparently there was then and still is little interest today in this phenomenon: the rings consist of concentric circles that appear on paper when an electric impulse is set off.

Priestley's scientific interests and work were not limited to electricity and its properties. His next project, which focused on drawing and perspective, in turn led him to investigate experiments relating to vision, light, and color. He hoped it would be the first major study of such matters since Newton's *Optics*—and that his scientific peers would accept it as the proper successor to the great work. He was sorely disappointed. His history, which appeared in 1772, was a major publication—indeed Franklin, still residing in London, ordered twenty copies—but the subject itself was formidable. At first, Priestley was uncertain whether he could ever complete it. He told Franklin, "I have just dispatched the discoveries of Newton and his Contemporaries, and from his time to the present have such a number of *Memoirs, dissertations, tracts,* and *books* on the subject of Light and colours to read, compare, and digest, as, I think, would make any person not practised in the business of arrangement, absolutely despair: Till I had actually taken a list of them, I did not think there had been a tenth or a twentieth part so much upon the subject. And other subjects, I see, will be much times more embarrassing than this." Perhaps he was no Newton.

Part of the problem was Priestley's confusion about the composition of light. One of his earliest intellectual and religious guides was the Christian philosopher/scientist David Hartley, whose ideas of the unity of mind and body led him to conclude that when the brain died and putrefied, so did the mind. This principle was the basis of Priestley's Unitarianism, because he denied the separate existence of mind and soul, an idea that had a profound impact on all of his scientific ideas. (In fact, he was so taken with Hartley's work, he later printed an abridged edition of Hartley's *Observations on Man, His Frame, His Duty, and His Expectations,* originally published in 1749.)

To Hartley's ideas about the body and mind, Priestley added some very odd notions he adopted from the Abbé Roger Joseph Boscovich. An Italian by birth, Boscovich was the director of optics for the French navy. More to the point, he had developed an unusual molecular theory. Basing his work on what he presumed were Boscovich's theories, Priestley claimed to have discovered what he thought was the key to the material universe:

the penetrability of matter. In a wild leap of eccentric thinking, he abandoned the idea that matter was solid. Mind and matter were so intimately related that one could not exist without the other; everything was part of this material world, surrounded by spheres of vital force. This concept led him to the startling and odd conclusion in his most important philosophical work, *The Disquisitions Relating to Matter and Spirit,* that there was in fact very little in the world that was material. Here he announced his famous "nutshell theory" of matter: "All the solid matter in the solar system might be contained within a nut-shell," he wrote in 1777, "there is so great a proportion of void space within the substance of most solid bodies."

Given the general acceptance today of the Big Bang theory, Priestley's nutshell theory now seems inspired and even prescient; still, at the time, it was a hard one for the scientific community to swallow. Boscovich himself was horrified at the use Priestley made of his work, especially the way Priestley appeared to have extended his ideas to deny the existence of the Holy Spirit. The Abbé was, after all, a Roman Catholic churchman. The two men carried on a heated exchange in 1778, after Priestley wrote on the subject of materiality. The situation became so bad that Boscovich at one point complained to Priestley's patron the Earl of Shelburne (an interesting twist, as if Priestley were a naughty child and Boscovich complaining to the parent). In fact, the dispute eventually came to nothing.

By the time he undertook his experiments on air, Priestley was residing in Leeds, preaching at the Mill Hill Chapel. While he was quite happy, because his congregation was comfortable with his Unitarian view, he was having some trouble with his personal finances. Thanks to a recommendation from Price, in 1773 he was offered the position as librarian and companion to Lord Shelburne, one of the leading liberal Whig politicians, who later served as head of the ministry for one year (1782–1783) and who later became the Marquis of Lansdowne. Before Priestley joined the Shelburne household, he equivocated about whether he should accept Shelburne's offer. For one thing, he was afraid he would lose his independence, to do both his own thinking and his research. Some of his friends—John Pringle, royal physician to the queen and president of the Royal Society from 1772 until 1778 when Banks succeeded him, and others—advised him against taking the position: it was just too political for an independent scientist.

In the meantime, Priestley told Franklin he found it difficult to leave Mill Hill, a place he found to be pleasant and conducive to his work. Franklin replied that while he could not tell Priestley *what* to do, he could tell him *how* to decide. His method was something he himself used when he faced important decisions, such as remaining in England or returning to Philadelphia. At any rate, Franklin now urged Priestley to undertake a "prudential or moral algebra," a system where he was to add up the pros and cons before deciding.

Franklin told Priestley to make two columns on a sheet of paper. At the top of the first column he was to write the word *pro,* and at the top of the second, *con.* Then for the next three or four days, he was to jot down in one or the other column "short Hints of the different Motives that at different Times occur to me for or against the Measure." At the end of this time, he was to weigh them. If there were two on a side, he scratched both of them out as equals, but it was more complex than that: "If I find a Reason *pro* equal to two Reasons *con,* I strike out the three. If I judge some two Reasons *con* equal to some three Reasons *pro,* I strike out the five; and thus proceeding I find at length were the Ballance lies; and if after a Day or two of farther Consideration nothing new that is of Importance occurs on either side, I come to a Determination accordingly."

No doubt this methodology had some weaknesses. After all, and Franklin realized this, it did not have the same precision as an algebraic proof. But it did prevent him from making what he called "a rash Step; and in fact I have found great Advantage from this kind of Equation, in what may be called *Moral* or *Prudential Algebra*."

Whether Priestley employed Franklin's method is lost to history; in any event, he decided to refused Shelburne's offer. But his friend Richard Price was enthusiastic about the prospects for Priestley and urged him to change his mind. He thought Priestley was just right for the position and that it would make him financially secure. Within two months of Price's urging, Priestley did change his mind, and he accepted the position. He remained with Shelburne for the next seven years, until he left for Birmingham in 1780.

Working for Shelburne allowed Priestley to spend the winters at Shelburne's London home and summers at his country estate in Calne. Priestley noted in his memoirs that Shelburne's "residence in London was the means of improving my acquaintance with Dr. Franklin. I was seldom many days without seeing him, and being members of the same club [the Honest Whigs], we constantly returned together." He noted that because tensions between Britain and America were becoming increasingly strained, most of their conversation focused on politics, not science. During this period, Priestley was also writing on politics, religion, and philosophy, and he even went with Shelburne for a monthlong journey to Paris, where he met his soon-to-be rival Antoine Lavoisier and other scientists.

It was in these years with Shelburne that Priestley was most creative in his scientific work—for it was his work on air and gases that made his reputation as a chemist. He had started his experiments years earlier while he was preaching in Leeds. At the time, he made annual visits to London to see his publisher, Joseph Johnson, who had close linkages with Dissenters and political reformers, and to present his findings to the Royal Society. (It was also there that he had produced sparkling water.) From Calne, he now wrote to Price about how air pollution had a negative impact on health. Price was convinced people who lived in the country lived longer. Priestley told him that he had been studying the impact of polluted air (or what he called "putrefied air") on animals and found he could purify it chemically. "I have been making many experiments on *putrefaction*, which is a most important process in nature, and which is little understood. The putrid effluvium, is neither *fixed air* [carbon dioxide] . . . nor *inflammable* effluvium . . . but a thing *sui generis*, which diminishes the bulk of any quantity of common air to which it is admitted, disposing it, I believe, to deposit its fixed air." He told Price he had sent his study of pollution to Franklin, who took it to the Royal Society, which published it the next year. That same year, in June 1772 Franklin and Pringle visited Priestley to witness his experiments on air, and they found he had made even more remarkable progress.

Priestley's most important experiment occurred in August 1774 with his discovery of oxygen. A longtime question has always been whether Lavoisier either started on the road to oxygen from his association with Priestley (when the two first met in Paris) or whether he came about it independently. This question has never been definitively answered. The problem is that more than twenty-five years after he discovered oxygen, we find an obstinate Priestley still defending the phlogiston theory. In 1796 he wrote an open letter to French chemists, saying nothing would ever convince him to give up the phlogiston theory, even if they threatened him with the guillotine itself. It would take more than force: "As you would not . . . have your reign to resemble that of *Robespierre*, few as we are who remain disaffected, we hope you had rather gain us [to Lavoisier's thesis] by persuasion, than silence us by your power."

Still, Priestley's studies of air led to several discoveries that most scientists and historians credit to him alone. In one of his more interesting observations, Priestley noted that while fire and inhalation destroyed air or oxygen (or as he preferred to call it, dephlogisticated air) and turned it into carbon dioxide, vegetation rejuvenated it. He wrote Franklin, "I have fully satisfied myself that air rendered in the highest degree noxious by breathing is restored by sprigs of mint growing in it. You will probably remember the flourishing state in which you saw one of my plants." He told Franklin he had placed a live mouse inside a closed vessel in which the mint was growing—perhaps reminiscent of his boyhood days of placing insects in closed containers. He took it out after five minutes and found it was "quite strong and vigorous." However, when he placed another mouse in the same closed chamber without the mint, the creature "died after being not two seconds" inside it. His conclusion? The mint restored properties to the air that made it habitable.

The following year, Priestley published his paper "Observations on Different Kinds of Air" in the Royal Society's *Philosophical Transactions*. It established him as "a leader of pneumatic chemistry, but not only because of the discoveries it announced—and there were many of these: the beginning observations leading to a knowledge of photosynthesis, the isolation and identification of nitrous air (nitric oxide) and vapor of spirit of salt (later called acid air or marine acid air; anhydrous hydrochloric acid); and the development of the nitrous air test (eudiometry)—but also because of the simple apparatus and manipulative techniques he had developed and described."

Like Franklin, an autodidact in science, Priestley may have made mistakes when he conducted his experiments—and when he refused to acknowledge his discovery of oxygen. But he did possess the courage to try new things to see what results he might achieve, and his vision was remarkably sound. In 1774 the first of his major books on air, *Experiments and Observations*, appeared and eventually grew over the years into six thick volumes. Here, he described oxygen and its properties as well as five more gases (ammonia, sulphur dioxide, nitrous oxide, and nitrogen dioxide). He also worked on how the blood works in the respiratory system and the phenomenon of photosynthesis. This period was his most productive time. It was also the moment Franklin left England for good. When Priestley heard of this, he wrote to his old friend he "shall be very sorry; as it will deprive me of one of the greatest satisfactions that used to make my annual visits to London agreeable."

In any case, Priestley's association with Shelburne was rapidly coming to an end. It was perhaps Shelburne's new wife, not the Marquis himself, who advocated Priestley's dismissal, because her strong religious views conflicted with his liberal Unitarianism. Shelburne had married her the year before Priestley was discharged. In 1780 Priestley moved to Birmingham. He remained there until the infamous Church and King Riots of 1791 destroyed his house, his laboratory, and almost cost him his life.

Birmingham was enormously appealing to Priestley, given its centrality in the English Midlands and its growing vibrancy as a commercial and industrial center. There Priestley truly flourished, but the physical distance that separated him from Franklin, now happily residing in Paris, saddened him. While they carried on a correspondence, it was no longer the same. When Franklin wrote to Priestley shortly after the move to Birmingham, he told him he was delighted to hear he was still engaged in his experiments. Franklin was so certain the future was unlimited for scientific inquiry that he envisioned a distant time when many diseases would be cured and new inventions made for the ease and comfort of humans. He told Priestley he was sorry he was born so soon, because of "the rapid Progress of *true* Science. We may perhaps learn to deprive large Masses of their Gravity, and give them absolute Levity, for the sake of easy Transport. Agriculture may diminish its Labour and doubt its Produce; all Diseases may by sure means be prevented or cured, not excepting that of Old Age, and our Lives lengthened at pleasure even beyond the antediluvian Standard." If inquiries into the natural world led to this prospect becoming a reality, he speculated that morality would not improve so well or so quickly as science. Franklin had already lived a long life when he wrote these words, especially by eighteenth-century (if not

Methuselah) standards. "O that moral Science were in as fair a way of Improvement," he told Priestley, "that Men would cease to be Wolves to one another."

In Birmingham, Priestley became minister at the New Meetinghouse (he had to supplement his income, because his lifetime pension from Shelburne amounted to only half of his previous salary). There he enjoyed the company of the leading scientists, physicians, and industrialists of the area as a member of the Lunar Society of Birmingham, which had been meeting monthly since 1766, when the full moon appeared, and was "the most brilliant of provincial intellectual gatherings." Calling themselves "the Lunatics," the men in the society—who were, like Priestley, liberal in their politics and fascinated by applied scientific inquiry (such as the chemical makeup of dyes, the building of canals, the use of the steam engine and windmills, and many other things)— gladly added to his income by financially supporting his experiments. The members included a mélange of businessmen, philosophers, physicians, and, of course, scientists: the industrialist and inventor Matthew Boulton, who was a founder of the steam engine industry along with his partner, the Scot James Watt, who in turn was a watch and instrument maker and who also coined the term *horsepower;* the corpulent and imaginative physician Erasmus Darwin, the grandfather of the more famous Charles and a scientist in his own right in botany and zoology; and the pottery and china maker Josiah Wedgwood, as well as other political and scientific luminaries of the town. The Lunar Society was for Priestley the natural intellectual successor to the Club of Honest Whigs.

Like Priestley, while many of the "Lunatics" were Dissenters, Darwin was not (he attended Cambridge), and Wedgwood was baptized in the Anglican Church. But they cared not a whit about their differences, whenever they arose: "We had nothing to do with the *religious* or *political* principles of each other," Priestley later recalled, in 1793. "We were united by a common love of *science*, which we thought sufficient to bring together

183

persons of all distinctions, Christians, Jews, Mohametans, and Heathens, Monarchists and Republicans."

Priestley's move to Birmingham was, he said, "the happiest event in my life." A rapidly growing city (its population grew from fifteen thousand to seventy thousand in the sixty-five-year period between 1735 to 1800), Birmingham was a bustling manufacturing town. Men like Boulton, Wedgwood, and Darwin grew famously rich there. For example, Boulton, with his factory at Soho, made finely crafted, filigreed trinkets of all sorts from gold and silver for the wealthy: toothpick cases, sword hilts, snuff boxes, and even tweezers, to name but a few. Wedgwood developed, among other ceramic finishes, his celebrated Queen's Ware for Charlotte, the wife of George III (and even developed a special finish for the king himself, which was known simply as Royal Pattern). And while Darwin was the best-known, wealthiest physician of the area, he, too, engaged in manufacturing, supporting his friends' interests in canalization and manufacturing (he developed what he called a "speaking machine," with lips that moved and made sounds when he blew into a tube with bellows that was attached to them).

Despite his association with these Lunatics, Priestley's happiness was not to last. Most likely, he would have lived the rest of his life in Birmingham had it not been for the extreme backlash in 1791 against the known supporters of the French Revolution, a reaction that the government itself likely stimulated and directed. With just a few minutes' warning, he was barely able to flee his house and laboratory in advance of an angry mob. The mob burned both buildings to the ground, and he lost everything. His Birmingham happiness was extinguished with the flames; the riots destroyed his life's work. From Birmingham he moved to London, where he lived for his last three years in England, succeeding Richard Price, who had died that very year, as schoolmaster at the Hackney Academy. Now, he remarked, "On the whole, I spent my time even more happily at Hackney than ever I had done before."

Richard Price's father, a strict Calvinist minister, originally planned for his son to become a businessman, but when the elder Price died suddenly in 1739, young Richard wanted an education. Just sixteen, he had already abandoned his father's austere Calvinism. Through his education in the Dissenting academy at Moorsfield, he became a Unitarian, more specifically an Arian. (Arianism was based on the religious beliefs of a fourth-century priest named Arius who advanced the idea that Jesus was not eternal and of the same divine substance as God the Father.)

While Price's writings primarily focused on philosophical, theological, and political topics, and his professional life centered on his congregation and students, he also wrote several exemplary works on probability and statistics. These led to his pioneering work on death rates and life insurance, making him an acknowledged founder of the modern life insurance industry and old-age pensions. While he studied mathematics as a student, he became particularly interested in statistics and probability when the family of the late Thomas Bayes invited him to organize Bayes's papers. Bayes, also a Dissenting minister and mathematician, who died in 1761, had written several tracts in philosophy and religion, but his work in mathematics had never been published. John Eames, Price's tutor at the Moorsfield Academy, who had also taught Bayes, introduced the two men. Price soon collected Bayes's works, but he went further, by writing several of his own papers on Bayes's work that he sent to the Royal Society. As it turned out, Price completed the mathematical formula Bayes had worked on, but not finished, concerning probability and chance in everyday affairs.

Specifically, Price investigated how we can reasonably forecast whether an event will occur or even reoccur when the same circumstances exist, knowing that sometimes it does occur, and sometimes it does not: how can we really predict that the sun will rise tomorrow simply because it rose today, for example?

(Or more precisely, how can we predict whether a forty-year-old man with consumption and a drinking problem will live to forty-five?) Because of his theoretical work on chance, probability, and Bayes, Price was elected a fellow of the Royal Society in 1765. Franklin was one of his six sponsors. As he was now a respected mathematician, life insurance companies consulted him about life expectancy rates, because they involved both retirement funds and annuities held by widows and widowers.

While we take life insurance for granted today, in late-eighteenth-century England it was a novel business. While provisions for old age, and for those who survived in a marriage, go back to ancient times, they were not the same thing for the early modern era. For one thing, in England, statistics on mortality rates were collected haphazardly, and the so-called statisticians of the day made numerous errors in trying to determine such facts as the accurate population of a given town or city.

One outcome of this inaccurate information and poorly run system was the birth of several societies, or companies, designed to insure lives with annuities and other instruments. But even these did not have accurate death rates and life expectancy tables. Some progress, however, was made when several statisticians developed new mortality tables. (Among these statisticians was Edmund Halley, the great English astronomer who discovered the comet named for him.) But while mortality tables were available, they were wildly inaccurate, and as a result, life expectancy could not be calculated.

This was the state of the so-called industry in the eighteenth century when in 1750 James Dodson, a fellow of the Royal Society, revolutionized the insurance industry. He figured out how to calculate premiums in a financially rational way. For the first time in history, he used mortality tables and probability studies of life expectancy to set premiums high enough to be fair to the policyholders and to keep life insurance companies solvent. Dodson died the next year and never completed his work. As it was an industry in its infancy, it needed ingenuity and direction. Price was just the man to give it both: his work in insurance was so precise and practical, so pragmatic and so superior, that he outdid Dodson.

Historian James Gibson Anderson says that Price's work was so profoundly original, he was truly the founder of the industry. Moreover, Price is also generally credited with improving existing death tables (his "study of life contingencies") for insurance and annuities. We see here an interesting confluence of two strains: the revolutionary idea that the growing English middle class might use the burgeoning commercial revolution in England to improve their own estate via insurance policies, an idea that paralleled the long-held benefit among the gentry of primogeniture (that is, the inheritance passed only to the eldest son). Even the name *Society for "Equitable" Assurances* rings for us today a cryptographic Jacobin chime.

The precise question was how to formulate policies that allowed for annuities in old age, annuities for survivorship, and annuities for both of these. In 1768, just six years after the establishment of the Society for Equitable Assurances, its directors, who were now well acquainted with Price's work, asked him to advise the company on a number of matters. At the very beginning, as he recalled, three men from the society asked him about some very practical problems having to do with the age of the people who purchased life insurance policies, their life expectancy, and the costs of the policy based on these two factors.

The society developed its policies based on the principle that everyone who was the same age was precisely in the same set of circumstances. They thought that in this way their clients were treated equitably (hence the name of the company). This, Price knew, was an inaccurate way of assessing a person's life expectancy: he quickly drew the society's attention "to the dangers of 'bad lives.'" His definition of people who lived "bad lives" included those whose life expectancy was seriously diminished by their hazardous occupations, their poor living habits, or other exigencies they faced that may lead to shorter lives. If all this were considered, then those whom we predict to live longer should pay higher premiums than those who do not—all perfectly mathematically correct.

On the basis of his association with the Society for Equitable Assurances, Price computed the values of the annuities in light of the probable deaths of their holders and concluded that the company had placed these values at too high a level. The company was in fact in danger of falling into bankruptcy. To forestall this possibility, he studied what today we call *demography*, along with mortality and birth rates. Several of his publications appeared in the Royal Society's *Philosophical Transactions*, most of them thanks to Franklin, who had them printed after Price forwarded them to him from Newington. By 1771 he had compiled so many detailed statistics, he published the work that made his name a respected authority in insurance matters, his *Observations on Reversionary Payments* ("reversionary payments" was the term he used for insurance claims). Dedicated to the Earl of Shelburne, this work has been called "the greatest classic in actuarial science."

Price set out to achieve two goals. First, he wanted to instruct the societies that provided annuities—both for survivors of marriages and old age—to set up a more rational approach to their businesses so that when they paid dividends to their investors, they had sufficient funds left over. He singled out two underperforming companies to show that "financial disaster was predictable if they failed to alter their scale of premiums [neither one was the Society for Equitable Assurances]. Their ineptitude could be seen in their failure to recognize that women tend to live longer than men, that they tend to marry earlier, and that, in consequence, they tend to outlive their husbands."

Price's second goal was to calculate life expectancy in the most rational and realistic way possible. He found the mortality tables the societies used were all inaccurate. After he presented ways they could remain solvent, he then set about trying to determine the best method to calculate death rates and, on the basis of these rates, life expectancy. He used common sense when he did not have access to hard figures. As he had earlier, he assumed that women live longer than men, that men generally marry women younger than themselves, and that life in the country is healthier than life in the city. He worked fast and furiously with the numbers he was able to obtain. An apocryphal story has it that Price's hair turned gray in a single night, when, in a storm of mathematical fervor, he tried to figure out these rates.

In the end, he developed mortality tables based on information about London and the nearby town of Northampton. The Equitable Society used the London tables for twelve years, from 1768 to 1780, at which point the directors realized that his life expectancy rates were actually too low. Thereafter, they switched to the more accurate Northampton tables that they and other life insurance companies used until well into the nineteenth century. Many companies that provided annuities and death benefits to their clients used Price's book on reversionary payments for many years. Maurice Edward Ogborn, the author of a history of the Equitable, notes that Price's study "had a profound influence on the annuity societies, material evidence of which is the handsome silver coffee-pot presented by the London Annuity Society to Price in 1790."

Price's book also included a section on what today we call a national social security program or old-age pensions. In 1772 such a plan based on Price's ideas was introduced into Parliament. In this case, workers were to deposit a small part of their income in a parish fund, which in turn invested in government bonds at a three percent interest rate. Its supporters claimed this plan would reduce poverty, especially among older people, and get people off poor relief. Although Price provided the statistical and actuarial materials, he was not in the forefront of the battle. The bill failed in the House of Lords, and that was the end of such social legislation until the next century.

Finally, although it did not exactly fit into a book about insurance, Price included a section concerning the dangers of England's growing national debt, one of the few areas where Hume and Price agreed (Hume feared a large national debt would bankrupt the country). This was also a subject that Price continually returned to (he published a pamphlet one year later on the subject). A national debt, he said, made every citizen a tributary of the Crown, it made the nation dependent on foreign countries, and it raised the price of goods and labor to an exorbitant level. In the end, such a debt reduced Britain's population because people died earlier in poverty or they emigrated when life was bad. Finally, it also had a negative impact on the balance of trade and the production of goods.

To avoid the growing national debt, Price advocated here and in other publications the creation of a sinking fund (designed literally to "sink" the debt): it was to be a compound fund to which the government annually contributed to ensure the eventual disappearance of the debt for good. Several years later, in a work on the population of England, he appended a section yet again decrying the debt, concluding that higher taxes—which, as a good eighteenth-century liberal, he dreaded—were the only solution to save the country from bankruptcy.

Price was quite proud of his book on reversionary payments and his contributions to the newly emerging insurance industry. He especially hoped his work revolutionized the industry so that companies made distinctions on the basis of age, location (differences between town and country), and other clearly identifiable and calculable matters. He also hoped the information he provided on life expectancy motivated people to move to the countryside, where people lived longer and where life was simpler, more virtuous, and luxury-free. He was so excited about his book—well, as excited as Richard Price ever could be—that he immediately sent Franklin a copy. In February 1772 Franklin sent him a note to thank him, "not only on my own Account for the Book itself you have so kindly sent me, but in Behalf of the

Publick for Writing it. It being in my Opinion, (considering the profound Study, and steady Application of Mind that the Work required, the sound Judgment with which it is executed, and its great and important Utility to the Nation) the foremost Production of Human Understanding that this Century has afforded us."

Price's book on life insurance and the national debt was very popular in America. In October 1778 Congress proclaimed Price a citizen of the United States and invited him to overhaul the country's finances. Congress resolved "That the Honourable Benjamin Franklin, Arthur Lee and John Adams [then in France] Esqrs or any one of them, be directed forthwith to apply to Dr Price, and inform him that it is the Desire of Congress to consider him as a Cityzen of the united States, and to receive his Assistance in regulating their Finances. That if he shall think it expedient to remove with his family to America and afford such Assistance, a generous Provision shall be made for requiting his Services." These three men sent Price this resolution from Passy on December 7, 1778, offering to pay his expenses for the journey to the United States. But Price declined. He told the three he was proud to have been asked, but he wasn't qualified for the job. Moreover, he was getting on in age (he was then fifty-five) and too attached to England. He hoped they would let Congress know his appreciation for the honor, and more important that he looked "to the American States as *now* the hope, and likely *soon* to become the refuge of mankind." His work on finances, he said, was a matter of amusement for himself—even if it did turn his hair gray.

Despite his decision not to become a United States citizen, American honors continued to accrue. Three years later, in April 1781, Yale University awarded him the honorary degree of LL.D., and in 1782 he was made a member of the American Academy of Arts and Sciences. In January 1785 he was elected a fellow of the American Philosophical Society. That year he advised a group of New Englanders about setting up an insurance company, which they did in the following months. The first in the New World, it was called the Massachusetts Congregational Charitable Society.

Price's last work on mortality tables, insurance matters, and the national debt appeared in 1786. Thereafter, he devoted his writings and preaching to the developments he saw taking place in the world. Most important to him was the French Revolution, an event that he likened to the American battle for independence. He died in 1791.

Priestley, in the meantime, did very little work of scientific value in London when he succeeded Price at Hackney. Instead, he, too, like Price, wrote about religion in works that contemplated the end of time and salvation of all mankind. He no longer had a laboratory as fully outfitted as the one he had lost in Birmingham. He had lost the society of conversation and sponsors he had enjoyed there, and he was convinced the Royal Society had become far too politicized, because opponents of the French Revolution now dominated its membership, making it difficult for those with liberal political views to feel welcome there. Besides, not only was Franklin dead, but so was Price, his best friend. A lonely man, Priestley contemplated leaving England for good, as the ministry began to crack down on supporters (or suspected supporters) of the French Revolution and conducted a number of show trials of those accused of sedition and treason.

In 1794, with France under the Terror and now embroiled in a full-scale war against most European countries, a move to that country was no longer an option. Priestley immigrated to America, because his son, young Joseph Priestley Jr.; his friend, scientist and lawyer Thomas Cooper; and several other men contemplated establishing a large English settlement for liberal Dissenters like themselves beside the Susquehanna River. He briefly contemplated accepting a chemistry professorship at the University of Pennsylvania and even corresponded with Rush about it. After he declined the offer (maybe he did another prudential algebra), Priestley chose to live the rest of his life in the country—along the Susquehanna River—because it was less expensive than Philadelphia, and he could not bear to be apart from his wife four months of the year. After he set up his laboratory in Northumberland, he devoted the rest of his life to science and religion, in particular to the imminent end of time, the return of Christ, and the coming Millennium. He died in 1804.

France

6

Marat and Mesmer, Charlatans
or Misunderstood Scientists?

Not all of Franklin's visionary friends were as close to
him as others. Certainly, Benjamin Rush, Joseph
Priestley, and Richard Price stack up among his
closest associates. The enjoyment he felt chatting or corresponding with them about political or scientific matters is evident.
Two other scientists, or at least two who claimed to be so, had
rather stormy relationships with Franklin. At first, he was fascinated and admired their work, but as time went on, he began
to see through their claims and became disenchanted with both
of them. First, there was Jean-Paul Marat, best known as one
of the leading spokesman for the French revolutionary Terror
from 1792 until his death a year later: as a member of the
National Convention, he called for blood every chance he
could get; he had begun his career as a physician and later
turned his attention to physics. And second, there was Franz-
Anton Mesmer, also trained as a physician: he concentrated

on a rather primitive field of psychotherapy, with an emphasis on hypnotism, to cure his patients of physical disorders that he thought sprang from psychological dysfunction. Both men wanted Franklin's friendship and, more importantly, his support, because they thought it was only through his influence that they would be admitted to the highest position in French scientific circles: the *Académie royale des sciences,* the Royal Academy of Sciences.

History depicts Marat as one of the most rabid, uncompromising advocates of the French revolutionary Terror of 1793–1794. By that fateful time, France was hopelessly divided into many factions. But the principal two were the moderate Girondins and the extremist Jacobins. The Girondins, also sometimes called the Brissotins after Jacques-Pierre Brissot, one of France's foremost political leaders, mostly led the government in 1792 and 1793 when France was under a constitutional monarchy. In June 1793 the Jacobins, led by Maximilien Robespierre, tried and executed many Girondins in power (those who were not executed committed suicide). Thus began the Terror. Marat, a member of the most radical wing of the Jacobins, spent the Revolution denouncing those whom he presumed to be the enemies of the republic, claiming he knew they lay beneath every stone and around every turn. In his radical paper *L'Ami du peuple* (The People's Friend), he wrote that the only way to ensure the success of the Revolution was to destroy all of its enemies. Blood must flow, he said, and the more the better.

In 1793 Marat himself was murdered by Charlotte Corday, a young Norman woman, who could not stand to see the Revolution destroy itself in the year before the Jacobins expelled the Girondins from the National Convention and demanded their arrest—and soon their execution as well. With her own Girondin sympathies intact, Corday was certain the democratic goals of the Revolution would soon become undone, and the only way to stop it was to eliminate the main antagonist of democracy.

Jean-Paul Marat (1743–1793) by H. Grévedon after J. Boze, 1793.
Courtesy of the Wellcome Library, London.

On July 13 Corday gained entry to Marat's well-guarded house, declaring that she wanted to give him a list of traitors. When she saw him, he lay soaking in his bath, something he perpetually did, having long suffered from pruritus, a dreadful skin disease he had contracted from hiding from the authorities in the filthy and wet sewers of Paris and in the damp basements of friends and collaborators. He also suffered from an undefined respiratory illness, and the steam from the bath helped his breathing. After Corday spoke a few words to him, he reputedly replied that her list was "good," and that "in a few days I will have them all guillotined." Without hesitation, she stabbed him to death, an act for which she was guillotined a few days later.

Charlotte Corday did not live to see the decree that the government enunciated two months later, which made the Terror "the order of the day" and began a ten-month-long nightmare of public executions. Thousands of people were caught in its maw.

How did Marat come to be such a bloodthirsty politician? It is no stretch to suggest, such was his passion for science, it has its origins in his earlier sour relationship with the French scientific establishment, which had rejected him and his ideas and caused him to hate everything and anything associated with Old Regime France.

Marat was trained as a physician in France and England and finished his medical degree in 1775, at the University of St. Andrews in Scotland (Benjamin Franklin had been awarded an honorary degree by St. Andrews in 1759). When he later became a full-time physicist, he was convinced his discoveries equaled Franklin's. Like the great American scientist, Marat experimented with electricity and lightning. He soon sought out Franklin, who, as the most respected and influential scientist in the world, had the political connections that could lead to Marat's admission to the *Académie royale des sciences*. All he needed was Franklin's endorsement.

There was a problem, however. Marat's views of contemporary physics and chemistry were out of the mainstream of eighteenth-century science. He was a maverick. And when his ideas were rejected, he took it personally, lashing out against those in authority and claiming they had a personal vendetta against him, disliked him, and were prejudiced against him and his theories. He thought he had some evidence for this, too, because he was often publicly characterized as a charlatan who demanded entry into a society of savants where he did not belong.

Marat's first book, *Essay on Man,* written in English in 1773, is a good example of his distinctive ideas. In this work he attempted to come to terms with human nature and human physicality by setting forth his theory (like that of Priestley) of the physical link between the human mind and body, a link he claimed was centered in the brain. Because the book was outrageous to some readers, it attracted wide attention, much of it derogatory. Its thesis struck Voltaire, for example, as presenting nothing new, and Denis Diderot thought it too materialistic. Marat, of course, believed he was absolutely correct and that no matter how important or well known his critics were, when it came to him and his work, they were all terribly mistaken. At the same time, he challenged accepted Newtonian ideas of the universe—the result was, unsurprisingly, that the *Académie royale des Sciences* again rejected his work.

Marat's contemporary critics and modern historians and biographers have criticized him for a variety of reasons: he lacked a true medical degree (but he actually did earn it legitimately at St. Andrews); he was a poor physician (but for years he was in the service of the Comte d'Artois, the king's brother), he was a poor scientist (while he was never admitted to the *Académie*, his ideas were continually published and widely circulated), and he was a crazed revolutionary (he did eventually lead the most extreme faction of the Jacobins during the Terror). And yet, Franklin, if only for a while, was an early supporter. He was among the first to endorse one of Marat's inventions, his *microscope solaire*, or solar microscope. Another early supporter was Jacques-Pierre Brissot, the journalist-turned-politician who was one of Marat's main allies in the 1780s. But the two split over the course of the Revolution in 1793 and became inveterate enemies.

So who was this complex, most likely paranoid man, this restless, ambitious opportunist who thought the scientific world had singled him out for persecution and ostracization? Marat was born in 1743 in a small town in Protestant Neuchâtel, an autonomous principality that became part of Switzerland in 1815. A smallish man, he has often been described as ugly, with a face that was pockmarked. His eyes were out of alignment. A portrait from the 1790s shows him with a broad forehead and widely set eyes (with the right one slightly sagging), a flat nose, and very thin lips.

The most famous portrait of Marat—that by Jacques-Louis David showing him lying dead in his bath—has become an icon of martyrdom. He lies peacefully in his tub, his head wrapped in a towel (probably soaked in vinegar to make his forehead feel better, by reducing the headache and inflammation of his pruritus). Blood flows everywhere, even on his chest. In his hand he holds a pen. It is legendary that he set up a writing table in his specially designed tub. In his other hand is the letter, now covered with blood, from Charlotte Corday. For art historian Stephen Miller, David painted Marat to look "like an angelic good-looking young man. . . . He seems serene—his eyes half closed, a slight smile on his mouth." In a Dorian Gray–like twist, David's idealized portrait does not reveal the true horridness of Marat's physical or spiritual being during the Terror.

Marat first practiced medicine as an apprentice, which was the custom, for many years in France and England until he finally secured his degree. He then served as the physician to the guards in the service to the Comte d'Artois, though he began to have doubts about continuing in that profession. In 1777, at the age of thirty-four, he began a new career as a scientist, although he remained in the Comte's service for another six years. He wanted to serve science, not only men, and turned his attention to three significant areas of inquiry, all popular in the eighteenth century: fire, light, and electricity. He thought he had something new to say in these areas, and he was convinced others would find his ideas interesting and revealing. It was his hope that the most prestigious scientists in France would accept them. He eventually wrote three volumes describing his theories and experiments, one for each of the three areas, and they were ultimately all united together in a single omnibus text.

Above all, Marat wanted a sympathetic hearing from Benjamin Franklin, in the hopes that the *Académie royale* would admit him among its immortal members. Within two years of devoting himself mainly to scientific inquiry, he asked Franklin to witness his experiments on fire. He claimed he had discovered the truth about fire, something no other scientist had ever achieved: fire contained an invisible fluid that, under controlled conditions, was visible to the human eye. He called it the *fluid igné,* or igneous fluid. Other scientists of the time said human beings could never see the fire's underlying material, since it was purely invisible. They believed fire was made of a substance that could be found in all material bodies and that could be freed by a shock: when two stones were struck together, for example, a flame appeared, and its warmth followed. But for Marat, the flame's matter was not the same as the original matter in fire; the original matter was invisible until Marat specially designed an instrument to view it; thus, his solar microscope. After Marat perfected the microscope so that the fluid itself was now visible, he believed he had finally revealed the truth about fire.

The first we know of a Franklin-Marat encounter appears in a 1779 journal entry that Franklin jotted down about receiving a letter in English "with a little tincture of French idiom" concerning Marat's experiments on fire. The unsigned correspondent (almost certainly Marat) had written, "The honour of your company at the repeating of the lately made discoveries on the igneous fluid is earnestly requested by the author. In an age where envy obstructs the way to the truth, ingenious and candid men are much wanted to support it." If indeed the anonymous letter was from Marat, whose handwriting bears a striking resemblance to the writing in question, the second sentence already reveals his growing fear (or paranoia) that mainstream scientists, jealous of his discoveries, would reject his work.

As it happened, the day was set, and a team from the academy attended the experiments, led by Jean Baptiste Le Roy, Franklin's old friend and scientific colleague. Le Roy was in charge of the king's laboratory in La Muette in Passy, near Franklin's Paris residence at the Hôtel de Valentinois. A physicist himself, Le Roy had experimented with electricity and had supported Franklin in his dispute with the physicist Abbé Nollet over its characteristics and nature. (Nollet had been the court physician during the reign of Louis XV, and Franklin and

Nollet differed over the nature and composition of electricity. Nollet held that electricity consisted of two effluvia, and these were the cause of attraction and repulsion, whereas Franklin emphasized the positive and negative charges emanating from a single electrical fluid.) As it turned out, Franklin could not attend Marat's demonstration—probably because of a flare-up of the gout. Franklin also missed several later displays of Marat's work before *Académie* judges because of illness or official duties on behalf of the United States.

Marat was so eager for Franklin to appear that he immediately wrote, "The representative of the author of the new experiments on fire has learned with mortification that you are indisposed. He wishes your gout to be immediately cured and hopes to have the honor of receiving you next Saturday, rue Bourgogne, at the home of the Marquis de l'Ausbespine. The gentlemen from the commission [of the *Académie royale*] will meet at 9:30 a.m. to take advantage of the sun"—his solar microscope, as the name suggests, only worked in sunlight. (It may be worth noting that the wife of the Marquis de l'Aubespine was Marat's patient and current mistress.) Franklin later apologized for being unable to attend, hoping he would be able to do so soon because of "the Honour done me in your obliging Invitation." When he finally did witness a demonstration, Franklin was intrigued but unimpressed; anxious to participate personally in the experiment, he asked Marat to shine the microscope on his bald head. The experiment was designed to prove Marat's claim that the movement of the igneous fluid actually caused heat to emanate from fire. He told Franklin and the other scientists they could see this fluid through his solar microscope in a darkened room.

Marat had actually designed 120 different experiments in a dark room with this device. The result of his experiment was it "gave off the emanations whose shadows Marat interpreted as visible evidence of igneous fluid." One member of the team, Balthazar Le Sage, who was the current director of the Monnaie and one of the few outspoken admirers of Marat's work, said he thought the "flame" created colors that "painters attributed to genius." Still, Olivier Coquard says that the mere presence of Franklin, Le Roy, and Le Sage gave Marat's theories a great deal of currency. Their report, though brief, was "rather favorable: it showed an interest that was more than polite for its experimental steps."

Despite the *Académie*'s interest, Marat was not awarded its highest distinction nor was he made a member. But he was not yet deterred. He next decided to submit his omnibus *Discoveries on Fire, Electricity, and Light* to the *Académie* in 1780, hoping to win approval for his views and gain for himself the great name in science he thought he deserved. His judges were again Le Roy and Le Sage, though this time Franklin could not join them. In Franklin's place the *Académie*'s permanent secretary, the Marquis de Condorcet, joined the group. What Marat could not achieve in quality, he tried to accomplish in quantity. Whereas he had earlier submitted some 120 experiments, he now asked the *Académie* to review an astonishing 5,000 experiments on light and vision. As might be expected, the commissioners were flabbergasted at his audacity; he was a waste of their time. Heaping insult upon injury, the commissioners said that because his work was anti-Newtonian, the *Académie* should condemn the author as a fool or, even worse, a fraud. Marat, in response, claimed he had actually been trying to build on Newton's incomplete work to find out why light passing through small objects was bent (although Newton had begun the investigation in 1672, he had never completed it). Still, Marat's initial conclusions were far different from the great English physicist.

So it was that the *Académie* treated Marat's work on optics "with disdain" and disgust; he had attacked Newtonian ideas, which the scientific establishment regarded as sacred. Anyone who argued against Newton was a mountebank. In many ways, Condorcet saw his job of permanent secretary to protect the integrity of the membership, or, as he himself put it, "to always be a barrier to charlatanism in every genre and it is for that reason that so many men complain." We can guess he had Marat in mind when he wrote these words.

Things deteriorated further when the *Académie* began simply to ignore Marat's studies of electricity, which now challenged Franklin's theory that electricity had to possess both attraction and repulsion (Marat said it was only attraction), and that electrical charges either consisted of a greater (or positive) charge or a lesser (or negative) one. As Clifford Conner puts it, "Franklin, together with most other physicists, conceived of the electric fluid as made up of particles that somehow repel each other. Marat was prepared to do battle against that opinion," but no one in the *Académie* cared to listen. Deeply hurt and insulted, he flew into a firestorm of rage.

Certain that the *Académie* had conspired against him, he now lashed out against it, accusing it of creating a cabal personally directed against him. He said the commissioners themselves were charlatans who failed to understand true science. He allied himself with others whom the *Académie* had rejected, including the physician/hypnotist Franz-Anton Mesmer and Jacques-Pierre Brissot. Marat and Brissot undertook a lengthy challenge to the *Académie*'s claimed authority to define scientific truth; but because all the firepower was arrayed against them and on the side of conventional science, their efforts were doomed.

Condorcet believed that the *Académie*'s two major purposes were, first, to combat charlatanism in all of its forms and, second, to uphold the best possible scientific methodology. Although Marat, he said, failed to meet these standards, the physician-turned-physicist was not deterred. In 1783 he wrote about the uses of electricity in medical therapy, his *Memoir on Medical Electricity.* While this book actually won first prize in a competition sponsored by the Rouen Academy of Sciences, Belles Lettres, and the Arts, the *Académie* simply ignored it. In this work Marat again rendered homage to Franklin and two other electricians. Franklin was actually very sympathetic to the idea that electricity might well be used in cures. There is even a report of Franklin's attempt to help a woman suffering from severe convulsions for over ten years. "Tortured almost to madness with a cramp in different parts of the body, then with more general convulsions of the extremities . . . and at times with almost the whole train of hysteric symptoms," she asked Franklin to help her. He complied by giving her two hundred strokes from his electric wheel every day and night. After two weeks he sent her home with her own apparatus to administer the shock therapy to herself, and she soon claimed that her condition had so improved that she would not now kill herself.

However, Marat's cures were not in the realm of pain therapy. He thought electrotherapy could cure all sorts of ailments, such as asthma, hypochondria, rheumatism, diabetes, and even obesity. He made a relatively successful medical practice in electrotherapy. All that Marat's "patients" needed to do was sit in a warm electrical bath. He used only human subjects in his experiments, because he opposed the use of animals for testing (he was an early advocate for animal rights). In his remedies he preferred to use different kinds of liquid as a conductor, beginning first with urine, then, in order of intensity, bile, blood, lymph, and finally something called *synovie*— whose true nature has been lost to time. After that he used solids, such as bone, muscle, nerves, tendons, and cartilage. Patients were subjected to an electric shock, not just static electricity, for at least twenty minutes a session, four or five times a day. He was fortunate that none of his patients were immediately and painfully electrocuted. Most likely, the shock was at a fairly low voltage. At any rate, when he reported his findings to the *Académie,*he was again laughed off. While Franklin might have been sympathetic to these medical uses, he apparently never witnessed them; he never commented on them.

If Marat's views of electrical medical remedies seemed strange to the *Académie,* but not to Franklin, his negative ideas about lightning rods sparked the first fires of resentment in the great scientist toward his work. Like many skeptics, Marat thought lightning rods were dangerous. Franklin, however, was absolutely convinced that lightning rods were not only safe, but that they protected life and property. He had been delighted in 1752 when they were erected under his direction on Philadelphia public buildings. He was even happier when they were later put on buildings in France. As he noted at the time, "I was pleased to hear of the success of my experiments in France, and that they there begin to erect points upon their buildings. We had before placed them upon our Academy and state-house spires."

A young, twenty-four-year-old Arras lawyer by the name of Maximilien Robespierre supported Franklin in this effort. In 1783 Robespierre, who ten years later would become the devil incarnate of revolutionary Terror, wanted to place a lightning rod on his own house, but a town law forbade him from doing so. When he erected one anyway, the local constables forced him to remove it. He argued that while scientific evidence proved the use of these rods, common sense demanded it. After all, everyone knew they worked: the king himself had placed a rod on the Château de la Muette. Why would the king do so if he thought it was dangerous? On May 13, 1783, the Artois council ruled that Robespierre could reerect his lightning rod.

But Marat vociferously objected to such things. He had already attacked the use of rods in his work on electricity when he claimed that Franklin had not really proved the rods staved off lightning attacks on buildings. He cited numerous examples of destroyed buildings that had lightning rods and suggested an alternate solution: place only one conductor beneath all of the houses and run the conductor into the street as far away as possible. One historian tells us that new buildings in Paris were actually constructed this way.

Marat's harsh opposition to lightning rods did not help his case with the *Académie*—or with Franklin. *Académie* members continued to react to his work with either outright disdain or condemnation, or they simply ignored it. For ten years he fought them, accusing them (as they did him) of "sterility, vanity, and charlatanism." He especially went after Condorcet, outrageously accusing him of selling his beautiful young wife, Sophie, into prostitution to cover his debts. If that were not enough, he was soon writing of his resentment of all academicians and learned societies throughout Europe.

Academicians, Marat said, "have tried to depreciate my discoveries throughout Europe, to raise the learned societies against me, and to shut down all my journals to the point of not being able to announce there the title of my works, to be forced to hide myself and to have a fake name [*prête-nom*], or pseudonym, so they could approve some of my productions." Ironically, he did have a few well-placed friends. Although many French scientists largely ignored his work, the popular journals, including the prestigious *Journal de Paris,* praised it. Scientists like Le Sage and the first crystallographer, Jean Baptiste Romé de Lisle, admired his work. Jean Baptiste Lamarck, the great classifier of invertebrates, accepted Marat's ideas of fire's igneous fluid. So it was not a complete loss for poor Marat.

Given this support, was there any merit to Marat's claim that he had been maliciously frozen out from membership in the *Académie royale des sciences*? Roger Hahn and Robert Darnton have investigated academy politics in these years and indeed all of the academic societies throughout Paris, such as the Academies of Surgery; of the Arts, Marine, Inscriptions and Belle-Lettres; of Inscriptions and Medals; of Painting and Sculpture; of Watch-Making; of Architecture as well as those academies throughout the country in such places as Lyon and La Rochelle. Jean Baptiste Colbert, Louis XIV's comptroller general of finances, had founded the *Académie royale* in 1666. Now, well over a century later, it was ruled by a scientific junta that was jealous of its authority and skeptical about men working on the cutting edge of science. They were especially suspicious of scientists like Marat who challenged accepted scientific knowledge and theories (such as Newtonian physics and optics). They either ignored or simply rejected hundreds of new experiments, simply because the experiments violated agreed-upon Newtonian ideas, or because they believed the experimenters, people like Marat or the famous proponent of the curative effects of animal magnetism, Franz-Anton Mesmer, were not part of the establishment.

Jacques-Pierre Brissot was one of Marat's most outspoken supporters. Brissot wished to end the narrow control over science that the establishment exercised. He wanted science and scientific inquiry to be truly open, democratic, and to reflect his own liberal politics. In his 1783 work, *De la verité* (On Truth), he offered Marat nearly unconditional support, based on his reading of Jean-Jacques Rousseau's work on the decline of morals and sensibility in a world increasingly overtaken by rationalism and science. This approach was precisely the opposite tack. Condorcet was just then attempting to find ways to apply scientific rationalism, not only to mathematics and statistics (his main academic disciplines) but also to politics and society. The worst offenders, for Brissot, were people like Condorcet and all of the men in the so-called learned societies. They corrupted the pure creative forces of humans by promoting the worst tendencies that we possess: their sole goal was to protect themselves and their own interests by keeping the societies closed to outsiders; thus they focused on intrigue and disputation, and they eliminated, or at least alienated, newcomers like Marat and Mesmer who had no real patrons and only a few intellectuals who had accepted their findings.

Brissot was certain Marat never had a chance because of narrow-minded academic prejudice. In *On Truth*, Brissot claimed that he himself was just the opposite of those despicable academics and that he was objective where they were not: "I swear to God, that in writing this chapter it is with the most disinterested spirit, with the greatest impartiality." Of course, he never wrote anything that was "disinterested" or "impartial." Brissot was actually a man of strong and spirited prejudice—though most of his prejudices favored more democracy, openness, and liberality.

Brissot argued that public opinion, not a small, closed cabal, should rule in matters of scientific and mathematical expertise. If the *Académie* were to reject Marat's experiments, it should do so because he had produced nothing new at all but had merely repeated old ideas in a new jargon. (He said in this work, "I will only cite here the story of the famous physicist, M. Marat. . . . I could cite a 100 others.") And yet, Condorcet saw things differently; he believed the supreme duty of the *Académie* was to keep science firmly in the hands of the acknowledged and tried professionals. Science was not a matter for the ravages and throes of public opinion. That would be the worst thing for science: making scientific knowledge a popularity contest when it should be based on the findings of the best and most rational minds of the nation. Public education was the only defense against attacks on the academy (and therefore science). Thus, the supreme and main duty of the *Académie* was to ensure that unscientific ideas, or ideas that were merely popular, would never make it into the public eye.

Franklin himself had become an associate member of the *Académie* in 1772 while he was in London, and once he moved to Paris he attended many meetings. His presence gave it additional prestige, which it probably did not need. Its conservatism aside, the *Académie* was truly dedicated to the advancement of science. Rigorous in its application of scientific standards, it was careful about whose experiments it endorsed: "If this meant assuming the role of an unpopular but benevolent despot, the academy was willing to suffer the consequences." Still, all of this led to increasing criticism of the *Académie*'s authoritarian ways, which undermined its credibility and contributed to its demise during the Revolution.

Like many of his unsuccessful predecessors, Marat was therefore both a pawn and a victim of the *Académie*. He believed to the very end of his life the *Académie* was a corrupt institution and had a corrupting influence on French life and thought. Disgusted, he gave up science and medicine altogether and entered politics full-time. Soon after the Revolution broke out, in 1789, he became the Revolution's *enfant terrible*, arguing in the most venomous manner against the king, the aristocracy, and naturally the scientists. In his underground newspaper he called for the blood of all of these people, and he allied himself with Robespierre. He and Brissot eventually had a falling out, when Brissot publicly praised Voltaire: Marat, who had been severely attacked by the great *philosophe*, brutally condemned his former friend. Writing his memoirs from prison, Brissot agreed with the members of the *Académie* when it noted Marat's "errors of logic . . . which reminded them of the charlatan-like attempts others had recently made in trying to discredit Newton."

Franz-Anton Mesmer (1734–1815), 1766. Courtesy of the Wellcome Library, London.

⚭

Marat was not alone in his criticism of the *Académie*. Another extraordinary eccentric whose path crossed Franklin's—and that of the scientific establishment—was the strange Austrian physician/hypnotist, Franz-Anton Mesmer.

Mesmer was one of the most peculiar physicians of the eighteenth century and maybe of all time. His place in history has depended on whether he has being assessed by his supporters or his adversaries. Some think of him only as a phony, while others regard him as a progenitor of modern psychiatry and psychotherapy. Some argue he was an early proponent of hypnosis. His successors, says Frank A. Pattie, a historian of psychoanalysis who is at the same time a critic of Mesmer, "freed themselves from the shackles of an irrelevant system of physics and opened the way to the discovery of the unconscious and the development of hypnotism and psychotherapy." By the end of the century, mesmerism, or animal magnetism as it was also called, was a sensational phenomenon practiced throughout the rest of France, England, Europe, and even as far away as Haiti. So was Mesmer a visionary, or was he a quack? Was he searching for fame and fortune for his own selfish ends, or was he trying to be a good medical practitioner? In fact, Mesmer's theories of health defied all known forms of eighteenth-century medicine. Some commentators believe his practice was consistent with today's faith healing: a patient is placed in a trance so that healing results through the power of suggestion—the success of mind over matter. But as far as Mesmer was concerned, none of these criticisms applied to him: his medical practice, so he claimed, was based on the firmest grounding in physics and physiology, medicine and psychology.

Even more important, Mesmer was responsible for the question of "mesmerism," one of the raging debates of the 1780s (thus taking his place with Machiavelli, Orwell, and the Earl of Sandwich, for contributing eponymously to the language). Interest in mesmerism matched the attention given to other curiosities, such as balloon flights and lightning rods. According to Robert Darnton, this interest distracted people from concentrating on Old Regime political corruption and economic failures—until the events of July 1789 refocused their attention. On the other hand, a revolutionary undercurrent, as we shall see, underlay the mesmerism debate: those who promoted it firmly believed it was a guide to utopia and the end of aristocratic corruption, a cure-all to every human psychic, medical, social, and political ill. In this way, says Darnton, mesmerism was a movement that contributed to both "the end of the Enlightenment" and the beginning of revolutionary politics.

Mesmer was a tall man for the time, standing almost five feet, ten inches. He had a high forehead, brown hair, and a round face. Few portraits of him exist, certainly none from when he was a young man, though he has been described as having been a handsome youth. Beyond science and medicine, Mesmer also wrote plays and satires. A self-confident man, he never resisted an argument. Always convinced he was right and his opponent wrong, he lashed out in the most vehement language, especially if someone disagreed with his medical treatments. When he wanted the *Académie royale* to review his methods, he demanded it merely affirm his principles willy-nilly without wasting time by witnessing his experiments. When Le Roy expressed skepticism of Mesmer's experiments, Mesmer called his comments "pitiful." Frank Pattie says that such remarks proved he was "haughty, touchy, self-important, and irritating." But Mesmer adored being in the public eye and was constantly reporting everything he did and inviting the learned community to witness his treatments.

Mesmer's relationship with Franklin was two-tiered: musical and scientific. First, Mesmer was deeply enamored with the glass armonica, a fascinating musical instrument that had been around for at least a century or more, which Franklin improved upon in 1761. In the eighteenth century, composers scored it into their work, so it became well known throughout Europe in this period. (Its sound was beautiful and haunting, serene and quieting. It has become increasingly popular in the twenty-first century, with scores of composers creating music for it and hundreds of new instruments being constructed to play it; there was even a glass armonica music festival in Paris in 2004.)

Franklin first met Mesmer in 1779 on a visit to his home. The young and beautiful Madame Brillon accompanied Franklin. Unsurprisingly, Franklin wanted to meet because of Mesmer's use of the glass armonica—and not because of his unusual medical treatments. Mesmer, however, wanted to talk to Franklin almost exclusively about fluids, medicine, animal magnetism, and such, and not the instrument. Madame Brillon was so astounded by the silliness of it all, she later told Franklin that when they all died and went to heaven, maybe "M. Mesmer will content himself with playing the armonica and will not bother us with his electrical fluid."

As he had for Jean-Paul Marat, Franklin investigated Mesmer's work. He led a joint commission from the *Académie royale* and the Faculty of Medicine, which was to determine whether Mesmer's medical techniques achieved his claimed results: were cures brought about by a combination of the music from the armonica, the attachment of magnets to the body, the submersions into warm baths, the touching by the master (Mesmer himself) of various parts of the body, and the swooning and fainting of the patients (mainly women)? Mesmer feared no one would understand his radical medical techniques, so he threatened Franklin that if he did not receive a proper hearing, he would leave town. In fact, his encounters with Franklin and the scientific establishment, like those of Marat, were hopeless (Franklin was skeptical from the beginning). They led to his ruin. When the commissions—a second commission had been set up by the Royal Society of Medicine—determined Mesmer's practices were a sham and he a fake, his practice failed, and he was forced to leave Paris. He fell into obscurity.

Apparently, Mesmer never actually claimed he could cure any diseases caused by organic disorders, such as infections or bacteria. He treated patients suffering from organic ailments with conventional methods, or he sent them to another physician. He claimed his cures applied only to "functional disorders," or what we today call mental illness. He believed the body and the mind were intimately connected to such a great degree that every human possessed a very subtle life-giving magnetic fluid. When this fluid was out of balance with the rest of the body's chemistry, a person fell ill. Once Mesmer restored the balance in the body through his medical-psychic techniques, the person's health returned.

He claimed he never used magic or faith healing. As a physician, he maintained he used only well-known medical practices, derived from science, to cure disorders by ways discovered by him alone. Darnton makes an important point: in an age when many people, including Franklin himself, Priestley, and Marat, as well as all chemists and physicists, talked about various fluids that pervaded electricity, fire, light, color, and even gases, why should not someone like Mesmer "discover" yet another fluid? After all, these were the years of Franklin's lightning rod experiments, forestalling and protecting against the electrical fluid that struck from the air; these were the years of Priestley's experiments on air in an attempt to unlock the secrets of God's universe; these were the years of the Montgolfier brothers' wondrous and magnificent hot air balloons. Just a year after Marat asked Franklin to witness his experiments on electricity, and five years after Mesmer arrived in 1778 in Paris from Vienna, the Montgolfier brothers performed their balloon feat before the royal family. Taking off from Faubourg St. Antoine near Paris, they carried with them in their balloon basket a sheep, a duck, and a rooster. For some, such an experiment defied everything about human beings, who were certainly not meant to fly like birds. As they soared skyward and half vanished into the clouds, they must have seemed to some like saints ascending to heaven. When asked what good would come from such an invention, Franklin reportedly responded in his characteristic humor-tinged-with-a-bit-of seriousness with a question of his own: "What is the use of a new-born baby?"

Franklin later came to think that such an invention had a practical application of "great Importance, and what may possibly give a new turn to human Affairs." Hot air balloons could even be used, he suggested, in air-mobile warfare, or what we now know as an air force. "Convincing Sovereigns of the Folly of Wars may perhaps be one Effect of it; since it will be impracticable for the most potent of them to guard his Dominions. Five thousand Balloons, capable of raising two Men each, could not cost more than Five Ships of the Line; and where is the Prince who can afford to cover his Country with Troops for its Defence, as that Ten Thousand Men descending from the Clouds might not in many places do an infinite deal of mischief, before a Force could be brought together to repel them?" So if air balloons were new, interesting, spectacular, and imaginative, what about other matters?

Mesmer came from the Lake Constance region in Swabia that borders Switzerland. At the University of Ingolstadt (today the University of Munich), he discovered the works of the sixteenth-century Swiss philosopher/physician Paracelsus, who used chemicals, such as mercury, sulphur, iron, and arsenic, for the first time, to treat disease. Mesmer was mainly attracted to Paracelsus's belief that the human body possessed an invisible magnetic force that was controllable through various chemical reactions. In medical school in Vienna, Mesmer wrote a thesis with distinctive Paracelsan allusions to magnetism and chemistry on how planetary movements affected a human being's health and welfare by means of a substance he called the "fluidum." This subtle magnetic fluid, present in all living beings, gave life force to human beings. It was already common knowledge that the planets influenced one another's orbits and that the phases of the moon affected the tides; Mesmer theorized that they likewise affected the human nervous system, because the fluids emanated from heavenly bodies penetrated directly into the body through a magnetic force.

Moreover, just as the ebb and flow of the tides occurred as a result of the pull of the moon, and just as the motion of one planet influenced the motion of other planets, so human beings, by means of magnetism, were connected to one another. Mesmer concluded that one person (namely Mesmer himself) could influence or cure other human beings when that person (Mesmer) understood how fluidum worked. If the flow of fluidum were somehow impeded or thrown out of kilter, then illness and disease resulted. If magnets were attached to the body, then the flow continued, and the patient was cured. Again, given the eighteenth century's obsession with fluids, it wasn't an absolutely absurd theory at the time.

But Mesmer went too far. He began to believe he could cure his patients without the magnets, by just the touch of his hands. He believed, or at least professed to believe, his own human or animal magnetism was so powerful that it alone produced a cure. His touch unblocked the obstructions to fluidum's passage into the body or its imbalance with other chemicals; however, he and he alone (and later one or two disciples) fully mastered the technique and understood the phenomenon enough to perform the cure. And it was this treatment that later got him into trouble with Franklin and the *Académie*.

Mesmer's Viennese mentors paid little attention to his thesis, and he passed his examinations with little acknowledgment and little fanfare. They simply agreed he would be a competent, hard-working doctor, a credit to the medical profession, who would likely devote his practice to providing good care to his patients. Always an imposing figure, he gave his patients the confidence and comfort that they would surely be cured of their maladies. His swaggering sense of self-confidence carried over to other interests in his life as well, especially music, because he used music in his treatment.

Mesmer played piano and the cello, and learning the glass armonica came natural to him. He believed the vibrations and the sounds the glass made were precisely related to the movement of the fluidum and the vibrations of the body. In Vienna, Mesmer met Leopold Mozart and his young prodigy son Amadeus, who was so taken by Mesmer's fascinating theories of animal magnetism and his admiration for the glass armonica that he eventually set some of his music to the instrument. Years later he would pay tribute to Mesmer in his 1790 opera *Così fan' tutte:*

> *Here and there a touch,*
> *Of the magnet,*
> *The stone of Mesmer,*
> *Who was born and bred*
> *In Germany's green fields,*
> *And who won great fame*
> *In France.*

Then again, maybe Mozart was making fun of the master of animal magnetism.

Just what was Mesmer's so-called medical technique? History has recorded a long series of stories of cures by touching—that is, cures by animal magnetism—that predate him. The famous or infamous "royal touch" was when the king or queen touched a person and healed him or her of some disease or malady. Queen Anne was said to be the last to perform such a cure in England. Another faith healer was the Irishman Valentine Greatraks, who participated in the 1641 Irish Rebellion and who was said to be able to cure the King's Evil, a swelling in the neck that we now know is due to such disorders as tuberculosis, scrofula, or goiter. Greatraks claimed he had to but touch the sick, and they were immediately cured. In his own healing practices, Mesmer first used magnets, as had Paracelsus, who claimed that magnets could even cure cancer. An Austrian astronomer, Maximilian

Hell, who was the first to compute the position of stars for every day of the year for use by navigators, claimed he had first induced Mesmer to use magnets to cure stomachaches and several nervous disorders. Hell had been engaged in manufacturing synthetic magnets as a hobby. Mesmer, however, denied the claim, and said he had come upon magnets through his own studies. Their debate became public, and a minor pamphlet war erupted between the two.

What really interested Mesmer was how the medical process worked: he claimed that his patients were cured when he used the magnetic force to concentrate fluidum on one single place on their body. In the course of his treatment, a patient experienced a whole raft of reactions: convulsions, bleeding, toothaches, earaches, inflammation of the intestines, despondency, hallucinations, fainting, temporary blindness, feelings of suffocation, and even paralysis that might last for days at a time. Mesmer said his goal was to produce these reactions, because they in turn provoked a crisis; it was this crisis that proved the patient was truly sick and the cure was working.

The therapy he used in both Vienna and Paris was really quite simple. By 1776 he had given up the use of magnets, claiming the human body possessed the same property contained in a magnet to bring about a cure. (It was also at this time he maintained that his own body, unlike those of most people, contained an endless supply of animal magnetism.) Second, he designed a new form of therapy with the use of water, iron bars, and music to cure his patients of disease. He used the word "disease" only in the singular, because he believed there was just one single disease in the world with a variety of manifestations. As mentioned, this disease occurred when the flow of a patient's animal magnetism became blocked or out of balance.

Mesmer initially treated his patients individually, but his practice grew so large that he devised a way to treat several of them together. Just as he had used his garden fountain in Vienna for his cures, in his Paris home he placed a large tub called a *baquet* with a layer of bottles on top. These bottles he "magnetized" by rubbing his hands on them. Sticking out of the tub were several iron bars. His patients stood in a circle around the *baquet,* where they were to be sure to touch both the bars and each other. Meantime, they were tied together with a cord, so the magnetic fluid reached the distressed parts of their bodies. Mesmer provided soft, soothing music for them on piano, wind instruments, or, more often, the glass armonica, and he dressed elegantly for the occasion, in lavender silk. He was often elegantly outfitted in lavender silk as he tied the patients together with the cord. Once he had filled the *baquet* with iron filings and powdered glass, he walked around his patients and touched whatever parts of their bodies that were ailing with an iron wand.

Some patients felt nothing, while others coughed or spit up phlegm. Others had more severe reactions. If one of his patients went into convulsions, he remarked that the animal magnetism was really working. Those in convulsive states were immediately taken to a "crisis" room filled with mattresses for the cure to work itself out. Jean-Sylvain Bailly, an influential astronomer and the mayor of Paris during the Revolution, described the scene: "Nothing is more astonishing than the spectacle of the patient's convulsions. . . . These convulsions are remarkable for their number, their duration, and their force; some of them have been known to last for three hours. These convulsions are characterized by involuntary jerking movements of the limbs, and of the whole body; by contractions of the throat; by twitchings in the hypochondriac and epigastric regions; by dimness and rolling of the eyes; by loud cries, weeping, hiccoughs, and uncontrolled laughter." Sometimes Mesmer prescribed more conventional treatments as a supplement, such as bleeding and purges, to clean out the bodily system, so that the animal magnetism could flow more freely through the body. That was the whole of it.

Was this a precursor of Freudian psychiatry? According to several historians, because Mesmer sometimes sat directly in front of his patients and threw them into a trance, he may be credited with having created what Claude-Anne Lopez calls "the germ of what would become hypnotism." It seems that even Franklin was wondering about this very question, although he, of course, would not apply the word *hypnosis* to Mesmer's treatment. In 1785 Franklin told Jan Ingenhousz, the Dutch physician who brought vaccination to England fifteen years later, that "we now have a fresh Folly" in Paris, concerning a "somnambule," that is, a person who has been placed in a hypnotic state by the mesmerist. "A Magnetiser pretends that he can by establishing what is called a *Rapport* between any Person and a Somnambule, put it in the Power of that Person to direct the Actions of the Somnambule, by a simple strong Volition only, without Speaking or making any Signs; and many People flock to see this strong Operation." Franklin would have had no idea that the spectacle was a hypnotic state or even a close-hypnotic state. But the incident certainly causes us to wonder whether Mesmer was ahead of his time. Some truly curious examples of his claimed cures are interesting, if not totally bewildering, to the contemporary, skeptical mind.

In a case in 1775, a patient called on Mesmer because no physician had been able to cure him of the horrible feeling his throat was closing in. He was certain he would suffocate. As he had done with his wife's cousin, Mesmer magnetized the man, who was, incidentally, a baron, and claimed he had cured him when the baron's seizures never recurred. Did Mesmer truly magnetize him under these circumstances, as reported by an eyewitness? "[The baron] was wearing a trout-gray suit decorated with gold braid. On one foot he wore a white silk stocking; the other foot was bare, and it was resting in a wooden washtub which was filled with water. . . . Beside the tub sat the baron's violinist with his face turned toward the bed. . . . He was holding in his left hand a piece of rattan, the lower end of which rested on the bottom of the tub. He was directed to grasp this rattan with his right hand and continually stroke it from the top downwards." Was the baron cured or was this "cure" the result of the power of suggestion? It is interesting to note that the baron's other physicians attributed his problem solely to his imagination.

Two years later, in what Mesmer claimed was one of his most spectacular Viennese "cures," he alleged that he healed a young pianist who had been blind since age three after no physician could help her. Eighteen-year-old Maria Theresa Paradis, the namesake of the empress, was the daughter of an Austrian bureaucrat. Mesmer brought her into his home so he could personally direct her care. Just after he began the treatment, so he said, she regained partial vision. In a turn of fate, however, once she could "see," if only a little, she lost her dexterity on the piano and kept hitting the wrong notes. At the same time, she was now in danger of losing the large pension the empress had awarded her. After five and a half months and after the constant prodding of her father, she returned to her family, where they found she had not regained any of her sight at all. She was still blind and remained so for the rest of her life. Was this a cure that lasted only while she lived with Mesmer, or was it a cure only in his mind? Were the accounts, and there were some, that she could see well enough under his care to identify objects actually true, or did he make them up? Frank Pattie concludes that perhaps "Miss Paradis may have appeared to see when she did not." There was never any conclusive evidence. In any event, she resumed her music career, which took her all over Europe, and eventually became a composer, perhaps best known today for *La Sicilienne.*

Eventually, the Viennese medical community lost all tolerance for these so-called cures, which were so far outside the boundaries of accepted treatment. Mesmer was expelled from the Vienna Medical Faculty. In 1778 he left his wife in Austria to handle the family affairs and moved to Paris. He never saw her again.

Paris was the one place where he thought he could openly

practice his medical theories, but he could not have miscalculated the situation worse. First, there was a problem in that his cures only occasionally worked; moreover, his critics claimed on these occasions there was no cure at all, but, rather, his patients hadn't been sick or disabled in the first place. On the occasions that his cures failed, Mesmer's response was that something had interfered with his work—either the spell he was casting was broken by outside influences, or the patient lost concentration, or the atmosphere itself was wrong. Second, Mesmer further incensed his critics by never bothering to become licensed in France; he just opened a practice without sitting for the required examinations and public disputations.

One thing is certain: he did have his supporters. One of the most important was a radical young Parisian lawyer, Nicolas Bergasse, who in 1781 wrote a pamphlet supporting Mesmer's medical theories. Bergasse began as Mesmer's patient when he appeared to have some sort of mental disorder (he might have been a manic depressive). Profoundly antiaristocratic and antimonarchical, Bergasse believed Mesmer's techniques would bring about a revolution in medicine so profoundly radical that health and prosperity would widely flourish and bring universal harmony to all humankind. With the help of another patient, Guillaume Kornmann, who was also Mesmer's banker and financial advisor, Bergasse set up the Society of Universal Harmony. It was designed to spread the truth of Mesmer's doctrines—at a subscription price that was designed to make them and Mesmer very rich men. The members all signed a pledge never to reveal the secrets of Mesmer's techniques or practice them without their mentor's written consent.

Another disciple was a young physician, Charles Deslon (or d'Eslon), though he, like so many of Mesmer's supporters, would later become an enemy when Mesmer accused him of stealing his doctrine and medical techniques. Mesmer had first enlisted Deslon's support soon after his arrival in Paris. At the time, Deslon was twenty-nine and a member of the Faculty of

Medicine. He was also the personal physician to the Comte d'Artois, the younger brother of the king. Through Deslon, whose "high standing with the faculty held out the hope that that august body might be persuaded to put its stamp of approval on Mesmer's discovery," Mesmer ingratiated himself with some of the great luminaries of Parisian society, including (aside from d'Artois), Marie Antoinette and the Marquis de Lafayette. Deslon was eventually dismissed from the medical faculty because of his adherence to Mesmer's bizarre medical techniques and was soon seeking to rehabilitate his reputation.

In the meantime, Mesmer's enemies were gathering. In 1784 the king appointed two commissions to investigate his work. The first team was a joint affair: *Académie royale* and the Faculty of Medicine of the University of Paris, which was widely known to oppose change in medical practice and to brand as a charlatan any physician with new treatments and methods. The second was a team from the Royal Society of Medicine, a newer group that fostered medical reform and the licensing of new medical practices. The first team included Benjamin Franklin, who by then was seventy-eight years old. Among the other members of this commission were the renowned astronomer Jean-Sylvain Bailly (who described the convulsions); Antoine Lavoisier, the great chemist; and Joseph Ignace Guillotin, credited with publicizing (though not himself inventing) the new machine to carry out humane executions. The resulting document is often referred to as the "Bailly Report," because while Franklin chaired the commission, Bailly served as its secretary. The second team included the botanist in the Jardin des Plantes, Antoine de Jussieu, who would be the only member to issue a dissenting opinion, because he believed the investigation was insufficiently thorough.

On the appointed day, members of the *Académie* commission set out to observe just how Mesmer operated. They met at Franklin's residence in Passy, because he was ill and could not travel. Lafayette, a Mesmer supporter, had hoped that Mesmer himself would attend, but instead Deslon, whose falling out with Mesmer was now public, wanted to justify and prove his use of animal magnetism to treat patients. Deslon, among other things, had not received written permission from Mesmer to treat patients with his techniques. Skeptical from the start, Franklin took a drastic step. He decided that he himself should be magnetized. As was typical with the treatment, there was complete silence, except for the music that was playing, while Deslon passed by the blindfolded Franklin with his magnetized instruments. Franklin was made to understand that the pain or heat, especially intense heat, that he could be expected to feel might well cause him to have a coughing fit, to perspire profusely, to become extremely dizzy, or to have convulsions. He might even faint dead away. But as he waited in the darkness, a curious thing happened: nothing. The commission reported that he "felt no sensation." Later, one of the commissioners disguised himself as Deslon and told a group of patients he was Dr. Deslon, the disciple of Dr. Mesmer. He soon found he could magnetize people as easily as Deslon did, or at least the patients reacted as if he could. Some of the commissioners believed the patients had simply talked themselves into believing they were ill and they suffered from a psychosomatic disorder easily cured through faith in their doctor. Deslon had failed, and with his failure, Mesmer also failed. The mesmerian system was totally discredited within the scientific community.

Published in August 1784, the commission report was an immediate best seller. Some twenty thousand copies were quickly bought up. The following year it was translated into English and printed in England and America. The commissioners determined there was little to Mesmer's medical prowess, a conclusion confirmed when the joint report of the medical faculty and Royal Society of Medicine concurred. The result was that the Faculty of Medicine formally outlawed animal magnetism, and Mesmer was largely disgraced. When Bergasse began to treat patients himself without written permission from his master, he was expelled from the Society of Universal Harmony.

Even so, animal magnetism continued to enjoy a modicum of success and celebrity, and several chapters of the Society were formed throughout America. It lasted until the Revolution, when it counted some 430 paid members in its ranks. To Franklin's consternation, his grandson Temple became a member of the Paris society and paid the one hundred *louis* subscription fee. The members met at the Hôtel de Coigny, Mesmer's residence (he had become quite wealthy by charging his clients dearly). On one occasion Mesmer asked Temple to help draft the bylaws of the society. Only in 1818 (twenty-eight years after Franklin's death), when Temple published his biography of his grandfather, did he finally renounce mesmerism and animal magnetism altogether.

At its height the Society of Universal Harmony included several friends and acquaintances of Franklin: the Girondin leaders, the Rolands; Jacques-Pierre Brissot; the Marquis de Lafayette, who in a 1784 America tour lectured on mesmerism to the American Philosophical Society; the Marquis de Chastellux, who along with Lafayette had fought in the American Revolution; and Claude-Louis Berthollet, the great chemist and member of the Faculty of Medicine, who was later embarrassed for having ever accepted the doctrine. When he finally changed his mind, Berthollet stalked out of a society meeting and publicly denounced Mesmer and mesmerism as being "perfectly illusory." Lafayette, however, remained a staunch adherent and a loyal member. He returned from America after his Philosophical Society lectures with what appeared to be a letter of support of or at least interest in mesmerism from George Washington himself. Thomas Jefferson, now Franklin's successor as the American minister in Paris, was so distraught on hearing of this letter that he sent anti-Mesmer pamphlets to America. He noted that Mesmer's doctrine was "a strange folly" and "a madness," "an imputation of so grave a nature as would bear an action at law in

America." As far as he was concerned, "Animal magnetism [is] dead, ridiculed."

However, the *Académie* commission left one possibility open about Mesmer's techniques, and this takes us back to where we began: the power of suggestion, or as they referred to it, the power of imagination. In its report the commission wanted to find out once and for all whether there was anything to Mesmer's ideas about magnetization.

Deslon brought a boy to Passy—there was nothing wrong with him—to test his reactions to Mesmer's practices. Deslon's task was to magnetize an apricot tree by pointing his cane at it. The boy was then led out, blindfolded, to see whether the magnetized tree, or those not magnetized, would have an effect on him. The commission reported what happened next: "The boy was . . . presented successively to four trees upon which the operation had not been performed, and caused to embrace each of them for the space of two minutes." Although Deslon had magnetized none of the four trees the boy embraced, he fell into a stupor and was thrown into contortions. He then passed out. The commissioners were astounded: because "the [boy's] crisis was . . . the effect of no physical or exterior cause," it had "to be ascribed solely to the influence of imagination. The experiment is therefore entirely conclusive: the boy knew that he was about to be led to a tree upon which the magnetical operation had been performed, his imagination was struck, it was exalted by the successive steps of the experiment, and at the fourth tree [where he collapsed] it was raised to the height necessary to produce the crisis."

Franklin himself had suspected this all along. Just before the beginning of the commission's investigation, he wrote to a man who was quite ill and who wanted to know whether he should try Mesmer's cure. Franklin replied:

As to Animal Magnetism, so much talk'd of, I am totally unacquainted with it, and must doubt its Existence till I can see or feel some Effect of it. None of the Cures said to be perform'd by it, have fallen under my Observation; and there being so many Disorders which cure themselves and such a Disposition in Mankind to deceive themselves and one another on these Occasions; and living long having given me frequent Opportunities of seeing certain Remedies cry'd up as curing everything, and yet soon after totally laid aside as useless, I cannot but fear that the Expectation of great Advantage from the new Method of treating Diseases, will prove a Delusion.

So it was that Franklin, who had discovered the subtle fluid in electricity, now denied the existence of Mesmer's universal fluid. But, and here is the interesting part, he acknowledged the delusion may be useful, because it might very well lead to a cure—if only because the patient *imagined* or *believed* it worked. Anticipating by almost two centuries the psychosomatic effect of placebos (first reported in 1955 by Dr. Henry K. Beecher at the Massachusetts General Hospital), Franklin said that the power of the mind might be enough to effect a cure: "There are in every great rich City a Number of Persons who are never in health, because they are fond of Medicines and always taking them, whereby they derange the natural Functions, and hurt their Constitutions. If these People can be persuaded to forbear their Drugs in Expectation of being cured by only the Physician's Finger or an Iron Rod pointing at them, they may possibly find good Effects tho' they mistake the Cause."

The commissioners pursued their line of reasoning that the results were psychosomatic. Such was the power of imagination, as Jan Goldstein has recently pointed out in her study of nineteenth-century French psychiatry. (It is as relevant today as it is for Franklin's time.) Years later even Thomas Paine marveled at Mesmer's power over his patients. In reviewing the biblical accounts of miracles, Paine concluded that the imagination was the sole source of a person's belief in them. "The force of the imagination is capable of producing strange effects," he wrote. "When animal magnetism began in France, which was while Dr. Franklin was Minister of that country, the wonderful accounts given of the wonderful effects it produced on the persons who were under operation, exceeded anything related [to miracles]. They tumbled down, fell into trances, roared and rolled about like persons supposed to be bewitched." But when the commissioners finally tested the doctrine, they found that "it was the effect of imagination only." Paine used mesmerism as a foil to promote his belief in deism; he argued it was particularly fortunate that mesmerism had not been around in New England a century earlier, for if it had, "this falling down and crying out" would have meant "the preachers would have been hung for witchcraft. . . . The progress that reason and Deism make in the world lessen the force of superstition and abate the spirit of persecution."

The commissioners themselves concluded, not without some trembling of their own, "the imagination is that active and terrible power, by which are operated the astonishing effects, that have excited so much attention to the public process." Even Deslon agreed. He told the commissioners, as they reported in their final assessment, "The imagination had the greatest share in the effects of the animal magnetism . . . this new agent might be no other than the imagination itself, whose power is as extensive as it is little known." Thus, the commissioners and Deslon both thought that medical cures might some day result only through the power of persuasion; though such cures, with their violent convulsions and crises, the commissioners felt, "are almost always destructive."

Even so, Nicolas Bergasse defended mesmerism in a long pamphlet in which he attempted to prove the relationship between Mesmer's doctrine and the fine arts, education, and moral philosophy. He even asked the Parlement de Paris to make an independent investigation of its own, and its members decided to do just that, but nothing came of it. Meanwhile, the police authorities were alerted to the underlying potential subversive power of the mesmerists and especially of Bergasse's society. Its meetings were reportedly filled with seditious attacks on the monarchy and aristocracy along with blasphemous attacks on religion. Lieutenant General of Police Jean-Pierre Lenoir noted that if he had had the authority, he would have shut down the entire society and arrested Mesmer—or at least seen him deported. In the end, the movement became, as Jefferson noted, a butt of ridicule, satire, and jokes. Bergasse and Mesmer had a falling out. In 1785 the Society for Universal Harmony split from Mesmer and denounced him. Soon after, Deslon set up his own clinic and went into competition with him.

Just before Franklin returned to the United States from France, he told Ingenhousz, the Dutch physician, that he noticed Mesmer was still in Paris and seemed to have some patients. Convinced now that Mesmer was a charlatan, Franklin concluded the whole point of the physician's doctrine was to enrich himself financially. "Mesmer continues here and has still some Adherents and some practice. It is surprizing how much Credulity still subsists in the world. I suppose all the Physicians in France put together have not made so much Money during the Time he has been here, as he has done." Soon, however, Mesmer took up a life of wandering, returning now and again to Paris, until his death twenty years later in 1815. He was eighty-one. For at least one modern historian, Mesmer was no charlatan, because he never once set out to deceive his patients. Mesmer thoroughly believed himself to be a well-trained and industrious physician and scientist intent on proving to the medical and scientific world that his treatments were not only novel but effective. Unfortunately for him, few others agreed.

Condorcet, Revolution, and la République Française

The Marquis de Condorcet is today mostly regarded as a founder of modern social science. Like Franklin, his interests were enormously wide ranging. He wrote on science, mathematics, politics, philosophy, and history. As an early supporter of the French Revolution, he became both a leader and victim of it, serving at the end of his life in the National Convention as a Girondin deputy and helping to draft both a universal system of public education and a new republican constitution; however, with the onset of the Reign of Terror in 1793, after escaping Paris, he was arrested—and later found dead, most likely a victim of suicide. He believed everyone was equal and, like Rousseau, thought everyone was born with a natural moral judgment and a sense of pity at seeing anyone suffer. He devoted his life to enhancing equality based on class, race, and gender, ideas that seem progressive by twenty-first-century standards. He even supported gay rights, as we call them today, saying at one point that because there are no victims in homosexual relations, "sodomy violates the right of no man." Moreover, he supported the rights of the accused in courts of law, and even demanded the appropriate treatment of children and animals (he hated hunting and would never even kill an insect).

Born in 1743, the same year as Jefferson, in Ribemont in the Picardy region of France, Condorcet came from a family with a tradition of military service. His father was killed on maneuvers shortly before Condorcet was born, and his widowed mother immediately dedicated the young boy's life to the Virgin Mary. Madame Condorcet dressed her son in a white dress until he was eight years old. As a grown man, he was quite tall for his era, almost six feet in height. He had a very high forehead, brown hair, gray eyes (a birthmark lay under his right eye), a broad, aquiline nose, and a round chin. In 1775 he contracted smallpox, which permanently scarred his face.

The Marquis de Condorcet (1743–1794) by François
Bonneville. Photo courtesy of The Newberry Library, Chicago.

He studied science and mathematics at the College of Navarre, where the famed electrician the Abbé Nollet held the chair in experimental physics. There he worked with scientist Georges Girault de Kéroudon, who remained his tutor even after Condorcet graduated in 1759. He moved to Paris three years later and, thanks to his association with Kéroudon (Condorcet lived with him for a time on the rue Jacob), was able to present his first paper (on mathematical probabilities) to the *Académie royale des sciences*. He became friendly with several Enlightenment thinkers, especially those engaged in the writing of the great *Encyclopedia*, such as Denis Diderot. But beginning in 1765 his most important intellectual contact would be with Jean le Rond d'Alembert, one of the great mathematicians of the century.

D'Alembert introduced Condorcet to Julie de Lespinasse, one of the most respected salonnières in Paris, who over time became like a "second mother" to Condorcet and called him "*le bon Condorcet*." D'Alembert, who was Julie's secretary and lover, served as coeditor with Diderot of the *Encyclopedia*. Although he later withdrew from the project, he wrote most of the articles on mathematics, philosophy, and science. He thought that scientists were often at odds with most of society, because in his view the scientist's duty was to reform society through enlightenment, even though the nobility were a coterie of ignorant men. Condorcet was deeply taken by these ideas and loved the notion that scientists have such a major, even commanding, role in society. As a member of both the *Académie royale des sciences* (elected in 1769, becoming its permanent secretary in 1776) and the French Academy (elected in 1782), Condorcet strove to achieve the independence and autonomy of the scientist/intellectual to lay out the path for society's improvement.

At Julie de Lespinasse's salon, through a combination of his ambition, vanity, and pride, Condorcet engaged in conversation with the leading philosophes of the French Enlightenment:

Anne-Robert-Jacques Turgot, who was to become his principal mentor and colleague in politics, and the philosophe the Abbé Etienne Bonnot de Condillac, founder of the psychology of sensationalism, who detested Condorcet (he claimed on his deathbed that he had become sick because of a cup of hot chocolate Condorcet had served him). At the salon, Condorcet cemented his ties to the scientific community. This was where he met several highly charged political liberals: the magistrate Malesherbes and the Toulouse archbishop Leménie de Brienne. One thing Condorcet said he had learned from d'Alembert was independent thinking, that is, not to be beholden to any one, especially the nobility, and therefore to be suspicious of men of wealth and power. Turgot reinforced these ideas later, and during the Revolution they became most important to Condorcet. He was shocked to learn the *Encyclopedia* had been suppressed in 1759 for its irreligion: Diderot and the Baron d'Holbach had become increasingly radicalized toward atheism and were convinced the priests were duping the kings. But instead of a head-on collision with the authorities, d'Alembert used guerrilla infiltration tactics. He knew political, social, and intellectual change would occur only when more people like him (such as the young Condorcet) infiltrated the established institutions, such as the *Académie royale des sciences,* and made subversive changes from within.

Condorcet also held the title of inspector general of the Monnaies (the mint and currency), a position created only in 1756 in the treasury department, which came with an annual salary of five thousand livres and a residence in the Hôtel des Monnaies on the quai de Conti. As only the second man ever to hold the office, Condorcet thought he could make a direct contribution to society by bringing a rational system of coinage to the realm.

First, he had to establish a rational and consistent system of weights and measures, then in a chaotic and miserable state. Agriculture, commerce, and science all suffered, because weights and measures differed throughout the nation.

Wood was sold by the corde, *wooden charcoal by the* tonne, *earthen charcoal by the* bacherelle; *ochre by the* tonneau, *woodwork by the* marque *or* solive. *Fruit made into cider was sold by the* poinçonée, *salt by the* muid *or* sétier *or* mine *or* minot *or* boisseau *or* mesurette. *Lime was sold by the* poinçon *and minerals by the* razière. *You could buy oats by the* picotin *and plaster by the* sac. *You could get wine by the* pinte, *by the* chopin, *by the* camuse, *by the* coquille, *in a* petit pot *and in a* demoiselle. *A person could buy eau-de-vie by the* portée *and wheat by the* muid *or the* écuellée.

And on and on and on. It was not until seven years later that Condorcet put a practical system of weights and measures into place.

If the "good Condorcet" offered observers a picture of a modest intellectual, he could also show a dark side to those who disagreed with him. In the spring of 1775 he plunged into a highly emotional public quarrel over free trade with the self-made Swiss banker Jacques Necker, whose ideas directly clashed with Condorcet's friend and mentor Turgot. Condorcet did not just defend the idea of free trade; he ruthlessly and personally attacked Necker with insult after insult. He called him the "Swiss moneylender" and attacked him for aiming to increase his own wealth at the expense of the poor. The depth of vituperation he dealt shocked his friends. Even Turgot called him "*le mouton enragé*" (the rabid or mad sheep), a name his enemies would use against him during the Terror. His friend Jean-Baptiste Suard once told him even the most honest men who did not know him personally thought he was "a vicious man, and even your own friends have found you to be unjust." His emotional mood shifts often gave him a peculiar look, something that was not lost on John Adams, who later recalled that on first meeting him he noticed Condorcet's face was "as pale, or rather as white, as a sheet of paper, I suppose from hard study." But

Adams hated Condorcet, as he did Condorcet's mentor Turgot, because they supported Franklin's single-chamber Pennsylvania legislature rather than Adams's Massachusetts's bicameral assembly: accordingly, for Adams, Condorcet was "ignorant, totally ignorant."

Condorcet's admiration for Franklin paralleled his veneration of the American Revolution and the liberty that the Americans achieved after tearing themselves from despotism. While their "natural genius" was not "extinguished" when they were a British dependency, as "Mr. Franklin is the proof of it," they improved even more so after the Revolution. Condorcet saw the American Revolution as inspiration for the French; once liberated from absolutism, they would likewise erect a republic, but not as the Americans had done. Condorcet favored the single-branch legislature that Franklin, Paine, and others created for Pennsylvania just after the break with England.

In an age when we are used to a two-house legislature, it seems almost given that power must be separated within the legislature just as it is between the various branches of government. In this way, with a house and senate, neither branch predominates over the other and corruption is best controlled. This is, in fact, why the United States Constitution provided for separate upper and lower houses. While this has become the convention of political organization in the United States and indeed in many democratic countries, it was not always the case. (Today only the state of Nebraska has a single-branch legislature, and its political leaders have long considered a change to a bicameral system.) The earliest American assemblies, those the Crown established in the seventeenth century, originally had only one house, whose only authority was to advise the royal governor. Most colonial legislatures did not have two branches until after 1680 (Connecticut was the last to change, in 1698). Whether a two-house system is more efficient than one or whether corruption is somehow reduced or eliminated with two houses remain open questions.

The great French philosopher the Baron de Montesquieu argued that the separation of powers was the best defense against despotism. Divided power prohibited royalty from aligning itself with the nobility, and it prevented both of them from becoming the sole beneficiaries of political power. With the exception of Connecticut and Pennsylvania, most of the new American states followed Montesquieu's recommendation after 1776 and divided state legislatures into two houses. (As described in the previous discussion of Price and Priestley, the roots of this principle lay in Aristotle's ideal that society was naturally divided into three classes of the one, the few, and the many, where each possessed a political counterpart to represent social standing and the interests of royalty, nobility, and the commoner. For practical purposes this translated into institutions of government: the king or executive, the aristocratic or upper house, and the many or the lower house.) As a follower of Turgot, Condorcet broke with this ideal and rejected the two-house principle.

In July 1776 all of the states began to write constitutions, because the Declaration of Independence invalidated their royal or proprietary charters. Elected to the Pennsylvania constitutional convention, Benjamin Franklin served as its president (without having to relinquish his membership in the Continental Congress, which was deeply involved in the final stages of drafting the first constitution of the new United States). For a couple of months, before he went off to France at the end of the year, Franklin padded back and forth between the two bodies, which were meeting in the same building. As president of the Pennsylvania constitutional convention, he argued for a unicameral legislature, because he believed such a body avoided party squabbles and would be more democratic than a bicameral legislature, which he called a beast. As his young friend and follower Thomas Paine later recalled, it was like a wagon being drawn by two teams of horses, one in the front, the other in the rear: "If the horses are of equal strength, the wheels of the cart, like the wheels of government, will stand still; and if the horses are strong enough, the cart will be torn to pieces." Franklin, as it turned out, was enormously successful in leading the convention to his way of thinking.

In the meantime, Paine always disavowed having anything to do with the drafting of the Pennsylvania constitution, though he joined Franklin in admiring the new unicameral legislature. For Paine, the convention "had the wisest and ablest man in the State, Dr. Franklin, for their President, whose judgment alone was sufficient to form a constitution, and whose benevolence of heart would never concur in a bad one." Moreover, the new constitution conferred on every male the right to vote—thus creating a republic that was far more radical than any other in America. After Franklin arrived in France at the end of 1776, he widely distributed translated copies of the new document. Dozens were printed and sent out, and the Pennsylvania constitution became the most well known constitution in France, better known even than the federal one. It is interesting to note that whenever Franklin's *Poor Richard* was reprinted in French translation after 1776, it typically included a copy of the Pennsylvania constitution. Most liberal French writers were delighted with it.

Among these admirers was Turgot. When Turgot had earlier written to Richard Price to congratulate him on the publication of his *Observations on Civil Liberty,* he used the occasion to lay out his own philosophy, especially why he believed he had been dismissed from the government. (He asked Price not to publish the letter, because it frankly depicted his true admiration for the Americans as they were establishing republican governments.) Turgot was notably disappointed to see that so many states had merely used the old English system as a political template. "Instead of collecting all authority into one center, that of the nation, they have established different bodies; a body of representatives, a council, and a Governour, because there is in England a House of Commons, a House of Lords, and a King.—They endeavour to balance these different powers, as if this equilibrium, which in *England* may be a necessary check to the enormous influence of royalty, could be of any use in Republics founded upon the equality of all the Citizens."

Turgot told Price, "In attempting to prevent imaginary dangers they create real ones." He predicted the result would be constant fighting, increasing bitterness, and statutorial gridlock. America was "the *hope* of the world," he said, but only if she broke free from the illusion that she needed to imitate Britain. The result in Europe had always been "a mass of divided powers contending for territory and commerce, and continually cementing the slavery of the people with their own blood." America deserved better than this, he said. Condorcet, naturally, agreed.

The Pennsylvania constitution stood as a model for the French constitution, which Condorcet would later help draft. As he wrote in his 1790 eulogy to Franklin, the Pennsylvania constitution "was in part [Franklin's] work. It was distinguished for the most part from others by a greatest equality and above all by the legislative power which was confided in a single chamber of representatives. The voice of Franklin alone decided this final arrangement." Long before that, Condorcet had written four letters from "a citizen of New Haven to a citizen of Virginia," which appeared in 1787 as part of Filippo Mazzei's history of the United States. (Condorcet was an honorary citizen of both New Haven and New York.) In these letters, without naming names, he responded to Adams's attacks on the now-deceased Turgot, who succumbed in 1781. Condorcet advocated the principles he had gleaned from Turgot on how to establish a government best representing the people's will. He argued that the opposing powers in a two-chamber government were dangerous, because they were always bullheaded or corrupt. "The history of every European government, which are not despotic, furnishes several striking examples," England principally among them. Parliamentary reform never took place, because the two houses consisted only of those who continued the abuses and those who did not reflect or represent the national will.

While Adams and others argued that England was the fount of liberty, with its heralded freedom of the press, its emphasis on habeas corpus, trial by jury, and the publication of all laws, Condorcet countered that England was not truly free because of the bifurcated legislative power of Lords and Commons. "It is easy to see," he said, "(and this is susceptible to a rigorous proof) that there is no particular advantage, relating to the truth of the decisions, by multiplying the legislative bodies. You will have the same advantage made simpler and surer when a majority is determined in a single body." And if there were any doubt about the source of this thought, the reader could consult "the work of M. le marquis de Condorcet," unabashedly citing his own work on the subject. (Condorcet never minded including a bit of self-congratulation or referring to himself in the third person.) His criticism even hit the Americans: their House of Representatives and Senate denied true equality and contradicted rational politics. Because America was yet young, however, she still could reform herself. "You can more easily in America than in Europe destroy this inequality or prevent its progress." The truth was, he felt, that a nation with a single leg-islature guaranteed its people would have good civil laws, free commerce, and the greatest equality. It was obvious to Con-dorcet that Adams was wrong and that his four letters put the argument to rest.

Condorcet's later friend and collaborator, the leader of the Girondins, Jacques-Pierre Brissot, also admired a single-house legislature. For Brissot, the Pennsylvania constitution was "the model of an excellent government." He reprinted the document in a multivolume work he wrote between 1782 and 1785, because he was convinced it was perfectly adapt-able to France. "It allows every citizen to examine and dis-cuss the laws and even to see them before they go into effect. Is that not the surest way to force our magistrates to be just and our legislators to be republicans?" Condorcet and Brissot later collaborated with Thomas Paine and others to design the French republic's new constitution in 1793 exactly along the same lines as the Pennsylvania document.

As consistent as he was throughout his career in admiring the republic, Condorcet just as consistently hated slavery, a subject he asked Franklin about. At the end of 1773, without ever having met the great man, Condorcet unexpectedly wrote Franklin, whom he called *"mon cher et illustre confrère"* (my dear and illustrious colleague). He asked him some questions he hoped members of the American Philosophical Society might be able to answer, thus beginning a friendship that lasted until the end of Franklin's life, seventeen years later. As might be expected, most of Condorcet's questions focused on science and mathematics, but he also asked about the status of freed blacks in America. He was obviously concerned with the similarities between the condition of American slaves and the misery of the class system in the French colonies created by the Code Noir (the French classification of white people, free blacks, black slaves, and the so-called *gens de couleur* or mulattoes in the French colonies, especially Saint Domingue, what is today Haiti). Three months later Franklin responded that in his judgment, "the Negroes who are free live among the White People . . . are not deficient in natural Understanding, but they have not the Advantage of Education." By then Franklin believed in the innate intelligence of black people. After making this remark, he immediately added that he thought "they make good musicians."

In 1781 Condorcet published his first major work on slavery, the *Reflections on Negro Slavery*. He did not sign the work: its author was listed as a Pastor Jacob Schwartz, but it was widely known that Condorcet wrote it (for what it's worth, *schwartz* means "black" in German, and may have been a deliberate, though weak, play on words by the author). Schwartz identified himself as the pastor of Saint-Evangile in Bienne, perhaps suggesting he was speaking with the moral and religious authority of a cleric; and he claimed he was originally from "Bienne," but he perhaps meant Vienne or Vienna, thus giving the work an international flavor. He tried to identify with those condemned to bondage. Dedicated to "the Negro Slaves," the essay began with the words, "Although I am not the same color as you are, I have always regarded you as my brothers. Nature formed you to have the same spirit, the same reason, the same virtues as whites." He argued that slavery constituted a criminal act, and the perpetrators had to be severely punished for claiming to own a human being: "To reduce a man to slavery, to purchase him, to sell him, to keep him in servitude, these are veritable crimes and they are crimes worst than theft. In effect, we strip the slave, not only of all mobile and financial property, but his ability to acquire it, including everything that nature has given him so he may conserve his life or satisfy his needs." He dismissed the conventional arguments in favor of slavery; for example, that slaves were better off in the West than in Africa, where if their enemies captured them, they would be eaten. Condorcet conceded that there was such a thing as cannibalism, but even so, if we assume we've saved people from being killed, what duties do we have to them now? To sell them would be like selling a person after we've saved him from an assassin. This made no moral or reasonable sense at all.

Condorcet thus condemned those who operated the great plantations in the French West Indies: "They have the perfidious art of exciting the greed and the passions of the Africans, to engage the father to deliver his children, the brother to betray his brother, the prince to sell his subjects. They have given to this unfortunate people the destructive taste of strong liquors. The have communicated to him this poison which, when concealed in the American forests [the West Indies], has become, thanks to the active voracity of the Europeans, one of the scourges of the globe, and they dare still speak of humanity!"

There was nothing good that the French overlords in the Americas could do to these people, short of emancipation.

As for the economic argument, Condorcet debunked the idea that slavery was necessary for the colonies to thrive. And here, as Pastor Schwartz, he offered his own credentials. Not only was he a minister of a reformed church, he was also "a member of the Economic Society of Bienne." Thus, it was with some authority that he could say it was far more costly to buy and keep slaves than to pay them for their labor. For the mathematician in Condorcet, it was a calculus of economic advantages and disadvantages. "The destruction of slavery would ruin neither the colonies nor commerce. It would render the colonies more flourishing and it would augment commerce." In fact, slavery really only helped the colonists produce their fortunes. For the *grands blancs*, for example, to own slaves, was like saying that one's human bondage was justified by another human's profit. Slavery conserved a fortune by means of a crime (the very conclusion Franklin was drawing at this time). Said Condorcet, just because the *grand blanc* needed to plow his fields, he did not have the right to steal his neighbor's plow horses.

But what could reasonably be achieved? What mechanisms could bring about the freedom of these people? One way to do it would be to free the black (and mulatto) children first, not the adults. But this solution would not work, because it would be inconvenient to both master and slave. Rather than freeing the slaves at the moment of their birth, an alternative proposal was to force the masters to educate them, as Franklin was advocating, but only on the condition that they would be freed when they reached the age of thirty-five. By that time, they would possess the requisite skills to live on their own, and they could even work for their former masters. For those who could no longer work because they were crippled or maimed by their masters (after having an affidavit signed by a physician attesting to the malady), the masters would have to provide them with pensions for life. To ensure masters did not try to force young mothers to have abortions (that is, to cut down on the numbers who would have to be released in the future and paid for later), the government would inspect the households every two months. Once the law freeing the slaves was published, all those under the age of fifteen would be freed in forty years. Those over fifteen would be freed when they reached the age of fifty. If they did not want to remain working for their master, he would have to pay whatever pension the law established.

In a postscript to the essay, Condorcet reviewed the progress in America, noting that in England a society to abolish slavery and the slave trade had been formed. The rejuvenated American society was still a few years off, of course, or he certainly would have mentioned it. He closed with a note of confidence that emancipation would succeed, "sooner or later."

Condorcet wanted to create a Parisian abolitionist society mirroring the British and American groups. As it turned out, the guiding force behind its creation was his friend Brissot, one of the most liberal writers in France and a follower of Rousseau and Voltaire in their quest for freedom and democracy. In 1788 Brissot founded the *Société des Amis des Noirs* (the Society of the Friends of the Blacks), or simply the *Amis des Noirs,* as it was informally known. The society grew out of his Gallo-American Society, a group that had been meeting since 1786 and that was devoted to fostering a better understanding of the new United States. The rights and liberties that the Americans enjoyed fascinated Brissot, and he was particularly interested when the American constitutional convention got under way, in the late spring of 1787. That same year he met Thomas Jefferson, the new American minister to France. He hoped France would soon be transformed into a government like the one the Americans were creating.

The same regard Condorcet had for political liberty drew him to become a leader of the *Amis des Noirs.* As Rousseau had taught, because human beings in the state of nature were free, their natural condition was to live without the bonds of slavery, and those of rank and privilege who enslaved humans were enemies. Curiously, however, social elites made up the majority of the society's membership. It soon included Condorcet's and Brissot's friends, such as the Swiss banker and later treasury minister Etienne Clavière; the lawyer and politician Nicolas Bergasse; the fiery orator the Comte de Mirabeau (Gabriel-Honoré Riquetti); and the mayor of Paris, Jérôme Pétion. Mirabeau had led a life of great excess in drinking and duels (so many in fact that his father had several lettres de cachet leveled against him, which meant he served time in jail). In the mid 1780s he was a changed (more mature) man when he became a powerful speaker loved both by liberal political thinkers and the masses. Because of this popularity and his standing as a nobleman (though he was elected to the Estates General by the Third Estate, no less), he was able to publish a journal ignored by the censors, in which he often included English translations of works concerning freeing the slaves.

In addition, Lafayette and the Duc de la Rochefoucauld soon joined the *Amis des Noirs,* as did the Abbé Grégoire, who wrote his *Letters to the Philanthropes* about freeing the blacks in Saint Domingue. Although Lafayette did not attend the first meeting, he told Brissot a few days later he regarded himself as a founder. He was soon helping alleviate the plight of the slaves in the French colonies by attempting to prove to the planters that their interests lay in freeing the slaves. In his memoirs Brissot saw the society as a means of stimulating a revolution in France much broader than freeing the slaves, leading to a republican constitution. He hoped he could use Mirabeau's uncensored paper as a model to launch his own journal that would have the same impact as Thomas Paine's *Common Sense* in America in 1776. Brissot's hopes for a revolution were almost immediately dimmed: he possessed neither a broad base beyond the aristocratic elites nor a network throughout the country (the society was active only in Paris).

In 1789, just before the king called the Estates General into session for the first time since 1614 to deal with the increasing financial crisis facing the country, Condorcet wrote another antislavery tract. In his *To the Electorate Against Black Slavery* he asked the voters to demand that the Estates General "destroy the trade and begin the process of ending slavery" in the colonies. He pretty much knew it was a lost cause, however, because he thought the Estates General was reactionary. Moreover, this work was mostly ignored, because the economic crisis was overwhelming. It was caused by the configuration of a variety of problems: a result of debts that had accumulated over a century of war, primarily with England and including the American Revolution, and disastrous crop failures after low harvests. Condorcet opposed the Estates General, believing instead that true liberty was founded in the provincial assemblies, not in the archaism and irrationality, i.e., the emotional assertion of power by the nobility and clergy, of the Estates General, especially when the Third Estate exercised no real power at all. Still, in a powerful address on behalf of the *Amis des Noirs* on the eve of the Estates General's first meeting, Condorcet linked the triumph of reason and liberty and called once again for the elimination of slavery. He took advantage of the moment to convince the nation's electoral districts that slavery in the French colonies must end: "Thus, the abolition of Negro slavery was considered by the several United States, and by the Congress which represents them, not only as a measure essential for a sound commonwealth, but as an act of justice, required by both honor and humanity. To be candid, how can we dare, without shame, to proclaim these declarations of rights, these inviolable bulwarks of freedom and of the security of all citizens, if every day we acquiesce in the destruction of these sacred principles?" The address had no effect.

Also in 1789 the English abolitionist Thomas Clarkson traveled to France to see for himself the new French abolitionist society. He met not only Condorcet and the leaders of the movement, but also secured through them an audience with the king. Louis XVI graciously accepted (though thereafter ignored) Clarkson's essay on the "impolicy" of the slave trade and the African artifacts he had collected on his trips around the English seafaring towns. When Mirabeau came to him for information to address the Constituent Assembly in favor of a bill to abolish the French slave trade, which was every bit as ghastly as the British trade, Clarkson was only too happy to comply. He sent him all the information he could. Clarkson later told one of the members of the assembly that if France did not abolish the slave trade, its new Declaration of the Rights of Man and Citizen would be "the Declaration of Hypocrites." In the meantime, Jacques-Pierre Brissot worked vainly on securing seats for the island mulattoes in the assembly, since the wealthy white planters, the so-called *grands blancs,* were the only representatives from the colonies.

With the outbreak of revolution in July 1789, Condorcet thought the time was ripe to take the first major steps toward achieving a republican constitution and universal suffrage and ending slavery and the slave trade. Like Clarkson, he wanted to move the assembly to act immediately on the latter two issues. He wrote a long article for the *Journal de Paris,* which appeared in two issues at the end of 1789. "We hope that the National Assembly, which has decreed that all men are free and equal in their rights, will no longer allow the buying and selling of an individual in the human race. We believe that slavery should be immediately abolished and suppressed from now on without ruining the [financial condition of] the colonies." Mirabeau introduced such a bill. It failed: the pro-slave trade, pro-slavery interests, especially those in the seaports of Bordeaux and Le Havre, effectively organized against it. When Mirabeau canvassed the deputies, three hundred favored abolition of the trade, but of the other nine hundred, five hundred said they would vote for its abolition if England did so too, simultaneously. Of course, the English did not: William Wilberforce's bill for abolition, despite the support of parliamentary leaders like William Pitt, Charles James Fox, and Edmund Burke, was defeated by a vote of 163 to 88. (It did not pass until 1807.) The outcome was just as dismal for France. In March 1790, despite lip service given by many deputies in favor of abolition of the trade and slavery, nothing happened. Condorcet was crushed, but undaunted, at least for the time being.

In the meantime, along with Brissot and others, Condorcet formed yet another society, the so-called Society of 1789. It included a random group of aristocrats, intellectuals, military officers, and Physiocrats. This was at the same time that the Constituent Assembly, which had emerged from the Estates General, was busily drafting a new constitution for France. (The king had called the Estates General into assembly for the first time in nearly 150 years because of the financial crisis in the 1780s; after the Revolution of 1789, the Estates General re-formed itself into a National Assembly. Then, because a new constitution was needed for the new political configurations—now that France was a constitutional monarchy—the Constituent Assembly was elected to write the new constitution.) It would not be a republican document, because the king was still in office; it was to confirm the new constitutional monarchy. Condorcet hoped the society would be a watchdog organization over the Constituent. He feared the new assembly would fail to fulfill its responsibilities and simply appoint itself a permanent, self-perpetuating body. If it did, the people would never have frequent elections and true rights and liberties. Only mob violence would result; and indeed bloodshed had already spilled when a mob forced the king and queen to return to Paris from Versailles. If it continued, the Revolution would be lost, and absolute monarchy would reemerge—if only to restore peace and order. To forestall this, the Society of 1789 was formed to be a watchdog organization.

The society's first meeting was held at the Palais Royal on

May 14, 1790. It was "a kind of academic club" that included several prominent politicians and scientists, such as the Marquis de Lafayette; the Comte de Mirabeau; the statesman and revolutionary the Abbé Sieyès; the great chemist and tax collector (as a member of the *Fermier Général* and Priestley's rival) Antoine Lavoisier; the diplomat, politician, and priest Charles-Maurice Talleyrand; the physician and inspirer of the death machine named for him, Joseph Ignace Guillotin; the naturalist Bernard Lacépède; the statesman/scientist the Duc de la Rochefoucauld; and the Duc de Montmorency. It was a curious mixture of royalists, republicans, and constitutional monarchists. The great Physiocrat theorist Dupont de Nemours, who believed that national wealth was based in agriculture, was a member, as was the engineer Jacques-Constantin Périer, who often opened his home to its meetings. These were all socially prominent men who held distinguished ranks in government. None of them was a liberal. The society monitored the assembly to make sure its members were doing what they were supposed to do, namely, writing a constitution for France that preserved elections but kept the king as the chief executive. Because Condorcet wanted to anticipate any major problems and issues before the assembly addressed them, he thought if the society came up with its own solutions, it could submit proposals to the assembly for approval. He (erroneously) assumed the society members unanimously agreed with him.

Among the more radical tactics of the society was its correspondence with other French popular societies to spread moderately liberal ideas throughout France. They believed if they could correspond with like-minded societies elsewhere within France, they could do so with the world. Condorcet started a periodical called the *Journal de la Société de 1789* that was to promote progress in the "social arts"—in industry, crafts, and such other useful trades, *"les travaux utiles"*—in order to stimulate the universal happiness.

Although Condorcet attracted several new members in the

first few months of the society's existence, it lasted only about a year. For more liberal-thinking members, it was not liberal enough, so they turned or returned to the Jacobin Club. For others, many of whom were financially well off and were drawn from "the court capitalism of the Old Regime," the society was too extreme. Some were constitutional monarchists and joined with more moderate or conservative constitutionalists who met at the former Feuillant convent and did not want a republic. Still others, the counterrevolutionaries who were beginning to wish for a return to absolutism, formed the Monarchical Club in late 1790.

While the society's main failure was ideological, it also had structural problems. Its rules required meetings to be held in secret, which meant its discussions were never made public. Moreover, it corresponded with only a few other societies, and it never expanded beyond its small base in Paris, despite Condorcet's vision that it would communicate with the world. Nor did it grow in membership: its constitution limited it to just six hundred members, hardly a mass movement. With its secrecy and small size, it was a closed organization that never challenged the power of the Jacobins. Republicans without a republican structure, they looked, at best, like an elitist, antipopular organization and, at worst, monarchical. It is no wonder its members quit as early as the fall of the same year it was founded.

Even worse was the infighting between its two titular leaders, the Comte de Mirabeau and the Marquis de Lafayette (Condorcet argued successfully that they were among the most prominent men in the society and thus should look like they were leading it). These two powerful men with robust personalities had very different political views and personal goals. Always a tireless critic of Lafayette, Mirabeau dismissed several of Lafayette's friends and associates from the ministry in October 1790 and returned to the Jacobin Club that same month. Condorcet would take the same step seven months later.

As a political actor, Condorcet not only formed the Society of 1789 after the fall of the Bastille, but he also entered into politics, being elected to the Paris Commune—along with many men of the radical bourgeoisie, tradesmen, and urban workers. There he collaborated with Brissot on an October 1789 address to the Constituent Assembly, warning the delegates that the ongoing violence threatened the Revolution. A constitutional monarchy could not stop a lawless and disorderly people, he said: the people had to be calmed to bring peace to the city. While Brissot was the principal author of the address, Condorcet edited it, so it clearly represented his thinking as much as Brissot's. The only choice was to get rid of the king and create a true republic.

Condorcet's support for political change was so stunningly seductive that by 1789–1790 he was a political figure on the make, or better, on the loose. For the good of his political principles, and indeed for the good of the republic, he abandoned his older aristocratic friends, no matter how liberal they were, and moved into yet more liberal circles. He grew closer to Brissot and eventually to Thomas Paine, the American firebrand himself.

Meantime, trouble was brewing both inside and outside the country. The weaknesses and infighting of the Constituent Assembly emboldened the royalist émigrés who had fled when the Revolution broke out but now dreamed of Louis's return. When the king and queen were returned from Varennes after their attempted escape to royalist lines, the assembly simply reconfirmed Louis as king and excused him for his ill-advised escape. In addition, the refractory clergy who had refused to adhere to the new Civil Constitution of the Clergy stirred up trouble, as they hoped for the restoration of the Church's former position of power and influence. Worst of all, foreign powers, especially Austria and Prussia, now considered invasion in a direct attempt to restore Louis to the throne (if revolution broke out in France, after all, it might occur in other Old Regime states as well). Besides, the Austrians never forgot that Marie Antoinette was an Austrian princess who was undoubtedly in danger—though how great a danger they had no way of knowing. Realizing that he had to unite the nation, Mirabeau attempted to reconcile with Lafayette and succeeded in attracting a number of Lafayette supporters to the government. He even named Condorcet a commissioner of the treasury. But then Mirabeau suddenly died of a heart attack on April 2, 1791. His life of debauchery and dissipation (he was fond of wine and women) had finally brought him down.

Two months later, with the new constitution providing for a constitutional monarchy completed, Condorcet was elected to the new Legislative Assembly. By then he had become so disgusted with the king's attempted escape earlier that June that he now created yet another political club. As far as Condorcet and his new close associates, Brissot, Paine, Achille Duchâtelet, and Nicolas de Bonneville were concerned, Louis had abdicated his throne when he abandoned Paris. Thus, for them, he had no moral or political authority to rule France.

These five men were attending Sophie de Condorcet's salon on the rue de Lille, when they formed the explicitly named Republican Society, with its journal, *Le Républicain*. As the first such society ever formed in France, it was designed to convince all Frenchmen that the best government was a republic. Paine and the young officer Duchâtelet went through town, posting the first notices promoting the new society. The unmentioned sixth initial member of *La Société Républicaine* was Sophie de Condorcet, whose republican views were as strong as her husband's and Paine's. Although she did not sign the document, she was delighted with the new liberal company her husband was keeping. Gone were the bankers and financiers and aristocrats: in other words, gone was the ancien régime's power elite. The four, plus Sophie, were now the people most frequently in Condorcet's company. His former associates in the Society of 1789 were meeting at La Rochefoucauld's residence without him.

Condorcet was outraged when the assembly restored Louis as a constitutional monarch after his return from Varennes, but he was even more appalled at the events that immediately followed. The government invited thousands of citizens to appear at the Champs-de-Mars to signal their allegiance to the newly reinstalled king. Thousands actually showed up, but most of them had no intention of supporting the king. Many of them were, like Condorcet, republicans; when they openly demanded the king's removal from office and the formation of a republican constitution, city authorities regarded their action as unlawful and a disturbance of the peace. Martial law was declared—even though some of the people on the Champs were just out for a stroll on a beautiful July afternoon, among them Sophie with her baby daughter, Eliza, then just fourteen months old.

With troops gathered on the side, stones were thrown, and the attack began, followed by a massacre, when thousands were callously mowed down and cleared out by the National Guard, under the command of General Lafayette and the mayor of Paris, Jean-Sylvain Bailly. At least fifty people died. Paris was now at war with itself; as Condorcet later recalled, in an overstatement (he suggested his daughter was injured or killed, but she survived): "I only knew about the petition at the Champs-de-Mars at the moment it appeared and I anticipated what followed from it. The opinion that martial law was necessary in order to carry out the order was no secret, and all knew that they were just looking for the right occasion. My only daughter, one year old at the time, was a victim of this atrocity and this circumstance only added to my indignation. I showed it rather haughtily and attracted hatred to myself from all those who held power." It was clear that as a result of the attack on the Champs-de-Mars, more military action might well be taken against the people. Marat, for example, went underground, and Georges Danton fled to London (he returned by the winter of 1791).

Despite the unrest in Paris, Condorcet was undeterred and showed up at the Legislative Assembly, though he was not exactly happy or optimistic about its prospects. As one of the few outspoken republicans in the new assembly, along with Brissot, Condorcet was especially miserable. Under the Old Regime and even during the early days of the Revolution, he had enjoyed a distinguished reputation as a scientist, philosopher, and statesman. And yet, while his greatest contribution was his report on a national educational system with its emphasis on equality and republican ideals, most of the assemblymen were, unlike Condorcet, new to national office: only a few had served, as he had, in the Paris Commune or in their local and regional assemblies. Robespierre had virtually ensured this inexperience when he persuaded the Constituent Assembly to enact a law making its members ineligible for service on the Legislative.

Most who observed political events in the capital did not recognize the names of the new assemblymen. Because few members of the aristocracy and no high churchmen were among them, the assembly was a truly bourgeois group of very young men: half of them under thirty years old and sixty-five members were under twenty-six. At forty-eight Condorcet was among the oldest. Most of these young, energetic men were quite satisfied with the new constitutional monarchy. As moderates, they placed great faith in and had high regard for the king and queen. Condorcet knew he could expect few changes from them. Besides, true power in Paris still resided in the commune, not the legislature, because the commune controlled the police and all matters of public safety.

Still, after he took the oath of allegiance, signifying his total loyalty to the king, Condorcet was seated even as the monarchists and those around the king knew he despised monarchy. Because he was so well known and respected, he was elected as one of the six secretaries of the assembly, and for the month of February 1792 he served as its presiding officer. For the most part, he sat with Brissot to the left of the dais, but not as far left as the Jacobins. They continued the battle against slavery and took vocal positions on all of the other issues of war and peace, revolutionary change or consolidation, education and constitution making that were facing the new government. Until that time, like Franklin, Condorcet devoted considerable time and energy advocating the end of the miserable plight of blacks in the French Caribbean colonies. His and Brissot's efforts came to nothing. He was sick at heart with memories of the king's flight and subsequent restoration and the despicable massacres on the Champs-de-Mars. As an often outspoken critic of the monarchy, he quickly became a favorite target of the royalist press.

Condorcet realized his worst fears when the nation went to war against Austria in April 1792. Even worse, despite his pacifism, he found himself voting in favor of the decision. The Girondins—currently heading the government—had been advocating war at least since the end of the previous summer (recall that the Girondins were led by Brissot and the Rolands, the Jacobins by Robespierre). Curiously, the royalists and leftist Jacobins formed an uneasy and curious alliance in opposing it. From the Jacobin left, Robespierre argued the war was a royalist plot designed to reimpose the king as an absolute ruler and crush liberty forever. From the conservative right, the supporters of the king believed an all-out war against Austria in fact forestalled the king's return to power and increased the danger that a republic might be formed. Brissot believed the war was the only way to decisively end the French monarchy and, he hoped, monarchies in other countries as well.

Condorcet detested war, calling it "a barbarian law" and "a kind of horror and repugnance." He had welcomed the antiwar decree of May 22, 1790, passed by the Constituent Assembly, renouncing war and conquest. But that was two years earlier. While he found some wars, like the American Revolution, to be "most legitimate and most just," he hoped that "the more civilization spread across the world, the more we will see the disappearance of war and conquest, like slavery and misery." The time would come, he felt, when war would forever end, when human reason would triumph, and when the perfect society finally came into being.

For now, he bit his lip and voted for war as a matter of necessity (and perhaps as a loyal Girondin and friend of Brissot), knowing that the Old Regime states of Austria and Prussia were intent on ending the Revolution lest it come to their doorsteps. And, he reasoned, a war would reveal the treasonous side to Louis's court, if indeed war came about. Besides, he believed, the war was initially only against Austria—England was still a friend. (Condorcet and his long-distance friend Richard Price saw eye-to-eye on the Revolution, as Price had demonstrated in his famous sermon to the Revolution Society in 1789.) So there were obviously some Englishmen who welcomed the French Revolution. A general war was probably unlikely, anyway, because Prussia was a truly enlightened nation under Frederick II, Spain was militarily powerless, and Russia was preoccupied with events in Poland.

Condorcet was deluding himself. As it turned out, the Prussians were as serious as the Austrians to restore Louis's absolute authority, and soon several other nations joined the fray. After the king's execution, France declared war on England on February 1, 1793, thus consolidating an actual European war against France, a large-scale war of a free people against tyranny perhaps for the first time in history. France's enemies had risen beyond Austria and Prussia to include Spain, Holland, and England, and soon Russia, Turkey, and Naples joined the anti-French coalition. It rapidly became a true royalist war against revolutionary France.

Condorcet was horrified by the acceleration and scope of the war, though he had initially thought the war could be used as part of an international struggle to complete the Revolution to bring truth, reason, and the republic to every nation of the world. It was nothing less than the "universal republic" that he now sought. But the war was eventually France's undoing as, internally, the moderates and radicals increasingly fought each other. Moreover, the war aggravated the economic crisis, now worsening over the course of the year. By August 1792 everything came to a head: France had been defeated at Longwy and Verdun, the monarchy was finally overthrown, the king and his family were now imprisoned, and elections had been scheduled for a National Convention to create the new republic that Condorcet longed for.

Elected to the convention, Condorcet, Brissot, and Paine, along with a few others, were immediately appointed to a committee to write the new constitution. As it turned out, "of all the French constitutions," their draft was "the most democratic" and, as mentioned, was consciously based on Franklin's 1776 Pennsylvania constitution.

Condorcet's report to the convention stated that the committee had considered the two competing views of designing a republic: with power located in a single body, as the Pennsylvanians with Franklin's urging had done, or divided into two or more legislative branches to achieve a balance of power, as the Americans did in the federal constitution of 1787. The committee members were convinced the latter configuration led to the proliferation of party politics, and "one of the most pressing needs of the French republic is to be wholly free of party." A government based on two houses of Parliament ended only in stalemate. Even a minority could hold up a law if it wanted to or, even worse, halt all innovation. France could not afford to have such an obstacle blocking the improvement of life. "The rapid passage from despotism to liberty, and the no less rapid passage from a so-called constitutional monarchy to a republic; the agitation occasioned by these successive revolutions and the spirit of distrust that necessarily results from the errors and mistakes into which so many men have been carried: these all render such arrangements impractical for us." Unsurprisingly, they opted for the simpler, cleaner model of a single legislature— a *corps législatif,* or National Assembly.

Following good traditional republican thinking, they also

argued that elections should be frequent and the length of service in office (again, term limits) short: these mechanisms were the best defenses against corruption. Moreover, the constitution preserved the right to file grievances and petitions against the government so that it could remedy problems quickly, efficiently, and rationally. Finally and most important, the constitution decreed, again like Franklin's Pennsylvania constitution, that the assembly must publish all bills in advance of any discussion. This meant that before a bill's final reading, the public would have a chance to review it and instruct their representatives to vote for or against it. This would ensure the direct participation of the people in political decision making, something Condorcet had long favored.

Once the assembly finished its work, a national council (the *Conseil exécutif*)—a kind of collective executive branch wholly dependent on the legislature—enforced the laws. Condorcet did not see it as having real power but only reflecting the national will, just the way the Executive Council in Pennsylvania operated (Franklin became president of the council when he returned home from France): "It must act in such a way that the national will, once expressed, is executed with precision, order, and certainty." In other words, the council had no life of its own; it embodied the people's general will as Rousseau had argued in *The Social Contract.* It would have a single head or leader, who was required to sign off on all decrees implementing new laws. Other members of the body would have the responsibility to carry out their functions in particular areas, such as finance, foreign affairs, and internal security.

The important thing was that the council would always be subordinate to the assembly. "This council must be the hand by which the legislators act, the eye with which they can observe the details of the execution of their decrees and of the effects which those decrees have produced." But council members would not be mere tools of the assembly, since the people annually elected one-half of its membership.

Capping everything off was a broad suffrage. The electorate consisted of all male citizens, not merely landholders, because "we have not thought it possible, in a nation enlightened as to its rights, to propose that half of the citizens abdicate some of these rights." (That women were not allowed to vote did not strike them as ironic.) Therefore, every man, upon reaching the age of twenty-one, was admitted into citizenship, so long as he was a native of France or had stated his desire to become a citizen and had lived in France for at least one year. Moreover, any male citizen was eligible to serve in any national office on condition that he was at least twenty-five years old. For those who thought the constitution should be amended, again like Franklin's Pennsylvania constitution, with its Council of Censors, the constitution of 1793 provided for auxiliary national conventions (*conventions nationales*) to make the necessary changes to the existing document when they were needed.

The constitution was a truly liberal and democratic document. Condorcet and his colleagues were justly proud of their work—even if just three years earlier the Pennsylvanians had scrapped their Franklinian single-chamber government for one that more directly mirrored the new American document. Condorcet's was, as he put it, "a constitution based on unity of action, frequent renewal of public officials by direct elections, and the most perfect equality between men."

As the committee debated these issues about the new constitution, the trial of the king in January 1793 took precedence over any discussion of the draft document (locked in the Temple prison with his family after August 1792, the king was now to be tried for treason by the convention). Condorcet had argued vehemently that the convention was the wrong place for a trial, that a legislative body was not a judicial forum. (Indeed, when the issue first arose, the question was whether the person of the king qua king was inviolable and not subject to trial at all; the convention easily answered that question when it decreed that the "nation" as a whole had terminated the monarchy; Louis

261

was responsible for his crimes and therefore had to answer to the people.) Still, reasoning on the premise of separation of powers, Condorcet persisted: the convention "could not be a legislature, a court of law, and a judge." While he raised this important question, he lost the argument, and the king was found guilty of crimes against France. The convention—serving as both judge and jury—condemned him to death. The vote for execution was close; Condorcet abstained, Brissot voted yea, and Paine advocated permanent banishment to America. The king was executed on January 21, 1793.

A few weeks later, just as Condorcet thought the convention was to debate the draft constitution, Robespierre suddenly set it aside. He said it would be reintroduced once the war ended. The revolutionary spark the people had ignited in the summer of 1789 was now rapidly running down the taper toward self-immolation. Time had drastically transformed the political and ideological makeup of the Revolution, changing in a short thirty months from the relatively upbeat feelings and harmony of 1789–1790 to the horrors of the Terror, which now began to steal into France like a viper rushing through the grass. The Terror would last for eleven months in 1793–1794 and claim between seventeen thousand and fifty thousand lives. Within three months of tabling the new constitution, the convention, on a motion by Robespierre, expelled all of the Girondin deputies; Condorcet himself was denounced on July 8 and went into hiding. There he spent his remaining months, writing his most famous work, the *Sketch for a Historical Picture of the Progress of the Human Mind,* which contains his faith in inevitable progress leading to human perfectibility—a remarkable sentiment, given that it was written during the Terror's darkest days.

This text remains one of the greatest works in political thought written during the French Enlightenment. As historian Jean-Pierre Schandeler notes, "More than previous notable works—Voltaire's *Essay on Morals,* Turgot's *Philosophical Table of the*

Successive Progress of the Human Spirit, and d'Alembert's *Preliminary Discourse*—the *Sketch* confirmed that the conquest of liberty was situated in a universal and unlimited movement where incremental progress assured the conditions of its success." Ironically, it is filled with the brightest optimism and most enduring hope about a future that heralded the most beneficent prospects for all people. In it, Condorcet describes nine stages of development that human beings had already passed through: each step represented a movement forward from the previous one, though of course there were always moments of regression, corruption, and decay. The first several stages, those before the invention of the alphabet and writing, were conjectural, because he had no records on which to base his conclusions. Still, he felt comfortable in assuming human beings had passed through successive periods, beginning with hunting and fishing and then on to a pastoral, and then an agricultural stage. People flourished during the fourth and fifth epochs, in Greece and Rome; the sixth stage lasted from the Middle Ages to the Crusades; and finally the seventh continued until the invention of printing. The eighth stage spanned from then until Descartes, and the ninth from Descartes until the outbreak of the French Revolution.

Like many utopian thinkers before and after him, Condorcet's belief in the periodization of history parallels our own understanding of history: antiquity, the medieval world, the Renaissance, the Enlightenment, and the early modern period on up to our own contemporary time. But Condorcet went further; convinced the history of the world was the history of the progress of the human mind, as his title suggested, the tenth and final stage embraced his vision of the future, when inequality between and within nations would end and mankind attain perfection.

Again, it is astonishing Condorcet could be so positive during such a terribly difficult time, in hiding from Paris authorities. As he forecast the coming perfection of human beings and the world, one can imagine his uttering a near-audible sigh when he said, "How consoling for the philosopher who laments the errors, the crimes, the injustices which still pollute the earth and of which he is often the victim is this view of the human race, emancipated from its shackles, released from the empire of fate and from that of the enemies of its progress, advancing with a firm and sure step along the path of truth, virtue, and happiness!" Contemplating a marvelous future was for him "an asylum, in which the memory of his persecutors cannot pursue him; there he lives in thought with man restored to his natural rights and dignity, forgets man tormented and corrupted by greed, fear, or envy."

The inevitable forward movement of history welded "an uninterrupted chain between the beginning of historical time and the century in which we live, between the first peoples known to us and the present nations of Europe." One single impediment stalled progress: men's failure to understand progress, because they lacked the education that allowed them to use their rational faculty. Even some misguided philosophers "harm the prejudice of truth" just as those in the less enlightened classes "retard the propagation of truths already known." Even worse, those in leading positions too often "place obstacles in truth's way." Our duty was to root out superstitions and mythologies that the enemies of progress placed in the way of the truly enlightened. His work showed the history of the ultimate triumph of truth over such obstacles. After all, *"man is a sentient being, capable of reasoning and of acquiring moral ideas"* (emphasis added).

The ninth stage of history already demonstrated that advances in physics, mathematics, and philosophy elevated humans to the greatest heights they had yet known. Some of the benefits of these advances redounded directly to people's health and welfare in medical science and education, architecture, and the fine arts. More important were the profound political and social ramifications, as the "noble" seventeenth-century English political activist and philosopher Algernon Sydney, a man who

264

paid with "his blood" in 1683, understood when he challenged the tyrannical authority of Charles II and was executed for it. Or John Locke, who later in that same century extended the ideals of liberty even further, leading ultimately to Rousseau, who "deserves renown for having established them among the truths that it is no longer permissible to forget or to combat."

With progress in science, mathematics, and philosophy, our minds are opened to the prospect that now "man could proclaim aloud his right . . . to submit all opinions to his own reason and to use in the search for truth the only instrument for its recognition that he has been given." The people based their ideas on their own opinions, not those of others who were more powerful than they were. Enlightened minds uprooted prejudice and superstition in government, in the schools, in the churches, everywhere.

The Americans in 1776 had taken the lead in the successful struggle for freedom. The French after 1789 went even further. The Revolution in France was far more violent and disruptive than the American one, because most political, social, and economic institutions were torn down and new ones created (as Burke in England was appalled to observe). While France, in the establishment of its republic, had achieved the highest level of human freedom to date, men and women had not yet reached perfection; some still suffered under the heavy burdens of slavery and ignorance, for "the philosopher is still afflicted by the spectacle of the stupidity, slavery, barbarism, and extravagance of mankind." They, too, however, would ultimately be free. In the tenth and final stage of history lay our "fantastic hope" ("*un espoir chimérique*") for the future—the inevitable progress of human reason, liberty, and rights.

Over time, the *Sketch* became the model for all books written about human progress, the standard by which all others are measured. Frank Manuel correctly observed that "the *Esquisse* was the form in which the eighteenth-century idea of progress was generally assimilated by Western thought. Condorcet wrote his manifesto with full awareness of its world revolutionary significance. Those who came after him had no choice but to affirm allegiance like Godwin or Saint-Simon or Comte, or to proclaim their hostility as did Malthus on the very title page of his pessimistic *Essay on Population,* which appeared as a formal refutation of the French *philosophe*'s work."

So how did Condorcet know what the future would hold? The short answer is he didn't, at least not for certain. He simply argued he could come close, because he knew the laws of history and he knew life from his own experience. A person who has learned the laws governing the universe also learned the laws governing human development—and its future. Now, we might wonder why his picture of the future was not gloomier (or, indeed, gloomy at all), since it was written during a time of such chaos and he would never again see Sophie and Eliza. Instead, he argued we could count on three basic truths about the future: we will see "the abolition of inequality between nations, the progress of equality within each nation, and the true perfection of mankind." His was an almost spiritual faith in human reason, a faith neatly and perfectly mirroring his scheme of the progress of society, politics, economics, and morals. He held out a special role for France to lead the people of all nations, because "we shall become for them the beneficent instruments of their freedom."

Education, the key to the ultimate progress of the human mind, was necessary if the least capable people were to achieve their greatest potential. Condorcet actually believed, naively one might say, such an achievement was possible:

> [B]y a suitable choice of syllabus and of methods of education, we can teach the citizen everything that he needs to know in order to be able to manage his household, administer his affairs and employ his labor and his faculties in freedom; to know his rights and to be able to exercise them; to be acquainted with his duties and fulfill them satisfac-

torily; to judge his own and other men's actions according to his own lights and to be a stranger to none of the high and delicate feelings which honour human nature; not to be in a state of blind dependence upon those to whom he must entrust his affairs or the exercise of his rights; to be in a proper condition to choose and supervise them; to be no longer the dupe of those popular errors which torment man with superstitious fears and chimerical hopes; to defend himself against prejudice by the strength of his reason alone; and, finally, to escape the deceits of charlatans who would lay snares for his fortune, his health, his freedom of thought, and his conscience under the pretext of granting him health, wealth, and salvation.

They would, in short, be a people of reason, a free people.

The result was that everyone would have the same basic understanding and capacity to enjoy freedom. In this perfected state of mankind, everyone would understand—through reason—how the world operated. Just as science and mathematics improved our health and welfare, so the social and political sciences improved our laws, morality, and public institutions. The "social arts," as he called them, ensured that only the best legislation would pass in the assemblies and the people would remain forever free. Finally and most obscurely, he foresaw the development of a universal symbolic scientific language "to set out the theory of a science or the rules of an art, to describe a new observation or experiment, the invention of a procedure, the discovery of a truth or a method." While Condorcet intended to develop this language on his own, he did not have the time left to do so. Still, he saw that humans would live far longer, and only war and revolution, if they still existed, would disrupt our longevity.

Condorcet was convinced his melioristic vision of the future was equally realistic. The philosopher would live "with his peers in an Elysium created by reason and graced by the purest pleasures known to the love of mankind." When the work was finally published in 1795, such talk led to criticism. Still burning from Condorcet and his friends' rejection of a bicameral legislature when he first visited France, John Adams exclaimed in the margins of his copy of the *Sketch*, "Thou art a Quack, Condorcet!" in addition to calling him "mischievous," "arrogant," and "wicked." The Revolution had come to a bad end, Adams believed, because of so-called geniuses like Condorcet: his death "was an effect of his own System, of a Government in one Assembly. It was the fruit of the Tyranny of his own pretended democratic Majority, without a Ballance [*sic*], or Check which he abhorred."

Others criticized Condorcet for having written a superficial work based solely on visionary nonsense that, it was always noted, had led France to a bad end. Still, we must not forget the work has a decidedly tentative nature. It is unfinished and incomplete; it is, after all, only a *sketch* of a historical picture, not the picture itself. It is a prospectus of what he would have written had Condorcet had more time. We thus find him always qualifying his statements with phrases like "we shall show" or "we shall point out," all at a later time.

But Condorcet never had a chance to write the full work. Ruthlessly pursued by the authorities, he was finally arrested on March 27, 1794, suffering from exposure and ill, just outside Paris, in the suburb of Bourg-la-Reine. He was transported back into the city and imprisoned. Two days later, on April 7, he was dead, probably by suicide. He had poisoned himself, rather than allow the murderous Jacobins to destroy him. His was a full though tragically shortened life.

8

⚭

Brissot, Revolutionary Politics, and Democracy

The French revolutionary journalist, philosophe, and statesman Jacques-Pierre Brissot greatly admired Franklin. Like the American scientist and diplomat, he not only wrote about the progress and ills of modern society and the virtues and corruptions of modern politics, but he also actively tried to fix them. He believed society corrupted the natural goodness of human beings; the stranglehold that tyrants and the Church maintained over the people was the root of all evil. Professionally, he was a newspaperman who started several papers throughout his career. Most of them failed. As a writer of legal and political tracts his works are voluminous, but he could barely afford to have them published. Moreover, they never sold very well, a fact that kept him, unlike Franklin, ever near poverty, looking for handouts from his friends and acquaintances. He was also a self-appointed organizer and created many associations: an intellectual literary club; a Franco-American friendship league to promote commerce between the two nations; an anti-slavery organization; a republican political action group. He audaciously defined himself as a philosophe whose progressive and liberal ideas would inevitably lead to French political and social reform.

Brissot's views of society may be traced to one of his earliest and most respected works, his commentary on criminal law, the *Théorie des lois criminelles*. Published in 1780 when he was just twenty-six, the work displayed his strong liberal views of how the law could be used to resolve social ills. First, it was necessary to end capital punishment. The death penalty was simply a practice that existed "only to protect the interests of the rich." He also advocated the end of laws against adultery, because only women were punished for violating them; men conventionally got away scot-free. The work also touched upon and opposed laws outlawing incest, arguing that because cultures were different, France need not prohibit it. Finally, he called for the legalization of prostitution: license the prostitutes, he said, and make certain they obey all health requirements. The government should contain and control it, not merely condemn it.

It may be a stretch to refer to the relationship between Franklin and Brissot as a "friendship," given that the two met only a few times. But Brissot's admiration and respect for the great statesman and scientist certainly made Brissot *think* they were friends, even if Franklin did not give it much thought. Brissot first met Franklin in 1780 at Jean-Paul Marat's house. At the time of the meeting, Brissot was helping Marat try to gain entry into the *Académie royale des sciences* as a member (as we have seen, when these efforts failed, Marat became an inveterate enemy during the Terror).

On one of the occasions when Franklin was reviewing Marat's scientific work, Marat introduced him to Brissot. Details of that first meeting have not been recorded, but the twenty-four-year-old Brissot had already translated into French Franklin's "Remarks concerning the Savages of North-America" and had it printed anonymously in the *Journal de Paris*. Franklin had written the essay because he thought even among American Indians we would find a polite people: should we look hard, he said, "we should find no People so rude as to be without any Rules of Politeness; nor any so polite as not to have some remains of Rudeness." And he was careful to define the term "savages" in referring to the Indian people. He meant to show that their customs were different, not inferior, to those of the Europeans: "Savages we call them, because their manners differ from ours, which we think the Perfection of Civility; they think the same of theirs." He illustrated this idea with a story of a group of Indians invited to send six of their young men to college in Virginia. After they politely declined, they suggested instead they would be delighted to train twelve young white men in Indian ways. Brissot was taken by Franklin's wisdom (which perhaps twined into memories of Rousseau's natural education in *Emile*).

Franklin and Brissot met again in 1788, this for the last time, when Brissot visited the United States for five months. Largely for financial reasons, Brissot was considering moving permanently with his family to America. Franklin wrote that "M. de Warville . . . is a most valuable man, and I hope his travels among us will be to his satisfaction." When Brissot later recounted his American visit, he described his Philadelphia encounter with Franklin:

> *I have met in America a great many enlightened statesmen and virtuous men, but none has possessed to such a high degree as Franklin the characteristics of the true philosopher. You know what these characteristics are, my friend: love of the human race to the extent that this love becomes the preoccupation of every waking moment; indefatigable zeal in the service of humanity; vast knowledge and understanding; simplicity of manners and purity of morals. . . . [O]ne more of his characteristics must be listed; namely,*

*that Franklin, in the very center of the broad stage where he
played so brilliantly a role, constantly has kept in view the
far vaster stage of heaven and the future life.*

So taken with Franklin, Brissot later attributed the outbreak of
the Revolution to the French translation of *Poor Richard's
Almanack,* which had appeared in France as *La Science du Bon-
homme Richard* with its naïve, direct style and simple wisdom.
At the Jacobin Club, prefiguring Emerson, Brissot announced
that "the patriot *par excellence* is a philosopher. Behold how
Poor Richard and Franklin were always friends of the people."

Born in Chartres in 1754 to a devout Catholic family, Brissot
possessed an overblown sense of self-importance about his
intellectual talent. Standing five feet five, he was of middle
height for the time. He was "slim, appearing older than his
age with a long nose compensated by a dimple in his chin,
the sole charm of his clean-shaven weasel face. His gray eyes
stared at his interrogators with a cold and piercing gaze,
which never showed the slightest glimmer of gaiety." Despite
his later criticism of monarchy, rank, and privilege, as a young
man he adopted "de Warville" as part of his last name—a
rather sad and certainly ill-advised attempt to sound aristocratic. It was an anglicized moniker derived from the nearby
town of Ouarville, where his father owned land; he would
later discuss it as "only Anglomania, a fashion."

Despite this general quirkiness, in many respects Brissot was
a typical Enlightenment liberal and philosophe. He believed the
new American republic was nearly perfect: it displayed a free
press, religious liberty (as he understood it), freedom of movement, open spaces close to nature (a very Rousseauist ideal),
and it was a place where the people had the right to vote and
participate in politics. Its main imperfections were the persist-
ence of black slavery and capital punishment, which were
rooted in a poisonous infection from the Old World. Once the

Jacques-Pierre Brissot (1754–1793) by N. F. Maviez after François Bonneville. Courtesy of the National Portrait Gallery, London.

Americans freed themselves of those two blights, the new land would be flawless.

Brissot was convinced to the point of self-delusion that he could reform France if only others would adopt his liberal ideas. Like Paine, Marat, Mirabeau, and other revolutionary writers and activists, Brissot made his contribution through journalism and politics. Through his writings, he became known as a fighter for republican government and soon made several important political connections, chiefly among the Girondins, that allowed him to enter politics, first as an elected member of the Paris Commune, then as a deputy in both the Legislative Assembly and the National Convention. Brissot's career can best be described as unsettled. He always wished to be accepted in the highest philosophe circles of Paris, to enjoy membership in the academies, and to be able to say his best friends were the leading liberal intellectuals and politicians of his time. He worked for several papers, founded many others, and wrote numerous books, which were often published at his own expense.

In 1782 Brissot went to London to become the editor of the

English edition of the French paper named the *Courrier.* There he met many important liberal activists, including those in Franklin's Club of Honest Whigs, such as Richard Price and Joseph Priestley, the novelist Frances Burney and historian Catherine Macaulay, the Dissenter David Williams, and even the young philosopher Jeremy Bentham. Brissot's friend and fellow Girondin Jean-Henri Bancal des Issarts, writing from London in 1790, later told Brissot, "Price spoke to me about you with highest esteem." And Brissot even once referred to Bentham as "my dear colleague."

Inspired by his surroundings, Brissot wanted to start an international literary society in London called the *Lycée de Londres.* It was to be a venue for French expatriates to discuss the issues of the day and philosophical (that is, republican) ideas. Most important, Brissot hoped to communicate these ideas to English and French intellectuals in London, Paris, and elsewhere. It was to be a truly enlightened international club, where thinking men talked about representative government and constitutionalism, a free press and religious liberty, including Brissot's hatred of anti-Semitism, the end of capital punishment, and the institution of a fair and equitable legal system. As Brissot put it, "one of the causes of the retardation of the progress in the sciences has been the lack of communication between intellectuals of different countries." With the new club, "in a word, we will advance more easily, more rapidly toward general truth because we will know all particular facts better." Sadly, he never established it.

While in England, Brissot associated not only with luminaries of the Royal Soceity and Franklin's Whig Club, but also with shady characters known for publishing pornography or libelous tracts attacking public figures. Some were even spies for the French police. When he returned to France in 1784, to his horror he was arrested and imprisoned in the Bastille, "accused of having written satirical pamphlets about highly placed government officials." It turns out that his expatriate enemies in London had spread lies about the king and queen and attached

Brissot's name to them. (Libelers like his London friends often used parody and satire as a favorite weapon to attack government officials. One favorite example was to refer to Marie Antoinette as the *Autrichienne,* which of course she was since she was an Austrian princess, and the word means "a woman from Austria." But the double entendre is as amusing as it was serious: the word for dog in French, *chien,* in its feminine form is *chienne;* thus, to call the queen by this moniker was to call her an Austrian bitch.)

In this case, the specific charge against Brissot was that he had printed a defamatory attack on the queen, claiming the dauphin was the product of an adulterous and even semi-incestuous affair between Marie Antoinette and the Comte d'Artois, the king's brother. In fact, Brissot almost certainly never wrote the story at all. It was likely written by one of his London enemies. The fact that Brissot was released from prison in just four months suggests he was innocent or at least that the police authorities had no evidence on which to hold him for a longer term. Although historian Robert Darnton was once certain that after Brissot's release he became a police spy for Lieutenant General Jean-Pierre Lenoir, he has now clearly softened his views about this subject. Lenoir wrote in his memoirs that Brissot, in fact, worked for him as an informer willing to expose his old enemies in England (the French expatriates) and France, the very ones who had most likely caused him to be incarcerated in the first place.

Once out of prison, Brissot heard of a peasant revolt in Transylvania (modern Romania) against the Hapsburg Empire. Emperor Joseph II had worked hard to lighten the laborious burdens on the peasants by placing limitations on the nobility's attempt to seize peasant lands. He even offered freedom to anyone who joined his border guards. But the nobility refused to allow the peasants to join the guards and clamped down on any attempt to transform the social order. Troops were brought in under royal command, despite Joseph II's initial desire to help the peasants. The revolt was brutally suppressed and its leaders executed. Their bodies were cut up and displayed as a deterrent to anyone who advocated reform.

The issues of the Transylvanian revolt were far more complex than land reform, though that surely sparked the revolt. Others included the religious question (the peasants were Orthodox, the government and nobility predominantly Catholic) and national prejudice (the peasants were Hungarian Magyars, their rulers primarily Romanian). That it was a complex matter was not lost on Brissot. He wrote open letters to Joseph II, whom he blamed for the peasants' problems, failing to recognize any of the progressive ideals the emperor displayed.

In any case, Brissot thought of the revolt in terms of an oppressed class of peasants rising against their cruel masters. Using perfectly good Rousseauist ideas, he argued that the general will of the peasant population demanded freedom, and the emperor was bound by the social contract and natural law to free them. He was especially appalled by Joseph II's refusal, after the end of the revolt, to allow the peasants to leave the empire. If they could not live well there, they should be able to live elsewhere. "I will tell you the truth about the people, for the people. I have studied their rights; they are the same as mine. I have to know these rights better than you know them in spite of the zeal in which you have tried to learn them. Your interest has had to be stronger than your humanity. It has been so. You are not a god. You are not even a man. You are a King. . . . You do not yet know the force of this word: *people,* of this word, *man.*" If Joseph II declined to let them leave, then they would simply fall into a worse lot, namely slavery, and Joseph II should not get away with that. "There comes a point when the irritated slave becomes so infuriated that he breaks his chains, immolates the tyrant, when he refuses to spill his blood and flees in spite of all of his efforts to a foreign asylum." Keeping to his views against capital punishment, Brissot said that the rebel leaders did not deserve the death penalty. Banishment was a better solution, even if land reform and freedom from serfdom were out of the question.

Brissot's hatred of slavery deepened when he read the Marquis de Chastellux's memoir, *The Voyage to North America*, recounting his military service during the American Revolution. Chastellux had served with Lafayette in the war, as part of French military forces fighting with the Americans. While Chastellux's memoir focused primarily on his experiences as a French officer, Brissot was shocked by Chastellux's view of black slaves as inferior people. His rejoinder, "A Critical Examination of the Voyages to North America of the Marquis de Chastellux," defended Quaker abolitionists and argued that blacks should be free and possess the same rights as whites.

Brissot's personal finances were in constant disarray and a source of great anxiety. In fact, at one point he was so poor, he threw his principles aside and worked for the Duc d'Orléans in November 1786 as the secretary-general of the chancellery at the Palais Royal. "My job," said Brissot, "was to examine all the projects that the prince could undertake with his vast fortune. He wanted to attract philosophers, encourage the arts, and so on." He stayed there for only a few months, leaving at the end of 1787. According to his friend Jérôme Pétion, who later served as mayor of Paris, Brissot grew restless working for an aristocrat, even one who later joined the revolutionary cause and dropped his noble status by renouncing his title as the Duc d'Orléans and adopting the name Philippe Egalité.

Before Brissot left d'Orléans's service, he got into trouble again when he and his patron supported the republicans against the stadtholder in the Netherlands, who was supported by the French foreign ministry. Brissot wrote some tracts favoring the Dutch republicans, which included an attack on the financial operations of the French government: Brienne, in charge of tax collections, had claimed that if the government was unable to collect its taxes, it would go bankrupt. Brissot objected and supported the Paris Parlement's attempt to raise revenues through the imposition of new taxes. He said the government must regularize taxes, and for that to happen, the king would have to call the Estates General into session. Once called, the Estates General, he hoped, would not only reform the tax structure, but also end the *lettres de cachet* process (which was how he earlier wound up in the Bastille). In any case, their support of the stadtholder got the house of Orléans and Brissot into trouble. The ministry thought the Duc d'Orléans, as the king's cousin, was about to denounce the government to the king.

All of them fled Paris—d'Orléans to Villiers and Brissot and others to England. It was there that Brissot met several Quakers and Anglican abolitionists through his association with men such as Price and Priestley, who were part of the Shelburne circle. These included the abolitionist Granville Sharp and the young Thomas Clarkson. Sharp and Clarkson, along with William Wilberforce and James Philips, founded an English abolitionist society that same year, and Brissot was invited to its meetings. He now thought he could do the same in France, which, in fact, he did the very next year in Paris. He proposed that the two societies—the English and the French—collaborate for greater effectiveness. "An important point that we set before the London committee is the affiliation of the two societies . . . to make them more respectable to public opinion, to create a solid front to oppose the particular [pro-slavery] interests and to the obstacles they pose to us."

At the same time, Brissot invited Thomas Jefferson, then in Paris as the American minister, to become a member of the new French society, the *Société des Amis des Noirs*. Jefferson, however, declined. He said in a most ambivalent way (not surprising, given Jefferson's general ambivalence about slavery) that he was genuinely bewildered by all the antislavery activity on both sides of the Atlantic. He was especially concerned about its effects in France. His response was diplomatic: "You know that nobody wishes more ardently to see an abolition not only of the trade but of the condition of slavery. But . . . I am here as a public servant; and those whom I serve having not yet been able to give their voice against this practice, it is decent for them to avoid too public a demonstration of my wishes to see it abolished. Without serving the cause here, it might render me less able to serve it beyond the water." William Short, Jefferson's chargé d'affaires, however, did join, and whether Jefferson approved of his doing so is not known.

At the same time that his rebuttal to Chastellux's book appeared, with many debts and very little money, Brissot decided he needed a change in scenery. He wanted to visit America to see for himself the conditions of blacks, and even considered a permanent move to the new United States. He thought perhaps he might engage in land speculation in the Ohio territory. In Paris he talked to Joel Barlow, the American agent in Paris for the Scioto Company, which was actively speculating on America's western lands. Brissot thought he might join the company on the American side. (Barlow is best known as one of the Connecticut Wits for his long epic poem about America, *The Columbiad,* and other works.) Before his departure, Brissot and his friend, the Swiss financier Etienne Clavière, discussed the feasibility of buying the war debt the Americans owed the French and capitalizing on it.

In May 1788 Brissot set off by himself for America "to serve the cause of the blacks and to extend the network of the society that he had just established in Paris." Leaving his wife and two children in Trouville, Brissot arrived in Boston on July 24, 1788. Traveling with the financial help of Clavière and other wealthy financiers, he visited a number of important men. Washington received him in Mount Vernon. St. John de Crève-coeur in New York gave him a cold reception. He was also scheduled to meet the Comte de Moustier, the French consul in America, who had little regard for Brissot. Moustier called him a "so-called *philosophe* who has produced some periodicals, some philosophical treatises, a pamphlet against the Marquis de Chastellux (filled with invectives) and another entitled *De France et des Etats-Unis* where he mixes criticisms of France with an exaltation of the English nation. Writing with a cutting and even sarcastic tone, he affects an enthusiasm for liberty and a hatred for tyranny. He therefore denounces France and values the English government and especially that of the United States which was not yet even set up. Such a man cannot, without inconvenience, be hosted by the minister of the King." Unsurprisingly, their meeting never took place, and Brissot did not much care. He had other people to see and other goals to accomplish in America.

He went to see Benjamin Rush and, of course, Franklin. First, he conversed with Rush about blacks and their condition in America: "He told me that it is much more difficult to treat and to cure Negro slaves than white people and that the Negroes have much less resistance to serious and prolonged illnesses. This is because they do not have the will to live; they are virtually without vitality and life force."

Brissot did not discuss these issues with Franklin, though he did devote a good deal of space in his *New Travels to North America* to the condition of blacks in America. He observed the school for black girls in Philadelphia started by Anthony Benezet, who, he said, had devoted himself "to public education, to the relief of the poor, and to the defense of Negro slaves. Benezet's philanthropy was of a universal sort still not very common at that time; he regarded all men of every country and of every color as his brothers." Like Franklin, after he accepted the native intelligence of blacks, Brissot thought blacks with an education were as smart as whites: "It was not enough to free the unfortunate Negroes from slavery; it was also necessary to educate them and to provide teachers for them. . . . It has been popularly believed until recently that Negroes are intellectually inferior to whites. Even respectable writers have supported this theory [and here he cited Chastellux]. . . . This prejudice is now beginning to disappear, and the Northern states can furnish examples to prove its falsity." He cited the case of Dr. James Derham, a black New Orleans physician visiting Philadelphia, who was as competent a doctor as any white physician.

After traveling in America for five months, Brissot learned that the financial and political situation in France had drastically deteriorated and that the king was convening the Estates General. He immediately abandoned his plans to settle in America and returned to France in January 1789. On his return to Paris, he and Condorcet first thought they could continue their efforts to gain freedom for blacks, as part of revolutionary liberation. But after July 14, 1789, everything changed. The Estates General's role in French politics became not only outmoded but irrelevant. A Constituent Assembly began the process of drafting a new constitution for the new constitutional monarchy.

With the Revolution, Brissot entered politics, first serving in elective office from September 18, 1789, to October 6, 1790, when he and Condorcet won seats on the Paris Commune. The commune administered the day-to-day operations of Paris that from 1789 onward had been divided into sixty electoral districts for the election of the Estates General (which after 1789 transformed itself into the Constituent Assembly). While each district had a representative in the municipal assembly, once seated, members of the commune claimed sovereignty over the entire city as a whole. Brissot and Condorcet became fast friends and worked together on several projects. One of them had to do with the members' assertion of control of their districts. Brissot wrote a manifesto on behalf of the commune asserting its control of the city, while the Cordeliers district (soon to be the location of the Cordeliers Club led by Georges Danton) opposed him. The conflict ended when the commune rejected his plan. The Cordeliers district and commune worked together to defeat the reelection of Jean-Sylvain Bailly as mayor of Paris (who was a friend to the Girondins). They were astonished when Bailly received almost 90 percent of the vote. Still, they were successful in reorganizing the City of Paris, and the commune replaced the sixty districts with forty-eight sections, which were designed to handle all matters of local government.

A month after their election, Brissot and Condorcet turned their attention to the ongoing unrest and violence in the city. They collaborated on an address to the new Constituent Assembly, which was elected in place of the National Assembly and charged with writing a new constitution for the nation. In their address, Brissot and Condorcet warned the delegates of the dangers that still existed in the Revolution. The main goal of the assembly should be to calm the people and bring peace to the city. The people must follow the law:

> Challenge therefore these turbulent spirits which breathe life into malcontents, discord, and riots. They only want your ruin. Riots heal no evil; they lead to scarcity instead of the opposite because the frightened farmers withhold their grain and the marks are deserted. . . . If you have been wronged, if you have to complain of abuses, address your complaints, your instructions to the legislative body, to your representatives and you will be satisfied. . . . The authority of the people cannot exist without their obedience . . . liberty cannot exist without obedience to the law and without respect of its organs. Representatives, being clothed with the most sacred character, therefore have the great right to your respect. To offend them would be a crime of high treason, of anti-brotherhood. A city that does not respect its deputies is dedicated to disgrace and to the gavel of those who do respect them.

Unlike his later advocacy of war against the Old Regime European states, after the Girondins took power in the spring of 1792, Brissot at this time supported peace and harmony. For any number of reasons, including possibly his outspokenness, he was not reelected in 1790 when his term ended.

At the same time, renewed political activity concerning the slave trade and slavery was stirring. Wealthy island planters initially viewed the Revolution with optimism: they thought they could use the Revolution to increase their own political and economic autonomy from France and to break the legal monopoly of French trading (the so-called Exclusive). Arriving in France in 1790 to serve as deputies in the Constituent Assembly, the planters formed a lobby to achieve these goals and to work against the efforts of the *Société des Amis des Noirs* and any reform movements challenging slavery. Known as the Corresponding Society of French Colonists, the lobby was housed in Marquis Mordant de Massaic's Paris mansion and became known informally as the Club Massaic. Consisting of both *grands blancs* living in Paris and sympathetic aristocrats, especially from the fiercely pro-slavery port town of Bordeaux, they were supported by the powerful, wealthy, and cumbersomely named Committee of the Extraordinary Deputies of Manufactures and Commerce of France.

This formidable group presented new challenges to Brissot, Condorcet, and the *Amis des Noirs*. Brissot knew that most delegates of the assembly had little interest in ending the slave trade and slavery. Even Mirabeau, the assembly's most powerful member, would not force the issue. Brissot and Condorcet shifted strategies: instead of seeking the end of the slave trade or slavery, since a mere one-quarter of the assembly actually favored full abolition of the trade, they decided to focus on the far narrower mulatto question, namely, whether it was possible to extend to the mulattoes the right to serve in the assembly. If they were successful in gaining this much, the new constitution might then recognize the official political status of the mulattoes—no small step in a society that recognized only three estates, none of which included them. From that moment on, Brissot and Condorcet argued that mulattoes (and they sometimes added free blacks) had full rights of citizenship as promised in the 1789 Declaration of the Rights of Man and Citizen.

From the colonies came an antislavery pressure group known as the *Colons Américains,* led by two mulattoes, Julien Raimond and Vincent Ogé, who were also members of the *Amis des Noirs.* Brissot complained that all thirty-seven delegates from the colonies were white, and that at least these two mulattoes should be allowed to serve. The *grands blancs* responded that the Declaration of Rights did not apply to slaves, since it addressed only human beings, and slaves could be considered inhuman and merely property. This argument was more difficult to make, however, when it came to the mulattoes: they were sometimes wealthy and were an increasingly powerful group (moreover, they were not slaves). When the assembly refused to go along with the *grands blancs*'s platform in the French West Indies, tensions increased. The *grands blancs* now changed course and said that their future lay not with Revolution after all, as they had originally thought, but with the Crown.

Not everything worked against the white planters. On March 2, 1790, they convinced the assembly to establish a colonial committee of twelve men to investigate the status of the islands. The head of this committee was the twenty-nine-year-old lawyer Joseph Barnave, a relative of a Saint Domingue planter and a high government official. Politically a liberal and initially a close associate and confidant to Mirabeau, Barnave had been a member of the Estates General and now the Constituent Assembly. According to Brissot, he was a cold, rational, and eloquent man. The *grands blancs* found in him a friend.

During his tenure in the assembly, Barnave worked tirelessly on behalf of the French trading monopoly and commerce. A fiery orator like Mirabeau, he was elected president of the assembly in October 1790, which, as it turned out, was the height of his very short career. He allied himself with two others, Adrien Duport, who wrote the famous August 4, 1789, decree ending feudal obligations in France, and Alexandre de Lameth, a young colonel who had once fought in the American Revolution. Together, the three were known as the "triumvirate," perhaps a deliberate attempt to compare them to the ancient Roman triumvirate. The Lameth brothers (Charles and Alexandre) were heavily involved in commercial trade with the colonies, and Barnave followed their lead to argue in favor of the status quo: white control over free mulattoes and black slaves and no representation for mulattoes in the assembly (and, correspondingly, no legal status for them in the new constitution). In essence, Barnave mouthed the term "the rights of man," but these rights were not for the mulattoes and free blacks, only whites.

On March 8, 1790, the report of the committee of twelve, written by Barnave, recommended that the colonies form their own local assemblies and present plans for internal control to the assembly for approval. As David Brion Davis notes, "the Assembly approved the report of the Committee on Colonies, which affirmed that the government had no intention of furthering innovation in any branch of colonial trade and which also outlawed any agitation that might endanger colonial property," including of course the slaves. In essence, white control continued. Brissot, Condorcet, Marat, and the Abbé Grégoire denounced the report and its author. Brissot's open letter accused Barnave of being a pawn of the white plantation owners, and he never forgave him for writing this report. In fact, Brissot's criticisms caused such a stir that Barnave rewrote it and presented a new report just twenty days later.

The revised report gave all taxpayers and property owners over the age of twenty-five the right to participate in a local version of the National Assembly. But the report did not name propertied mulattoes in the instructions. The *grands blancs* were delighted with this omission. When a new National Assembly was elected in Saint Domingue, its first job was to write a new constitution for the island. Shortly, however, it became clear there was no unity of opinion between the *grands blancs* and the *petits blancs*. Whereas the *grands blancs* wanted a closer association with France, the *petits blancs* (the poorer whites who worked for the plantation owners or filled clerical positions), now calling themselves the Patriots, sought greater independence. There were so many more *petits* than *grands blancs*. The result was civil war in Saint Domingue—*grands blancs* against *petits blancs,* mulattoes and free blacks against both of them.

When Vincent Ogé, who had left Paris disgusted with the inaction of the Constituent Assembly, arrived back in Saint Domingue, he joined the insurrection on the side of the mulattoes and free blacks, an act that Brissot openly supported in January 1791. Ogé secretly planned a general slave insurrection, so that all the *gens de couleur* and former slaves would dominate any future assembly. However, the slaves failed to support him; he was sorely outnumbered and outgunned. With a remnant of his forces, Ogé fled to the Spanish sector of Saint Domingue. Brissot noted, "Ogé had everything to fear from these agents of despotism," and he was right. Captured by the Spanish governor of San Rafaël, Ogé was sent back to Saint Domingue, where he was hanged. His death was followed by two hundred other executions. Brissot later compared Ogé's treatment to that of Cato and Brutus at the hands of Nero and Caligula. In tribute to his revolutionary fearlessness, the Girondin Charles Barbaroux named his son, born the following year, in honor of Ogé.

Meantime, Joseph Barnave began a curious relationship with the queen. After the king and queen fled Paris in June 1791, Barnave was sent along with several others to Varennes to escort them back to the capital. While riding in the coach, he became an ardent admirer of Marie Antoinette and subsequently began a rather frank (and secret) correspondence with her; he also sent her copies of his essays. Back in Paris, he established the Feuillants, those who supported a constitutional monarchy, not a republic, effectively abandoning the Jacobins to Robespierre and increasing extremism. He wanted to forestall the Revolution from going any further than a constitutional monarchy, which he now hoped would be a permanent feature of the new French government. He feared people like Condorcet, Brissot, and other like-minded republicans who, he felt, wanted to pull down the king. The American republic simply could not be duplicated in France, as the liberals claimed, and it was time for the Revolution to end. Robespierre, who worked tirelessly against Barnave, proposed that the new constitution prohibit all members of the Constituent Assembly from serving in the new Legislative Assembly or from holding any governmental office. This was a deliberate attempt to exclude Barnave, who was a delegate in the Constituent. The bill easily passed.

Once the king and queen fled Paris into the arms of their royalist brethren in Varennes, Brissot, Condorcet, and Paine planned to bring about a republic for France, an idea that was very different from Barnave's. For Brissot, Barnave was a hypocrite (the word he actually used was *escobarderie,* a hypocritical priest). In his attack, the *Letter of J-P Brissot to M. Barnave on his reports concerning the colonies,* Brissot claimed to see a thousand dangers in the assembly's treatment of the colonies and said only a republic could solve the problems. He asserted that Barnave "possessed the logic of a lawyer, but not the thinking skills of a politician" and called Barnave "empty-headed," a man having light political ideas (*"la légèreté de ses idées en politique"*).

The influential salonnière Madame Roland also despised Barnave. Brissot frequented her salon along with Pétion, Robespierre, Paine, and several other important liberal politicians and writers. She spoke of *"le petit Barnave,"* as she called him, while at the same time praising Brissot, who opened the columns of his paper to her. Still, she thought him a bit naive and simple: "He is the best of human beings; a good husband, a tender father, a faithful friend, a virtuous citizen, his friendship is as sweet as his character is facile; confident to the point of imprudence, gay, naive, an ingénue as one is at fifteen, he was destined to live with the wise men and to be the dupe of evil ones." Brissot's wife, Félicité, seconded this sentiment in a letter, writing of her husband's selflessness: "My husband acquires much glory, but fortune is not for us. His patriotism, his style of life to be useful, burdens him with expenses that only he knows."

With France's political landscape wide open, Brissot took advantage of the moment to create a new outlet for his views. While he worked for many newspapers in France and England, his greatest success began in May 1789, when he launched his *Patriote français*. It is said that his paper "was justifiably considered one of the best pro-revolutionary newspapers" and "the best propaganda instrument" during the Revolution. It also proved to be his downfall. Brissot's was among some 140 new papers started in 1789, with only 34 of them lasting one year. Eighteenth-century books and pamphlets reached only a limited audience, whereas with the newspapers, "one can teach the same truth at the same moment to millions of men; through the press, they can discuss it without tumult, decide calmly and give their opinion." Brissot's careers in politics and journalism were so intertwined they were indistinguishable. *Le Patriote français* became the first unofficial (or unlicensed) publication of its kind. Published thereafter every day except Sunday, Brissot's paper lasted until June 2, 1793, the day the Girondins were expelled from the convention.

It was during these years that Brissot became the most influential member of the Roland circle, meeting in the salon of Madame Roland and her husband Jean-Marie Roland de la Platière, who controlled two consecutive governmental ministries in 1792 and 1793. In fact, Brissot became Roland's principal advisor. Roland, who was twenty years older than his wife, had been a municipal officer in Lyon and then a former inspector general for manufactures. He first came to Paris in February 1791 to request that the Lyon debt become part of the national debt. He and his wife were soon holding court on the rue Guénégaud. When the Rolands returned to Lyon in September, they found his job as inspector general had been eliminated. So they returned to Paris to the same street, but in a different, less expensive location in the Hôtel Britannique.

Brissot used his newspaper and his political associations to enhance his advances in politics and at the same time promote his political principles. On his success as a journalist and editor, one of his enemies once posed, and then answered, the following question: "How does it happen that this petty individual does so much harm to the public welfare? It's because he has a newspaper . . . it's because Brissot and his friends have all the trumpets of renown at their disposal." The French revolutionary newspaper was an instrument of civic instruction for the new free French citizen. "The point is to spread the enlightenment which prepares a nation to receive a free constitution, by instructing the people about the National Assembly's operations," and to defend "the rights of the people." It will not "be led into continual fermentation, which would perpetuate disorder and postpone the constitution."

Even after Brissot became a deputy in both the Legislative Assembly in 1791 and the National Convention the following year, he remained the editor in chief and publisher of his paper until it closed when the Jacobins came to power in June 1793. His goal, as a major leader of the Girondin party, was to establish a French republic. By 1792 he had abandoned his former pacifist principles, and he concluded the best means to achieve a French republic was for France to go to war against Austria and perhaps other Old Regime states in Europe. After all, the marriage of Louis XVI and Marie Antoinette, the daughter of the Austrian Archduchess Marie Theresa and the German Emperor Francis I, was designed to strengthen the relationship between France and Austria. Moreover, the Austrians should be punished for harboring proroyalist French émigrés, the French aristocrats who fled France to await the end of the constitutional regime and the restoration of the absolute monarchy, and the refractory priests who refused to accept the Civil Constitution of the Clergy and the reduced role of religion in the new nation. These matters put the Girondins into a collision course with the Crown.

Meantime, Condorcet and Brissot continued to work on behalf of the mulattoes and free blacks in the West Indies. Having been elected to the new Legislative Assembly in the fall of 1791, Brissot addressed the body in the most vociferous terms. He called the colonists "dissipaters" (*dissipateurs*), "crushed by debts," who hated both the people of color and the law and wanted only to maintain "the despotism of white flesh." His speech deserves quoting at length for its eloquent vehemence:

> So, Gentlemen, you must regard the enemies of these men of color as the most violent enemies of our Constitution. They detest it because they see it as the annihilation of pride and prejudice; they are sorry [because] they would bring back the former state of things if they saw the guarantees which they could with impunity oppress without being themselves oppressed by the ministers. The cause of the men of color is the cause of the patriots, of the former Third Estate, of the people so long oppressed. Here I must warn you, Gentlemen, I will portray for you these colonists who, for three years, use the most criminal maneuvers to break the bonds which link them to the mother country, to crush the people of color; I speak only of this class of poor colonists in spite of their immense property, factious [factieux] in spite of their indigence, proud despite their profound ineptitude, audacious despite their cowardice, factious without means of being, these colonists despite their vices and their debts unceasingly carry their troubles and who for three years have directed the diverse colonial assemblies toward an independent aristocracy. . . .
>
> These kinds of men possess the greatest empire over another class no less dangerous, that called "the petits-Blancs," composed of adventurers, men without principles and nearly all of them without morals. This class is the true curse of the colonies because it is recruited from the dregs of Europe. This class looks with jealousy on the men of

color, be they artisans because those working better and to the best market are more sought after, be they proprietors because their wealth excites their envy and debases their pride. This class sighs only after the troubles because it loves to pillage, which after independence, because masters of the colony, the petits–Blancs hope to share the spoils of the men of color.

In a tour de force, Brissot claimed that the *gens de couleur* were actually more European than the French might realize. "They are not the black slaves," but people who "owe their days to European blood mixed with African blood." He who condemned the blood of mulattoes therefore condemned his own blood. And the slaves? "The last class is that of the slaves, the numerous class, since it amounts to more than 400,000 souls, while the mulattoes, and free negroes form hardly a sixteenth part of this population. I will not stop to paint for you a picture of these misfortunate ones yanked from their freedom, from their country, to water a foreign soil with their sweat and their blood, with no hope and under the blows of the whips of their barbarian masters." Two days later Brissot described how debtors from the colonies and creditors from France (the *negociants* and shipowners) were in fact allied in this nefarious business of withholding rights from mulattoes and free blacks.

Brissot thought, quite rightly, that enemies within and without the nation endangered the French Revolution. First, there were the Old Regimes states (which soon would try to forestall revolution in their own countries by waging war against France in an effort to restore Louis to his throne). Second, French émigrés living abroad in those countries, who were often abroad to the revolutionary changes at home, stirred up hatred toward the revolutionary regime. For Brissot, war created the possibility of a "permanent revolution," an idea that a century and a half later would be used by Leon Trotsky to stimulate the onward push of the Russian Revolution after 1917.

Robespierre became one of the most vocal opponents of Brissot's war mongering (recall that Paris politics was becoming increasingly riven, with Robespierre and the Jacobins on the one side and Brissot and the Girondins on the other). Likewise, Marat chimed in against a general European war in an article in *L'Ami du peuple*. On two occasions in December 1791, Robespierre and Brissot debated war. Using patriotic language, Brissot proclaimed, "For a people who have conquered its liberty after twelve centuries of slavery, war is necessary to consolidate it; to purge despotism, to make disappear the men who would still corrupt them." Insulted by neighboring powers for two years, it was now time to act. "Destroy Coblence [Johann Ludwig, Count of Coblentz, a leading Austrian general]. Coblence destroyed, all will be tranquil abroad, all tranquil within." Three days later Robespierre argued that the enemies of France were internal, not external. "Extinguish the internal enemies, and then the external ones, if they still exist," he said: an echo of the coming Terror that he himself would lead. A few weeks later, in January 1792, Robespierre said again that the enemies were inside France, and not the foreign powers threatening France.

Brissot began to win over both the Jacobins and the assembly, and soon the opponents of war were isolated: Danton thought war should be only a last resort, not a means to spread revolution to all European nations; Barnave's moderate Feuillants wanted to continue to work with the king and queen to make the new constitutional monarchy work and maintain peace in Europe. Brissot, undeterred, said it was time for "another crusade" to achieve "universal liberty." Reluctantly, as we have seen, the antiwar Condorcet agreed. On January 25, 1792, the assembly decreed that Louis had to demand that the German emperor Leopold, Louis's brother-in-law, state his attitude about the new French constitution and whether he accepted peace with France. The decree said that if the king received no response by March 1, or if the response was inconclusive, then France would consider it a declaration of war.

The first Girondin government, which entered office in March 1792, included, as expected, only members from that faction. Brissot wanted to be the minister of foreign affairs, but found himself edged aside when General Charles-François Dumouriez, who had made a name for himself as a successful commander in putting down a rebellion in the Vendée, was appointed in his stead. Roland got the position of minister of the interior. Brissot successfully nominated his old friend, the wealthy Etienne Clavière, for the finance ministry (he had been in Mirabeau's brain trust on financial affairs). Pierre Victurnien Vergniaud nominated his friend Antoine Duranthon, who had been a prosecutor in the Gironde, for the ministry of justice. This was the embryo of a modern parliamentary cabinet. Although Brissot received no appointment, as a member of the assembly and later a convention deputy, he maintained a powerful influence on the Roland government.

That same month, the Girondin government at long last used its powers of persuasion in the Legislative Assembly to see that a decree was passed giving the *gens de couleur* full rights. The king signed it into law on April 4, 1792. A new group of commissioners was dispatched to Saint Domingue to enforce it (and, it was hoped, stop the insurrection there). Condorcet wrote: "For the first time in this era of liberty, the representatives of the French nation have rendered to the colonies a decree that was worthy of it and its century." Justly delighted by this development, he also added that the battle must continue: "We must hope for the honor of humanity that the interests of the blacks will not be entirely forgotten."

Ominously, just as the commissioners were preparing to depart for Saint Domingue, the assembly declared war on Austria; and then Prussia promptly declared war on France in support not just of Austria, but of royalism. The efforts in the colonies were no longer a priority in Paris. Even worse, the delegation sailed just a few days before the monarchy came crashing down on August 10. That collapse would plunge France into political disarray.

⧯

The Girondins' final break with the Jacobins came over war policy in late March when France declared war on Austria. (There was a famous moment in the assembly when the king arrived to ask for support of a declaration of war while Condorcet was at the podium submitting his program on education, which had to wait.) While the king was lukewarm about going to war, the queen was won over by the prospect that once France lost, the Austrians would restore absolute monarchy to France. Only seven deputies voted against the declaration. Robespierre's split with Brissot was now final—Robespierre had opposed the war from the beginning—and his Jacobin colleague, Marat, was soon denouncing French losses and arguing the only recourse was to massacre the generals.

The Jacobins denounced the king, the court, the generals, and, above all, the new ministry—which, of course, included Brissot. Hatred of Brissot spread to the other clubs, including the Cordeliers, once led by Camille Desmoulins but now by Jacques-René Hébert, and the popular press. Hébert was the leader of the *enragés* (the madmen), one of the most extreme groups to emerge during the Revolution. With his newspaper, *Père Duchesne,* Hébert was one of the founders of a new revolutionary religion, which he called the Cult of Reason. After Robespierre achieved absolute power in the Committee of Public Safety, he adopted Hébert's religion as his own, terming it the Cult of the Supreme Being. (By the spring of 1794 it was clear to Robespierre that Hébert was a potential threat to his authority; consequently, in March, Hébert was arrested and guillotined soon afterward.)

If this infighting were not enough, Roland increased tensions even more by sending a letter (actually written by Madame Roland) to the king that demanded he order the stationing of twenty thousand National Guardsmen around Paris for protection. The letter also demanded all refractory priests be forced to swear allegiance to the constitution or face dismissal. Predictably, the king found the letter to be impudent. In June 1792, just three months after the Roland government began, the king dismissed it. With the Girondins temporarily out of office (they returned within two months), another attempt was made to reconcile all of the radical Jacobins, because the accusation that Brissot and his colleagues had joined with the king against the Revolution was now patently absurd. It now appeared the king wanted to lose the war on purpose, so he could once again rule as an absolute monarch.

With the battles going against France, with the Roland ministry dismissed, and with the Revolution in disarray, on June 20, 1792, a large group of armed men from the sections of Paris peacefully petitioned the assembly. We do not know for sure whether they had the approval of Brissot, Condorcet, and others, but their goals were clear: to force the king to rescind his vetoes favoring the refractory priests. They also wanted the king to force the émigré leaders to return to France. One immediate result of this display of support for Girondin positions was the king's decision, under some pressure from Brissot and his colleagues, to restore the Roland ministry. Louis thought this would forestall an insurrection that would destroy him.

Everyone, it seemed, from the king to Brissot to the extremists, anticipated a violent uprising against the monarchy. They weren't disappointed. Less than two months after the beginning of the second Roland ministry, led by the extremists of the Cordeliers, the Jacobins, and the guardsmen from the provinces (and not by more outspoken moderate leaders like Brissot and Condorcet or even Marat and Robespierre), this, the second French Revolution, took place on August 10, 1792. The king was permanently suspended from the throne and imprisoned. Marat reportedly was so frightened he left town, disguised as a jockey.

For his intrigue with the queen and his hesitancy to support republicanism, Barnave was arrested just after the August 10 insurrection. The authorities found in the Tuileries all the writings he had sent to Marie Antoinette, indicating his improper relationship with the court. Brissot called this work Barnave's "iron casket," an allusion to Louis XVI and Marie Antoinette's so-called bin of letters to French émigrés living abroad and conspiring against the Revolution, thus contributing to their ultimate downfall and execution. Arrested on August 19, 1792, Barnave spent a year in prison in Dauphiné, until he was transferred to Paris in November 1793, tried by the Revolutionary Tribunal, and executed on the 29th. He was thirty-two.

Perhaps the worst outcome for Brissot after the August uprising was Robespierre's further (and fatal) alienation from him. Robespierre had already disagreed with Brissot about fighting a foreign war. Now he feared that Brissot wanted to seize power for himself. His fears were reinforced when, as the new minister of justice, Georges Danton joined the second Roland or, as it was also known, Brissotin government; and they were further reinforced when Danton saw that government funding was provided for only some propaganda journals and papers (like Brissot's) and not for others (like Marat's *L'Ami du peuple*). Robespierre was determined to engage his allies, such as Marat and Desmoulins, to stop Brissot.

Robespierre's first major step was to vigorously denounce Brissot in a meeting of the Paris Commune. His September 1 attack was not limited to singling out Brissot alone. Robespierre went after the entire Girondin faction, calling them all enemies of the Revolution, demanding their ouster from government, and accusing them of treason. He outrageously further accused them of aiding the Prussian commander in chief, the Duke of Brunswick, whose forces were just then threatening Paris (the threat was so real that the Paris government, under a suggestion by Roland, then minister of the interior, contemplated moving to Blois). Danton accused Roland of cowardice, and from that time on, the Rolands and Danton barely spoke to one another. As a close friend of the Rolands, Brissot supported them against Danton; the alliance between these two men began to fade, and Danton grew closer to Robespierre.

Over the next several days, in the infamous September Massacres, hundreds of so-called suspects (estimates reach up to thirteen hundred) were slaughtered in Paris prisons. Many extremists like Marat accused those incarcerated of having betrayed the Revolution, though many of the victims were simply common criminals or prostitutes. As minister of justice, Danton was charged with protecting them, but when asked to do so, he reportedly callously remarked, "Fuck the prisoners." The incarcerated were denounced as traitors, who were no better than the foreign armies attacking the nation, with the goal of reestablishing absolutism in France. When news of the massacres reached Saint Domingue, the insurrection was spurred on; and when the commissioners arrived, black leaders, including Toussaint L'Ouverture, withdrew to the Spanish quarter of the island to await a more propitious moment for revolution.

The commune, under Robespierre's insistence (and probably Marat's, too, though he was not a member), now issued an arrest warrant for Brissot and several of his associates, including Condorcet, Roland and his wife, and other Girondin leaders. The split between Brissot and Robespierre was now at its meanest point; they were playing a deadly game of low politics. Had Brissot and the others been arrested, they surely would have perished during the September Massacres. Only the intervention by the mayor of Paris, Jérôme Pétion, and Danton, who thought the quarrel between Robespierre and Brissot was purely personal, spared them. Danton failed to see it was a matter of bald political power.

When the elections were held for the National Convention in September 1792, it was clear that no Paris district would elect Brissot, because the commune under Robespierre's direction controlled the city convention deputies. Desmoulins, who on July 14, 1789, had led the crowds to the Bastille, now published his nefarious *J.-P. Brissot demasqué.* The rumors abounded about Brissot's history as a police spy, which Desmoulins, Marat, and Louis Saint-Just all eagerly spread. Unsurprisingly, Louis and the right wing also opposed Brissot's election. Even worse, just at this time, Brissot's old nemesis Théveneau de Morande returned to the picture, accusing Brissot of wanting to be an aristocrat because he had added "de Warville" to his name as a young man. Brissot disingenuously responded that the name of a nearby village simply distinguished him from his brothers.

But because Brissot was still popular in the provinces, three regions elected him as their deputy to the convention, and he accepted the call from Eure-et-Loire. The same was true for Condorcet: no Paris district would elect him because of his close ties to Brissot, and he took his seat as a deputy representing Aisne. Several non-Frenchmen, such as Richard Price, Joseph Priestley, Thomas Paine, George Washington, James Madison, and others from other nations, were given French citizenship and elected to the convention, but only two accepted: Paine and the Prussian baron and writer Jean-Baptiste "Anarcharsis" Clootz, who called himself "the orator of the human race, representative of the oppressed sovereign peoples of mankind." Paine, like Brissot and Condorcet, was not elected by any Paris district, but from four provincial districts. He chose to represent Pas-de-Calais, because it was the first to do so.

In the convention, Brissot served as one of the secretaries along with Condorcet, Paine, and Lanthenas. Jérôme Pétion was named president. The committee to create a new constitution—the whole aim of the convention—was headed by Condorcet. It included Girondins like Brissot, Paine, Danton, and others. Brissot also served on the committee on general defense, which was eventually overhauled without him and became the infamous Committee of Public Safety. Opening on September 20, 1792, the same day that Brunswick's Prussian forces were defeated at Valmy and began their retreat from the capital, the convention now declared France to be a republic, one, indivisible, and democratic. But it was "one" in name only: the ruthless divisions that separated the leadership were never repaired, even with the work on the new republican constitution and the eventual trial and execution of the king.

Neither Robespierre nor Brissot yielded on any point. Brissot's newspaper was successful in placing his point of view before the people, and not just the people of Paris: *Le Patriote français* was read throughout the country. Robespierre had no alternative press to combat Brissot's positions. Working closely with Marat (now a convention deputy and daily calling for more heads to roll), Desmoulins, and Saint-Just, Robespierre convinced the Jacobin Club to expel Brissot, who, they said, had been divisive when he advocated war the previous year against the European monarchies. For his part, Brissot for the first time really lamented the September Massacres, saying they were not only unnecessary but also immoral and destructive of a united France. The *septembriseurs* should all be brought to justice, Brissot said, which suggestively and wrongly blamed the commune (and thus Robespierre) for the bloodshed.

Condorcet and Danton tried to find ways to bring the two sides together, but to no avail. Robespierre would not budge, and neither would Brissot. They quarreled over whether grain and bread prices should be capped or whether the government should allow free trade in grain (Robespierre despised price controls, Brissot favored government regulation to forestall poverty and famine). As a leading member of the Committee on General Security, Brissot first proposed to the convention that war be declared against England, which happened on February 1, and a few weeks later Spain and Holland were added to France's enemies. It was now a full European war against revolutionary France.

By this time, Robespierre, who was lukewarm about the war's expansion, went along reluctantly with its extension to these three countries. Still, he and his faction almost daily attacked Brissot's newspaper and the press that supported the Girondins, claiming that since the August 10 insurrection

Brissot had acted against the interests of the Revolution and the people and was corrupting public opinion. Even more damning, French troops faced serious military difficulties against the Austrians and Prussians in Belgium and Holland, especially after General Dumouriez's entire army deserted in March 1793. The Jacobins simply blamed Brissot and the Brissotins, and some even demanded his resignation and arrest for being counterrevolutionary. They regarded Dumouriez, who had overseen important French victories in the Argonne, Valmy, and Jemmapes, as a traitor, even though he himself did not defect until a few weeks later.

Dumouriez, now with a change of heart, vigorously attacked the convention and demanded an end to the war. He also denounced Condorcet's draft republican constitution: to many Jacobins, he had turned into a royalist—which might well have been true. He wanted to turn his troops against Paris and dissolve the convention, but his forces refused, and he unceremoniously fled to the Austrian camp. Danton denounced Dumouriez after first supporting him as one of the few military men who knew how to run a war. He, too, then blamed all of France's ills on Brissot and his followers, especially Roland.

At the same time, mobs of citizens attacked several so-called moderate presses and permanently shut them down. Even the Jacobins were appalled at such lawlessness (Robespierre claimed they were undertaken by riotous women who represented no one but themselves). On the other hand, the Jacobins were also secretly delighted, because they used the uprising against the press to eliminate Brissot and all of the other so-called moderates. Brissot now gave up editorial control of his paper and turned it over to his associate, the young Joseph Marie Girey-Dupré (he was just twenty-three). A March 9, 1793, decree forbade members of the convention from running newspapers. Brissot was clearly shaken. "The rights of man are no more," he wrote, "all natural laws are trampled under foot; one night has overturned the work of four years: individual liberty, the freedom of the press. . . . A faction that wishes to reign among shadows has banned thinking deputies from enlightening their citizens."

Marat was now calling for the elimination of anyone whom he suspected of being unfaithful to "revolutionary principles." In his view, Brissot was clearly an apostate. Along with Danton, Robespierre, and Desmoulins, Marat condemned Brissot for his early support of Dumouriez, charging Brissot with royalism in light of Dumouriez's betrayal. Marat, now a leading figure among the *enragés,* leveled daily harangues against Brissot and the Girondins. Even worse, law and order broke down when the sansculottes, those who wanted harsh actions against those whom they considered unfaithful to the Revolution, forced themselves onto the convention floor and disrupted its proceedings (which were now becoming increasingly chaotic). The sansculottes wanted to eliminate moderate and even liberal leaders whom they said were "suspect," that is, who failed to exhibit sufficient faith in revolutionary principles. The new radicals invaded the convention floor with petitions supporting agitators like Marat, who was himself demanding a law of suspects (eventually approved on September 17, 1793) to condemn to death anyone the convention or its Revolutionary Tribunal found guilty of treason, no matter the vague evidence or unreliable testimony against the charge.

Robespierre now accused Brissot and his followers of working directly with foreign armies to restore the king to the throne. He urged Desmoulins to publish his *Histoire des Brissotins,* a scurrilous attack on Brissot, which appeared in April 1793, advocating the expulsion of the Girondins from the convention (the full title in English was "history of the Brissotins, or fragments of the secret history of the Revolution and the first six months of the Revolution"). Brissot saw that his influence was drastically declining as Robespierre and his faction, which now included both Marat and Danton, increasingly marginalized him. He rarely spoke in the convention, limiting himself to replying in his former paper, at which he still had friends and supporters, to the charges against him.

When Marat, then serving as president of the convention, signed a decree advocating the arrest and trial of the Girondins, Brissot momentarily turned things around by having Marat impeached. All the charges against Marat were undoubtedly true: he was the divisive force in the convention, and his newspaper was endlessly filled with attacks on whomever he thought were enemies of the Revolution (which meant whomever he did not like). Brissot was certainly one of them. Writing in his memoirs, he would give this final testament about Marat:

> I confess that I believed that Marat was a mediocre writer, an inconsequential logician, someone who did not believe in morality, someone ambitious and the enemy of all talent. But I do believe that he violated all the principles, all the laws to the point of viciously attacking the most virtuous men and to preach massacre and pillage. I stop here and end with this thought: whatever evil Marat did to me, I forgive him, but I will never forgive him for having corrupted the morality of the people and of having inspired their taste for blood. Without morality and without principles, there is no republic.

At the same time, many deputies—though, curiously, few Girondins—demanded new provincial elections to determine which side (the Jacobins or the Girondins) could attract the most support. Had these maneuvers succeeded, they might have saved Brissot and his allies, but they never garnered enough support. The elections were never held. A few months later Marat was acquitted.

The second Roland government—and thus Brissot's standing—now disintegrated in the face of mounting French defeats (the loss of Belgium and the fall of the northern army), a massive food shortage in Paris as prices for meat and bread rose astronomically (with the requisite call for maximum prices on these and other goods), the fall of the value of the assignat, and the internal rebellion when the Vendée and eventually three other regions (Lyon, Marseille, and Normandy) blew up into civil war against the central government. These events, all converging at the same moment in April and May, doomed the Girondins, especially as the convention floor was now constantly invaded by Parisian mobs of not only the sansculottes, but also the working poor and women, who were demanding economic relief from rising inflation and food shortages.

The convention issued the first decree of accusation against twenty-two Girondin deputies in the middle of April. On June 2, 1793, the order was made final, and the convention, under Robespierre's undisputed leadership, expelled twenty-nine Girondin deputies, including Brissot. Like so many Girondins, they almost all immediately went into hiding. (Sadly, all of this took place when Condorcet and Brissot's last battle on behalf of rights for mulattoes and slaves was coming to an end and years after Franklin's death in 1790. The Girondin government under Roland's leadership, but clearly directed by Condorcet's and Brissot's ideas, was powerless to help the blacks in the islands.) Robespierre and his faction seized control of the government in June of 1793.

Arrested on June 10, Brissot was returned to Paris under police guard, where he spent 104 days in the Abbaye, a former convent turned into a prison. He and his colleagues had to know they were in a far more precarious position after Marat's murder by Charlotte Corday in July: the radicals now viewed the Brissotins as dangerous rebels. Bartrand Barère, a member of the Committee of Public Safety who survived the Terror and lived, incredibly, until 1841, declared, "Terror shall be the order of the day."

Brissot's interrogation before the Revolutionary Tribunal took place a month later. Along with Armand Gensonné,

Joseph-Marie Girey-Dupré, Pierre Victurnien Vergniaud, and other Girondins, he was executed on October 31, 1793. He was thirty-nine.

9

Learning in the New Era

L ike most of the men of the Enlightenment, many of Benjamin Franklin's visionary friends understood that widespread and available education was crucial to an emerging liberal society. His associate Noah Webster, with whom he developed a new shorthand, for example, believed in a strong civic education for the youth of the new country, and George Washington went so far in his *Farewell Address* to call for the creation of a national university. Franklin himself is most well known in this respect for his founding of the Philadelphia Academy, which, by the end of the century, became the University of Pennsylvania. Thomas Jefferson was so proud of his work to create the University of Virginia that he drafted this epitaph just before his death:

> *Here was buried*
> *Thomas Jefferson*

Author of the Declaration of Independence
Of the Statute of Virginia for religious freedom
& Father of the University of Virginia

Benjamin Rush, like Franklin, Jefferson, Washington, and Webster, believed that only a fully educated citizenry ensured the continuation of the republic; otherwise, the people would not recognize corrupt, power-seeking men, and the republic would decay into tyranny. The Marquis de Condorcet echoed these ideas in France when he claimed that only an educated people guaranteed rational decision making. Among all of these men, Condorcet stands out by advocating universal education not only for every man but for every woman as well.

Many of Franklin's visionary friends fought to create strong national institutions, especially of higher learning; but they also sought the spread of free public schools so that the entire citizenry could achieve its greatest potential, from tradesman to the head of the government. With the exception of Franklin, all of these men enjoyed the benefits of some level of higher education: Rush at Princeton and then the Edinburgh School of Medicine; Jefferson at the College of William and Mary; Condorcet at the College of Navarre; and Brissot at the College of Chartres and then the law school at Reims (the latter was widely known as a degree mill). While they all developed schemes of education, and some of their ideas were actually implemented, none ever directed a school or college in its day-to-day operations. Like our own contemporary educational institutions, theirs often experienced severe financial and internal political problems from which it took years to recover.

Thirty years after Franklin founded the Philadelphia Academy, his young friend Benjamin Rush devoted considerable time and energy to establishing two colleges in Pennsylvania: one named for John Dickinson, the Pennsylvania governor (Dickinson College in Carlisle), and the other for the great man himself,

Franklin College (today Franklin and Marshall) in Lancaster. Like Franklin, Rush was vitally interested in creating colleges for Americans who, once educated, would become "republican machines." The first college he planned was in Carlisle. Franklin agreed. He, too, had long thought the western lands of Pennsylvania would soon be teeming with people and that the colony (and later the state) must provide them with every conceivable service. In 1763 Franklin wrote his friend Richard Jackson, a London barrister and also a friend of Dr. (Samuel) Johnson, "There are already several Schemes on foot among the People in different Parts of this and the neighbouring Provinces for Removal Westward, and great Numbers show a strong Disposition to go and settle on the Ohio or Missisipi [*sic*]." Rush chose western Pennsylvania for the very reasons Franklin enumerated. He also thought it was in a less expensive part of the state; besides, the area was beautiful. Perhaps most important of all, Rush wanted to start his own Presbyterian college—in a kind of competition with the medical school in Philadelphia.

His first announcement of the plan came in September 1782 when he wrote a small pamphlet called "Hints for Establishing a College at Carlisle in Cumberland County, Pennsylvania." By that time, he said, the Presbyterians had become a strong political force in the state, but because others, mainly Quakers and Episcopalians, had united against them, it was time to start schools, "the true nurseries of power and influence." Because the Presbyterians enjoyed a majority in the Pennsylvania Assembly, now was the time to draft a charter for a new college.

Accordingly, Rush set out to raise money for a church, a chapel, a library, a laboratory, and a classroom building. He specifically left out dormitories, because he thought they were only for monks; the boys would live with families instead. The legislature was initially hostile to his plan. Many members thought a college in Cumberland County would divide the Presbyterians and would ultimately fail financially. Besides, they said, Rush was obviously in high dudgeon because of his recent departure from the medical college over his opposition to its medical practices, and they cited in particular his dispute over the efficacy of smallpox inoculation.

Although the Philadelphia leadership opposed the Presbyterians of Cumberland County, the Presbyterians themselves, after a period of some uncertainty, finally asked Rush to draw up a petition for a charter, which he did and sent to the legislature. Crucial to the project, he knew, was to persuade John Armstrong, a wealthy landowner and influential member of the assembly who did not want competition with Princeton. In March 1783 Rush appealed to Armstrong's pecuniary interests; he told him if the commonwealth agreed a college was crucial for central Pennsylvania, men like Armstrong could capitalize on its construction by purchasing land in the area. This was, after all, precisely what had happened in the area around Princeton, New Jersey. "The value of the land in the neighborhood of Princeton before the College was erected there was from £3/0/–4/0/ an acre. It has risen in the space of five years to £8/0/0 and £10/0/0 per acre, which is £5/0/0 an acre more than land sells for in the neighborhood of most of the villages in New Jersey." Shortly afterward, Rush's friend John Montgomery, a Scotch-Irish emigrant to Carlisle and also a member of the assembly, suggested that if Armstrong were promised a place on the college's board of trustees, he would support the project. A month later the Carlisle Presbytery approved the plan, and twenty-four trustees, including Armstrong, were appointed to the board, which soon expanded to thirty when the board added a group of Germans whom they intended to solicit for funds. The final board totaled forty people and included several ministers from thirteen denominations.

Six months later, on September 9, 1783, the state assembly finally passed the college charter: "An Act for the Establishment of a College at the Borough of Carlisle, in the County of Cumberland, in the State of Pennsylvania." Rush told Granville Sharp that Dickinson College had been named for "the illustrious Pennsylvania farmer, who is now Governor of our state, and who has contributed very liberally towards the institution. It bids fair from its situation to spread the light of science and the gospel over those parts of our country that are at present inhabited by savages. Its charter is truly catholic—all religious societies having equal claims to the power and honors of the College." He asked Sharp to help him raise money in England, or at least to find people willing to contribute books or scientific instruments. There is no indication that Sharp was able to help him, but Richard Price told Rush that while he was delighted to learn not only of the success of establishing a college "in the back parts of Pennsylvania," he was thrilled that it was erected on "so liberal a plan as you describe." A year later Price sent the college a three-volume collection of Bishop Benjamin Hoadly's works. It is not exactly the collected works of Shakespeare or a Guttenberg Bible, but Price admired Hoadly, who died in 1761, as an opponent of divine right and an advocate of the consent of the governed, and it seems a fitting gift to the college.

Although underfunded, the college opened in the fall of the following year with ten students. Its first president, or principal—Rush preferred the Scottish usage—was Charles Nisbet, a Presbyterian minister from Scotland whom Rush had met when he was a student in Edinburgh. His salary was to be 250 pounds a year plus a house and 50 pounds for moving expenses. When Nisbet arrived in June 1785, Rush introduced him to Franklin, who had just returned from France and had just succeeded John Dickinson as president of the Executive Council.

Unfortunately, all was not well in Carlisle. Nisbet was shocked to find how poorly funded the college was, and he detested the house provided for him. Moreover, when he arrived in Carlisle he found the warm, humid July weather to be quite unpleasant. Even worse, he felt sick. So in October he resigned, and the college agreed to reimburse him for his expenses for his return to Scotland. However, he never left. As the fall weather was approaching and turning considerably cooler, and because he did not know whether his pulpit was still open in Montrose, Scotland, he decided to stay in Carlisle for a while. His relationship with the board was never good after that, and he often had conflicts with the liberal Rush (Nisbet was very conservative). But the college was launched.

Four years later Rush helped found another college, this one for the German population of Central Pennsylvania. The stimulus came from the German-speaking Lutherans who were prevalent throughout the area but feared if their children were admitted to Dickinson, the faculty would segregate them from the English-speaking students; this had been their experience at the University of Pennsylvania, when a separate department had been created just for them. Thus, they lobbied for a college in the heart of German-speaking or Pennsylvania Dutch country (the "Dutch" in "Pennsylvania Dutch" has nothing to do with Holland at all, but is a corruption of *Deutsch,* meaning German). These people were from a conglomeration of settlements, estimated to be at least half the entire population in the central part of the state; they included the Amish, the Mennonites, the Dunkards, the River Brethren, the Lutherans, the Moravians, and the Schwenkfelders. They wanted to locate their college in either Mannheim or Lancaster.

In 1785, under the pseudonym of "A Friend to Equal Liberty and Learning in Pennsylvania," Rush wrote a short argument in favor of a college for German-speaking students. He claimed and advocated it should be sectarian, because that would encourage learning, and if each religious sect "takes care of its own youth, the whole republic must soon be well educated. It has been found by experience that harmony and Christian friendship between the different religious societies is best promoted by their educating their youth in separate schools."

Reminiscent of recent debates in contemporary American politics about making English the official language of the United

States (or even individual states), some Pennsylvanians asked whether it was a good idea to create a college for its German-speaking citizens. How dedicated were these people to their own language rather than to English, and would not such a college perpetuate their separateness to the extent that they never learned English? Rush met this argument head-on: "Some narrow-minded people have said that if the Germans have a college of their own, it will be the means of keeping up their *language* in our country, and therefore advise that they should send their sons to the English colleges in Philadelphia and Carlisle. But this objection should have no weight."

They would learn a great many things in college, yes, in their own native language, Rush argued, but in the end they would also learn the necessity of knowing English: "A thirst for learning excited by German books will naturally lead them to study the English language for the sake of becoming acquainted with English authors who abound with knowledge in all arts and sciences." When Rush's opponents asked whether such a college led to the decline in the number of farmers by turning them into scholars, he incredulously responded, this was nonsense: "What! The agriculture of the state will always keep pace without improvements in the arts and sciences." Within a year, a charter was drawn up, and the Pennsylvania Assembly approved it in March 1787. Named in honor of Benjamin Franklin, it was called Franklin College (it only became Franklin and Marshall after its merger with Marshall College in 1853). Like Dickinson, it had little money and could boast of only good (though unknown) prospects and a good will for the future—similar to Franklin, Rush was an expert at founding institutions but not at running them; this, he left to others and to future generations.

Like Rush, the Marquis de Condorcet believed education was necessary to republican training. He envisioned a new day with a state-sponsored civic educational system from primary grades through university training.

Interestingly, Condorcet hated his early Jesuit training, which he said was the surest method "for reducing man to the intellectual level of the beast." In a moment of surefire rage and overstatement, he claimed it was "a moral education fit to make debauched and hypocritical atheists or fanatically bigoted imbeciles; a philosophical education comprised of scholastic jargon and theological dreams; a close educational environment calculated to foster and perpetuate the adolescent tendency to homosexuality." Things were different for him at the College of Navarre, largely because of his friendship with the mathematician the Abbé Georges Girault de Kéroudon, whose enormous influence started him on probability theory and a spectacular academic career.

Condorcet's disgust at his early educational experiences was not unique. Debate about the proper course of education had been seething in France since mid-century as a reaction to Jesuit-controlled instruction in the schools. Railing against an education system dominated by the Church and its clergy, some intellectuals, and Condorcet counted himself among them, demanded a good education focused on secular subjects that promoted moral and political values. For Condorcet, education should ultimately be founded on human reason, and not on the "superstitions" of religion. The court physician François Quesnay, the founder of the Physiocratic school, and other Physiocrats, such as the Marquis de Mirabeau and La Mercier de la Rivière, all a generation older than Condorcet, had earlier argued along these same lines: education should sharpen a man's reason to prepare him to challenge not only the established church but governmental policies as well: "Enlightened public opinion, perpetuated by instruction, would oppose the errors of the administration; and an administration recruited only for its knowledge of the natural social order would oppose the errors of the government."

One indication of high achievement in education in eighteenth-century France was admission to one of the academies of science; for Condorcet, that meant the *Académie royale des sciences*. Serving in the *Académie* was tantamount to a second positive educational experience and he understood it was an institution that furthered the scientific and technical goals of the government. If we compared the major publications of the English Royal Society of London and the French *Académie royale*, we would see that the *Philosophical Transactions* often consisted of letters and material written by amateur rather than professional scientists, whereas the *Histoire et Mémoires* was a journal solely dedicated to the publication of work by professional scientists. As the *Académie* fell under the domain of the scientific establishment, it became increasingly difficult for non-professional or nonworking scientists, or scientists whose ideas were outside the mainstream, to break through its barriers to become members. (This is precisely why Marat and Mesmer had so much difficulty with the *Académie* in the 1780s.)

To further the interests of the scientific profession, the French government provided subsidies in the form of stipends to senior scientists to pursue their work and fund their attendance at meetings of the *Académie*. The *Académie*'s members were grouped into divisions, depending on their specialty, with a hierarchy of rank, dependent on the prestige and seniority of the scientists (*pensionnaires,* associates, and adjuncts or foreigners). After he became the *Académie*'s permanent secretary, Condorcet received no stipend. Actually only the *pensionnaires* (those counted as the senior scientists) were compensated, receiving one thousand livres a year. The permanent secretary's duties included the collection of data from those who claimed to have made new scientific discoveries, and organizing them chronologically so there was clear evidence of who submitted material first. In this way, if there ever were disputes, an *Académie* commission or committee could scrutinize the published material.

On the other hand, the *Académie* awarded no degrees or certificates, nor did it financially support full-time professional scientists on a day-to-day basis. Its main function was to allow for the interchange of ideas and for younger scientists to work with and share their work with the more senior members. The single most important element in its admission process was competence, not birth, wealth, status, or rank (which was directly in line with Condorcet's politics of rationality). Hence, one of the most important and crucial roles that the *Académie* played was to distinguish sense from nonsense and to determine which scientific efforts were truly expert and which were fraudulent. This was its duty to the state and for the public good. The *Académie* had a scientific responsibility. It also clearly possessed an educational and social role as well, and Condorcet lathered in the bath of the *Académie*'s rich intellectual waters.

While true savants like Condorcet desperately wanted to see the free exchange of ideas, such an exchange under the ancien régime was regarded as a threat to the status quo and the government's authority. This was especially true when new ideas created a sense of skepticism about truth and, ultimately, about the government itself. The professional scientist did not care about riches, whereas the aristocrat cared only about wealth and the means of increasing it. The man of letters sought truth for the good of society, while the nobleman sought only his own truth for his own interests. The man of knowledge lived outside the court beyond the constricting social norms of society and among his fellow scientists in a community that was geared to the improvement of society. This open scientific community stimulated Condorcet's desire for universal education, but since the *Académie* was so restricted in its members, it remained the redoubt only for the elite scientific few.

In the mid-1780s Condorcet entered the forefront of the battle for an educated citizenry. Once there was an educated public, he believed, the new national and provincial assemblies could pass laws codifying the social and political goals of the middle class, who could participate in the political and social decision making through their vote. As he wrote in his 1786 panegyric biography of Turgot, "It is easy to establish assemblies; but their usefulness depends entirely on the education of their members and the spirit that animates them; and it was a question in France of giving a new education to an entire people, of creating in them new ideas while, at the same time, as they were being called to take on new functions."

No one in France called for universal education as strongly as Condorcet, not even the Physiocrats. Turgot had once advocated universal, free education, but no one went as far as Condorcet. He drafted his great work on public instruction when the 1791 constitution recognized France as a constitutional monarchy. He conceded that while this form of government was acceptable for the time being, it was only temporary. Only in a true republic (without a king) would the people be certain the law of reason applied to all educational policy. In other words, the nation would flourish only with enlightened bureaucratic institutions based on Condorcet's "technocratic creed": "The creed of men who are confident in their expertise, easy in the tradition of power, convinced that the problems of politics are susceptible of rational answers and systematic solutions." The educated and enlightened expert provided rational answers to most of the social and political ills society faced. Education, as a truly transforming agent for all people, was designed to end their public lives as *subjects* and change them into *citizens.* These new citizens concentrated not on the ancient languages and classics the Church had provided, but on the moral and physical sciences. The education of priests was no longer relevant (if it ever was).

Enlightened education was therefore imperative. Just look, Condorcet said in his report on public instruction, at what happened when ignorant men in power failed to understand how to oversee good government. Political breakdown, corruption, and ultimately collapse would occur, causing the terrible loss of life and property. This was revealed most explicitly and frighteningly during the 1775 bread riots after the disastrous grain harvest in France the previous year. This harvest led to a huge rise in the cost of wheat. In the Physiocratic tradition, Turgot, with Condorcet's insistence and support, implemented through the local *parlements* a new free market system, which directly opposed the old medieval "just" price system, a system that relied on fixed prices set by the governing authorities and beyond which no grain merchant could legally exceed. Now, prices were allowed to fluctuate higher or lower on the basis of market forces. When the harvest was bad (as it was in 1774), the price of bread suddenly shot up sky-high, and many people were hurt when their stores of grain and the bakeries were cleaned out. One result was that peasants often seized control of the grain storage racks, rioted and burned buildings and homes, and even attempted to murder (or even succeeded in murdering) their landlords. Many people were arrested and a few executed once the troops restored order.

Turgot was disgraced, but Condorcet threw all of the blame for the resulting chaos and upheaval on Turgot's rival and successor, Jacques Necker, who had denounced free trade in grain just two months before the riots broke out. For Necker, price regulation and controls were imperative, because they kept everything "standardized." Even better, they kept the poor in their place. Besides, he argued, free trade in grain only hurt the poor, because prices were always rising anyway.

Condorcet vehemently disagreed. He took Necker on directly, arguing times had changed, it was a time of freedom, and free trade was the order of the day. He said it was now time to revise the tax laws, so the burden fell on the rich, not the poor; it was time to make the laws more amenable to the poor; it was time to revise the criminal justice system so that it was fair and equitable; and finally, it was time to create a system of free public education to raise the poor into the mainstream of society. Progress and the improvement of mankind were possible only if we dared take the right steps to educate the citizenry. "If hope of the people's happiness is a mistake, it is the only useful one, the only one that must not be taken away from mankind."

For Condorcet, education held the key to freedom and a rational society. Through education and enlightenment, the poor would become citizens and would respect property and property rights even more. They would become firm supporters of all social structures and institutions. Not least, as good republicans, they would become good citizens.

Condorcet had only a brief opportunity to try to implement his ideas of universal education and link the academies to it. During the short-lived Girondin ministry in the spring of 1792 with the moderates in power, Condorcet set to work on his ideas about public instruction. On October 30, 1791, he became the head of the Committee of Public Instruction. The 1791 constitution decreed free public education for all citizens, and Charles-Maurice Talleyrand had initially submitted a plan along these lines, but the assembly failed to act on it. Earlier that year, Condorcet had prepared for this assignment in five essays that appeared as *La Bibliothèque de l'homme public* (the library of the public man). At the committee's first meeting, in April 1792, he submitted "The Report and Project on the General Organization of Public Instruction" to the assembly. He was optimistic the delegates would accept his ideas exactly as he proposed them. But he would be sorely disappointed.

Based in part on Talleyrand's failed plan, Condorcet's vision surpassed it in scale and vision. Its basic principle was, as he had argued all along, that education should be universal, free, equal, and complete. An enlightened system of education promoted individualism and progress in ways that allowed people to achieve their greatest potential in whatever occupation or profession they chose. A primary school for all children between the ages of six and ten years old would teach them to read, write, and count, and learn about elementary morality. A secondary education for children ten to thirteen (today's contemporary French *lycées*) would teach them history, geography, the principles of the mechanical arts, drawing, mathematics, physics, natural history, and a foreign language. Secondary schools would also build on the primary schools' lessons on morality and social science.

In addition, there would be professional institutes to train people in particular trades and industry, because some citizens would be less capable of going on to the highest level, the university (which he actually called, by the way, the *lycée*), where students would prepare for careers in teaching and research, the two key elements of a wholly enlightened society. Above this educational scheme reigned the academies, one in every capital city of each department. In Paris there was the supreme academy, which he said should be called the "National Society for the Arts and Sciences." This society covered "the entire realm of the former academies, front and center of Enlightenment, playing in education a double role of inspiration and regulation."

All of this was to be without cost to families who sent their children to these schools. Poor children would receive the same education and opportunities as children from wealthy families. Children in the countryside would be treated no differently than those in the cities. While Condorcet claimed that public education served no particular political doctrine, because it was politically neutral, he truly meant for it to be the foundation of a republic. Education in the social sciences—that is, in politics and society—would be as precise and perfect as that in the natural sciences. Now it was time to stop humanity from being divided into two groups: those who reasoned and those who believed; those who were masters and those who were slaves.

Condorcet maddeningly declined, or refused, to say how it all could be paid for. Perhaps he never really gave the financial aspects of his national public educational plan much thought. In any case, he designed what he thought was a truly enlightened education not for a monarchy, but for a republic, toward which France was rapidly moving. The Legislative Assembly officially declared France a republic in August 1792 after the king was finally overthrown. Men and women who were able to perform the simplest mathematical calculations were now no longer dependent on anyone for their health and happiness. Men and women who were familiar with the rudiments of civil law were no longer dependent on a corrupt legal profession. Corrupt and tyrannical politicians could never again dupe the men and women equipped with reason. In short, these men and women possessed everything necessary to be at once fathers and mothers to their families and citizens of their country. It was to be *"l'école de la République,"* the school for the republic.

Condorcet did not live to see this plan implemented or even much discussed. The Legislative Assembly never seriously considered it, because a new national convention was elected to write a republican constitution. When the convention finally got around to discussing a variant of Condorcet's educational plan, the deputies misunderstood it and simply dismissed it as being too elitist and hierarchical, lacking in equality, "an insidious effort to replace the corporate tyranny of priests with that of an aristocracy of savants." By then, other pressing matters rapidly came before the fragile government: the trial of the king and his execution, the external war with the European powers, the internal war with the counterrevolutionaries, and a badly failing economy. And the Reign of Terror was looming in the near future. Only in 1795, in Year III of the Republic, did the Directory finally put Condorcet's ideas into effect.

As we have seen, for all of Benjamin Franklin's visionary friends (and for Franklin himself), a good education produced an informed, public-spirited citizenry. How else could the people know the issues confronting them, how to discuss them in public places, or even vote for a candidate who was most capable of solving social and economic ills? Education was most often defined in terms quite different from how Americans define it now (as a system of stepped levels leading to a university or graduate degree); a more expansive concept, eighteenth-century education included life experiences; broad reading in literature, science, and history; and a focused attention on current events at home and abroad.

For Mary Wollstonecraft, radical feminist writer and herself a governess and schoolmistress, education should be equal for boys and girls; after all, they both faced the same hostile and unforgiving world. In 1786 her *Thoughts on the Education of Daughters* was an unusual and even startling work for its time, focusing on the inherent equality of boys and girls. She would later develop this idea even further in her famous *A Vindication of the Rights of Woman*, the earliest response to Burke's *Reflections*: "If girls were encouraged from their earliest to develop their minds, nourish ambitions and exercise their bodies exactly as boys were, said Mary, they would develop equal capacities and talents."

And yet, it would have been most unusual even for the most enlightened of Enlightenment men, the Englishman Daniel Defoe excepted, to advocate an absolute equal education for boys and girls, especially at the university level. Most eighteenth-century men argued that women's education began and ended by learning the stay-at-home tasks of homemaker and mother. They need not be educated for education's sake, as Wollstonecraft suggested, because they had no need to know about politics and government. Those affairs were exclusive to men, and, besides, women did not vote, hold office, or serve on juries.

While Franklin, Rush, and Jefferson were liberal thinkers who actively promoted educational institutions and even participated in founding new institutions of higher education, they argued that education for women should be limited to learning how to run the home and nurture the children, and little else. This meant learning to read and write and handle financial matters, but it did not mean receiving the same intensive education as boys. Women were to be adjuncts and helpmates to their husbands. At most, added Rush, women must approve a patriotic hero's work, indicating that women were part of homeland defense only as cheerleaders, and not as foot soldiers or line officers.

However, things were changing, as the duties of mothers changed; increasingly their task was to ensure the moral development of their children so that they, or the boys at least, were prepared to succeed their fathers in the running of the republic. Still, only the Marquis de Condorcet, among Franklin's most visionary friends, agreed with Wollstonecraft that men and women were fundamentally equal and deserved fundamentally equal treatment. In his *Journal of the Society of 1789,* he demanded that the government grant women full citizenship rights. What use was the Revolution, after all, if only men gained their rights, while some twelve million women were forgotten? "Women," he wrote, "having these same qualities [as men], must necessarily possess equal rights."

On this score he was alone among his colleagues. His examples were marvelous choices of the deeds of women and the misdeeds of men, projected onto a scrim that he himself had invented. Thus, Elizabeth I of England, Maria Theresa of France, and the two Catherines of Russia, all of whom rose to power by virtue of their royal birth, possessed great political leadership and courage. And Catherine Macaulay, the great Whig historian of England, would have "expressed her opinions in the House of Commons better than many representatives of the British nation," especially Edmund Burke; just after the appearance of Burke's *Reflections,* Condorcet wrote that Macaulay was obviously "as enthusiastic for liberty as Mr. Burke could be for tyranny." Indeed, Michel Montaigne's adopted daughter would have defended the rights of French citizens far better than the king's counselor, the Duc de Courtin, who still believed in magic and the occult. Madame Lambert would never have drafted the absurd laws that the Keeper of the Seals did when he criminalized "Protestants, robbers, smugglers, and Negroes." In short, women "know how to love liberty, although they do not share all its advantages," and they never shirked their civic responsibilities, even when men did. "They have demonstrated the virtues of citizens whenever chance or civil troubles have brought them upon a scene from which the pride and the tyranny of men have excluded them in all nations."

If education were not reformed to include women at all levels of public instruction, then Condorcet advocated stripping from all ignorant workingmen the rights denied to women, because those workmen, too, were uneducated. They were too busy either to "acquire knowledge [or] exercise their reason. Soon, little by little, only persons who have taken a course in public law would be permitted to be citizens. If such principles are admitted, we must, as a natural consequence, renounce any idea of a free constitution," leaving government only to "aristocracies," which "have had nothing but similar pretexts as their foundation or excuse" to exclude others. In the end, "Condorcet affirmed the necessity of immediately dispensing a public education to women, and this would not merely guarantee the good fortune of the household. When he set forth the different levels of instruction, he made the education of girls in the primary years a social obligation and introduced the idea of mixed classes."

Condorcet's ideas of women's civic and political equality were met mostly with a cold silence, and his political reputation suffered for it. On the other hand, these ideas stimulated some discussion, and a few new societies for the advancement of women's rights were formed (though the Jacobins shut them all down in October 1793, at the height of the Terror).

A Dutch-born widow whose husband had been a baron founded one of them: Etta Palm d'Aelders created a women's patriotic society in 1790, but she became the target of such calumny that she left France permanently in 1793. The doomed activist Théroigne de Méricourt, who cofounded the *Société des Amies des Lois,* wanted to see armed women fighting at the front for *la République.* No one listened; she died in prison at the Salpêtrière. And the great feminist and radical Olympe de Gouges, herself a victim of the Terror, rewrote the Declaration of the Rights of Man and Citizen as *"Les droits de la femme et de la citoyenne,*" substituting the word "woman" wherever "man" appeared. Like these women, Condorcet was ahead of his time. According to his biographers, "the times were just not ripe for the cause of the equality of the sexes." But he was what a later century would call a feminist, something we might again attribute in part to the influence of his young, intellectual and liberal wife, Sophie.

At any rate, it was clear to Condorcet that a woman's right to vote depended on her being adequately educated. Moreover, educational equality improved the schools and universities, because it allowed the meritocracy to flourish. Along those lines, Condorcet advocated women as teachers, and there already were women teachers in Italy. "Several women," he pointed out, "have occupied chairs in the most famous Italian universities. They have fulfilled with distinction the duties of professor in the most elevated sciences without causing the slightest inconvenience or encountering the slightest opposition—without even being the butt of humor— in a country which can scarcely be regarded as free from prejudices or characterized by a simplicity of purity of manners." He noted that Laura Bassi had been an anatomy professor, and Françoise Agnesi had been a mathematics professor at the University of Bologna.

If women deserved education, and if they could even become professors, then why not allow them to participate in government? Here Condorcet equivocated. As noted, he included no right of women to vote or hold office in his draft of the new republican constitution of 1793. Perhaps it was because the politics of the time told him proposing women's suffrage was pointless. Or perhaps it was because of his theories of mathematics and education. Women first needed to have a minimum intellectual ability, which they did have, but also to acquire a general education, which very few possessed. In his 1785 essay "On the application of Mathematics to the Theory of Decision Making," Condorcet had argued that legislators would make the right decision only if they understood what to do as a matter of justice and truth, that is, if they had a fully developed rational faculty. This required at least an elementary level of education. They must therefore be a fairly homogeneous group. Women did yet not fit in, which was why he said that women must have an opportunity to acquire equal education. Once there was an educated class of women, they would certainly gain the right to vote and hold office. Nonetheless, though they could be citizens in the short term, they would only get the vote in the long term.

Condorcet was clearly ahead of his time, as full equality in education had to wait until the twentieth century. While Franklin, Jefferson, and Rush at least considered the role of women's education in the new republic, only Condorcet was thinking and writing about the full and equal education of women.

Epilogue

⣰⣰⣰

A Future of Progress, Liberty, and Justice

Benjamin Franklin was an optimist, a curious optimist fascinated by the unlimited possibilities a human being could achieve. Just perform good deeds, as Cotton Mather had taught him, and the world in its entirety would improve. Franklin undertook this enormous task in the three main venues of his life: America, England, and France. Proud as he was to be an American, his bonds to England and France were deeply and affectionately rooted. There is no doubt he enjoyed the company of the rich and famous. As the son of a candle and soap maker, he was wolfishly upwardly mobile. While he always strove to improve his lot, to call him a social climber does him an injustice, though he probably saw himself that way. He was always trying to better himself intellectually, professionally, and financially, and he did just that, just as he wanted to help stimulate progress—with his inventions and scientific discoveries, his statesmanship at home and abroad, his writings on politics and society. He was a visionary. Unlike those in this book, however, Franklin was never really at heart a true revolutionary. He might have revolutionized science, developed revolutionary ideas to coincide with the American and French Revolutions, and invented revolutionary items, but he was no social or even political radical.

He was, after all, a late bloomer when it came to opposing slavery. (Here he was not alone; so was his younger visionary friend Benjamin Rush, and Thomas Paine rarely addressed the issue.) But once Franklin fully understood how despicable slavery and the slave trade were, he attacked both of them on moral principles; as he always said, it was never too late to act on good moral principles. In this respect, others of his friends and colleagues were far in advance of him. Benezet and Sharp and the Frenchmen Condorcet and Brissot never hesitated to undermine the institution as vigorously as they possibly could.

Of the events in Franklin's life, none had greater impact on him than the revolutions in America and France. Despite his lack of a revolutionary frame of mind, he reveled in them. He hoped with all his might that they would be successful in overthrowing tyranny and privilege. Largely because they did triumph, he was convinced that a general progression throughout the world toward liberty and justice was inevitable. And yet, an underlying ambivalence always seemed to overtake him. He was not an immediate sponsor of America's separation from Britain, for example, and once the revolution in France was under way, in the last year of his long life, he hesitated. He marveled that the French had acted at all to bring freedom to a nation dominated by royalty and nobility, but in the same breath he hoped it would all work out in the best interests, as he put it, of both king and the nation.

As for the first of these, in January 1774, he was still a strong supporter of the British Empire and believed America should remain a strong anchor in the imperial regime. This began to change when, as the agent for Massachusetts, he was called before the Privy Council in the Cockpit (so-called because it had once been the location in Henry VIII's palace reserved for cock-fighting) to present arguments why the royal governor, Thomas Hutchinson, should be removed from office at the request of the Masschusetts Assembly. Shortly after his arrival, instead of addressing the issue itself directly, the Privy Council turned matters over to the solicitor general, the ambitious Scotsman Alexander Wedderburn, whose behavior was more conducive to a prosecutor than a hearing officer. Wedderburn was "one of the most formidable lawyer-orators in Britain." Franklin was shocked to listen to severe charges against him (the crux of the problem was that Franklin had stolen several incendiary letters between Hutchinson and Andrew Oliver, his son-in-law, who was the colony's lieutenant governor; while Franklin had insisted that the letters not be published, they were, and they served as the grounds on which the Massachusetts Assembly had acted).

Lashing out at Franklin in the most insulting language he could muster, Wedderburn spoke for over an hour. His blustery speech was full of insinuation and scorn: "My Lords, Dr. Franklin's mind may have been so possessed with the idea of a Great American Republic, that he may easily slide into the language of a minister of a foreign independent state." This "true incendiary" expected the letters to "blow up the province into a flame, which from thence was to have been spread over the other provinces." His small coterie of New England followers, who were now preparing a general uprising, learned their outrageous lessons well "in Dr. Franklin's school of Politics." But then Wedderburn shifted his position, turning contradictory. He accused Franklin of secretly wanting to have "Mr. Hutchinson displaced, in order to make room for Dr. Franklin as a successor." Could the solicitor general have it both ways: that Franklin wanted rebellion and the governor's chair? For Wedderburn, there was no inconsistency. The men of Boston wanted independence, and Franklin wanted the executive office, far from British control. In response to this invective, Franklin simply said nothing.

But even this remarkable event did not deter him from trying to reconcile England and America. After this humiliating moment, perhaps the lowest in Franklin's diplomatic career, he worked with the aging William Pitt, the Earl of Chatham, to convince the Lords to negotiate a deal with the Americans that would be equitable to both sides. When that effort failed, he spoke to Lord Admiral Richard Howe (who soon would be the commander in chief of British naval forces against the Americans during the Revolution); they secretly worked together to find a middle road that would satisfy both sides. But the British were simply uninterested.

When Franklin finally returned to America in January 1775, he was still convinced that the problems between America and England could be settled. In July he wrote to Howe saying he was deeply saddened that it appeared a break between the two sides was now inevitable: "Long did I endeavor with unfeigned and unwearied Zeal, to preserve from breaking, that fine and noble China Vase the British Empire: for I knew that being once broken, the separate Parts could not retain even their Share of the Strength or Value that existed in the Whole, and that a perfect Re-Union of those Parts could scarce even be hoped for." In the very next month, the king proclaimed the colonies to be in rebellion. Franklin was elected to the Second Continental Congress, where he drafted the Articles of Confederation.

In France, Franklin enjoyed the same noble company he had in London. He often met with the foreign minister, the Comte de Vergennes, and he often dined with his Passy neighbor, Louis-Guillaume Le Veillard. He had long conversations with the Physiocrat comptroller general, Anne-Robert Jacques Turgot, the finance minister, and he mingled with nobility at Madame Helvétius's salon and flirted with and wrote bagatelles (light essays usually containing a lesson) for Madame Brillon and others. He quite enjoyed attending the meetings of the *Académie royale des sciences,* where he talked with Condorcet, Le Roy, and Turgot. In 1767, when he traveled with the royal English court physician, John Pringle, to Versailles, he was presented to King Louis XV. He was obviously deeply moved and impressed: "He spoke to both of us very graciously and cheerfully [*sic*], is a handsome Man, has a very lively Look, and appears younger than he is." When in Paris as the American envoy to negotiate French support for America's war against England, Franklin could not but highly acclaim Louis XVI for agreeing to enter into a treaty of friendship and alliance with the Americans. "The friendly disposition of this court towards us continues. . . . This is really a generous nation, fond of glory, and particularly that of protecting the oppressed."

By the time the revolution broke out in France, in 1789, Franklin was already back in America with but a year left of his life. Even so, he heralded the coming of greater freedom to the nation he loved so dearly. Despite the initial violence and the deaths of many people, he was, as usual, optimistic. He told his English friend Benjamin Vaughn, "The revolution in France is truly surprising. I sincerely wish it may end in establishing a good constitution for that country." When the tumults became increasingly dangerous to life and limb, he still retained the hope that the outcome would be positive, but not to the extent that the revolutionaries would remove, or even attempt to remove, his hero, Louis XVI, who had helped the Americans during their war against Britain. And yet, he was clearly worried and wrote Vaughn, "The mischiefs and troubles it suffers in the operation, however, give me great concern." He told his old friend, Le Roy, who had not written to him in a year, "A great part of the news we have had from Paris, for near a year past, has been very affecting. I sincerely wish and pray it may all end well and happy," and notably, "for the King and the nation."

Missing from the equation in France's revolution, he went on, was a good dose of *philosophy,* by which he meant good rational, liberal, and progressive thinking. Once the French realized this, he later told David Hartley, then France, like America, would be a fit place for any Enlightened man. "God grant, that not only the Love of Liberty, but a thorough Knowledge of the Rights of Man, may pervade all the Nations of the Earth, so that a Philosopher may set his Foot anywhere on its Surface and say, 'This is my Country.'" Thomas Paine could not have said this any better. Nor, for that matter, could any of Franklin's Atlantic cousins. The only difference was that Franklin was still an admirer of Louis XVI; had Franklin lived, he undoubtedly would have mourned the king's execution.

Then again, Franklin's quite unvisionary friend Edmund Burke, raged against the Revolution, proclaiming that the Revolution in France had caused that nation to enter a period of "chaos and darkness." America in 1776 had been different. The American war against Britain never once threatened the English monarchy or social hierarchy of rank and privilege. If the Americans wanted to go it alone, said Burke, and withdraw from the empire, then let them. No real harm would be brought to Britain. On the other hand, Burke's famous attack on the revolution in France roundly condemned not only revolutions that destroyed centuries of institutional and cultural development, but also attacked the very people who fervently believed, as did Franklin and his Atlantic cousins, in the inevitability of human progress. For Burke, abstract ideas of freedom, rights, and justice ignored the long history of how the established order came into existence. Revolution, he predicted, led only to tragedy: "This new, and hitherto unheard of bill of rights, though made in the name of the whole people, belongs to those gentlemen and their faction only. The body of the people of England have no share in it. They utterly disclaim it." Revolutionaries therefore courted anarchy, war, upheaval, and confusion along with internecine and world war. The outcome ultimately, he predicted, was dictatorship.

Was Burke accurate in his forecast? After all, internal and

foreign enemies soon beset France, as war and civil war split the nation. And the nation fell into tyranny and, finally, the great Reign of Terror in 1793–1794, which ultimately led to the empire of Napoleon Bonaparte.

But Burke was not so right in the very end. Benjamin Franklin and his visionary friends—Rush and Paine in America, Price and Priestley in England, and Condorcet and Brissot in France—had the last word; England, France, and the rest of Western Europe, like the United States before them, became democratic nations that have recognized the centrality of human rights and human freedom. Even in light of continuing class and racial divisions, these nations have taken steps, however incremental, to achieve social equality and social justice. Burke might well have advocated change and reform that would take place so gradually over long periods of time that a person rarely discerns it in a lifetime. But Franklin's Atlantic cousins sought immediate changes, through revolution if necessary: the end of slavery and the slave trade; practical improvements for us to enjoy our daily life through developments in science, medicine, and technology; and the end of monarchy and rank and privilege.

Above all stood the increasingly critical role of education for all citizens, not just for the leisured and wealthy few. New ways of thinking were born in Franklin's eighteenth century, ways that promoted enlightenment and progress for the common people, those who, like Franklin himself, mostly came from humble origins or from middle-class backgrounds. It was the start of the modern era, with an emphasis on the worth of the individual human being. The goal was for all people to have the opportunity to achieve their greatest potential in whatever way they wanted to undertake. This is the visionary legacy left to us by Franklin and his Atlantic cousins.

Short Titles

Autobiography of Benjamin Rush. Corner, George W., ed. *The Autobiography of Benjamin Rush.* Princeton, NJ: Princeton University Press for the American Philosophical Society, 1948.

Autobiography of Joseph Priestley. Lindsay, Jack, ed. *Autobiography of Joseph Priestley.* Teaneck, NJ: Fairleigh Dickinson University Press, 1970.

Brissot, *Correspondance.* Perroud, Claude, ed. *J.-P. Brissot, Correspondance et papiers.* Paris: Librarie Alphonse Picard, 1911.

Brissot, *Mémoires.* Brissot, Jacques-Pierre. *J.-P. Brissot: Mémoires, publiés avec Étude critique et notes,* ed. Claude Perroud, 2 vols. Paris: Librarie Alphonse Picard, 1911.

Condorcet: Selected Writings. Baker, Keith Michael, ed. *Condorcet: Selected Writings.* Indianapolis: Bobbs-Merrill, 1976.

Correspondence of Richard Price. Peach, W. Bernard, and D. O. Thomas, ed. *The Correspondence of Richard Price,* 3 vols. Durham: Duke University Press, 1981, 1983, 1994.

Letters of Benjamin Rush. Butterfield, L. H., ed. *Letters of Benjamin Rush,* 2 vols. Princeton, NJ: Princeton University Press for the American Philosophical Society, 1951.

Oeuvres de Condorcet. Condorcet-O'Connor A., and M. F. Arago, ed. *Oeuvres de Condorcet,* Nouvelle impression en facsimile de l'édition Paris, 1847–1849, 12 vols. Stuttgart-Bad Cannstatt: Friedrich Frommann Verlag, 1968.

Papers. Labaree, Leonard W., et al., eds. *The Papers of Benjamin Franklin,* 36 vols. to date. New Haven, CT: Yale University Press, 1959– .

Works of Joseph Priestley. Rutt, John Towill, ed. *The Theological and Miscellaneous Works of Joseph Priestley,* 25 vols. in 26. Hackney, 1816–1831.

Writings. Lemay, J. A. Leo., ed. *Benjamin Franklin: Writings.* New York: Library of America, 1987.

Writings of Benjamin Franklin. Smyth, Albert Henry, ed. *The Writings of Benjamin Franklin,* 10 vols. New York: Macmillan, 1905–1907.

Writings of Thomas Paine. Foner, Philip S., ed. *The Complete Writings of Thomas Paine,* 2 vols. New York: Citadel Press, 1945.

Notes

Prologue

p. 2. Radical was a term: *The Oxford English Dictionary (O.E.D.)*, 8:99. See J. C. D. Clark, 2000, 374–422, and Burke, 2001, 110 (from Jonathan Clark's introduction).

p. 3. Rights and privileges by heredity: Franklin to Sarah Bache, Jan. 26, 1784, in *Writings*, 1085–86. See Wills, 1984, for the Washington connection.

p. 4. First, we find him among his friends: Kammen, 1968.

p. 6. All were intellectual men of action: Pocock, 1999, 1:5.

p. 7. They were what the eighteenth century called: Postman, 1999, 103, and generally 103–11. See also Commager, 1978, 257, and generally 256–66, which comprises his definition of "philosophe."

p. 7. Based on ideas that Franklin: Isaacson, 2003, 55–60, E. Morgan, 2002, 49–49, Brands, 2000, 92–93, and I. Cohen, 1953, 113–14. As a boy, Franklin was deeply impressed by Mather's *Bonifacius: An Essay Upon the Good*. Cohen sees Mather's work as one of the influences that stimulated Franklin to form the Junto; the other one was Defoe's *Essay upon Projects*. See I. Cohen, 1953, 146–47, and D. Anderson, 1997, 16–24. For a full-length study, see Breitwieser, 1984.

p. 7. As he bluntly told: Franklin to Joseph Huey, June 6, 1753, in *Writings*, 476. See de Lagrave, 2003.

p. 7. Church ministers in the eighteenth century: On Latitudinarianism, see Kroll, Ashcraft, and Zagorin, 1992.

p. 8. All of them wholly encompassed Washington's adage: Washington to George Washington Parke Custis, Nov. 28, 1796, in ed. J. Fitzpatrick, 1931–1944, 35:295.

p. 8. Because Franklin lived: For an account of his British friendships alone, see Labaree, "Benjamin Franklin's British Friendships," 423–27.

p. 8. Historian Daniel Royot said: Royot, 1993, 91.

p. 9. Nor is there any evidence: Fortune and Warner, 1999, 9–11.

p. 9. History presents him as having: Jennings, 1996, and Middlekauff, 1996. See also Wood, 2004, 4–8, for the criticism that he was "lacking elegance" or wound up being "a lackey of capitalism."

p. 9. Everyone knows that no matter: D. Morgan, 1996.

p. 9. As a model of the good citizen: George Washington, *Farewell Address*, Sept. 19, 1796, in ed. J. Fitzpatrick, 1931–1944, 35:229 (for the *Address* in its entirety, see 35:214–28).

p. 10. He negotiated treaties: Ketchum, 2002.

p. 10.   But as his inclination: On the role of the colonial agent, see Kammen, 1968.

p. 11.   His numerous inventions: I. Cohen, 1956, 29. For a modern edition of Franklin's scientific work, see I. Cohen, 1941.

p. 11.   Most Americans know Franklin: Tucker, 2003.

p. 11.   As a prolific writer: On the difficulty in determining which anonymous pieces Franklin might have written, see Lemay, 1986.

p. 11.   *Poor Richard's Almanack:* Franklin's *Autobiography* has become part of American literary iconography. See Seavey, 1988. For the latest annotated edition, including excerpts from Franklin's journal and correspondence, see Zall, 2000. For the "generic" text, see Lemay and Zall, ed., 1981, and for the standard text, see Labaree, et al., ed., 1964.

p. 12.   There was hardly a subject: On the bagatelles, see Brands, 2000, 566–69, Granger, 1964, 181–208, Aldridge, 1957, 159–87, and Lemay, "The Public Writings and the Bagatelles," 1979, 153–60.

p. 12.   Some claim he embellished: C. Jordan, 1989, 27–57 (the quotation is on page x), and Granger, 1964, 209–38.

p. 12.   Perhaps his obsession: Jennings, 1996.

p. 12.   When Adams arrived in France: Middlekauff, 1996, and McCullough, 2001.

p. 12.   Franklin himself once noted: Franklin, *Autobiography,* in *Writings,* 1463, and Paine, "Address and Declaration at a Select Meeting of the Friends of Universal Peace and Liberty" (1791), in *Writings of Thomas Paine,* 2:536.

p. 13.   It was a time of innovation: Franklin's scientific work has been widely explored, but no one has investigated this subject, especially the electrical side of Franklin, with greater elegance, detail, or depth than the preeminent historian of science, I. Bernard Cohen. See his unsurpassed edition of 1941, and his books (1956 and 1990). For the general background, see Fara, 2002.

p. 13.   Alexis de Tocqueville could have been thinking: De Tocqueville, "Philosophical Method of the Americans," 1945, Pt. II, Bk.I, 4.

p. 14.   With the Revolution in France: For a comparative treatment of the American and French Revolutions, see Dunn, 1999.

p. 16.   Unlike its French counterpart: Hunter, 1982, 6.

p. 17.   Franklin called it: The classic study remains Crane, Apr. 1966, 210–33.

p. 17.   There you would also find: For a full list of the members, see D. Thomas, 1977, 142–43.

p. 17.   Once Boswell noted: Boswell, 1956, 319.

p. 17.   Franklin did not smoke: Quoted in Van Doren, 1938, 422, 770.

p. 18.   One of the most fascinating aspects: Lopez, 2000, ch. 17, where she argues that Franklin's change from slave owner to abolitionist did not fully take place until after he met Condorcet in France in the 1780s, and Lopez and Herbert, 1975, 291–302.

p. 18.   In time, however: Waldstreicher, 2004.

p. 18.   Attitudes began to change: Soderlund, 1985.

p. 18.   According to David Brion Davis: D. Davis, 1975, 44.

p. 19.   "For it is self-evident": Price, 1784, 68.

Chapter 1. Three Men and the Horrors of Slavery:
Whitefield, Benezet, and Sharp

p. 23.   Each in his own way: For many people, the slave trade was far worse than slavery; the transport of thousands of blacks from Africa under the most horrid conditions imaginable outweighed their enslavement, because people actually believed that living as a slave in a white world actually improved their living conditions when compared to their life in Africa.

p. 23.   The great outdoor English Methodist: Stout, 1991, 220–33.

p. 24.   Dedicating themselves: Lambert, 1999, 93.

p. 24.   A thunderous and charismatic speaker: Butler, 2000, 202–03, who includes the comparison with modern evangelists.

p. 24.   He found that Whitefield: Franklin, *Autobiography*, in *Writings*, 1406.

p. 25.   In recovering from the measles: Belcher, 1857, 470. A squint, or what in medical terms is called *strabismus*, means that one of the eyes is directed obliquely. To say a person is "cross-eyed" is therefore not quite accurate, but this phrase is used in ordinary language in the United States. For an analysis of the squint, culture, and personality in this period, see West, Fall 1999, 65–84, esp. 71, when she deals with Whitefield's squint and its depiction in artistic, dramatic, or comedic caricature by one's enemies as a feature indicating deception and dishonesty.

p. 25.   It is said that Whitefield's severe comportment: It was not always this way with Franklin, because he once thought Whitefield was a fraud and possibly an embezzler, but that was before he met him. See Heimert, 1966, 161 n299, 368. The Walpole remark is to be found in ibid., 229. For the view that after 1741, Franklin opposed Whitefield and the Awakening preachers, see Buxbaum, 1975. For their friendship, see D. Morgan, 1985, 208–18.

p. 26.   Here we see the origins: Bonomi, 1986.

p. 26.   According to a contemporary of Whitefield's: Belcher, 1857, 459–60, for both the Garrick and Beaumont remarks.

p. 26.   A friend of his once claimed: Lambert says that Whitefield made the claim. See Lambert, 1999, 100, whereas Dallimore, 1971, 1:296, says others made it.

p. 26.   From this distance: Franklin, *Autobiography*, in *Writings*, 1409.

p. 27.   In Philadelphia, his words: Belcher, 1857, 102, citing John Watson, *Annals of Philadelphia, and Pennsylvania, in the Olden Time* (Philadelphia, 1857).

p. 27.   On hearing him preach: Franklin, *Autobiography*, in *Writings*, 1406 (emphasis in the original). That Whitefield actually used this phrase (from Luke 18:9–14), see Zall, 2000, 139.

p. 27.   He once wrote: Dallimore, 1971, 1:433, quoted from *George Whitefield's Journals, 1737–41*, William V. Davis, intro. (Gainesville, FL: 1969), 345.

p. 27.   He said if the building: Dallimore, 1971, 1:568–69, from the *Pennsylvania Gazette*, Dec. 4, 1740.

p. 27.   The building was also to house: Apparently two groups working together were able to fund the construction of the New-Building: one that had an interest in the education of children, the other that wanted a place for Whitefield to preach. The former group won out in 1750 with the establishment of the Philadelphia Academy. See *Papers*, 2:290, nt.

p. 28. Writing in 1747: Quoted in Dallimore, 1980, 2:222, from a letter at the American Philosophical Society.

p. 28. In 1765 the young Benjamin Rush: Rush to Ebenezer Hazard, May 21, 1765, in *Letters of Benjamin Rush*, 1:14.

p. 28. One woman remarked: Quoted in Belcher, 1857, 465.

p. 28. Not so Franklin: Franklin, *Autobiography*, in *Writings*, 1408. Nor apparently did his preaching affect Dr. Johnson. See ed. Pottle and Bennett, 1936, 20.

p. 28. Or, as one of Whitefield's biographers: Stout, 1991, 2202–21.

p. 29. In fact, the preacher often: On the western colony with Whitefield, see D. Morgan, 1996, 73.

p. 29. Whitefield continually reported: *George Whitefield's Journals*, 357, and *Letters of George Whitefield for the Period 1734–1742*, 226.

p. 29. By May of 1740: Lambert, 1994, 114–22.

p. 29. As Frank Lambert: Ibid., 128. For an account of how Whitefield used the press, especially Franklin's *Pennsylvania Gazette* and other news outlets and then how Franklin, in turn, used Whitefield for his own enterprises, see Lambert, 1994, ch. 3.

p. 29. "Your dogs are caressed": Quoted in Dallimore, 1971, 1:496, from, *To the Inhabitants of Maryland, Virginia, and North and South Carolina Concerning Their Negroes, Works of George Whitefield*, 4:35–41.

p. 30. We could, of course: Shyllon, 1977, 13–14.

p. 30. We do have, however: Franklin, *Observations Concerning the Increase of Mankind*, 1751, in *Writings*, 367–74.

p. 32. In 1723: D. Morgan, 1996, 63, 94.

p. 32. Samuel Johnson: On Franklin and Johnson, see Korshin, 1993, 33–48.

p. 32. The first schools for blacks: See Thompson, 1951, and idem., 1954.

p. 32. Deborah Franklin: Deborah Franklin to Franklin, Aug. 9, 1759, in *Papers*, 8:425 and n6.

p. 32. Like Whitefield: Franklin to John Waring, Dec. 17, 1763, in *Writings*, 799–800.

p. 33. Whitefield "held": Lambert, 1994, 204.

p. 33. As Whitefield himself noted: Cited in Dallimore, 1971, 1:495.

p. 33. Worse, he himself: Henry, 1957, 117.

p. 34. In 1770: Soderlund, 1985, 175.

p. 34. He was nearly always frail: G. Brookes, 1937, 38.

p. 34. He is also said: Whitney, 1942, 178.

p. 35. He was widely admired: Quoted in G. Brookes, 1937, 155.

p. 35. Benezet's wife: Ibid., 23–24.

p. 35. Rush, a devout Presbyterian: Rush to Sharp, May 13, 1774, and Rush to Sharp, Apr. 27–May 15, 1784, in ed. Woods, 5, 23.

p. 35. He said that he was deeply: Brissot de Warville, 1964, 217–18, 229.

p. 36. According to Rush: Quoted in G. Brookes, 1937, 138, 155.

p. 36. Franklin first came to know: Editor's Note, *Papers,* 2:125.

p. 36. He was also an early: Ibid., 5:327.

p. 36. A year later: Ibid.,6:369, n9; 424, n3.

p. 36. After some experience: Vaux, 1969, 22.

p. 37. He told Secker: Quoted in ibid., 25–26.

p. 37. Benezet's first major contribution: Anstey, 1975, 214–17.

p. 38. By 1772: Ibid., 239–41.

p. 39. The American (Franklin): Franklin, *A Conversation on Slavery,* Jan. 26, 1770, in *Writings,* 647–48.

p. 39. "To instruct, advise": Franklin, "An Address to the Public," Nov. 9, 1789, in *Writings,* 1154–55.

p. 39. Two years after: Nadelhaft, July 1966, 193–208. For a study of Sharp that appeared after the completion of this book, see Wise, 2005.

p. 39. "I am glad to hear": Franklin to Benezet, Aug. 22, 1772, in *Writings,* 876. According to Lopez and Herbert, Benezet may have been Deborah's cousin. See Lopez and Herbert, 1975, 298. The editors of the Franklin *Papers,* however, say that Deborah's cousin Elizabeth North married Anthony Benezet's brother, Daniel, making Elizabeth the cousin, not Anthony. See *Papers,* 18:90, n8.

p. 40. "By a late computation": Benezet to Franklin, Apr. 27, 1772, in *Papers,* 19:115.

p. 40. In May of 1772: Benezet to Granville Sharp, May 14, 1772, in G. Brookes, 1937, 291.

p. 40. By February of the next year: Franklin to Benezet, Feb. 10, 1773, in *Papers,* 20:41.

p. 40. Benezet immediately wrote: Benezet to Sharp, Apr. 4, 1773, in G. Brookes, 1937, 298.

p. 40. Franklin had already indicated: Franklin cited Sharp's work, *A Representation of the Injustices and Dangerous Tendencies of Tolerating Slavery,* in his *A Conversation on Slavery,* which appeared in the London *Public Advertiser,* June 26, 1770, reprinted in *Writings,*647.

p. 42. There were several mainstream Britons: Hudson, Summer 2001, 559–76.

p. 42. The family played: Lascelles, 1928, 119–26, 92.

p. 42. Sharp's American friend: Rush to Sharp, July 9, 1774, and then Rush to Sharp, Apr. 27–May 15, 1784, in Woods, ed., 1967, 6, 23. The second letter is in *Letters of Benjamin Rush,* 1:330–31. The first convention of the Protestant Episcopal Church of America met in Philadelphia in 1785.

p. 43. Sharp was deeply: Lascelles, 1928, 15.

p. 43. In *Taxation No Tyranny:* S. Johnson, in ed. Donald J. Greene, 1957, 10:454.

p. 43. He argued with all of them: Prince Hoare, 1828, 1:43, 53.

p. 45. It now appeared: For profiles of Sharp and Mansfield, see Gerzina, 1995, 90–132.

p. 45. Though undeterred: Prince Hoare, 1828, 1:66 note.

p. 45. He had written that: See Shyllon, 1977, 24. Shyllon points out that in a series of cases beginning in 1694, the chief justice Sir John Holt argued that slaves were free whenever they set foot on English soil, because "by the common law no man can have a property in another." But in 1729 these decisions were not regarded as precedent. (See Shyllon, 17.) The Blackstone quotation comes from Blackstone, 1978, 1:123.

p. 46. Catherine Macaulay called him: Quoted by Kulisheck, 1997, 437.

p. 46. More spectacularly: Hibbert, 1958.

p. 46. He was regarded: Gerzina, 1995, 95, 97.

p. 47. It was a curious: Heward, 1979. See also Oldham, 1992.

p. 47. Perhaps this is ultimately why: Oldham, Jan. 1988, 45. For the case law background of Somerset, see 48–49.

p. 47. "There have been many instances . . . . an age of darkness": Granville Sharp, *A Representation of the Injustice and Dangerous Tendency of Tolerating Slavery; of, or Admitting the Least Claim of Private Property in the Persons of Men in England* (London, 1769), 4–5, 112,126 cited in Hudson, Summer 2001, 569–70.

p. 48. Lord Mansfield, who heard the case: Oldham, Jan. 1988, 51–52.

p. 49. If Mansfield's attitude: See Prince Hoare's comment, 1828, 1:104 ("At length, the important case of James Somerset presented itself;—a case which is said to have been selected, at the mutual desire of Lord Mansfield and of Mr. Sharp").

p. 49. As historian Mark Weiner: Weiner, Apr. 2002, 127. Weiner points out that Stewart ultimately rose through the customs service to become the receiver-general of the Eastern Middle District covering a territory from Quebec to Virginia (p. 128). Stewart's name in the historical record also appears as "Steuart" and is even sometimes cited as "Stuart."

p. 50. In a note: Sharp to Hargrave, January 26, 1772, in Prince Hoare, 1828, 1:110. For the impact of the case in the American patriot press, see Bradley, 1998, 66–80.

p. 50. Hargrave was a perfect addition: Hargrave to Sharp, Jan. 31, 1772, in Prince Hoare, 1828, 1:111.

p. 50. In all: Prince Hoare listed them as Serjeant William Davy, Serjeant John Glynn, Francis Hargrave, James Mansfield (no relation to the chief justice, but a barrister who later became chief justice of the Court of Common Pleas), and a Mr. Alleyne (no first name was given). See Prince Hoare, 1828, 1:139; Shyllon, 1977, 28.

p. 50. Sharp himself: Weiner, Apr. 2002, 124.

p. 50. It was "a Brief": Quoted in Shyllon, 1977, 13.

p. 50. Would England allow a bashaw: Everyone understood the term "bashaw" in the English eighteenth century. It was used as an early variant of "pasha," a term of distinction. For Noah Webster, 1838, who used it in his famous "blue-backed" speller, it was a Turkish governor (see p. 72).

p. 52. "in the most wretched shaped . . . the man must be discharged": Prince Hoare, 1828, 1:116, 125, 126–27, 129, 132. The information concerning Dido comes from Oldham, Jan. 1988, 67, n74.

p. 52. In short: Quoted from the Mansfield decision in Nadelhaft, July 1966, 199. The actual legal meaning of this phrase as reported by five sources at the time is beyond the scope of this book, but see Oldham, Jan. 1988, 57–60, who settles on the report by Serjeant Hill, and Cotter, Feb. 1994, 31–56, esp. 39, who settles on court reporter Capel Loftt.

p. 52. He complained to Benezet: Franklin to Benezet, Aug. 22, 1772, in *Writings*, 876.

p. 52. The slave trade would not end: Historians have long debated the impact of Mansfield's 1772 ruling. For an argument that it in fact did not free the slaves, see Nadelhaft, July 1966, 193–94, 198; for an opposing view, see Lascelles, 1928, 33–34. For a full discussion of the debate, see Oldham, Jan. 1988, who argues that in the end, Mansfield fully believed "in the validity of slavery in England," even after Somerset.

p. 53. Still, his ruling: On the impact of Somerset in American law, see Wiecek, 1977, and Cover, 1975.

p. 53. "that the same humanity . . . on their posterity": Franklin, *The Somerset Case and the Slave Trade,* in *The London Chronicle,* June 20, 1772, in *Writings*, 677–78.

Chapter 2. Benjamin Rush, Religion, Revolution, and Medicine

p. 56. "Yes . . . I anticipate": Rush to Jeremy Belknap, June 21, 1792, in *Letters of Benjamin Rush,* 1:620.

p. 57. An admirer: The admirer was lawyer William Rawle. See Wharton, 1840, 57.

p. 58. In considering: Kloos, 1991, 1, 18–20. Kloos takes his title from a phrase Rush often used and derived from Lord Kames (see Kloos, 56).

p. 58. His writings attacked: *Letters of Benjamin Rush,* 1:lxviii, lxx.

p. 58. Rush thought that humans: Kloos, 1991, 46–49.

p. 59. He told his friend John Adams: Rush to Adams, Aug. 20, 1811, in *Letters of Benjamin Rush,* 2:1095. Although he suggested Adams write a posthumous address setting forth these virtues, he could have been addressing himself as well.

p. 59. As Benjamin Franklin once told him: Quoted in Van Doren, 1938, 770.

p. 59. While many physicians: "To His Fellow Citizens: Treatment of Yellow Fever," Sept. 12, 1793, and "To the College of Physicians: Use of the Lancet in Yellow Fever, Sept. 12, 1793, both from the *Federal Gazette,* in *Letters of Benjamin Rush,* 2:660–62.

p. 59. "He was idolized": N. Goodman, 1934, 402, who said that Rush's friend Thomas Ruston first called Rush "the Sydenham of America," and Flexner, 1939, 113. The Fothergill in this quotation was the Quaker Dr. John Fothergill, Franklin's London physician and friend, who in 1770 was elected to the American Philosophical Society. He always welcomed young medical students who came to Edinburgh to study, including Rush as well as John Morgan and William Shippen. Thomas Sydenham was a seventeenth-century physician, known as the "English Hippocrates," as a founder of clinical medicine and epidemiology.

p. 60. The stethoscope: Kervran, 1960.

p. 61. In 1736: Fruchtman, 2002.

p. 61. Sixty years later: LeFanu, 1951, and Fenn, 2001.

p. 61. In 1768: Rush to John Morgan, Oct. 21, 1768, in *Letters of Benjamin Rush,* 1:66.

p. 61. It was called heroic: Fissell, 2000, 601.

p. 63. Some actually thought: Franklin was successful in part during his first tour of duty from 1757 to 1762 to convince the Privy Council and the king to allow Pennsylvania to tax some of the Penns's estates. See D. Morgan, 1996, 47–68. Now he sought their removal entirely by requesting that the king transform the colony into a royal one. See Hutson, 1972.

p. 63. But Franklin knew: D. Morgan, 1996, 93–109.

p. 63. He wrote to his boyhood friend: Rush to Ebenezer Hazard, Nov. 8, 1765, in *Letters of Benjamin Rush,* 1:18.

p. 64. In Edinburgh: Reid-Maroney points out that between 1750 and 1790, some 177 American physicians studied at the Edinburgh Medical School, and "the enclave of graduates in Philadelphia provided a direct link to ideas flowing out of the Scottish Enlightenment." See Reid-Maroney, 95.

p. 64. Rush learned from Cullen: *Autobiography of Benjamin Rush,* 80–82.

p. 64. He wrote to a Philadelphia friend: Rush to Jonathan Bayard Smith, Apr. 30, 1767, in *Letters of Benjamin Rush,* 1:41.

p. 65. Rush later recalled: *Autobiography of Benjamin Rush,* 55.

p. 65. So impressed: Quoted in D'Elia, 1974, 35, from David F. Musto, "Benjamin Rush's Medical Thesis, 'On the Digestion of Food in the Stomach,'" *Transactions and Studies of the College of Physicians of Philadelphia,* 44th series, 33 (Oct. 1965): 121–38. The thesis was also dedicated secondarily to other scientists and physicians as well.

p. 66. He had gotten the idea: Rush to Jeremy Belknap, Jan. 8, 1768, in *Letters of Benjamin Rush,* 1:447–48.

p. 66. He later recalled that "these exercises": *Autobiography of Benjamin Rush,* 32, 82.

p. 67. His essay: See Franklin to Rush, July 22, 1774, in *Papers,* 21:247–48, for Franklin's warning that he would not be admitted.

p. 67. "From the amiable character": Rush to Sharp, May 11, 1773, in ed. Woods, 1967, 2.

p. 68. "It did me harm": *Autobiography of Benjamin Rush,* 83.

pp. 68–70. "foreign" that "the moral faculties . . . to be just or merciful": All quoted from Rush's *Address* in Runes, ed., 1947, 3–18.

p. 69. It is worth noting: Rush to Sharp, Oct. 29, 1773, in ed. Woods, 1967, 3. No London edition of either pamphlet was apparently printed.

p. 70. Nisbet eventually: *Autobiography of Benjamin Rush,* 83, n12.

p. 70. In May: Rush to Franklin, May 1, 1773, in *Papers,* 20:193.

p. 70. In July 1773: Franklin to Benezet, July 14, 1773, in *Papers,* 20:296, and Franklin to Rush, July 14, 1773, in *Papers,* 20:314.

p. 71. Rush predicted: Rush to Sharp, Nov. 1, 1774, in ed. Woods, 1967, 13.

p. 71. Though termed a "revolutionary gadfly": Hawke, 1971.

p. 71. He told Granville Sharp: Rush to Sharp, July 9, 1774, and Rush to Sharp, Sept. 20, 1774, in Woods, 1967, 9, 12.

pp. 72–73.   "The battle of Lexington": *Autobiography of Benjamin Rush,* 114, 112, 46.

p. 73.   Rush had earlier opposed: Rush to Ebenezer Hazard, Nov. 8, 1765, in *Letters of Benjamin Rush,* 1:18.

p. 73.   Though baptized: Tennent, a close friend of Franklin's, became one of the first trustees of the College of Philadelphia. See Coalter, 1986. When Tennent came to Franklin seeking money to build a new meetinghouse, however, Franklin, who had just completed fundraising for so many of his charitable institutions (the Library Company, the Association, the fire department, the academy, and the hospital), refused because he did not want to ask the same people over and over again to contribute to his projects. See Franklin, *Autobiography,* in *Writings,* 1424.

p. 74.   In the fourth decade: Heimert, 1966, 2, points out that the split in the Presbyterian Church was constituted by Old Sides and New Sides, while in the Congregationalist Church it was the Old Lights and the New Lights. On the character and significance of the Great Awakening, see Lambert, 1999. For a reassessment of the New Sides/Old Sides schism, see Reid-Maroney, 2001, 17–20.

p. 74.   "[W]hen I consider": Franklin to Joseph Galloway, Feb. 25, 1775, in *Papers,* 21:509.

p. 75.   In the fall of 1773: [Rush] "Hamden," "To His Fellow Countrymen: On Patriotism," Oct. 20, 1773, in the *Pennsylvania Journal,* in *Letters of Benjamin Rush,* 1:83. Rush told William Gordon he had written the essay. See Rush to Gordon, Oct. 10, 1773, in *Letters of Benjamin Rush,* 1:82.

p. 76.   Rush had always admired him: *Autobiography of Benjamin Rush,* 110.

p. 76.   By 1775, with Ruston: Rush mentioned Ruston in his autobiography as his Nottingham Academy classmate. See *Autobiography of Benjamin Rush,* 34, 35, n26, 253.

p. 77.   British troops in America: Rush to Ruston, Oct. 29, 1775, in *Letters of Benjamin Rush,* 1:91–92.

p. 78.   As a growing number of Americans: Paine, *Common Sense,* 63.

p. 78.   Only, Rush added: Rush to Mrs. Rush, May 29, 1776, in *Letters of Benjamin Rush,* 1:99 (emphasis in the original).

p. 78.   And just in case: Rush to Mrs. Rush, June 1, 1776, in *Letters of Benjmain Rush,* 1:102.

pp. 78–79.   As he told Granville Sharp: Rush to Granville Sharp, July 9, 1774, in ed. Woods, 1967, 6–9. This letter, it must be recalled, was written just before the Apr. 1775 battle of Lexington, so Rush was still hoping for some last-minute resolution of the disputes between Lord North and the colonies.

p. 79.   He might well have torn: Corner, ed., "Introduction," in *Autobiography of Benjamin Rush,* 6–7.

p. 80.   In one of the few surviving: Rush to John Adams, Oct. 21, 1777, in *Letters of Benjamin Rush,* 1:159–60.

p. 80.   The general should be dismissed: Quoted in Flexner, 1939, 73. On the Conway Cabal, led by General Thomas Conway in an attempt to replace Washington as commander in chief, see Flexner, 1969, ch. 15. Rush, accused of giving aid and comfort to the cabal, always denied it.

p. 80. As he told John Adams: Rush to Adams, Oct. 21, 1777, in *Letters of Benjamin Rush*, 1:161.

p. 80. He told a friend, Anthony Wayne: Rush to Anthony Wayne, Apr. 2, 1777, and May 19, 1777, in *Letters of Benjamin Rush*, 1:137, 148.

p. 81. Writing in opposition: Rush, "Letter II in Observations on the Government of Pennsylvania," in Runes, 1947, 57.

p. 81. Besides smallpox: Fissell, 2000, 601, from which the statistics are taken.

p. 82. Franklin replied: Franklin to Benjamin Rush, July 14, 1773, in *Writings*, 884.

p. 82. "Another means of preserving health": Franklin, "The Art of Procuring Pleasant Dreams," in *Writings*, 1119.

p. 83. He described them: Quoted in N. Goodman, 1934, 88, from Benjamin Rush, *Medical Inquiries and Observations*, 4 vols. (1789 and 1793), 1:269–78.

p. 83. "I was crushed": *Autobiography of Benjamin Rush*, 136.

p. 84. "The hospital's physicians": Hawke, 1971, 267.

p. 84. In 1780: Nadelhaft, July 1966, 203.

p. 84. Rush learned that Nathanael Greene: Rush to Greene, Sept. 16, 1782, in *Letters of Benjamin Rush*, 1:286.

p. 84. Other states hesitated: Benezet to Franklin, Mar. 5, 1783, quoted in D. Davis, 1975, 317–18.

p. 85. It was now called: D. Davis, 1966, 216.

p. 85. When Clarkson wrote: Armistead, 1971, 62 nt.

p. 86. Five years after: Rush to Richard Price, Oct. 15, 1785, in *Letters of Benjamin Rush*, 2:371.

p. 86. "fully satisfied . . . ninety four": Quoted in Hawke, 1971, 104–05 (and 361, where Rush's manumission is quoted from the Philadelphia Manumission Book of 1780–1793).

p. 87. He noted that at least fifty whites: Biddle, ed., 1905, 138.

p. 87. In addition to the rapidly changing: Kloos, 1991, esp. 29–33.

p. 87. As he later told Richard Price: Rush to Richard Price, June 2, 1787, in *Letters of Benjamin Rush*, 1:419. The year 1780 was when Rush read Fletcher's *An Appeal to Matter of Fact and Common Sense* on universal salvation.

p. 87. As he noted: *Autobiography of Benjamin Rush*, 163.

p. 87. Rush reconciled: Reid-Maroney, 2001.

p. 88. He told John Bayard: Rush to John Bayard, July 2, 1783, in *Letters of Benjamin Rush*, 1:303. Hawke says this letter should have been dated Aug. 2. See Hawke, 1971, 439, n24.

p. 89. He sent a copy: Price to Rush, July 22, 1785, in *Correspondence of Richard Price*, 2:294, where Price estimated that two-fifths of the population was disenfranchised.

p. 89. Just before Franklin: Rush to Price, Oct. 15, 1785, in *Letters of Benjamin Rush*, 2:371. Rush's examples are interesting and somewhat ironic: Francisco Ximenes de Cisneros was a fifteenth-century Spanish cardinal and statesman; Hercule André de Flery, a seventeenth and eighteenth-century French cardinal and statesman; and William Murray, the first earl of Mansfield, was chief justice.

p. 89.   In April of 1786: Rush to Price, Apr. 22, 1786, in *Letters of Benjamin Rush*, 1:385.

p. 90.   Franklin told him: Rush to Price, June 2, 1787, in *Letters of Benjamin Rush*, 1:418.

p. 90.   But we know: Rakove, 1996.

p. 90.   He wanted him to know: Rush to John Adams, June 4, 1789, in *Letters of Benjamin Rush*, 1:514 (his emphasis).

p. 90.   He told Granville Sharp: Rush to Granville Sharp, Apr. 2, 1799, in ed. Woods, 1967, 32–33 (see also his letters to Sharp, Oct. 8, 1801, and June 20, 1809, in Woods, 35–37, where he expressed the same sentiment).

p. 91.   Rush argued that even if no cure: Rush to the Managers of the Pennsylvania Hospital, Nov. 11, 1789, in *Letters of Benjamin Rush*, 1:529.

p. 91.   Still, he tried to cure: Rush to John Coakley Lettsom, Sept. 28, 1787, ibid., 1:443.

p. 92.   His last years: Kloos, 1991, 87–109.

p. 92.   About one hundred white people: Biddle, ed., 1905, 146.

p. 93.   By then: For the argument that Rush applied his theory of the "unitary" causes of disease to the problems in the American political system in the 1790s, see Kloos, 1991, 71–85.

p. 93.   As he put it: Rush to Lettsom, in *Letters of Benjamin Rush*, 102.

p. 93.   In his 1811: Mease, 1811, 37–38.

p. 94.   The result was: N. Goodman, 1934, 168–69.

p. 95.   Not only: The purge treatment became known as "Rush's ten-and-ten," because he prescribed a "cocktail" of ten grains of calomel mixed with ten grains of jalap.

p. 95.   Bloodletting was a controversial: For bloodletting in our own time, see Root-Bernstein, 1997, 84, 85–97. See also Mestel, Aug. 6, 2001, S2. In 2000 the National Museum of Health and Medicine at Walter Reed Hospital in Washington, D.C., installed an exhibit titled "From Lancets to Leeches: A Brief History of Bloodletting."

p. 95.   Publicist William Cobbett: Appendix III, The Cobbett-Rush Feud," in *Letters of Benjamin Rush*, 2:1213–18. See Spater, 1982.

p. 95.   He called him: For the documents, see ed. D. Wilson, 1994.

p. 95.   "I have bled twice": Quoted in N. Goodman, 1934, 178.

p. 98.   He wrote his friend, John R. B. Rodgers: Rush to Rodgers, [Oct. 16, 1797], in *Letters of Benjamin Rush*, 2:794.

p. 98.   On October 20: *Autobiography of Benjamin Rush*, 95, n34.

p. 98.   He instructed Rodgers: Rush to Rodgers, Nov. 6, 1797, in *Letters of Benjamin Rush*, 2:795.

p. 99.   Two years later: All quoted from "Appendix II: John Adams' Appointment of Rush as Treasurer of the Mint," in *Letters of Benjamin Rush*, 2:1209–12.

p. 99.   "In reviewing": *Autobiography of Benjamin Rush*, 97.

Chapter 3. Paine, Revolutionary Zeal, and Engineering

p. 101.   "I am willing": Adams to Waterhouse, Oct. 29, 1805, in ed. Ford, 1927, 31. The "disastrous meteor" quotation is from ed. Butterfield, 1961, 3:330.

p. 102.   She apparently remarked: Franklin, "Speech in the Convention at the Conclusion of its Deliberations," Sept. 17, 1787, in *Writings*, 1140.

p. 102.   His ideas of government and society: Fruchtman, 1994, and Keane, 1995.

p. 103.   Despite a lack of formal education: Paine, *The Age of Reason*, 1974, 78.

p. 104.   "as the money raised in Britain . . . sever us forever": Franklin, *Causes of the American Discontents Before 1768*, Jan. 17, 1768, but reprinted Aug. 30 and Sept. 1, 1774, in *Writings,*608, 615.

p. 104.   The first appearance of Paine's interest: Some have speculated that Paine's inauguration into political and social reform began when he was a Methodist preacher in Dover and Sandwich in the 1760s. Keane, 1995, 45–49, 60–62, is at fault here. But the idea that Paine was a preacher of any coloration makes little sense until we have far more evidence than thin speculation. Keane hedges only slightly when he quotes Oldys's charge from 1791 that Paine thought about seeking ordination until he realized his formal education was defective in Latin (see Keane, 1995, 547, n63).

p. 105.   Paine's participation: Kramnick, 1990, esp. ch. 5, "Tom Paine: Radical Liberal."

p. 107.   "One shilling and ninepence farthing a day . . . the severity of their distress": Paine, "The Case of the Officers of Excise, with Remarks on the Qualifications of the Officers, and on the Numerous Evils Arising to the Revenue, from the Insufficiency of the Present Salary: Humbly Addressed to the Members of Both Houses of Parliament" (1772), in *Writings of Thomas Paine*, 2:3–15. The piece, though printed for parliament, was published only in 1793. It is not known whether Paine revised it in the meantime.

p. 108.   Franklin agreed: Conway, 1892, Appendix B, 2:468.

p. 108.   "The bearer": Franklin to Richard Bache, Sept. 30, 1774, in *Papers*, 21:325–26.

p. 109.   Finding a residence: Paine to Franklin, Mar. 4, 1775, in *Writings of Thomas Paine*, 2:1131.

p. 109.   They were meeting: See Black, 1963, on illegal extra-parliamentary association meetings.

p. 110.   But as he later remarked: Paine to a Committee of the Continental Congress, Oct. 1783, in *Writings of Thomas Paine*, 2:1227.

p. 110.   When he arrived in America: [Paine] "Common Sense," *The American Crisis*, Nov. 21, 1778, in *Writings of Thomas Paine*, 1:143. In this number, Paine outlined his reasons why he thought Britain was intent on conquest, which in his mind was the moral equivalent to slavery. Paine signed his *Crisis* papers with the pseudonym "Common Sense" or "C. S.," which will not be noted.

pp. 111–113. "Now is the seed time . . . at hand": Paine, *Common Sense*, 82, 84, 87, 98, 121.

p. 112.	As early as 1776, just a few months: [Paine], *Letters on Four Interesting Subjects,* Letter IV, in ed. Kammen, 1986, 3. These letters were published anonymously in the spring of 1776, but after careful research, A. Owen Aldridge, the most dedicated Paine scholar in America, has determined conclusively that Paine wrote them. See Aldridge, 1984, 219–21. Eric Foner, unconvinced that Paine wrote these essays, declined to include them in his Library of America collection.
p. 113.	"one honest man . . . the brute of Britain": Paine, *Common Sense,* 81 (emphasis added), 92, 114. See also Paine, *The American Crisis,* Mar. 5, 1782, in *Writings of Thomas Paine,* 1:192: "Like the Pharaoh on the edge of the Red Sea, he [George III] sees not the plunge he is making, and precipitately drives across the flood that is closing over his head."
p. 113.	"The cause of America . . . the Power of feeling": Paine, *Common Sense,* 63–64.
p. 114.	"Common sense will tell us": Ibid., 72–73, 76, 69, 79, 80–81, 105; Jordan, Sept. 1973, 294–308. On Milton, see Fish, 2001, 564, on the Fall.
p. 114.	Later, in an open letter: [Paine], *The American Crisis,* Jan. 13, 1777, in *Writings of Thomas Paine,* 1:72.
p. 115.	"I have as little superstition": Ibid. Dec. 23, 1776, in *Writings of Thomas Paine,* 1:50–51.
p. 116.	"in his project . . . it contemplates": Quoted in Armytage, Jan. 1951, 16–17.
p. 117.	"With such circumstantial evidence": Kemp, 1977– 1978, 23.
p. 117.	"What weight it will bear . . . by that circumstance": Paine to Franklin, June 6, 1788, in *Writings of Thomas Paine,* 2:1026–27.
p. 118.	He wrote to George Clymer: Paine to George Clymer, Nov. 19, 1786, in *Writings of Thomas Paine,* 2:1258.
p. 119.	"The bearer of this": Franklin to the Duc de la Rochefoucauld, Apr. 15, 1787, in *Writings of Benjamin Franklin,* 9:565–66. See Franklin to Le Veillard, Apr. 15, 1787, 9:562; to Comte d'Estaing, Apr. 15, 1787, 9:566–67; and to the Marquis de Chastellux, Apr. 17, 1787, 9:568.
p. 119.	Franklin also alerted: Franklin to Thomas Jefferson, Apr. 19, 1787, in *Writings of Benjamin Franklin,* 9:574–75.
p. 119.	Once in Paris: Paine to Franklin, June 22, 1787, in *Writings of Thomas Paine,* 2:1263.
p. 119.	Without a single reservation: Quoted by Paine to Sir George Staunton, Spring of 1789, in *Writings of Thomas Paine,* 2:1241.
p. 120.	Paine decided: Armytage, Jan. 1951, 16, n1.
p. 120.	As he told Jefferson: Paine to Jefferson, Sept. 9, 1788, in *Writings of Thomas Paine,* 2:1269.
p. 120.	A local squire: On Foljambe, see Paine to Jefferson, Feb. 19, 1789, in *Writings of Thomas Paine,* 2:1035–40. The Foljambe quotation is in Paine to Jefferson, Feb. 26, 1789, in *Writings of Thomas Paine,* 2: 1281.
p. 121.	Again Paine went: Paine to Thomas Walker, Jan. 16, 1789, quoted in Armytage, Jan. 1951, 20.

p. 121.   He found that the arch: Paine to Staunton, Spring of 1789, in *Writings of Thomas Paine*, 2:1043.

p. 121.   By July of 1789: Paine to Jefferson, July 13, [1789], in *Writings of Thomas Paine*, 2:1294; Paine to Jefferson, Sept. 15, 1789, in *Writings of Thomas Paine*, 2:1295.

p. 121.   He hoped to erect: Paine to Jefferson, Sept. 18, 1789, in *Writings of Thomas Paine*, 2:1296.

p. 122.   He wrote to Walker: Paine to Walker, Sept. 19, 1789, quoted in Armytage, Jan. 1951, 24.

p. 122.   At the same time: Paine to Jefferson, Sept. 15, 1789, in *Writings of Thomas Paine*, 2:1295.

p. 123.   He also told Walker: Paine to Walker, Apr. 14, 1790, in *Writings of Thomas Paine*, 2:1305.

p. 123.   He wanted desperately: Paine to Washington, May 31, 1790, in *Writings of Thomas Paine*, 2:1305.

p. 123.   As he later told Jefferson: Paine to Jefferson, Oct. 1, 1800, in *Writings of Thomas Paine*, 2:1411. (Paine quoted Monroe in his letter to Jefferson.)

p. 124.   Paine never received anything: Kemp, 1977–1978, 32. Kemp includes a document that indicates that while Paine's design was considered for the Sunderland Bridge, Burdon did not choose it, because "Burdon's design is in marked contrast to the Paine design proposed for the same site." See Kemp, 34–35. That parts of Paine's bridge at Paddington were used in the construction of the Sunderland Bridge is attested to in Armytage, Jan. 1951, 29.

p. 124.   The man of little formal education: Kemp, 1977–1978, 36.

p. 124.   "Why may we not suppose": Paine, *Rights of Man* (1791–1792), 1984, 271 (emphasis added).

p. 125.   In the first part: For the Burke-Paine controversy, see Morris, 1998, and Fennessy, 1963.

p. 125.   "These are the materials of a superb edifice": Jefferson to Paine, Sept. 15, 1789, in ed. Boyd, et al., 1950——, 15:269.

p. 126.   He even told Burke: Paine to Burke, Jan. 17, 1790, in Boulton, Mar. 1951, 49.

p. 126.   As a member of the convention: Paine, "On Preserving the Life of Louis Capet," speech before the French National Convention during the trial of Louis XVI, Jan. 15, 1793, in *Writings of Thomas Paine*, 2:553.

p. 127.   "There was formed among the crowned brigands . . . the monarchical system": Paine, "On Bringing Louis XVI to Trial," speech before the French National Convention on Nov. 21, 1792, in ibid., 2:548, 551. Louis XVI was tried by the Convention, which first met in September of 1792 specifically to write a new republican constitution for France after the fall of the monarchy on August 10, 1792; Paine was elected as a member from Pas-de-Calais and three other jurisdictions as well.

p. 127.   But there was a world of difference: Ibid. 2:552 (emphasis added).

p. 128.   "it requires but a very small glance": Paine, *Rights of Man*, 44.

p. 128.   This was Paine's: Jefferson to James Madison, Sept. 6, 1789, in ed.

Boyd, *Papers of Thomas Jefferson, 1950–*, 15:392, where he made the famous remark that "I set on this ground, which I suppose to be self-evident, *that the earth belongs in usufruct to the living*" (emphasis in the original). For a recent interpretation of that remark, see Ellis, 1998, 131–32.

p. 128.   "The objects that now press . . . the spring is begun": Paine, *Rights of Man*, 171, 266, 272–73.

p. 129.   In the meantime, he crafted: Thomas Spence, for one. See Fruchtman, 2000.

p. 130.   "employment buildings . . . but of a right": Paine, *Rights of Man* (1792), in ed. P. Foner, 1984, 246, 247, 243. See Claeys, June 1994, 249–90, although Claeys is concerned with Paine's last great work, *Agrarian Justice* (1797).

p. 131.   Two years earlier: Paine to Condorcet, de Bonneville, and Lanthenas, June 1791, in *Writings of Thomas Paine*, 2:1317. For five years Paine lived with Bonneville, a prominent journalist, after he recovered from his illnesses, and wrote for his paper. Lanthenas translated Paine's works into French.

p. 131.   In December 1793: Paine was imprisoned from December 28, 1793, until November 4, 1794. He related the story of his "miraculous" escape of the scaffold in Letter Three of "Letters to the Citizens of the United States," Nov. 26, 1802, in *Writings of Thomas Paine*, 2:921–92. Robespierre himself had signed his death warrant. See Fruchtman, 1994, 317–24.

p. 132.   *Common Sense* had opened: Paine, *Common Sense*,65.

p. 132.   "The right which any man": Paine, *Dissertation on the First Principles of Government* (1795), in *Writings of Thomas Paine*, 2:571, 573.

p. 133.   "nothing therefore can justify . . . to take away property": Ibid. 2:587, 588, 589 (emphasis in the original).

p. 135.   "There could be no such thing . . . any national measures": Paine, *Agrarian Justice* (1797), in *Writings of Thomas Paine*, 1:608, 611, 610, 612, 618, 613, 621; Fruchtman, 2000, 30–40.

p. 136.   Paine, clearly, was a man: Claeys, Winter 1988, 21–31.

Chapter 4. Price and Priestley, Religious Dissent and Revolution

p. 141.   And yet, as close as they were: Price and Priestley, *A Free Discussion of the Doctrines of Materialism, and Philosophical Necessity, in a Correspondence between Dr. Price and Dr. Priestley*, 1778. Priestley provided the introduction, giving the context of the debate where Price argued for free will, Priestley for determinism.

p. 142.   This largely took the form: The classic study that illuminated the origins and development of the opposition movement is Robbins, 1959. Studies that move beyond 1776 include Cone, 1968, and Goodwin, 1979.

p. 142.   Price and Priestley came from Dissenting religious backgrounds: M. Fitzpatrick, 2000, 30–31.

p. 142.   Price and Priestley, as had many Dissenters before them: On the Dissenting tradition, see Rupp, 1986, and Watts, 1978.

p. 144.   "When I think of your present crazy Constitution": Franklin to Richard Price, Aug. 16, 1784, in *Correspondence of Richard Price,* 2:224–25.

p. 145.   Most importantly, they wanted to transform: On the reforming spirit, see Pocock, 1975, now the classic study of the republican tradition from Aristotle to the American Revolution. Pocock has not been without his critics, notably Kramnick, June 1982, 629–64, in an article Pocock later answered in March 1981, 49–72. See also the criticism underlying the work of J. C. D. Clark, 1994, J. C. D. Clark, 2000, and Hulliung, 2002. The debate is summarized in Fruchtman, May 1996, 94–103. For a discussion of how Franklin fit into Pocock's Machiavellian moment in the American eighteenth century, see Jehlen, 1993, 61–74.

p. 145.   This was not a rare concept: Fruchtman, 1983, and Wood, 2004, 117–20.

p. 145.   He also claimed: *Autobiography of Joseph Priestley,* 92.

p. 145.   His friends commented: Gibbs, 1968, 16.

p. 146.   He adopted the Socinian: The Socinians originated in the antitrinitarian religious beliefs of Faustus Socinus in the sixteenth century when he attempted to reconcile religion, humanism, and rationalism.

p. 146.   "a man like ourselves": Quoted in Porter, 2000, 409.

p. 146.   a bitter exchange with the grand historian: Pocock, 1999, 1:67.

p. 147.   "the widespread demonstration": Golinski, 1992, 66.

p. 147.   Price's first philosophical work: The work is *A Review of the Principal Questions and Difficulties in Morals* (1758).

p. 148.   "The power within us": R. Thomas, 1924, 35. The best discussion of Price's philosophy is Laboucheix, 1970, 64–121, or in English translation, 1982, 41–81.

p. 149.   "Perhaps, I do not go too far": Price, *Observations on the Importance of the American Revolution, and the Means of Making it a Benefit to the World,* 1784, 7.

p. 150.   Price would later retract: Price to Rush, July 22, 1785, in *Correspondence of Richard Price,* 2:293–94. See the chapter on Rush in the section on political reform below.

p. 150.   "would often drop in": Quoted in Ogborn, 1962, 88.

p. 153.   "I am then for": O. Goldsmith, 1987, 117.

p. 153.   The greatest commentator: Blackstone, 1978.

p. 153.   "do what Englishmen are renown": Priestley, *An Essay on the First Principles of Government, and on the Nature of Civil, Political, and Religious Liberty,* 1768, in *Works of Joseph Priestley,* 22:37. The first volume is actually in two parts, so there are twenty-six volumes in all.

p. 154.   "If there is any higher will . . . wise form of government": Price, *Additional Observations on the Nature and Value of Civil Liberty, and the War with America,* 1777, 7, 19, 17.

p. 155.   To refine their thoughts: Fruchtman, 1983.

p. 156.   Edmund Burke, in a forecast: Burke, who advocated reconciliation with the colonies, never denied that Britain had a right to tax the Americans, and he replied with his *Letter to the Sheriffs of Bristol* (London, 1776).

See R. Thomas, 1924, 75–76. The Revolution Society commemorated the English Revolution of 1688–1689, and it had met for almost a century every year on November 4. Its full title was "The Society for Commemorating the Revolution in Great Britain."

p. 157. "the power of a *Civil Society* . . . his own legislator": Price, *Observations on the Nature of Civil Liberty,* London, 1776, 3, 6.

p. 158. "consists in the power . . . must not infringe": Priestley, *An Essay on Government,* in *Works of Joseph Priestley,* 22:11, 13.

p. 159. Price agreed: Price, *The Evidence for a Future Period of Improvement in the State of Mankind,* London, 1787, 19–20.

p. 159. His title said it all: Osborne, 1972.

p. 159. He also told Cartwright: Price to Cartwright, Nov. 27, 1776, in *Correspondence of Richard Price,* 1:250–51. In 1778 the two works were published together in a single volume.

p. 160. In September 1777: Shelburne to Price, Sept. 24, 1777, in *Correspondence of Richard Price,* 1:260.

p. 161. He told Benjamin Rush: Price to Benjamin Rush, June 26, 1783, in *Correspondence of Richard Price,* 2: 185.

p. 161. As mentioned: Price, *Observations on the Importance of the American Revolution,* 1784, 7.

p. 161. Price responded: Price to Benjamin Rush, July 30, 1786, in *Correspondence of Richard Price,* 3:55. And of course Franklin within ten months was to join the Constitutional Convention in Philadelphia.

p. 161. He told Price: Franklin to Price, Aug. 1, 1784, in *Correspondence of Richard Price,* 2:225.

p. 162. When Jefferson arrived in Paris: Jefferson to Price, Feb. 1, 1785, in *Correspondence of Richard Price,* 2:261.

p. 162. "No part of America . . . such things as these": Quoted in Gibbs, 1968, 188–89. Priestley, *An Address to Protestant Dissenters of all Denominations,* 1774). See Lincoln, 1938, 57.

p. 162. Worse yet: Cone, 1952, 92; Lincoln, 1938, 49.

p. 163. "We should love our country . . . moved him to tears": All quotations from Price, *A Discourse on the Love of Our Country,* 1790, 13, 15, 30, 40. The Priestley quotation is cited in R. Thomas, 1924, 10.

p. 164. His attack: Burke, *Reflections on the Revolution in France,* 10.

p. 164. "What candour": All quoted in D. Thomas, 1977, 339, 341–42.

p. 165. In a 1790 letter to Price: Priestley to Price, Aug. 29, 1790, *Works of Joseph Priestley,* 1, Pt. 2:79–81.

p. 166. "some important prophecies": Priestley to Lindsey, Nov. 12, 1794, in *Works of Joseph Priestley,* 1, Pt. 2:280.

p. 166. "Upon one occasion": Belsham, 1873, note on 248. After the Birmingham Riots, Priestley moved to London and taught at the New College from 1791 until he left for America in 1794. Like many Dissenting academies of the time, it failed financially and finally closed in 1796.

p. 166. "The late events": Priestley to Lindsey, Jan. 19, 1795, in *Works of Joseph Priestley,* 1, Pt. 2:290.

p. 166. "I never was a believer": Rush to John Adams, Aug. 22, 1806, in *Letters of Benjamin Rush,* 2:927.

p. 166.   Such a strong: For the Hemphill affair, see Walter, 1999, 136–40.

p. 167.   Even so, the ministry criminalized: M. Davis, ed., 2000; Philp, ed., 1991; and Dickinson, 1985.

p. 167.   Some men were convicted: Barrell, 2000; Wharam, 1992; and Black, 1963.

p. 168.   In 1791: Rose, Nov. 1960, 68–88, and Robinson, 1960, 173–75.

p. 168.   "remember me affectionately": Franklin to Benjamin Vaughn, Oct. 24, 1788, in *Writings*, 1169.

Chapter 5. Price, Priestley, and Scientific Inquiry

p. 169.   Priestley is known: An older, though serviceable, biography is Gibbs, 1968.

p. 170.   Priestley's younger brother: Schofield, 1966, 1, and *Autobiography of Joseph Priestley*, 12.

p. 171.   "burnt up": *O.E.D.*, 7:785.

p. 171.   who taught Benjamin Rush: *Letters of Benjamin Rush*, 1:80, n1.

p. 172.   "My method of impregnating water": Quoted in *Autobiography of Joseph Priestley*, 95.

p. 172.   Priestley's theory was based: Schofield, 1997, 256–57.

p. 172.   "a rare honor": Badinter and Badinter, 1988, 157, n1.

p. 172.   "The strong striving state": Franklin to Joseph Priestley, July 1772?, in *Papers*, 19:215–16.

p. 173.   Seddon had long known John Canton: Canton, also a Fellow of the Royal Society, is famous for his proof of the compressibility of water.

p. 173.   "For the most amiable simplicity": *Autobiography of Joseph Priestley*, 98.

p. 174.   "The club of *honest whigs*": Priestley to Franklin, Feb. 13, 1776, in Schofield, 1966, 156.

p. 174.   "the greatest, perhaps": Quoted in Wood, 2004, 65.

p. 174.   "It is to be lamented" and "I do not believe": *Autobiography of Joseph Priestley*, 117.

p. 174.   "great ambition would be to be": Priestley to Franklin, Mar. 25, 1766, *Papers*, 13:200.

p. 175.   Priestley had written the first: Schofield, 1966, 47.

p. 175.   In his nomination letter: Schofield, 1997, 152.

p. 176.   "I have just dispatched": Priestley to Franklin, Nov. 21, 1770, *Papers*, 17:290.

p. 177.   "All the solid matter": Quoted in Fruchtman, 1983, 26. The full title of Priestley's work was *Disquisitions Relating to Matter and Spirit. To which is Added, the History of the Philosophical Doctrine Concerning the Origin of the Soul, and the Nature of Matter, with Its Influence on Christianity* (London, 1777).

p. 177.   The situation became so bad: Schofield, 1966, 166–71.

p. 178.   His method was something: D. Morgan, 1996, 19.

p. 178.   "short Hints of the different Motives": Franklin to Joseph Priestley, Sept. 19, 1772, in *Writings*, 878.

p. 179.   "residence in London": *Autobiography of Joseph Priestley*, 116.

p. 179.   From Calne, he now wrote to Price: D. Thomas, 1977, 136.

p. 180.   "I have been making many experiments": Priestley to Price, Oct. 3, 1771, in *Correspondence of Richard Price*, 1:103.

p. 180.   This question has never: Ihde, 1980, 62–91. For two recent treatments, see White, 2001, 57–95, and Horvitz, 2001, 11–23.

p. 180.   "As you would not": Quoted in *Autobiography of Joseph Priestley*, 44 (and generally at 52–59), his emphasis.

p. 180.   In one of his more interesting: In Schofield's view, Priestley's work on the restoration of air from vegetation was his major contribution. Schofield, 1997, 266.

p. 180.   "I have fully satisfied myself": Priestley to Franklin, July 1, 1772, in Schofield, 1966, 104–05.

p. 181.   "a leader of pneumatic chemistry": Schofield, 1997, 259.

p. 181.   Here, he described oxygen: Schofield, 1966, 139.

p. 182.   "shall be very sorry": Priestley to Franklin, Sept. 26, 1773, in Schofield, 1966, 143.

p. 182.   "the rapid Progress": Franklin to Joseph Priestley, Feb. 8, 1780, in *Writings*, 1017.

p. 183.   "the most brilliant": Schofield, 1966, 198, and Porter, 2000, 428.

p. 183.   Calling themselves: On "Lunatics," see Brewer, 1997, 599.

p. 183.   The members included: Uglow, 2002, 544, n1, who says that Wedgwood may not have been a formal member.

p. 183.   The Lunar Society was: Golinski, 1992, 599.

p. 183.   "We had nothing to do": Quoted in Uglow, 2002, xiv.

p. 184.   "the happiest event in my life": *Autobiography of Joseph Priestley*, 120.

p. 184.   And while Darwin: Uglow, 2002, 142–43, for the speaking machine. For Darwin, see Porter, 2000, 438–45.

p. 184.   Most likely, Priestley: Black, 1963, and Cone, 1968.

p. 184.   "On the whole": *Autobiography of Joseph Priestley*, 130 (Priestley wrote this in 1795 after the Church and King Riots forced him from Birmingham).

p. 185.   These led to his pioneering work: J. Anderson, 1937, 42. Roland Thomas agrees with Anderson that Price was a founder of life insurance but adds that he was also a founder of old-age pensions, or social security. See R. Thomas, 1924, 58, 60, and also Ogborn, 1962, 85–97.

p. 185.   On Thomas Bayes: For Price's full description of his work on Bayes's mathematics, drawn with heavily analytical formulation, see Price to John Canton, Nov. 10, 1763, in *Correspondence of Richard Price*, 1:6–35. Bayesian theory is still used today in modern social science forecasting, and Richard Swinburne, a contemporary philosopher, has used Bayesian ideas to prove to his satisfaction that the chances that the Resurrection actually occurred stand at 97 percent. For its application to political science, see the critique by Erikson, Bafumi, and Wilson, Dec. 2001, 815–19. For philosophy, see Swinburne, 1979, esp. 64–69, and for the proof of the Resurrection, see Eakin, May 11, 2002, A17, A19, for a discussion of Bayes's work in relation to contemporary proofs of religious beliefs.

p. 187.   Historian James Gibson Anderson: J. Anderson, 1937, 42.

p. 187.   "study of life contingencies": Raynes, 1950, 133. This is such a cold, impersonal phrase. My colleague at Towson University, George Hahn, suggested the phrase "cryptographic Jacobin chime."

p. 187.   In 1768: For examples of the questions posed to Price, see "Calendar with extracts of the Correspondence of Richard Price and John Edwards, Actuary of the Equitable Society, contained in MS Letter-book belonging to the Equitable Life Assurance Society," in *Correspondence of Richard Price*, 1:277–83.

p. 187.   "to the dangers of 'bad lives'": Quoted in D. Thomas, 1977, 216.

p. 188.   Several of his publications: Price to Franklin, Apr. 3, 1769, in *Correspondence of Richard Price*, 1:58–79, and also in *Papers*, 16:81–107.

p. 188.   "the greatest classic": Raynes, 1950, 133.

p. 188.   "financial disaster": D. Thomas, 1977, 138.

p. 189.   "had a profound influence": Ogborn, 1962, 92; see also D. Thomas, 1977, 58, and Cone, 1952, 43.

p. 189.   The bill failed: Cone, 1952, 45–46.

p. 190.   Hume feared a large national debt: Pocock, 1975, 496–98, and Pocock, 1999, 2:256, where he specifically cites Price and Hume together.

p. 190.   To avoid the growing national debt: His pamphlet devoted to the debt alone was titled *An Appeal to the Public on the Subject of the National Debt*, 1772.

p. 190.   Several years later: This work, *An Essay on the Present State of Population in England and Wales*, 1780, was originally appended to a book on insurance written by his nephew, William Morgan, who lived with the Price family and who was then the actuary at the Equitable Life Assurance Society. The work was his *Treatise on the Doctrine of Annuities*, 1779. There followed several other tracts on public indebtedness for the rest of his life, including his advice to the short-lived Shelburne ministry in 1782. See D. Thomas, 1977, 234–59, R. Thomas, 1924, 58–63, and Cone, 1952, 131–51.

p. 190.   "not only on my own Account": Franklin to Richard Price, Feb. 10, 1772, in *Papers*, 19:77.

p. 191.   "That the Honourable Benjamin Franklin": Franklin, Lee, and Adams to Price, in *Correspondence of Richard Price*, 2:29–30.

p. 191.   "to the American states": Price to Franklin, Arthur Lee, and John Adams, Jan. 18, 1779; he also wrote separately to Lee, Jan. 18, 1779, both in *Correspondence of Richard Price*, 2:34–36.

p. 192.   The first in the New World: Cone, 1952, 49.

p. 192.   He had lost the society of conversation: Golinski, 1992, 55–56, 69.

p. 192.   A lonely man: Barall, 2000, and Wharam, 1992.

p. 192.   For the settlement in Pennsylvania, see S. Cohen, 1982, 301–15.

Chapter 6. Marat and Mesmer, Charlatans or Misunderstood Scientists?

p. 199.   After Corday: Quoted in Miller, 2001, 123.

p. 199.   Without hesitation: The most recent and sympathetic biography in English is Conner, 1998. See also the classic study by Gottschalk, 1927, and Fayet, 1960. For Corday, see Melchior-Bonnet, 1989.

p. 199. Terror "the order of the day": That "terror shall be the order of the day" was the call of Bertrand Barère in a proposal to the Convention on Sept. 5, 1793. See Guerlac, 1931, 270. Simon Schama attributes the saying to Georges Danton. See Schama, 1989, 807.

p. 201. Marat, of course: Conner, 1998, 37, and Miller, 2001, 132. Schama concludes that Marat enjoyed the role of outcast, one that he successfully played until his death, and loved the idea that he was always perfectly rude, interrupting people, breaking up their dinner parties, or just being outrageously crude. Schama, 1989, 734.

p. 202. For art historian Stephen Miller: Miller, 2001, 125, acknowledges the universal agreement about Marat's ugliness.

p. 203. But for Marat, the flame's matter: Cabanès, 1920.

p. 203. "with a little tincture of French idiom": Franklin, *Papers*, 28:226.

p. 203. "The honour of your company": Marat to Franklin, Mar. 13, 1779, in *Papers*, 29:107.

p. 203. A physicist himself: Heilbron, 1979, 359–62.

p. 203. Nollet had been: For historian of science Clifford Conner, Franklin's theory was "a classical Newtonian elastic fluid." Conner, 1998, 117. See I. Cohen, 1956, and Franklin's "Jean-Antoine Nollet: Letters on Electricity," in *Papers*, 4:423–28.

p. 204. "The representative of the author": Marat to Franklin, Mar. 25, 1779, in *Papers*, 29:106 and n4.

p. 204. "the Honour done me": Franklin to Marat, Mar. 29, 1779, in *Papers*, 29:228–29.

p. 204. "gave off the emanations": Conner, 1998, 77.

p. 205. "painters attributed to genius": Quoted by Cabanès, 1920, 175.

p. 205. "rather favorable": Coquard, 1993, 136.

p. 205. "with disdain": Cabanès, 1920, 340. Conner notes that Newton's reflections on the bending of light and the production of color as a result of this bending were only "preliminary answers in the queries appended to his *Opticks*" and that Marat was genuinely trying to build on Newton's work, while at the same time building a case against Newtonian optics. Conner, 1998, 92–112.

p. 206. "to always be a barrier": Quoted by Badinter and Badinter, 1988, 164. There is a dispute whether Condorcet was addressing this letter to d'Alembert or Brissot (see ibid., 164, n30).

p. 206. "Franklin, together with most other physicists": Conner, 1998, 124.

p. 206. Deeply hurt and insulted: Bougeart, 1865, 1:39.

p. 207. "Tortured almost to madness": Quoted in Lopez and Herbert, 1975, 50, from [Cadwallader Evans], report in *Medical Observations and Inquiries*, 2 vols. (London, 1757), 1:84–85.

p. 207. He used only human subjects: Cabanès notes that "our anti-vivisectionists are not waiting to find out whether Marat is a champion of their cause." See Cabanès, 1920, 284.

p. 208. Like many skeptics: Ibid., 235–57, and I. Cohen, 1990, ch. 8.

p. 208. "I was pleased to hear": Quoted in I. Cohen, 1990, 68.

p. 208. After all, everyone knew they worked: Cabanès, 1920, 249.

p. 208. One historian tells us: Ibid., 257.

p. 209.   "sterility, vanity, and charlatanism": Quoted in Badinter and Badinter, 1988, 164, from Marat, *"Les Charlatans modernes, ou Lettres sur le charlantanisme académique,"* in *L'Ami du peuple,* 1791.

p. 209.   "have tried to depreciate my discoveries": Quoted in Coquard, 1993, 144.

p. 209.   So, it was not a complete loss: Cabanès, 1920, 223–28.

p. 209.   Roger Hahn and Robert Darnton: Hahn, 1971, and Darnton, 1968.

p. 210.   "I swear to God . . . I could cite a 100 others": Brissot, 1792, 163. See Loft, Mar.–May 1993, 265–87, esp. 266–70.

p. 211.   And yet, Condorcet saw things differently: Baker, 1975, 77–80.

p. 211.   "If this meant assuming": Hahn, 1971, 115.

p. 212.   "errors of logic": Brissot, *Mémoires,* 1:142.

p. 213.   His place in history: See the discussion in Crabtree, 1993, 3–72; Gauld, 1992, 16–17; Hughes and Rothovius, 1996, 13–60; Wyckoff, 1975; and Buranelli, 1975.

p. 213.   "freed themselves": Pattie, 1994, 282–83. Pattie also concludes that Mesmer was a charlatan, because he claimed knowledge he really didn't have and refused to use scientific investigative tools then available to find out what really worked, what didn't. He calls him "a charlatan who was also a humanitarian" (Pattie, 1).

p. 213.   By the end of the century: For the English context, see Fara, June 1995, 127–77, and for the cities outside of Paris in the rest of France, Europe, and even Haiti, see Gauld, 1992, 8–9.

p. 213.   In fact, Mesmer's theories of health: Lopez, 2000, ch. 9, and Lopez, 1966, 163–73.

p. 213.   Even more important: Crabtree, 1993, 1.

p. 214.   According to Robert Darnton: Darnton, 1968.

p. 214.   Mesmer was a tall man: All of his biographers describe the contents of his identity card from 1798 when he was sixty-four: "Age 64; height, five feet nine inches; hair and eyebrows, brown; eyes, the same; chin, double; face, full; forehead, high; nose and mouth, medium." See, for example, Wyckoff, 1975, 124.

p. 214.   Frank Pattie says: Pattie, 1994, 85, where the quotation may be found.

p. 215.   For a recent news account on the glass armonica, see Pollak, Dec. 12, 2001, E2, which recounts much of the contemporary interest in the glass armonica but also the strange disappearance of the world's most prolific makers of the instrument, Gerhard Finkenbeiner in Massachusetts in 1999. On the instrument itself, see Miley, Christmas 1998.

p. 215.   "M. Mesmer will content himself": Quoted in Lopez, 1966, 170.

p. 216.   Darnton makes an important point: Darnton, 1968, 15–17; and for Franklin's involvement, see Lopez and Herbert, 1975, 215–24.

p. 217.   "What is the use": Quoted in Lopez and Herbert, 1975, 269.

p. 217.   "great importance . . . to repel them": Franklin to Jan Ingenhousz, Jan. 18, 1785, in *Writings of Benjamin Franklin,* 9:155–56.

p. 217.   In medical school in Vienna: Pattie, 1994, 5–27, who argues that Mesmer plagiarized the thesis from a work by Richard Mead, who died in 1754, and other English and European physicians whose works he had read at Ingolstadt. Mead was the personal physician to Isaac Newton and Queen Anne.

p. 218. Again, given the eighteenth century's obsession: see Darnton, 1968, 2–45.

p. 219. Years later, he would pay tribute: Quoted in Wyckoff, 1975, 17, and Buranelli, 1975, 57.

p. 219. Then again: Lopez, 2000, 125–26.

p. 221. "Nothing is more astonishing": *Report of Dr. Benjamin Franklin*, 1785, 49.

p. 222. "the germ of what would be called hypnotism": Lopez, 2000, 117, but see also Pattie, 1998, 271–83, and Buranelli, 1975, 205–17.

p. 222. In 1785, Franklin told Jan Ingenhousz: Franklin to Jan Ingenhousz, Apr. 29, 1785, in *Writings of Benjamin Franklin*, 9:320–21.

p. 222. In a case, in 1775: The eyewitness was Ernst Seyfert, a tutor of the Baron Hareczky de Horka's household. It is quoted at length in Pattie, 1994, 49–51, but see also Buranelli, 1975, 68–69.

p. 223. Two years later, in what Mesmer claimed: The Paradis story appears in all the standard Mesmer biographies. For the quotation, see Pattie, 1994, 65.

p. 224. One of the most important was a radical young Parisian lawyer: On Bergasse and the Society of Universal Harmony, see Darnton, 1968, passim, and Pattie, 1994, 117–41.

p. 224. The members all signed a pledge: Gauld, 1992, 8.

p. 225. "high standing with the faculty": Crabtree, 1993, 16.

p. 225. The resulting document: Ibid., 26–27.

p. 227. It lasted until the Revolution: Gauld, 1992, 10.

p. 227. "perfectly illusory": Quoted in Pattie, 1994, 133.

p. 227. "a strange folly . . . dead, ridiculed": These are actually from different letters: Jefferson to John Page, Nov. 11, 1784; Jefferson to David Rittenhouse, Nov. 11, 1784; Jefferson to Francis Hopkinson, Jan. 13, 1785; Jefferson to James Currie, Feb. 5, 1785; in Boyd, 1950–, 7:514, 517, 602, 635, respectively.

p. 228. "The boy . . . was presented": *Report of Dr. Benjamin Franklin*, 69.

p. 228. "As to Animal Magnetism . . . they mistake the cure": Franklin to La Sablière de la Condamine, Mar. 19, 1784, in *Writings*, 1091.

p. 229. It is as relevant today: According to Goldstein, 1987.

p. 229. "The force of the imagination . . . abate the spirit of persecution": Paine, "Remarks by Mr. Paine," in *The Prospect* (1804), in *Writings of Thomas Paine*, 2:829–30. Paine wrote some seventeen pieces for this deistic journal, which failed in the spring of 1805.

p. 230. "the imagination is that active . . . are almost always destructive": *Report of Dr. Franklin*, 98, 100, 102.

p. 231. In 1785, the Society: Darnton, 1968, 72, 84–86.

p. 231. "Mesmer continues here": Franklin to Jan Ingenhousz, Apr. 29, 1785, in *Writings of Benjamin Franklin*, 9:320.

p. 231. For at least one modern historian: Gauld, 1992, 16.

Chapter 7. Condorcet, Revolution, and la République Française

p. 233. The Marquis de Condorcet is today: See, for example, McLean and Hewitt, ed., 1994, esp. 32–48, 73–78.

p. 234. "sodomy violates the right": Quoted in Robb, 2003, 176.

p. 234. For the birth and description of Condorcet, see Badinter and Badinter, 1988, 13–17, 33–34. In the past fifteen years, there has been virtual explosion of new interpretations of Condorcet's life and thought: conferences in Paris and Rome devoted to him, new books and articles, and even (in 1991) a new statue erected in his honor in Paris. Moreover, political scientists and mathematicians find his work in probability and statistics highly informative in terms of the science of rational choice theory. See, for example, Goodell, 1990.

p. 235. "second mother . . . *le bon Condorcet*": Badinter and Badinter, 1988, 41, 88, and Charlet, 1997, 59–70. According to the Badinters, Amélie Suard was his "third mother," though they were practically the same age, and his three "fathers" were d'Alembert, Turgot, and Voltaire (ibid., 44–54).

p. 237. "Wood was sold": Guedj, 1987, 9–10. This work tells of the work and adventures of two astronomers. The subtitle is "How Jean-Baptiste Delambre and Pierre Méchain, crossing revolutionary France with one another, came to define the new universal standard, the meter." For a recent treatment in English, see Alder, 2002.

p. 237. *"le mouton enragé"*: For a recent critique of how Condorcet's image fared during the nineteenth century, see Schandeler, 2000.

p. 237. "a vicious man": Jean-Baptiste Suard to Condorcet, May 18, 1775, in ed. Badinter, 1988, 163.

p. 237. "as pale, or rather as white": Quoted in Haraszti, Dec. 1930, 479. Haraszti published the marginalia he found in Adams's personal copy of Condorcet's posthumous *Sketch for a Historical Picture of the Progress of the Human Mind* (1795), which will be considered below in chapter seven.

p. 238. "ignorant, totally ignorant": Quoted by Huggins, 1997, 220, n12. Huggins has found this quotation, along with many others about Condorcet, in the marginalia that Adams had written in Condorcet's books and letters sent to him by the philosopher/mathematician that have been preserved in the Adams's library.

p. 239. On Aristotle and the republic, see Pocock, 1975, but also Bailyn, 1967, Wood, 1969 (revised 1992).

p. 239. "If the horses are of equal strength": Quoted by Paine, in *Constitutional Reform* (1805), in *Writings of Thomas Paine*, 2:1006.

p. 240. "had the wisest and ablest man": Paine, "A Serious Address to the People of Pennsylvania on the Present Situation of Their Affairs," Dec. 1, 1778, in the *Pennsylvania Packet*, and Paine, "To the People" (where he denied responsibility for the document), Mar. 18, 1777, in the *Pennsylvania Packet*, in *Writings of Thomas Paine*, 2:280, 270. For Franklin's actual role in the finalization of the Pennsylvania Constitution, see Editorial Notes on the Pennsylvania Constitution, *Papers*, 22:512–15.

p. 240. It is interesting to note: Dippel, 1997, 203.

p. 240. "Instead of collecting . . . with their own blood": Turgot to Richard Price, Mar. 22, 1778, in *Correspondence of Richard Price*, 2:13, 17.

p. 241. The Pennsylvania constitution: The entire document may be found in *Oeuvres de Condorcet*, 12:423–501.

p. 241. "was in part": Condorcet, "Eloge de Franklin," in *Oeuvres de Condorcet*, 3:401.

p. 241. "a citizen of New Haven . . . prevent its progress": Condorcet, *Lettres d'un bourgeois de New Haven à un citoyen de Virginie sur l'inutilité de partager le pouvoir legislatif entre plusieurs corps* (1787), in *Oeuvres de Condorcet*, 9:69, 76, 92.

p. 242. "the model of an excellent government . . . to be republicans": Brissot, *Bibliothèque philosophique du législateur, du politique, du jurisconsulte*, 10 vols. (Paris, 1782–1785), 3:243, 244. See Selsam, Jan. 1948, 25–43.

p. 243. "*mon cher and illustre confrere*": Condorcet to Franklin, Dec. 2, 1773, in *Papers*, 20:489.

p. 243. On the Code Noir, see Ott, 1973, Winock, 1991.

p. 243. "the Negroes who are free": Franklin to Condorcet, Mar. 20, 1774, in *Papers*, 21:151.

p. 243. He did not sign the work: Jurt, 1989, 388.

pp. 244–246. "Bienne . . . sooner or later": *Oeuvres de Condorcet*, 7:69–140.

p. 246. In 1788, Brissot: Resnick, Fall 1972, 558–59.

p. 247. Because of this popularity: Brissot, *Mémoires*, 2:79.

p. 247. In addition, Lafayette: Lafayette is not on the list in Ellery, 1915, 442–47, but see Brissot to James Philips, Mar. 19, 1788, in Brissot, *Correspondance*, 169–70, when Lafayette declared to Brissot and Claviére that "he regarded himself as one of the members of our society." For Abbé Grégoire, see Brissot, *Mémoires*, 2:87.

p. 247. He was soon helping: Brissot, *Mémoires*, 2:77. For the entire list, see Appendix B, Ellery, 1915, 442–47, or Brissot, *Mémoires*, 2:74–75.

p. 247. He hoped he could use: Brissot, *Mémoires*, 2:80–81.

p. 248. "destroy the trade": Quoted in Jurt, 1989, 393.

p. 248. "Thus the abolition of Negro slavery": Quoted in D. Davis, 1975, 97, n16, from Condorcet, *Lettre écrit par la Société des Amis des Noirs en France, aux differens bailliages et districts ayant droit d'envoyer les deputés aux Etats-Generaux* (letter written by the Society of the Friends of the Blacks in France to the different bailliages and districts having the right to send deputies to the Estates General), Feb. 3,1789.

p. 249. "We hope that the National Assembly": Quoted in Badinter and Badinter, 1988, 294.

p. 249. Wilberforce's bill for abolition: E. Wilson, 1989, ch. 5, and Griggs, 1970, ch. 1. The last several passages on Clarkson are drawn from these two works, the latter by one of the leading socialist historians of the twentieth century.

p. 251. "a kind of academic club": Cahen, 1904, 237–38, who lists the members.

p. 251. The great Physiocrat: Baker, 1975, 272.

p. 252. "the court of capitalism": Ibid., 279.

p. 254. These five men: Aldridge, Jan. 1958. The full title was *Le Républicain, ou le défenseur du gouvernement représentatif*.

p. 255. "I only knew about the petition . . . all those who held power": Condorcet, "Fragment" (1794), in *Oeuvres de Condorcet*, 1:610.

p. 256. At forty-eight: Badinter and Badinter, 1988, 354.

p. 257. "a barbarian law . . . a kind of horror": Quoted in ibid., 374.

p. 257. "most legitimate and most just": Condorcet, *Lettres d'un bourgeois de New Haven, in Oeuvres de Condorcet*, 9:46, for the first quotation, Condorcet, *Vie de Voltaire, Oeuvres de Condorcet*, 4:147, for the second.

p. 258. "universal republic": Bénot, 1997, 251.

p. 259. "of all the French constitutions . . . the most democratic": Dippel, 1989, 2:61–73, with the quotation on 61. Dippel cites similar comments about the 1793 constitution made by the great French historians Alphonse Aulard, Jacques Godechot, Jean-Jacques Chevallier, Maurice Deslandres, and Jacques Ellul.

pp. 259–261. "one of the most pressing needs . . . perfect equality between men": Condorcet, et al., "On the Principles of the Constitutional Plan Presented to the National Convention" (1793), in Baker, ed., 1976, 156, 158–59, 163, 164, 166, 178. The original may be found in Condorcet, *Exposition des principes et des motifs du plan de constitution* (1793), in *Oeuvres de Condorcet*, 12:333–415.

p. 262. "could not be a legislature": Quoted in Whaley, 2000, 107.

p. 262. The vote for execution: Patrick, 1972, esp. part 2.

p. 262. A few weeks later: Within days of the fall of the Girondins, May 31–June 2, 1793, a new constitutional committee was formed under the leadership of Hérault de Séchelles, who reported a new document to the Convention on June 24. It was almost exactly like Condorcet's in that it reflected the manner and style of his work and was a mirror image of the Pennsylvania Constitution. See Dippel, 1989, 2:68–69.

p. 262. The Terror would last: Higonnet, 1998, 15. See Dunn, 1999, 92, for estimates of those killed during the Terror.

p. 262. "More than previous notable works": Schandeler, 2000, 7.

pp. 264–265. "How consoling for the philosopher . . . extravagance for mankind": Condorcet, *Sketch* (1795), 1955, 201–02, 8, 11, 128 (his emphasis), 130, 136, 169.

p. 265. "fantastic hope": Condorcet, *Esquisse d'un tableau historique des progrès de l'esprit humain, in Oeuvres de Condorcet*, 6:20.

p. 265. "the *Esquisse* was the form": Manuel, 1962, 61.

pp. 266–268. "the abolition of inequality . . . the love of mankind": Condorcet (1795), 1955, 172, 177, 182, 193, 194, 196. 198. We will not deal here with Condorcet's important and complex scientific calculus of progress. The *Sketch* appeared in 1795, almost two years after his death, and was widely distributed by the Directory.

p. 267. While Condorcet: Rey, 1997, 137–46.

p. 267. "with his peers in an Elysium": Condorcet, *Sketch*, 202.

p. 268. "Thou art a Quack!": Haraszti, Dec. 1930, 474, 478, Haraszti, 1952, 241–42, and Dunn, 1999, 40–43.

Chapter 8. Brissot, Revolutionary Politics, and Democracy

p. 269. The French revolutionary journalist: For Brissot's life and work, see

Brissot, *Mémoires*. For modern studies, see the works (noted here) of the most prolific Brissot scholar, Loft, 2002, who believes he deserves the stature of Voltaire and Rousseau, and D'Huart, 1986. For an older but still serviceable study, see Ellery, 1915. Robert Darnton has been anticipating writing a full-length study of Brissot's life and work. The population of Chartres was around 13,500 inhabitants. See François-Primo, 1932, 7, n1.

p. 269. Most of them failed: For Brissot's development as a writer and revolutionary journalist, especially within the context of the eighteenth-century book trade, see Darnton, 2001, 7–47. A copy of Darnton's essay may also be found online at the Voltaire Foundation Web site: *www.voltaire.ac.uk*. See also Loft, Mar.–May 1993, 265–85.

p. 270. "only to protect the interests": Loft, Sept.–Oct. 1989, 247. The work was published in 1781.

p. 270. Finally, he called for: Loft, Sept.–Oct., 1989, 247–53.

p. 270. At the time of the meeting: Brissot, *Mémoires*, 1:142. There is also a reference to the meeting in Bougeart, 1885, 1:38, and in Cabanès, 1920, 228, who cited Brissot's *Mémoires*.

p. 271. "we should find no People . . . the same of theirs": Franklin, "Remarks Concerning the Savages of North-America" (1783), in *Writings*, 969.

p. 271. Brissot was taken by Franlin's wisdom: Warner, 1993, 75–87.

p. 271. "M. de Warville . . . is a most": Franklin to Flainville, Oct. 23,1788, in *Writings of Benjamin Franklin*, 9:667.

p. 271. "I have met in America": Brissot de Warville, 1964, 182.

p. 272. "the patriot *par excellence*": Quoted in Aldridge, 1957, 45–46, citing P. J. B. Buchez and P. C. Roux, *Histoire parlementaire de la Révolution Française*, 40 vols. (Paris, 1834–1838), 14:139.

p. 272. Born in Chartres: Darnton, 2001, 7–47.

p. 272. "slim, appearing older": D'Huart, 1986, 40.

p. 272. "only Anglomania": Winock, 1991, 123.

p. 274. There he met: Brissot to David Williams, 1783, in Brissot, *Correspondance*, 77–78.

p. 274. "Price spoke to me": Bancal des Issarts to Brissot, 1790, in Brissot, *Correspondance*, 259.

p. 274. "my dear colleague": Brissot to Jeremy Bentham, July 8, 1783, in Brissot, *Correspondance*, 64.

p. 274. Most important, Brissot hoped: Loft, Jan. 1993, 7–37, and D. Goodman, 1994, 281–88. Loft cannot determine why Brissot insisted on the spelling of the word "licée" (rather than the more commonly used and correct "lycée"), though it is clear that he thought of it as a modern parallel to Aristotle's famous Lyceum. See Loft, Jan. 1993, 33, n6.

p. 274. It was to be a truly enlightened: For Brissot's attack on anti-Semitism, see Loft, 2002, 223–33; Loft, 1990, 465–75; and Loft, 1991, 605–22.

p. 274. "one of the causes of the retardation . . . all particular facts better": Quoted in Loft, Jan. 1993, 8.

p. 274. "accused of having written": Quoted in Loft, 2002, 11.

p. 275. Although historian Robert Darnton: Darnton, July 1970, 532–59, and Darnton, 1982, ch. 2, Darnton, 2001, 36. Darnton has been challenged by DeLuna, Spring 1991, 159–90, to which Darnton replied (Spring 1991, 191–205). In his latest essay, 2001, Darnton has definitely lightened in views about whether Brissot was a police spy and now suggests that he was merely speculating that he may have been.

p. 275. He even offered freedom: Loft, Spring 1991, 209–18.

p. 276. "I will tell you the truth . . . a foreign asylum": Quoted in Loft, Spring 1991, 212, 214, from Brissot's anonymously published *Un défenseur du people à l'Empereur Joseph II, sur son réglement concernant l'émigration, ses diverse réformes, &c.* (Dublin [Paris], 1785).

p. 277. His rejoinder: Jacques-Pierre Brissot, *Examen critique des voyages dans l'Amérique septentrionale, de M. le marquis de Chastellux* (1786), translated into English and published in Philadelphia in 1788. See Loft, 2002, 216–17, D'Huart, 1986, 93–96, and Ellery, 1915, 59–60.

p. 277. "My job": Perroud, Brissot, *Correspondance*, xli.

p. 278. It was there that Brissot met: Brissot, *Mémoires*, ch. 16 in vol. 2.

p. 278. "An important point": Brissot to James Philips, Mar. 19, 1788, in Brissot, *Correspondance*, 168 (see also the rest of the letter, 168–71). See Loft, 2002, 207–16.

p. 278. "You know that nobody wishes": Jefferson to Brissot, Feb. 11, 1788, Brissot, *Correspondance*, 164–65.

p. 279. "to serve the cause of the blacks": Brissot, *Mémoires*, 2:74.

p. 279. "so-called *philosophe*": "Recommandation de M. de Montmorin en faveur de Brissot," Apr. 29, 1788, in Brissot, *Correspondance*, 176–77.

p. 280. "He told me that it is much more difficult": Brissot de Warville, 1964, note on 233.

p. 280. Brissot did not discuss: Brissot devoted six letters to a description of the life of blacks in America. See Brissot, 1964, 217–52.

p. 280. "to public education, to the relief . . . to prove its falsity": Brissot, 1964, 218, 234.

p. 281. He cited the case: Brissot's information, he said, came from Benjamin Rush's report on Derham in an address Rush made to the Philadelphia Society for Promoting the Abolition of Slavery, which was later printed in *American Museum 5* (1789): 61–62 (see ibid., 234, n5).

p. 281. On Brissot entering politics, see Whaley, 2000, 27–29. Bailly received 12,500 votes out of a total 14,000 cast.

p. 282. "Challenge therefore these turbulent spirits": Quoted in Cahen, 1904, 142–43.

p. 283. This formidable group: for detail, see Winock, 1991, 173–75.

p. 284. According to Brissot, he was a cold, rational, and eloquent man: Brissot, *Mémoires*, 2:116.

p. 285. In essence, Barnave mouthed: Chill, ed., 1971, 6–8.

p. 285. "the Assembly approved the report": D. Davis, 1975, 99–100.

p. 285. Brissot's open letter: Furet, 1989, 188.

p. 286. "Ogé had everything to fear": Brissot, *Mémoires*, 2:98.

p. 286.	Captured by the Spanish governor: Ott, 1973, 37.
p. 286.	In tribute to his revolutionary fearlessness: On the *Mémoires de Barbaroux*, see Brissot, *Mémoires*, 1:97, n1, and 100.
p. 286.	On Barnave and the Queen, see Chill, ed., 1971, 11–12.
p. 287.	"possessed the logic of a lawyer": Brissot, *Mémoires*, 2:102–14.
p. 287.	"*le petit Barnave* . . . the dupe of evil ones": De Roux, ed., 1966, 129.
p. 287.	"My husband acquires much glory": Félicité Brissot to her sister, Apr. 1792, in Brissot, *Correspondance*, 283.
p. 288.	While he worked for many newspapers: Originally called *Le Patriote français*, according to eighteenth-century usage, the paper lasted from July 28, 1789, to June 2, 1793.
p. 288.	"was justifiably considered . . . the best propaganda instrument": Popkin, 1990, 113, and Winock, 1991, 125. See also Loft, 2002, 17, 135.
p. 288.	"one can teach the same truth": Popkin, 1990, 33, 28.
p. 288.	Published thereafter every day: Perroud, ed., Brissot, *Correspondance*, li.
p. 289.	"How does it happen . . . postpone the constitution": Quoted in Popkin, 1990, 55, 113.
pp. 290–291.	"dissipaters" (*dissipateurs*) . . . their barbarian masters": Brissot's speech of Dec. 1, 1791, quoted in Winock, 1991, 176.
p. 291.	"a permanent revolution": Quoted from French historian Jean Jaurès in Winock, 1991, 144–45; see also 145–46.
p. 292.	"For a people who have conquered . . . if they still exist": Quoted in Winock, 1991, 148–49.
p. 292.	"another crusade" to achieve "universal liberty": Quoted in ibid., 152.
p. 293.	Brissot successfully nominated: For the financial and political relationship between Brissot and Clavière, see Darnton, 2003, ch. 7.
p. 293.	Pierre Victurnien Vergniaud nominated his friend: Winock, 1991, 186.
p. 293.	"For the first time . . . not be entirely forgotten": Quoted in Badinter and Badinter, 1988, 395.
p. 295.	Marat reportedly so frightened: Whaley, 2001, 74.
p. 296.	Brissot called this work: Brissot, *Mémoires*, 2:113.
p. 297.	"Fuck the prisoners": Quoted in Higonnet, 1998, 37 and 338, n23 (*"je me fous bien des prisonniers; qu'ils deviennent ce qu'ils pourront"*).
p. 297.	when the commissioners arrived: James, 1989.
p. 297.	Had Brissot and the others been arrested: No one is certain of the origins of the September Massacres, except that no radical club, such as the Jacobins, the Cordeliers, or even the Girondins, disassociated itself from them until they were over. Nor is it clear why Pétion, the Paris mayor, did not call out the National Guard until it was too late. It is important to bear in the mind that those murdered included common criminals and the poor. See Whaley, 2000, 81–84.
p. 298.	"the orator of the human race": Avenel, 1865.
p. 299.	Still, he and his faction almost daily: Whaley, 2000, 123.
p. 300.	"The rights of man are no more . . . enlightening their citizens": Quoted in Baczko, 1994, 85.
p. 302.	"I confess that I believed . . . there is no republic": Brissot, *Mémoires*, 1:207.

p. 303. "Terror shall be the order of the day": Guerlac, 1931, 270, and Schama, who attributes the phrase to Danton (Schama, 1989, 807).

Chapter 9. Learning in the New Era

p. 305. "Here was buried": Peterson, ed., 1984, 706. See Wills, 2002.

p. 306. With the exception of Franklin: See Whaley, 2000, 3. David Bell points out that Brissot was not alone in using Reims for a law degree. Danton, Roland and several other prominent "lawyers" during the Revolution also purchased their degrees there as well. Bell, 1994, 34.

p. 307. "republican machines": Blinderman, 1976, 18.

p. 307. "There are already several Schemes": Franklin to Jackson, Apr. 17, 1763, in *Papers*, 10:255.

p. 307. "the true nurseries of power": Quoted in N. Goodman, 1934, 322.

p. 308. "The value of the land": Rush to Armstrong, Mar. 19, 1783, in *Letters of Benjamin Rush*, 1:297.

p. 309. "the illustrious Pennsylvania farmer": Rush to Sharp, Nov. 28, 1783, in Woods, ed., 1967, 20–21.

p. 309. "the back parts of Pennsylvania": Price to Rush, Jan. 1, 1783, and Oct. 14, 1784, in *Correspondence of Richard Price*, 2:162, 2:235.

p. 310. "takes care of its own youth . . . the arts and sciences": [Rush], "To the Citizens of Pennsylvania of German Birth and Extraction: Proposal of a German College," Aug. 31, 1785, *Letters of Benjamin Rush*, 1:364–68.

p. 312. "for reducing man . . . tendency to homosexuality": Quoted in Baker, 1975, 3–4, and in Badinter and Badinter, 1988, 17–21.

p. 312. "Enlightened public opinion": Keith Baker conclusively points out, Condorcet's ideas were rooted in the secular vision of education that Louis-René Caradeuc de la Chalotais had proposed as early as 1763, La Mettrie in 1767, Quesnay and others afterward. See Baker, 1975, 288–93, with the quotations on 291 and 10.

p. 314. "It is easy to establish assemblies": Condorcet, *Vie de M. Turgot* (1786), in *Oeuvres de Condorcet*, 5:122.

p. 315. "technocratic creed . . . systematic solutions": Baker, 1975, 291–92. See the recent contemporary analysis by Boulad-Ayoub, 1997, 109–19.

p. 315. Education, as a truly transforming agent: Livesey, 2001, 168–70, who sees the Rousseauist background in Condorcet's ideas of education.

p. 316. When the harvest was bad: See the now-classic study by Rudé, 1964, esp. ch. 1.

p. 316. "If hope of the people's happiness": Condorcet, *Réflexions sur le commerce des blés* (1776), in *Oeuvres de Condorcet*, 11:194.

p. 318. "the entire realm of the former academies": Badinter and Badinter, 1988, 398.

p. 318. Condorcet maddeningly declined: Niklaus, 1989, 265.

p. 319. "l'école de la république": Badinter and Badinter, 1988, 400.

p. 319. "an insidious effort": Baker, in ed. Furet and Ozouf, 1989, 207.

p. 320. "If girls were encouraged": Tomalin, 1985, 139. See Sapiro, 1992,

237–49, where Sapiro outlines in detail the rationale for many of these ideas, especially the different definitions of education.

p. 320. At most, added Rush: Rush, "A Plan for the Establishment of Public Schools and the Diffusion of Knowledge in Pennsylvania; to Which are Added Thoughts upon the Mode of Education, Proper in a Republic. Addressed to the Legislature and Citizens of the State" (1786), in Rudolph, 1965, 3–8, 9–21, 21–22. Rush hoped that his "Thoughts on Female Education" would be published in England, but he told John Coakley Lettsom that he thought it was "too trifling to be reprinted in a separate pamphlet. I therefore beg it may not be obtruded upon the public eye in that form in Great Britain." Rush to John Coakley Lettsom, Sept. 28, 1787, in *Letters of Benjamin Rush*, 1:443. Goodman and Hawke say that Rush lifted the guts of this essay from François Fénelon's *Treatise on the Education of Daughters*. See N. Goodman, 1934, 314, and Hawke, 1971, 333. For disagreement, see Straub, 1967, 149–50, who sees some similarities but says that Rush was disinclined to include the study of classics, whereas Fénelon disagreed, and Rush included some of the sciences, like arithmetic and bookkeeping, whereas Fénelon chose not include them.

p. 321. Still, only the Marquis de Condorcet: On Condorcet's feminism, see Williams, 1976, 151–63, B. Brookes, 1980, Niklaus, 1987, 119–40, and de Lagrave, 1989, 434–42. Williams argues that the ideas of Diderot and d'Holbach were antecedents to Condorcet's feminism.

p. 321. "Women," he wrote, "having these same qualities": The essay appears in translation as "On the Admission of Women to the Rights of Citizenship," in ed. Baker, 1976, 97–104, with the quotation appearing and the citation of the twelve million women at p. 98.

pp. 321–322. "expressed her opinions" . . . to exclude others: Condorcet, "On the Admission of Women to the Rights of Citizenship," in ed. Baker, 1976, 99, 100.

p. 322. "Condorcet affirmed": Fauré, 1989, 352.

p. 323. "the times were just not ripe": Badinter and Badinter, 1988, 297–98. See Niklaus, 1987, 121–26 and 130, n19, for a list of the clubs started by women advocating women's rights.

p. 323. "Several women . . . purity of manners": Some of Condorcet's essays on education are reprinted in translation in ed. Baker, 1976, 105–42, with the quotations on 142, n1.

p. 323. Perhaps it was because: Fauré, 1989, 351.

p. 324. Nonetheless, though they could be citizens: Condorcet indicated as much in his last known work, called *A Fragment on the New Atlantis*. For a discussion on how Condorcet saw women and blacks differently, see Fricheau, 1989.

Epilogue: A Future of Progress, Liberty, and Justice

p. 327. "one of the most formidable lawyer-orators": Editors, *Papers*, note on 21:20.

p. 327. "My Lords, Dr. Frankin's mind . . . as a successor": "Wedderburn's Speech

Before the Privy Council," Jan. 29, 1774, in *Papers*, 21:58–59, 60–61, 64, 66. The speech runs some twenty-five pages in the collection.

p. 328. "Long did I endeavour": Franklin to Lord Howe, July 20, 1776, in *Writings*, 993.

p. 329. "He spoke to both of us": Franklin to Mary Stevenson, Sept. 14, 1767, in *Writings*, 824.

p. 329. "The friendly disposition of this court": Franklin to Robert R. Livingston, Mar. 4, 1782, in *Writings*, 1043.

p. 329. "The revolution in France . . . give me great concern": Franklin to Vaughn, Nov. 2, 1789, in ed. Smyth, *Writings of Benjamin Franklin*, 10:50.

p. 329. "A great part of the news . . . for the King and nation": Franklin to Le Roy, Nov. 13, 1789, in ed. Smyth, *Writings of Benjamin Franklin*, 10:68–69.

p. 330. "God grant . . . 'This is my Country'": Franklin to David Hartley, Dec. 4, 1789, in ed. Smyth, *Writings of Benjamin Franklin*, 10:72.

p. 330. "chaos and darkness": Burke to Charles Jean François Depont, Nov. 1789, in ed. Copeland, 6:46.

p. 330. "This new, and hitherto unheard of bill of rights": Burke, *Reflections on the Revolution in France* (1790), 1987, 14.

Works Cited

Primary Sources

Adams, Charles Francis, ed. *The Works of John Adams, Second President of the United States*, 10 vols. Freeport, NY: Books for Libraries Press, 1969, orig. publ. Boston: Little, Brown, 1850–1856.

Armistead, Wilson. *Anthony Benezet, from The Original Memoir*. Freeport, NY: Books for Libraries Press, 1971, orig. publ. 1859.

Badinter, Elisabeth, ed. *Correspondance inédite de Condorcet et Madame Suard, 1771–1791*. Paris: Fayard, 1988.

Belsham, Thomas. *The Memoirs of the Late Reverend Theophilus Lindsey*. London, 1873.

Bentham, Jeremy. *The Works of Jeremy Bentham*, published under the superintendence of his executor, John Bowling, 11 vols. Bristol, UK: Thoemmes, 1995, orig. publ. 1843.

Blackstone, William. *Commentaries on the Laws of England*, 4 vols. Oxford, 1765–1769, reprt. New York, 1978.

Biddle, Louis Alexander, ed. *A Memorial Containing Travels Through Life or Sundry Incidents in the Life of Dr. Benjamin Rush*. Philadelphia, 1905.

Boswell, James. *Boswell in Search of a Wife*, 1766–1769, ed. Frank Brady and Frederick A. Pottle. New York: McGraw-Hill, 1956.

_____. *Boswell's Journal of a Tour to the Hebrides with Samuel Johnson, LL.D.*, Frederick A. Pottle and Charles H. Bennett. New York: McGraw-Hill, 1936.

Boulton, J. T. "An Unpublished Letter from Paine to Burke," *Durham University Journal* 43 (Mar. 1951): 49–50.

Boyd, Julian P. ed. *The Papers of Thomas Jefferson*, 30 vols. to date. Princeton, NJ: Princeton University Press, 1950–.

Brissot de Warville, Jacques-Pierre. *De la verité, ou Méditations sur les moyens de parvenir à la vérité dans toutes les connaissances humaines*, Nouvelle Edition. Neuchâtel, 1792.

_____. *New Travels in the United States of America, 1788*, ed. Durand Echeverria. Cambridge, MA: Harvard University Press, 1964.

Burke, Edmund. *The Writings and Speeches of Edmund Burke*, ed. Paul Langford, 12 vols. Oxford: Oxford University Press, 1981, 1989.

_____. *Reflections on the Revolution in France* (1790), ed. J. C. D. Clark. Stanford, CA: Stanford University Press, 2001.

_____. *Reflections on the Revolution in France* (1790), ed. J. G. A. Pocock. Indianapolis: Hackett, 1987.

Butterfield, Lyman H., ed. *The Diary and Autobiography of John Adams*. 4 vols. Cambridge, MA: Harvard University Press, 1961.

[Chalmers, George]. *Life of Thomas Pain, Author of Rights of Men* [sic], *with a Defence of his Writings, by Francis Oldys, A. M. of the University of Pennsylvania*

(London, 1791). Second edition: *Life of Thomas Pain, Author of the Seditious Writings, entitled Rights of Man*. London, 1793.

Chill, Emanuel, ed. "Introduction: Barnave as Philosophical Historian," *Power, Property, and History: Barnave's "Introduction to the French Revolution" and Other Writings*. New York: Harper and Row, 1971.

Condorcet, Antoine-Nicolas de. *Sketch for a Historical Picture of the Progress of the Human Mind* (1795), trans. June Barraclough. London: Weidenfeld and Nicolson, 1955.

Copeland, Thomas W., ed. *The Correspondence of Edmund Burke*, 10 vols. Cambridge: Cambridge University Press, 1958–1978.

Farrand, Max, ed. *The Records of the Federal Convention of 1787*, 4 vols. New Haven, CT: Yale University Press, 1937.

Fitzpatrick, John C., ed. *The Writings of George Washington*, 39 vols. Washington, D.C.: Government Printing Office, 1931–1944.

Ford, Worthington Chauncey, ed. *Statesman and Friend: Correspondence of John Adams with Benjamin Waterhouse, 1784–1822*. Boston: Little, Brown, 1927.

Gillies, John, ed. *Works of the Reverend George Whitefield*, 4 vols. London, 1771.

Goldsmith, Oliver. *The Vicar of Wakefield*. Harmondsworth: Penguin Books, 1987, orig. publ. 1766.

Greene, Donald J., ed. *The Yale Edition of the Works of Samuel Johnson*, 16 vols. to date. New Haven, CT: Yale University Press, 1957–.

Johnson, Samuel. *Dictionary of the English Language*, 2 vols. London, 1832.

Labaree, Leonard W., et al., ed. *The Autobiography of Benjamin Franklin*. Ithaca, NY: Cornell University Press, 1964.

Lemay, J. A. Leo, and P. M. Zall, ed. *Autobiography of Benjamin Franklin: A Genetic Text*. Knoxville: University of Tennessee Press, 1981.

Mease, James. *The Picture of Philadelphia, Giving an Account of Its Origin, Increase and Improvements in Arts, Sciences, Manufactures, Commerce and Revenue*. New York: Arno Press, 1970; orig. publ. Philadelphia, 1811.

Paine, Thomas. *Common Sense*, ed. Isaac Kramnick. Harmondsworth: Penguin, 1976.

_____. *Rights of Man* (1792). Introduction by Eric Foner and notes by Henry Collins. Harmondsworth: Penguin, 1984.

_____. *The Age of Reason* (1794–1795) in two parts, ed. Philip S. Foner. New York: Citadel Press, 1984.

Peterson, Merrill D., ed. *The Portable Thomas Jefferson*. New York: Viking, 1984.

Price, Richard. *Additional Observations on the Nature and Value of Civil Liberty, and the War with America*. London, 1777.

_____. *A Discourse on the Love of Our Country, Delivered on Nov. 4, 1789, at the Meeting House in the Old Jewry, to the Society for Commemorating the Revolution in Great Britain*. London, 1790.

_____. *An Appeal to the Public on the Subject of the National Debt*. London, 1772.

_____. *An Essay on the Present State of Population in England and Wales*. London, 1780.

_____. *A Review of the Principal Questions and Difficulties in Morals* (1758), ed. David Daiches Raphael. Oxford: Clarendon, 1974.

_____. *Observations on the Nature of Civil Liberty, the Principles of Government, and the Justice and Policy of the War with America*. London, 1776; reprt. as *Two Tracts on Civil Liberty*, New York: Da Capo Press, 1972.

_____. *Observations on the Importance of the American Revolution, and the Means of Making it a Benefit to the World.* London, 1784.

_____. *The Evidence for a Future Period of Improvement in the State of Mankind, with the Means and Duty of Improving It, in a Discourse Delivered on Wednesday, the 15th of Apr., 1787, at the Meeting-House in the Old Jewry, London, to the Supporters of a New Academical Institution Among Protestant Dissenters.* London, 1787.

_____, and Joseph Priestley. *A Free Discussion of the Doctrines of Materialism, and Philosophical Necessity, in a Correspondence between Dr. Price and Dr. Priestley.* London, 1778.

Prince Hoare. *Memoirs of Granville Sharp, Esq.,* 2 vols. London, 1828.

Report of Dr. Benjamin Franklin and other Commissioners, charged by the King of France, with the Examination of the Animal Magnetism, as now practised at Paris. Translated from the French. With an Historical Introduction. London, 1785.

Rickman, Thomas Clio. *The Life of Thomas Paine.* London, 1819.

Roux, Paul de, ed. *Mémoires of Madame Roland.* Paris: Mercure de France, 1966.

Runes, Dagobert D., ed. *The Selected Writings of Benjamin Rush.* New York: Philosophical Library, 1947.

Schofield, Robert E., ed. *A Scientific Autobiography of Joseph Priestley, 1733–1804.* Cambridge, MA: Harvard University Press: 1966.

Smith, Adam. *Théorie des sentiments moraux . . . ,* 3rd edition, trans. Sophie de Grouchy Vve Condorcet. Paris, 1860.

Swift, Jonathan. *Gulliver's Travels.* New York: Signet Classics, 1960.

Tocqueville, Alexis de. *Democracy in America,* 2 vols. New York: Vintage, 1945.

Vaux, Roberts. *Memoirs of the Life of Anthony Benezet.* Philadelphia: B. Franklin, 1969; orig. publ. in 1817.

Webster Noah. *The Elementary Spelling Book; Being An Improvement on the American Spelling Book.* Cazenovia, NY, 1838.

Wharton, Thomas Isaac. *A Memoir of William Rawle.* Philadelphia, Vol. 4, Part 1, 1840.

Whitefield, George. *George Whitefield's Journals, 1737–41,* William V. Davis, intro. Gainesville, FL: Scholars' Facsimiles and Reprints, 1969.

_____. *Letters of George Whitefield for the Period 1734–1742.* Edinburgh: Banner of Truth Trust, 1976; orig. publ. 1771.

Wilson, David A., ed. *William Cobbett, Peter Porcupine in America: Pamphlets on Republicanism and Revolution.* Ithaca, NY: Cornell University Press, 1994.

Woods, John A., ed. "The Correspondence of Benjamin Rush and Granville Sharp, 1773–1809," *Journal of American Studies 1 (1967)* : 1–38.

Secondary Sources

Alder, Ken. *The Measure of All Things: The Seven-Year Odyssey and Hidden Error That Transformed the World.* New York: Free Press, 2002.

Aldridge, Alfred Owen. *Benjamin Franklin and His French Contemporaries.* New York: New York University Press, 1957.

_____. *Benjamin Franklin: Philosopher and Man.* Philadelphia: American Philosophical Society, 1965.

_____. "Condorcet et Paine: leurs rapports intellectuals," *Revue de literature comparée* 32 (Jan. 1958): 47–65

_____. "Jacques Barbeu-Dubourg, A French Disciple of Benjamin Franklin," *Proceedings of the American Philosophical Society* 95 (Aug. 17, 1951): 331–92.

_____. *Thomas Paine's American Ideology*. Newark: University Press of Delaware, 1984.

Anderson, Douglas. *The Radical Enlightenments of Benjamin Franklin*. Baltimore: Johns Hopkins University Press, 1997.

Anderson, J. G. *The Birthplace and Genesis of Life Assurance*. London: F. Muller, 1937.

Anstey, Roger. *The Atlantic Slave Trade and British Abolition, 1760–1810*. London: Macmillan, 1975.

Armytage, W. H. G. "Thomas Paine and the Walkers: An Early Episode in Anglo-American Co-operation," *Pennsylvania History* 18 (Jan. 1951): 16–30.

Ashe, Geoffrey. *The Hell-Fire Clubs: A History of Anti-Morality*. London: Ashe, 1974.

Avenel, Georges. *Anacharsis Cloots, l'Orateur du genre humain: Paris! France! Univers!* Paris, 1976, facsimile reproduction of the 1865 edition.

Ayer, A. J. *Thomas Paine*. London: Secker and Warburg, 1988.

Backscheider, Paula R. *Daniel Defoe: His Life*. Baltimore: Johns Hopkins University Press, 1989.

Baczko, Bronislaw. *Ending the Terror: The French Revolution after Robespierre*, trans. Michel Petheram. Cambridge: Cambridge University Press 1994.

Badinter, Elisabeth, and Robert Badinter. *Condorcet (1743–1794), Un intellectuel en politique*. Paris: Fayard, 1988.

Bailyn, Bernard. *To Begin the World Anew: the Genius and Ambiguities of the American Founders*. New York: Alfred A. Knopf, 2003.

_____. *The Ideological Origins of the American Revolution*. Cambridge, MA: Harvard University Press, 1967.

Baker, Keith Michael. "Condorcet," in ed. François Furet and Mona Ozouf, *A Critical Dictionary of the French Revolution*, trans. Arthur Goldhammer. Cambridge, MA: Harvard University Press, 1989, 204–12.

_____. *Condorcet: From Natural Philosophy to Social Mathematics*. Chicago: University of Chicago Press, 1975.

_____. "L'unité de la pensée de Condorcet," in dir. Pierre Crépel and Christian Gilain, *Condorcet: mathématicien, économiste, philosophe, homme politique*, Actes du colloque. Paris: Minerve, 1989, 515–24.

Banning, Lance. *The Sacred Fire of Liberty: James Madison and the Founding of the Federal Republic*. Ithaca, NY: Cornell University Press, 1995.

Barrall, John. *Imagining the King's Death: Figurative Treason, Fantasies of Regicide, 1793–1796*. Oxford: Oxford University Press, 2000.

Barrett, Andrea. "Rare Bird," in *Ship Fever*. New York: W. W. Norton, 1996.

Belcher, Joseph. *George Whitefield: A Biography*. New York: American Tract Society, 1857.

Bell, David A. *Lawyers and Citizens: The Making of a Political Elite in Old Regime France*. New York: Oxford University Press, 1994.

Bénot, Yves, "Condorcet et la République universelle," in ed. Anne-Marie Chouillet and Pierre Crépel, *Condorcet, homme des Lumière et de la Révolution*. Fontenay/Saint Cloud: ENS Editions, 1997, 251–61.

Berkin, Carol. *A Brilliant Solution: Inventing the American Constitution*. New York: Harcourt, 2002.

Berlin, Ira. *Many Thousands Gone: The First Two Centuries of Slavery in North America*. Cambridge, MA: Harvard University Press, 1998.

Black, Eugene Charlton. *The Association: British Extraparliamentary Political Organization, 1769–1793*. Cambridge, MA: Harvard University Press 1963.

Blinderman, Abraham. *Three Early Champions of Education: Benjamin Franklin, Benjamin Rush, and Noah Webster*. Bloomington, IN: Phi Delta Kappa Educational Foundation, 1976.

Boissel, Thiérry. *Sophie de Condorcet: Femme des lumières, 1764–1822*. Paris: Presses de la Renaissance, 1988.

Bonomi, Patricia U. *Under the Cope of Heaven: Religion, Society, and Politics in Colonial America*. New York: Oxford University Press, 1986.

Boorstin, Daniel. *The Lost World of Thomas Jefferson*. Chicago: University of Chicago Press, 1981

Bougeart, A. *Marat, l'ami du peuple*, 2 vols. Paris: A. Lacroix, 1885.

Boulad-Ayoub, Josianne. "*Le moyen le plus sûr. . . ou les parti-pris de Condorcet, président du premier comité révolutionnaire d'instruction publique*, in ed. Marie Chouillet and Pierre Crépel, *Condorcet, homme des Lumières et de la Révolution*. Fontenay/Saint Cloud: ENS Editions, 1997, 109–19.

Bowen, Catherine Drinker. *The Most Dangerous Man in America: Scenes from the Life of Benjamin Franklin*. Boston: Little, Brown, 1974.

Bradley, Patricia. *Slavery, Propaganda, and the American Revolution*. Jackson: University Press of Mississippi, 1998.

Brands, H. W. *The First American: The Life and Times of Benjamin Franklin*. New York: Doubleday, 2000.

Brett-James, Norman G. *The Life of Peter Collinson, F.R.S., F.S.A.* London: Edgar G. Dunstan, 1926.

Breitwieser, Mitchell Robert. *Cotton Mather and Benjamin Franklin: The Price of Representative Personality*. Cambridge: Cambridge University Press, 1984.

Brewer, John. *The Pleasures of the Imagination: English Culture in the Eighteenth Century*. Chicago: University of Chicago Press, 1997.

Brookes, Barbara. "The Feminism of Condorcet and Sophie de Grouchy," *Studies on Voltaire and the Eighteenth Century*, SVEC 189. Oxford: Voltaire Foundation, 1980, 297–361.

Brookes, George S. *Friend Anthony Benezet*. Philadelphia: University of Pennsylvania Press, 1937.

Buranelli, Vincent. *The Wizard from Vienna*. New York: Coward, McCann & Geoghegan, 1975.

Butler, Jon. *Becoming America: The Revolution before 1776*. Cambridge, MA: Harvard University Press, 2000.

Buxbaum, Melvin H. *Benjamin Franklin and the Zealous Presbyterians*. University Park, PA: Penn State University Press, 1975.

Cabanès, Augustin. *Marat inconnu: l'homme privé, le médecin, le savant*, 3rd ed. Paris: Albin Michel, 1920.

Cahen, Léon. *Condorcet et la Révolution française*. Paris: F. Alcan, 1904.

Campbell, James. *Recovering Benjamin Franklin: An Exploration of a Life of Science and Service*. Chicago: Open Court, 1999.

Carr, William G. *The Oldest Delegate: Franklin in the Constitutional Convention*. Newark: University of Delaware Press, 1990.

Cassara, Ernest. *The Enlightenment in America*. New York: Twayne, 1975.

Charlet, Christian. "Condorcet, inspecteur général des Monnaies de France

(1775–1790)," in ed. Anne-Marie Chouillet and Pierre Crépel, *Condorcet: homme des Lumières et de la Révolution.* Fontenay/Saint Cloud: ENS Editions, 1997, 59–70.

Christensen, Morton A. "Franklin on the Hemphill Trial: Deism Versus Presbyterian Orthodoxy," *William and Mary Quarterly*, 3rd Series, 10 (July 1953): 422–40.

Claeys, Gregory. "The Origins of the Rights of Labor: Republicanism, Commerce, and the Construction of Modern Society Theory in Britain, 1796–1805," *Journal of Modern History* 66 (June 1994): 249–90.

_____. *Thomas Paine: Social and Political Thought.* Boston: Unwin, Hyman 1989.

_____. "Thomas Paine's *Agrarian Justice* (1796) and the Secularization of Natural Jurisprudence," *Society for the Study of Labour History* 52 (Winter 1988): 21–31.

Clark, J. C. D. *English Society, 1660–1832: Religion, Ideology and Politics During the ancien regime.* Second edition. Cambridge: Cambridge University Press, 2000.

_____. *The Language of Liberty, 1660–1832: Political Discourse and Social Dynamics in the Anglo-American World.* Cambridge: Cambridge University Press, 1994.

Clark, Ronald W. *Benjamin Franklin: A Biography.* New York: Random House, 1983.

Coalter, Milton J. Jr. *Gilbert Tennent, Son of Thunder: A Case Study of Continental Pietism's Impact on the First Great Awakening in the Middle Colonies.* Westport, CT: Greenwood, 1986.

Cohen, I. Bernard. *Benjamin Franklin's Experiments: A New Edition of Franklin's Observations and Experiments on Electricity.* Cambridge, MA: Harvard University Press, 1941.

_____. *Franklin and Newton: An Inquiry into Speculative Newtonian Experimental Science and Franklin's Work in Electricity as an Example Thereof.* Philadelphia: American Philosophical Society, 1956; reprt. 1966.

_____. *Benjamin Franklin: His Contribution to the American Tradition.* Indianapolis: Bobbs-Merrill, 1953.

_____. *Benjamin Franklin's Science.* Cambridge, MA: Harvard University Press, 1990.

Cohen, Seymour S. "Two Refugee Chemists in the United States, 1794: How We See Them," *Proceedings of the American Philosophical Society* 126 (1982): 301–15.

Commager, Henry Steele. *The Empire of Reason: How Europe Imagined and America Realized the Enlightenment.* New York: Anchor, 1978.

Cone, Carl B. *The English Jacobins: Reformers in Late-Eighteenth-Century England.* New York: Scribners, 1968.

_____. *Torchbearer of Freedom: The Influence of Richard Price on Eighteenth-Century Thought.* Lexington: University Press of Kentucky, 1952.

Conner, Clifford D. *Jean Paul Marat: Scientist and Revolutionary.* Amherst, NY: Humanity Books, 1998.

Conway, Moncure D. *The Life of Thomas Paine*, 2 vols. New York: G. P. Putnam's Sons, 1892.

Coquard, Olivier. *Jean-Paul Marat.* Paris: Fayard, 1993.

Cormack, Patrick. *Wilberforce: The Nation's Conscience.* Basingstoke: Pickering, 1983.

Cotter, William R. "The Somerset Case and the Abolition of Slavery in England," *History* 79 (Feb. 1994): 31–56.

Cover, Robert M. *Justice Accused: Antislavery and the Judicial Process.* New Haven, CT: Yale University Press, 1975.

Cowherd, Raymond G. *The Politics of English Dissent: The Religious Aspects of Liberal and Humanitarian Reform Movements from 1815 to 1848.* New York: New York University Press, 1956.

Crabtree, Adam. *From Mesmer to Freud: Magnetic Sleep and the Roots of Psychological Healing.* New Haven, CT: Yale University Press, 1993.

Crane, Verner W. *Benjamin Franklin's Letters to the Press.* Chapel Hill: University of North Carolina Press, 1950.

_____. "The Club of Honest Whigs: Friends of Science and Liberty," *William and Mary Quarterly*, 3rd series, 23 (Apr. 1966): 210–33.

Dallimore, Arnold A. *George Whitefield: The Life and Times of the Great Evangelist of the Eighteenth-Century Revival*, 2 vols. London: Banner of Truth Trust, 1971, 1980.

Darnton, Robert. *George Washington's False Teeth: An Unconventional Guide to the Eighteenth Century.* New York: W. W. Norton, 2003.

_____. "J-P Brissot and the Société Typographique de Neuchâtel (1779–1787)," in ed. Anthony Strugnell, et al., *From letter to publication: Studies on correspondence and the history of the book.* SVEC 2001:10. Oxford: Voltaire Foundation, 2001, 7–47.

_____. *Mesmerism and the End of Enlightenment in France.* Cambridge, MA: Harvard University Press, 1968.

_____. "The Brissot Dossier," in "Forum: Interpreting Brissot," *French Historical Studies* 17 (Spring 1991): 191–205.

_____. *The Literary Underground of the Old Regime.* Cambridge, MA: Harvard University Press, 1982.

_____. "The Memoirs of Lenoir: Lieutenant de Police of Paris, 1774–1785," *English Historical Review* 336 (July 1970): 532–59.

Davidson, Edward H., and William J. Scheick. *Paine, Scripture, and Authority: "The Age of Reason" as Religious and Political Idea.* Bethlehem, PA: Lehigh University Press, 1994.

Davis, David Brion. *The Problem of Slavery in the Age of Revolution, 1770–1823.* Ithaca, NY: Yale University Press, 1975.

_____. *The Problem of Slavery in Western Culture.* Ithaca, NY: Yale University Press, 1966.

Davis, Michael T., ed. *Radicalism and Revolution in Britain, 1775–1848: Essays in Honour of Malcolm I. Thomis.* London: Macmillan, 2000.

D'Elia, Donald J. *Benjamin Rush: Philosopher of the American Revolution.* Philadelphia: American Philosophical Society, 1974.

DeLony, Eric. "Tom Paine's Bridge: The Man Who Wrote *Common Sense* Was Just as Much of Revolutionary in the Field of Engineering," *American Heritage of Invention and Technology* 15 (Spring 2000): 38–45.

DeLuna, Frederick A. "The Dean Street Style of Revolution: J.-P. Brissot," *Jeune Philosophe*," in "Forum: Interpreting Brissot," *French Historical Studies* 17 (Spring 1991): 159–90.

D'Huart, Suzanne. *Brissot: La Gironde au pouvoir.* Paris: Robert Laffont, 1986.

Dickinson, H. T. *British Radicalism and the French Revolution, 1789–1815.* Oxford: Blackwell, 1985.

Dippel, Horst. "Aux origines du radicalisme bourgeois: De la constitution de Pennsylvanie de 1776 à la constitution jacobine de 1793," *Francia* 16 (1989) 2:61–73.

_____. "Condorcet et la discussion des constitutions Américaines," in ed. Anne-Marie Chouillet and Pierre Crépel, *Condorcet, homme des Lumières et de la Révolution*. Fontenay/Saint Cloud: ENS Editions, 1997, 201–06.

Drescher, Seymour. *Econocide: British Slavery in the Age of Abolition*. Pittsburgh: University of Pittsburgh Press, 1977.

_____. *Capitalism and Antislavery: British Mobilization in Comparative Perspective*. New York: Macmillan, 1986.

_____. *From Slavery to Freedom: Comparative Studies in the Rise and Fall of Atlantic Slavery*. New York: Macmillan, 1999.

Dull, Jonathan R. *Franklin the Diplomat: The French Mission*. Philadelphia: American Philosophical Society, 1982.

Dunn, Susan. *Sister Revolutions: French Lightning, American Light*. New York: Faber & Faber, 1999.

Eakin. Emily. "So God's Really in the Details, *New York Times*, May 11, 2002, A17.

Ellery, Eloise. *Brissot de Warville: A Study in the History of the French Revolution*. Boston: Houghton Mifflin, 1915.

Ellis, Joseph. *American Sphinx: The Character of Thomas Jefferson*. New York: Alfred A. Knopf, 1998.

_____. *Founding Brothers: The Revolutionary Generation*. New York: Alfred A. Knopf, 2000.

Erikson, Robert S., Joseph Bafumi, and Bret Wilson. "Was the 2000 Presidential Election Predictable?" *PS: Political Science and Politics* 4 (Dec. 2001): 815–19.

Fara, Patricia. "An Attractive Therapy: Animal Magnetism in Eighteenth-Century England," *History of Science* 33 (June 1995): 127–77.

_____. *Entertainment for Angels: Electricity in the Enlightenment*. Cambridge, MA: Icon Books, 2002.

_____. *Sympathetic Attractions: Magnetic Practices, Beliefs, and Symbolism in Eighteenth-Century England*. Princeton, NJ: Princeton University Press, 1996.

Fauré, Christine. "La pensée de Condorcet et le suffrage féminin," in dir. Pierre Crépel and Christian Gilain, *Colloque international. Condorcet: Mathématicien, économiste, philosophe, homme politique*. Paris: Minerve, 1989, 349–54.

Favret, Mary A. *Romantic Correspondence: Women, Politics, and the Fiction of Letters*. Cambridge: Cambridge University Press, 1993.

Fayet, Joseph. *La Révolution française et la science, 1789–95*. Paris: M. Rivière, 1960.

Fenn, Elizabeth A. *Pox Americana: The Great American Smallpox Epidemic, 1775–82*. New York: Hill and Wang, 2001.

Fennessy, R. R. *Burke, Paine, and the Rights of Man: A Difference of Political Opinion*. The Hague: M. Nijhoff, 1963.

Ferguson, Robert A. "'We Hold These Truths': Strategies of Control in the Literature of the Founders," in ed. Sacvan Bercovitch, *Reconstructing American Literary History*. Cambridge, MA: Harvard University Press, 1986, 1–28.

Ferling, John. *A Leap in the Dark: The Struggle to Create the American Republic*. Oxford: Oxford University Press, 2003.

_____. *Setting the World Ablaze: Washington, Adams, Jefferson, and the American Revolution*. Oxford: Oxford University Press, 2000.

Fish, Stanley. *How Milton Works*. Cambridge, MA: Harvard University Press, 2001.

Fissell, Mary E. "Medicine before and after the Revolution," in ed. Jack P. Greene and J. R. Pole, *A Companion to the American Revolution*. Oxford: Blackwell, 2000, 600–04.

Fitzpatrick, Martin. "Toleration and the Enlightenment Movement," in ed. Ole Peter Grell and Roy Porter, *Toleration in Enlightenment Europe*. Cambridge: Cambridge University Press, 2000, 23–68.

Flexner, James Thomas. *Doctors on Horseback: Pioneers of American Medicine*. New York: Garden City, 1939.

_____. *Washington: The Indispensable Man*. Boston: Little, Brown, 1969.

Fohlen, Claude. *Benjamin Franklin: L'Américain des Lumières*. Paris: Biographie Payot, 2000.

Foner, Eric. *Tom Paine and Revolutionary America*. Oxford: Oxford University Press, 1976.

Foner, Philip S., ed. *The Democratic-Republican Societies, 1790–1800: A Documentary Source-Book*. Westport, CT: Greenwood Press, 1976.

Fortune, Brandon Brame, with Deborah J. Warner. *Franklin & His Friends*. Washington, D.C.: Smithsonian Institution, 1999.

François-Primo, Jean. *La jeunesse de J.-P. Brissot*. Paris: B. Grasset, 1932.

Frey, Sylvia R. "Slavery and Anti-Slavery," in ed. Jack P. Greene and J. R. Pole, *A Companion to the American Revolution*. London: Blackwell, 2000, 402–12.

Fricheau, Catherine. "Les femmes dans la cité de l'*Atlantide*," in dir. Pierre Crépel and Christian Gilain, *Colloque internationale. Condorcet: Mathématicien, économiste, philosophe, homme politique*. Paris: Minerve, 1989, 355–69.

Fruchtman, Jack Jr., ed. *An Eye-Witness Account of the French Revolution by Helen Maria Williams: Letters Containing a Sketch of the Politics of France*. New York: Peter Lang, 1997.

_____. "Death and Benjamin Franklin," in ed. Kevin L. Cope, *1650–1850: Ideas, Aesthetics, and Inquiries in the Early Modern Era*, vol. 7. New York: AMS Press, 2002, 209–22.

_____. "Public Loathing, Private Thoughts: Historical Representation in Helen Maria Williams's *Letters from France*," *Prose Studies* 18 (Dec. 1995): 223–43.

_____. "Review article–Classical Republicanism, Whig Political Science, Tory History: The State of Eighteenth-Century Political Thought," *Eighteenth-Century Life* 20 (May 1996): 94–103.

_____. "The Aesthetics of Terror: Burke's Sublime and Helen Maria Williams's Visions of Anti-Eden," in ed. Kevin L. Cope, *1650–1850: Ideas, Aesthetics, and Inquiries in the Early Modern Era*, vol. 6. New York: AMS Press, 2001a, 211–31.

_____. *The Apocalyptic Politics of Richard Price and Joseph Priestley: A Study in Late Eighteenth-Century English Republican Millennialism*. Philadelphia: American Philosophical Society, 1983.

_____. "The Politics of Sensibility: Helen Maria Williams's *Julia* and the Terror in France," in ed. Linda V. Troost, *Eighteenth-Century Women: Studies in Their Lives, Work, and Culture*, vol. 1. New York: AMS Press, 2001b, 185–202.

_____. *Thomas Paine and the Religion of Nature*. Baltimore: Johns Hopkins University Press, 1993.

_____. *Thomas Paine: Apostle of Freedom*. New York: Four Walls Eight Windows, 1994.

Furet, François. "Barnave," in ed. François Furet and Mona Ozouf, *A Critical Dictionary of the French Revolution*, trans. Arthur Goldhammer. Cambridge, MA: Harvard University Press, 1989, 186–95.

Gauld, Alan. *A History of Hypnotism*. Cambridge: Cambridge University Press, 1992.

Gerzina, Gretchen. *Black England: Life before Emancipation*. London: J. Murray, 1995.

Gibbs, F. W. *Joseph Priestley: Adventurer in Science and Champion of Truth*. London: Thomas Nelson and Sons, 1968.

Goldstein, Jan. *Console and Classify: The French Psychiatric Profession in the Nineteenth Century*. Cambridge: Cambridge University Press, 1987.

Golinski, Jan. *Science as Public Culture: Chemistry and Enlightenment in Britain, 1760–1820*. Cambridge: Cambridge University Press, 1992.

Goodell, Edward. *The Noble Philosopher: Condorcet and the Enlightenment*. Buffalo, NY: Prometheus Books, 1990.

Goodman, Dena. *The Republic of Letters: A Cultural History of the French Enlightenment*. Ithaca, NY: Cornell University Press, 1994.

Goodman, Nathan G. *Benjamin Rush: Physician and Citizen, 1746–1813*. Philadelphia: University of Pennsylvania Press, 1934.

Goodwin, Albert. *The Friends of Liberty: The English Democratic Movement in the Age of the American Revolution*. Cambridge, MA: Harvard University Press, 1979.

Gopnik, Adam. "American Electric: Did Franklin Really Fly That Kite?" *New Yorker*, June 30, 2003, 96–100.

Gordon-Reed, Annette. *Thomas Jefferson and Sally Hemings: an American Controversy*. Charlottesville: University Press of Virginia, 1997.

Gottschalk, Louis. *Jean-Paul Marat: A Study in Radicalism*. London: Allen & Unwin, 1927, reprt. 1967.

Granger, Bruce Ingham. *Benjamin Franklin: An American Man of Letters*. Ithaca, NY: Cornell University Press, 1964.

Green, Daniel. *Great Cobbett: The Noblest Agitator*. London: Hodder and Stoughton, 1983.

Griggs, Earl Leslie. *Thomas Clarkson: The Friend of Slaves*. Westport, CT: Negro University Press, 1970; orig. publ. 1936.

Guedj, Dennis. *La Méridienne, 1793–1799*. Paris: Seghers, 1987.

Guerlac, Henri. *Les Citations françaises*. Paris: A. Colin, 1931.

Hahn, Roger. *The Anatomy of a Scientific Institution: The Paris Academy of Sciences, 1666–1803*. Berkeley: University of California Press, 1971.

Haraszti, Zoltán. *John Adams and the Prophets of Progress*. Cambridge, MA: Harvard University Press, 1952.

_____. "John Adams on Condorcet: His Comments on 'The Outline of the Progress of the Human Mind' Now First Published," *More Books: The Bulletin of the Boston Public Library* 5 (Dec. 1930): 473–79.

Hawke, David Freeman. *Benjamin Rush: Revolutionary Gadfly*. Indianapolis: Bobbs-Merrill, 1971.

Heilbron, J. L. *Electricity in the Seventeenth and Eighteenth Centuries: A Study of Early Modern Physics*. Berkeley: University of California Press, 1979.

Heimert, Alan. *Religion and the American Mind: From the Great Awakening to the Revolution*. Cambridge, MA: Harvard University Press, 1966.

Hellenbrand, Harold. *The Unfinished Revolution: Education and Politics in the Thought of Thomas Jefferson*. Newark: University of Delaware Press, 1990.

Henry, Stuart C. *George Whitefield: Wayfaring Witness*. New York: Abingdon Press, 1957.

Heward, Edmund. *Lord Mansfield*. Chichester, UK: Barry Rose, 1979.

Hibbert, Christopher. *King Mob: The Story of Lord George Gordon and the London Riots of 1780.* London: Longmans Green, 1958.

Higonnet, Patrice. *Goodness beyond Virtue: Jacobins during the French Revolution.* Cambridge, MA: Harvard University Press, 1998.

Honeywell, Roy J. *The Educational Work of Thomas Jefferson.* New York: Russell and Russell, 1964; orig. publ. 1931.

Honour, Hugh. *The Image of the Black in Western Art*, vol. 4 with various parts, *From the American Revolution to World War I.* Houston: Menil Foundation, 1989.

Horvitz, Leslie Alan. *Eureka! Scientific Breakthroughs that Changed the World.* New York: Wiley, 2001.

Huang, Nian-Sheng. *Life of a Colonial Boston Tallow Chandler, 1657–1745.* Philadelphia: American Philosophical Society, 2000.

Hudson, Nicholas. "'Britons Never Will Be Slaves': National Myth, Conservatism, and the Beginnings of British Antislavery," *Eighteenth-Century Studies* 34 (Summer 2001): 559–76.

Huggins, Dorette. "John Adams et ses réflexions sur Condorcet," in ed. Anne-Marie Chouillet and Pierre Crépel, *Condorcet: homme des Lumières et de la Révolution.* Fontenay/Saint Cloud: ENS Editions, 1997, 207–21.

Hughes, John C., and Andrew E. Rothovius. *The World's Greatest Hypnotists.* Lanham, MD: University Press of America, 1996.

Hulliung, Mark. *Citizens and Citoyens: Republicans and Liberals in America and France.* Cambridge, MA: Harvard University Press, 2002.

Hunter, Michael. *The Royal Society and Its Fellows, 1660–1700: The Morphology of an Early Scientific Institution.* Bucks, UK: British Society for the History of Science, 1982.

Hutson, James H. *Pennsylvania Politics, 1746–1770: The Movement for Royal Government and Its Consequences.* Princeton, NJ: Princeton University Press, 1972.

Ihde, Aaron J. "Priestley and Lavoisier," in ed. Lester Kieft and Bennett R. Willeford Jr., *Joseph Priestley: Scientist, Theologian, and Metaphysician.* Lewisburg, PA: Bucknell University Press, 1980, 62–91.

Isaacson, Walter. *Benjamin Franklin: An American Life.* New York: Simon & Schuster, 2003.

James, C. L. R. *Black Jacobins: Toussaint L'Ouverture and the San Domingo Revolution*, 2nd rev. ed. New York: Vintage, 1989; orig. publ. 1938.

Jehlen, Myra. "Benjamin Franklin: or, Machiavelli in Philadelphia," in ed. Gianfranca Balestra and Luigi Sampietro, *Benjamin Franklin: An American Genius.* Rome: Bulzoni, 1993, 61–74.

Jennings, Francis. *Benjamin Franklin, Politician.* New York: W. W. Norton, 1996.

Johnson, Herbert A. "Thomas Jefferson and Legal Education in Revolutionary America," in ed. James Gilreath, *Thomas Jefferson and the Education of a Citizen.* Washington, D.C.: Library of Congress, 1999, 103–14.

Jordan, Cynthia S. *Second Stories: The Politics of Language, Form, and Gender in Early American Fictions.* Chapel Hill: University of North Carolina Press, 1989.

Jordan, Winthrop D. "Familial Politics: Thomas Paine and the Killing of the King." *Journal of American History* 60 (Sept. 1973):294–308.

Jurt, Joseph. *"Condorcet: l'idée de progrès et l'opposition à l'esclavage,"* in dir. Pierre Crépel and Christian Gilain, *Condorcet: mathématicien, économiste, philosophe, homme politique*, Actes du colloque. Paris: Minerve, 1989, 385–95.

Kammen, Michael G. *A Rope of Sand: The Colonial Agents, British Politics, and the American Revolution*. Ithaca, NY: Cornell University Press, 1968.

_____, ed. *The Origins of the American Constitution: A Documentary History*. Harmondsworth: Penguin, 1986.

Kates, Gary. *The "Cercle Social," the Girondins, and the French Revolution*. Princeton, NJ: Princeton University Press, 1985.

Kaye, Harvey J. *Thomas Paine: Firebrand of Revolution*. New York: Oxford University Press, 2000.

Keane, John. *Tom Paine: A Political Life*. Boston: Little, Brown, 1995.

Kelley, Mary. "Petitioning with the Left Hand: Educating Women in Benjamin Franklin's America," in ed. Larry Tise, *Benjamin Franklin and Women*. University Park, PA: Penn State University Press, 2000, 83–101.

Kemp, E. L. "Thomas Paine and his 'Pontifical Matters,'" *Transactions of the Newcomen Society for the Study of the History of Engineering and Technology*, vol. 49 (London, 1977–1978): 21–35.

Kennedy, Deborah. *Helen Maria Williams and the Age of Revolution*. Lewisburg, PA: Bucknell University Press, 2002.

Kervran, Roger. *Laënnec: His Life and Times*, trans. D. C. Abraham-Curiel. Oxford: Pergamon, 1960.

Ketchum, Richard M. "The Spirit of '54," *American Heritage* 53 (Aug.–Sept. 2002): 57–62.

Kloos, John M. Jr. *A Sense of Deity: The Republican Spirituality of Dr. Benjamin Rush*. Brooklyn, NY: Carlson Publications, 1991.

Korshin, Paul J. "Benjamin Franklin and Samuel Johnson: A Literary Relationship," in ed. Gianfranca Balestra and Luigi Sampietro, *Benjamin Franklin: An American Genius*. Rome: Bulzoni, 1993, 33–48.

Kramnick, Isaac. *Republicanism and Bourgeois Radicalism: Political Ideology in Late Eighteenth-Century England and America*. Ithaca, NY: Cornell University Press, 1990.

_____. "Republican Revisionism Revisited," *American Historical Review* 87 (June 1982): 629–64.

Kroll, Richard, Richard Ashcraft, and Perez Zagorin, ed., *Philosophy, Science, and Religion in England, 1640–1700*. Cambridge: Cambridge University Press, 1992.

Kulisheck, P. J. "Mansfield, Earl of (William Murray)," in ed. Gerald Newman, *Britain in the Hanoverian Age, 1714–1837: An Encyclopedia*. New York: Garland, 1997, 437.

Labaree, Leonard W. "Benjamin Franklin's British Friendships," *Proceedings of the American Philosophical Society* 108 (Oct. 20, 1964): 423–27.

Laboucheix, Henri. *Richard Price: théoricien de la Révolution américaine, le philosophe et le sociologue, le pamphlétaire et l'orateur*. Paris: Didier, 1970, and in English translation as *Richard Price as Moral Philosopher and Political Theorist*, SVEC 207, trans. Sylvia and David Raphael. Oxford: Voltaire Foundation, 1982.

Lagrave, Jean-Paul de. "L'influence de Sophie de Grouchy sur la pensée de Condorcet," in dir. Pierre Crépel and Christian Gilain, *Condorcet: mathématicien, économiste, philosophe, homme politique*, Actes du colloque. Paris: Minerve, 1989, 434–42.

_____. *La Vision cosmique de Benjamin Franklin*. Sillery: Septentrion, 2003.

Lambert, Frank. *Inventing the "Great Awakening"*. Princeton, NJ: Princeton University Press, 1999.

_____. *"Pedlar in Divinity": George Whitefield and the Transatlantic Revivals, 1737–1770*. Princeton, NJ: Princeton University Press, 1994.

Larivière, Michel. *Pour tout l'amour des hommes: anthologie de l'homosexualité dans la littérature*. Paris: Delétraz, 1998.

Lascelles, E. C. P. *Granville Sharp and the Freedom of the Slaves in England*. London: Oxford University Press, 1928.

Leaf, Munro. *The Story of Ferdinand*. New York: Viking Press, 1936.

Le Fanu, W. R. *A Bio-Bibliography of Edward Jenner, 1749–1823*. London: Harvey & Blythe, 1951.

Lemay, J. A. Leo. *The Canon of Benjamin Franklin, 1722–1776: New Attributions and Reconsiderations*. Newark: University Press of Delaware, 1986.

_____. "Franklin's 'Dr. Spence': The Reverend Archibald Spencer (1698?–1760), M.D.," *Maryland Historical Magazine* 59 (1964): 199–216.

_____. "The Public Writings and the Bagatelles," in ed. Brian M. Barbour, *Benjamin Franklin: A Collection of Critical Essays*. Englewood Cliffs, NJ: Prentice-Hall, 1979, 153–60.

Lerat, Christian. *Benjamin Franklin: quand l'Amérique s'émancipait*. Bordeaux: Presses universitaires de Bordeaux, 1992.

_____. "Essay at Revisiting Benjamin Franklin as a Philogynist," in ed. Gianfranca Balestra and Luigi Sampietro, *Benjamin Franklin: An American Genius*. Rome: Bulzoni, 1993, 99–119.

Lerner, Ralph. *Revolutions Revisited: Two Faces of the Politics of Enlightenment*. Chapel Hill: University of North Carolina, 1994.

Lessay, Jean. *L'Américain de la convention, professeur de révolutions, député de Pas-de-Calais*. Paris: Perrin, 1987.

Lewis, Jan. "Jefferson, The Family, and Civic Education," ed. James Gilreath, *Thomas Jefferson and Education of a Citizen*. Washington: Library of Congress, 1999, 63–75.

_____. *The Pursuit of Happiness: Family and Values in Jefferson's Virginia*. Cambridge: Cambridge University Press, 1983.

Lincoln, Anthony. *Some Political and Social Ideas of English Dissent, 1763–1800*. New York: Octagon, 1971; orig. printed 1938.

Link, Eugene P. *Democratic-Republican Societies, 1790–1800*. New York: Columbia University Press, 1942.

Livesey, James *Making Democracy in the French Revolution*. Cambridge, MA: Harvard University Press, 2001.

Loft, Leonore. "J.-P. Brissot and the Problem of Jewish Emancipation," *Studies on Voltaire and the Eighteenth Century* SVEC 278. Oxford: Voltaire Foundation, 1990, 465–75.

_____. "J.-P. Brissot and the Evolution of Pamphlet Literature in the Early 1780s," *History of European Ideas* 17 (Mar.–May 1993): 265–85.

_____. "*La Théorie des loix criminelles*: Brissot and Legal Reform," *Australian Journal of French Studies* 26 (Sept.–Oct. 1989): 242–59.

_____. "*Le Journal du Licée de Londres*: A Study in the Pre-Revolutionary French Press," *European History Quarterly* 23 (Jan. 1993): 7–37.

_____. "Mirabeau and Brissot Review Christian Wilhelm Von Dohm and the Jewish Question," *History of European Ideas*, "Contemporary Historians on the French Revolution," 13 (Special Issue, 1991): 605–22.

_____. *Passion, Politics and Philosophie: Rediscovering J.-P. Brissot*. Westport, CT: Greenwood Press, 2002.

_____. "Toward a More Just Criminal Code in Pre-Revolutionary France: J.-P. Brissot (1754–1793)," *Journal of Criminal Justice* 20 (1992): 121–33.

_____. "The Roots of Brissot's Ideology," *Eighteenth-Century Life* 13 (May 1989): 21–34.

_____. "The Transylvanian Peasant Uprising of 1784, Brissot and the Right to Revolt: A Research Note," in "Forum: Interpreting Brissot," *French Historical Studies* 17 (Spring 1991): 209–18.

_____. "'Un de ces esprit aieriens decendu sur la terre': Félicité Dupont and the Paradox of Sensibility," in ed. Roland Bonnel and Catherine Rubinger, *Femmes savantes et femmes d'esprit: Women Intellectuals of the French Eighteenth Century*. New York: Peter Lang, 1994, 297–320.

Lopez, Claude Anne. *My Life With Franklin*. New Haven, CT: Yale University Press, 2000.

_____. *Mon Cher Papa: Franklin and the Ladies of Paris*. New Haven, CT: Yale University Press, 1966.

_____, and Eugenia W. Herbert. *The Private Franklin: The Man and His Family*. New York: W. W. Norton, 1975.

Maier, Pauline. *American Scripture: Making the Declaration of Independence*. New York: Alfred A. Knopf, 1997.

Malone, Dumas. *Jefferson and His Time: The Sage of Monticello*, 6 vols. Boston: Little, Brown, 1948–1981.

Manuel, Frank. *The Prophets of Paris*. Cambridge, MA: Harvard University Press, 1962.

Maspero-Clerc, Hélène. "Une Gazette anglo-française pendant la guerre d'Amérique," *Annales historiques de la Révolution française*. Reims, 1976, 572–94.

Matthews, Richard K. *If Men Were Angels: James Madison and the Heartless Empire of Reason*. Lawrence: University Press of Kansas, 1995.

_____. *The Radical Politics of Thomas Jefferson: A Revisionist View*. Lawrence: University Press of Kansas, 1984.

May, Henry F. *The Enlightenment in America*. New York: Oxford University Press, 1976.

McCullough, David. *John Adams*. New York: Simon & Schuster, 2001.

McGrath, Patrick. "Writers on Writing: Heroism in Trying Times," *New York Times*, Mar. 25, 2002.

McLean, Iain, and Fiona Hewitt, ed. *Condorcet: Foundations of Social Choice and Political Theory*. Aldershot: Elgar, 1994.

MacQuitty, Betty. *Victory over Pain: Morton's Discovery of Anaesthesia*. New York: Raplinger, 1971.

Melchior-Bonnet, Bernardine. *Charlotte Corday*. Paris: Perrin, 1989.

Menand, Louis. *The Metaphysical Club*. New York: Farrar, Straus and Giroux, 2001.

Mestel, Rosie. "Booster Shots: Modern Bloodletting and Leeches," *Los Angeles Times*, Aug. 6, 2001, S2.

Middlekauff, Robert. *Benjamin Franklin and His Enemies*. Berkeley: University of California Press, 1996.

Miley, Mary R. "The Glass Armonica," *Early American Homes* (Christmas 1998).

Miller, Stephen. *Three Deaths and Enlightenment Thought: Hume, Johnson, Marat*. Lewisburg, PA: Bucknell University Press, 2001,

Morgan, David T. "A Most Unlikely Friendship—Benjamin Franklin and George Whitefield," *This Historian: A Journal of History* 47 (Feb. 1985): 208–18.

_____. *The Devious Dr. Franklin, Colonial Agent: Franklin's Years in London*. Macon, GA: Mercer University Press, 1996.

Morgan, Edmund S. *Benjamin Franklin*. New Haven, CT: Yale University Press, 2002.

Morris, Marilyn. *The British Monarchy and the French Revolution*. New Haven, CT: Yale University Press, 1998.

Nadelhaft, Jerome. "The Somersett Case: Myth, Reality, and Repercussions," *Journal of Negro History* 51 (July 1966): 193–208.

Nattrass, Leonora. *William Cobbett: Politics of Style*. Cambridge: Cambridge University Press, 1995.

Neilson, Winthrop, and Frances Neilson. *Verdict for the Doctor: The Case of Benjamin Rush*. New York: Hastings House, 1958.

Newcomb, Benjamin H. *Franklin and Galloway: A Political Partnership*. New Haven, CT: Yale University Press, 1972.

Newman, Stephen. "A Note on *Common Sense* and Christian Eschatology," *Political Theory* 6 (Feb. 1978): 101–08.

Niklaus, Robert. "Condorcet's Feminism: A Reappraisal," in ed. David Williams, *Condorcet Studies II*. New York: Peter Lang, 1987, 119–40.

_____. "Idéalisme philosophique dans les *Cinq Mémoires sur l'instruction publique*," in dir. Pierre Crépel and Christian Gilain, *Condorcet: mathématicien, economiste, philosophe, homme politique*, Actes du colloque. Paris: Minerve, 1989, 262–68.

Oberg, Barbara B., and Harry S. Stout, ed. *Benjamin Franklin, Jonathan Edwards, and the Representation of American Culture*. New York: Oxford University Press, 1993.

Ogborn, Maurice Edward. *Equitable Assurances: The Story of Life Assurance in the Experience of the Equitable Life Assurance Society, 1762–1962*. London: Allen and Unwin, 1962.

Oldfield, J. R. *Popular Politics and British Anti-Slavery: The Mobilisation of Public Opinion Against the Slave Trade, 1787–1807*. Manchester: Manchester University Press, 1995.

Oldham, James. "New Light on Mansfield and Slavery," *Journal of British Studies* 27 (Jan. 1988): 45–68.

_____. *The Mansfield Manuscripts and the Growth of English Law in the Eighteenth Century*, 2 vols. Chapel Hill: University of North Carolina Press, 1992.

Osborne, John. *John Cartwright*. Cambridge: Cambridge University Press, 1972.

Ott, Thomas O. *The Haitian Revolution, 1789–1804*. Knoxville: University of Tennessee Press, 1973.

The Oxford English Dictionary, 12 vols. Oxford: Oxford University Press, 1933.

Park, Mary Catherine. "Joseph Priestley and the Problem of Pantisocracy," *Proceedings of the Delaware County Institute of Science* 10 (1947): 1–60.

Patrick, Alison. *The Men of the First French Republic*. Baltimore: Johns Hopkins University Press, 1972.

Pattie, Frank A. *Mesmerism and Animal Magnetism: A Chapter in the History of Medicine*. Hamilton, NY: Edmonston, 1994.

Philp, Mark T. *Paine*. Oxford: Oxford University Press, 1989.

_____. ed. *The French Revolution and British Popular Politics*. Cambridge: Cambridge University Press, 1991.

Pilcher, George William. *Samuel Davies: Apostle of Dissent in Colonial Virginia*. Knoxville: University of Tennessee Press, 1971.

Pocock, J. G. A. *Barbarism and Religion: The Enlightenments of Edward Gibbon, 1737–1764*, vol. 1. Cambridge: Cambridge University Press, 1999.

_____. *Barbarism and Religion: Narratives of Civil Government*, vol. 2. Cambridge: Cambridge University Press, 1999.

_____. *The Machiavellian Moment: Florentine Political Thought and the Atlantic Republican Tradition*. Princeton, NJ: Princeton University Press, 1975.

_____. *"The Machiavellian Moment* Revisited: A Study in History and Ideology," *Journal of Modern History* 53 (Mar. 1981): 49–72.

_____, ed. *The Varieties of British Political Thought, 1500–1800*, with the Assistance of Gordon J. Schochet and Lois G. Schwoerer. Cambridge: Cambridge University Press, 1993.

_____. *Virtue, Commerce, and History: Essays on Political Thought and History, Chiefly in the Eighteenth Century*. Cambridge: Cambridge University Press, 1985.

Pollak, Michael. "Glass, Wet Fingers and a Mysterious Disappearance," *New York Times*, Dec. 12, 2001, E2.

Popkin, Jeremy. *Revolutionary News: The Press in France, 1789–1799*. Durham, NC: Duke University Press, 1990.

Porter, Roy. *The Creation of the Modern World: The Untold Story of the British Enlightenment*. New York: W. W. Norton, 2000.

Postman, Neil. *Building a Bridge to the 18th Century: How the Past Can Improve Our Future*. New York: Vintage, 1999.

Powell, David. *Tom Paine: The Greatest Exile*. New York: St. Martin's Press, 1985.

Rakove, Jack N. *Original Meanings: Politics and ideas in the Making of the Constitution*. New York: Vintage, 1996.

Raynes, Harold E. *A History of British Insurance*. New York: Garland, 1983; orig. publ. London, 1950.

Reid-Maroney, Nina. *Philadelphia's Enlightenment, 1740–1800: Kingdom of Christ, Empire of Reason*. Westport, CT: Greenwood Press, 2001.

Resnick, Daniel. "The Société des Amis des Noirs and the Abolition of Slavery," *French Historical Studies* 7 (Fall 1972): 558–69.

Rey, Roselyne. "Sur L'*Essai d'une langue universelle* de Condorcet," in ed. Anne-Marie Chouillet and Pierre Crépel, *Condorcet: homme des Lumières et de la Révolution*. Fontenay/Saint-Cloud: ENS Editions, 1997, 137–46.

Robb, Graham. *Strangers: Homosexual Love in the Nineteenth Century*. New York: W. W. Norton, 2003.

Robbins, Caroline. *The Eighteenth-Century Commonwealthman: Studies in the Transmission, Development and Circumstance of English Liberal Thought from the Restoration of Charles II until the War with the Thirteen Colonies*. Cambridge, MA: Harvard University Press, 1959.

Robinet, Dr. (Jean François Eugène). *Condorcet, sa vie, son oeuvre*. Paris: Librairies-imprimeries réunies, 1893; reprt. Geneva, 1968.

Robinson, E. "New Light on the Priestley Riots," *Historical Journal* 3 (1960): 173–75.

Robiquet, Paul. *Théveneau de Morande*. Paris: A. Quantin, 1882.

Roosevelt, Theodore. *The Life of Gouverneur Morris*. New York: Houghton Mifflin, 1888.

Root-Bernstein, Robert, and Michèle Root-Bernstein. *Honey, Mud, Maggots, and Other Medical Marvels: The Science Behind Folk Remedies and Old Wives' Tales*. Boston: Houghton Mifflin, 1997.

Rose, R. B. "The Priestley Riots of 1791," *Past and Present* 18 (Nov. 1960): 68–88.

Rosenfeld, Richard N. "The Adams Tyranny: Lost Lessons from the Early American Republic," *Harpers* (Fall 2002): 82–86.

Royot, Daniel. "Humor and Sex: The French Connection in Franklin's Lovelife," in ed. Gianfranca Balestra and Luigi Sampietro, *Benjamin Franklin: An American Genius* Rome: Bulzoni, 1993, 89–98.

_____. "Long Live *La Différence*: Humor and Sex in Franklin's Writings, in ed. Carla Mumford and David S. Shields, *Finding Colonial Americas: Essays in Honor of J. A. Leo Lemay*. Newark: University of Delaware Press, 2001, 307–15.

Rudé, George. *The Crowd in History: A Study of Popular Disturbances in France and England, 1730–1848*. New York: Wiley, 1964.

Rudolph, Frederick. *Essays on Education in the Early Republic*. Cambridge, MA: Harvard University Press, 1965.

Rupp, Gordon. *Religion in England, 1688–1791*. Oxford: Oxford University Press, 1986.

Safire, William. *Scandalmonger: A Novel*. New York: Simon & Schuster, 2000.

Sapiro, Virginia. *A Vindication of Political Virtue: The Political Theory of Mary Wollstonecraftl*. Madison: University of Wisconsin Press, 1992.

Schama, Simon. *Citizens: A Chronicle of the French Revolution*. New York: Alfred A. Knopf, 1989.

Schandeler, Jean-Pierre. *Les interpretations de Condorcet: symboles et concepts (1794–1894)*. SVEC: 2000–2003. Oxford: Voltaire Foundation, 2000.

Schofield, Robert E. *The Enlightenment of Joseph Priestley: A Study of His Life and Work from 1733 to 1773*. University Park, PA: Penn State University Press, 1997.

_____. *The Lunar Society Birmingham: A Social History of Provincial Science and Industry in Eighteenth-Century England*. Oxford: Oxford University Press, 1963.

Scheuermann, Mona. *In Praise of Poverty: Hannah More Counters Thomas Paine and the Radical Threat*. Lexington: University Press of Kentucky, 2002.

Seavey, Ormond. *Becoming Benjamin Franklin: The Autobiography and the Life*. University Park, PA: Penn State University Press, 1988.

Selsam, J. Paul. "Brissot de Warville on the Pennsylvania Constitution of 1776," *Pennsylvania Magazine of History and Biography* 72 (Jan. 1948): 25–43.

Sheldon, Garrett Ward. *The Political Philosophy of Thomas Jefferson*. Baltimore: Johns Hopkins University Press, 1991.

Shuffelton, Frank. "Binding Ties: The Public and Domestic Spheres in Jefferson's Letters to His Family," in ed. James Gilreath, *Thomas Jefferson and the Education of a Citizen*. Washington, D.C.: Library of Congress, 1999, 28–47.

Shyllon, Folarin. *Black People in Britain, 1555–1833*. London: Oxford University Press, 1977.

Skemp, Sheila L. *Benjamin Franklin and William Franklin: Father and Son, Patriot and Loyalist*. Boston: St. Martin's Press 1994.

_____. *William Franklin: Son of a Patriot, Servant of a King*. New York: Oxford University Press, 1990.

Smith, Jeffrey A. *Franklin and Bache: Envisioning the Enlightened Republic*. New York: Oxford University Press, 1990.

Soderlund, Jean. *Quakers and Slavery: A Divided Spirit*. Princeton, NJ: Princeton University Press, 1985.

Spater, George. *William Cobbett: The Poor Man's Friend*, 2 vols. Cambridge: Cambridge University Press, 1982.

Srodes, James. *Franklin: The Essential Founding Father*. New York: Regnery, 2002.

Stout, Harry S. *The Divine Dramatist: George Whitefield and the Rise of Modern Evangelism*. Grand Rapids, MI: W. B. Eerdmans, 1991.

Straub, Jean S. "Benjamin Rush's Views on Women's Education," *Pennsylvania History* 34 (1967): 147–57.

Swem, E. G. *Brothers of the Spade: Correspondence of Peter Collinson, London, and of John Custis, of Williamsburg, Virginia, 1734–1746*. Barre, MA: Barre Gazette, 1957; reprinted from the Proceedings of the American Antiquarian Society.

Swinburne, Richard. *The Existence of God*. Oxford: Clarendon Press, 1979.

Symposia on Slavery and the Slave Trade in the *William and Mary Quarterly* 56 (Apr. 1999) 2 and 58 (Jan. 2001).

Thomas, D. O. *The Honest Mind: The Thought and Work of Richard Price*. Oxford: Oxford University Press, 1977.

Thomas, Roland. *Richard Price: Philosopher and Apostle of Liberty*. Oxford: Oxford University Press, 1924.

Thompson, Henry Paget. *Into All Lands: The History of the Society for the Propagation of the Gospel in Foreign Parts, 1701–1950*. London: S. P. C. K., 1951.

_____. *Thomas Bray*. London: S. P. C. K., 1954.

Tise, Larry E. "Liberty and the Rights of Women: Sarah Franklin's Declaration of Independence," in ed. Larry Tise, *Benjamin Franklin and Women*. University Park, PA: Penn State University Press, 2000, 37–49.

Tomalin, Claire. *The Life and Death of Mary Wollstonecraft*. London: Weidenfeld and Nicolson, 1974.

Tourtellot, Arthur Bernon. *Benjamin Franklin: The Shaping of Genius—The Boston Years*. Garden City, NY: Doubleday, 1977.

Townsend, Sara Bertha. *An American Soldier: The Life of John Laurens*. Raleigh, NC: Edwards & Broughton, 1958.

Troyansky, David G. "Condorcet et l'idée d'assurance viellesse: risque, dette sociale et générations," in dir. Pierre Crépel and Christian Gilain, *Colloque international, Condorcet: mathématicien, économiste, philosophe, homme politique*. Paris: Minerve, 1989, 174–80.

Tucker, Tom. *Bolt of Fate: Benjamin Franklin and His Electric Kite Hoax*. New York: Public Affairs, 2003.

Uglow, Jenny. *The Lunar Men: Five Friends Whose Curiosity Changed the World*. New York: Farrar, Straus and Giroux, 2002.

Vail, Gilbert. *The Life of Thomas Paine*. New York: Privately printed, 1841.

Van Doren, Carl. *Benjamin Franklin*. New York: Viking, 1938.

Vincent, Bernard. *Thomas Paine, ou la religion de la liberté*. Paris: Aubier, 1987.

Wagoner, Jennings L. Jr. "'That Knowledge Most Useful to Us': Thomas Jefferson's Concept of Utility in the Education of Republican Citizens," in ed. James Gilreath, *Thomas Jefferson and the Education of a Citizen*. Washington, D.C.: Library of Congress, 1999, 115–33.

Waldstreicher, David. *Runaway America: Benjamin Franklin, Slavery, and Revolutionary America*. (New York: Hill and Wang, 2004).

Walters, Kerry S. *Benjamin Franklin and His Gods*. Urbana: University of Illinois Press, 1999.

Warner, Michael. "Savage Franklin," in ed. Gianfranca Balestra and Luigi Sampietro, *Benjamin Franklin: An American Genius*. Rome: Bulzoni, 1993, 75–87.

_____. *The Letters of the Republic: Publication and the Public Sphere in Eighteenth-Century America*. Cambridge, MA: Harvard University Press, 1990.

Watts, Michael R. *The Dissenters from the Reformation to the French Revolution*. Oxford: Oxford University Press, 1978.

Weiner, Mark S. "New Biographical Evidence on *Somerset's Case*," *Slavery and Abolition* 23 (Apr. 2002): 121–36.

West, Shearer. "Wilkes's Squint: Synecdochic Physiognomy and Political Identity in Eighteenth-Century Print Culture," *Eighteenth-Century Studies* 33 (Fall 1999): 65–84.

Whaley, Leigh. *Radicals: Politics and Republicanism in the French Revolution*. Phoenix Mill, UK: Sutton, 2000.

Wharam, Alan. *The Treason Trials, 1794*. Leicester: Leicester University Press, 1992.

White, Michael. *Rivals: Conflict as the Fuel of Science*. London: Vintage, 2001.

Whitney, Janet. *John Woolman, American Quaker*. Boston: Little, Brown, 1942.

Wiecek, William. *The Sources of Antislavery Constitutionalism in America, 1760–1848*. Ithaca, NY: Cornell University Press, 1977.

Wilkins, Roger. *Jefferson's Pillow: The Founding Fathers and the Dilemma of Black Patriotism*. Boston: Beacon Press, 2001.

Williams, David. "Condorcet, Feminism, and the Egalitarian Principle," in ed. Ronald C. Rosbottom, *Studies in Eighteenth-Century Culture*. Madison: University of Wisconsin Press, 1976: 5:151–63.

Wills, Garry. *Cincinnatus: George Washington and the Enlightenment*. Garden City, NY: Doubleday, 1984.

_____. *Mr. Jefferson's University*. Washington, D.C.: National Geographic Society, 2002.

Wilson, David A. *Paine and Cobbett: The Transatlantic Connection*. Kingston: McGill-Queen's University Press, 1988.

Wilson, Ellen Gibson. *Thomas Clarkson: A Biography*. London: Macmillan, 1989.

Winock, Michel. *L'Echec au roi, 1791–92*. Paris: O. Orban, 1991.

Wise, Steven M. *Though Heavens May Fall: The Landmark Trial That Led to the End of Human Slavery*. Cambridge, MA: Da Capo Press, 2005.

Wood, Gordon S. *The Americanization of Benjamin Franklin*. New York: Penguin Press, 2004.

_____. *The Creation of the American Republic, 1776–1787*. Chapel Hill: University of North Carolina Press, 1969.

_____. *The Radicalism of the American Revolution: How a Revolution Transformed a Monarchical Society into a Democratic One Unlike Any That Had Ever Existed*. New York: Alfred A. Knopf, 1992.

Wright, Esmond. "Benjamin Franklin: The Old Englishman," in ed. Gianfranca Balestra and Luigi Sampietro, *Benjamin Franklin: An American Genius.* Rome: Bulzoni, 1993, 9–19.

_____. *Franklin of Philadelphia.* Cambridge, MA: Harvard University Press, 1986.

Wyckoff, James. *Franz Anton Mesmer: Between God and Devil.* Englewood Cliffs, NJ: Prentice Hall, 1975.

Zall, Paul M., ed. *Ben Franklin Laughing: Anecdotes from Original Sources By and About Benjamin Franklin.* Berkeley: University of California Press, 1980.

_____. *Franklin on Franklin.* Lawrence: University Press of Kansas, 2000.

Index

Sharp, William, 42, 44
Shelburne, Lord, 149, 160,
    177–79, 182–83, 188, 278
Shippen, William, Jr., 62–65, 83
Short, William, 279
Siciliènne, La, 223
Sieyès, Abbé, 251
single-branch legislature,
    238–43, 259
*Sketch for a Historical Picture of
    the Progress of the Human
    Mind,* 262–66
slave trade
    ending, 14, 18–20, 54–55,
        69, 84–86, 244–50, 331
    views on, 18–20, 23, 53–54,
        243–50, 283–86, 291
slavery
    Benezet's views on, 23, 33,
        36–40
    Brissot's views on, 249,
        256–57, 276–81,
        283–86, 290–91
    Condorcet's views on,
        243–50, 256–57
    ending, 14, 18–20, 54–55,
        69, 84–86, 244–50, 331
    Franklin's views on, 23,
        30–31, 38–40,
        53–54, 326
    Rush's views on, 67–70
    Sharp's views on, 4, 23,
        39–41, 47
    Whitefield's views on, 4,
        23–24, 29–30, 33
    see also abolitionists
*Slavery not Forbidden by Scrip-
    ture,* 70
social arts, 251, 267
Social Contract, The, 260
social programs, 7, 129–31, 136
social sciences, 233, 267
social security program, 189
societal change, 3–4, 269–70
Société des Amies des Lois, 322
Société des Amis des Noirs, 19,
    246–48, 278, 283–84
Société Républicaine, La, 254

Society for Equitable Assurances,
    187–89
Society for Promoting Christian
    Knowledge, 31–32
Society for Promoting Constitu-
    tional Information,
    154–55, 160
Society for the Propagation of
    the Gospel in Foreign Parts,
    31–32
Society of 1789, 250–52
Society of Friends, 19
Society of the Friends of the Blacks,
    19, 246–48, 278, 283–84
Society of Twelve, 105
Society of Universal Harmony,
    224, 227, 231
Socinianism, 146
Solander, Daniel, 171
"Somerset Case and the Slave
    Trade, The," 53
Somerset, James, 39, 49–53
Spain, 258, 299
Stamp Act, 63, 73, 160
Stewart, Charles, 49, 51–52
Strahan, William, 17
Strong, Jonathan, 44–45
Suard, Jean-Baptiste, 237
suffrage, 261, 323
Sunday, Billy, 24
Sussex Weekly Advertiser, 106
Sydney, Algernon, 264–65

T
*Take Your Choice! Representation
    and Respect; Imposition and
    Contempt. Annual Parliaments
    and Liberty. Long Parliaments
    and Slavery,* 159
Talbot, Charles, 45, 49, 52
Talleyrand, Charles-Maurice,
    251, 317
Taxation No Tyranny, 43
technological discoveries, 3, 14,
    18, 325–26, 331. *See also* sci-
    entific inventions
Tennent, Gilbert, 73
Terror. *See* Reign of Terror

Acknowledgments

This book began with a telephone call in the winter of 1996. Larry Tice, who was then the director of the Benjamin Franklin National Memorial at the Franklin Institute, called to invite me to participate in a symposium on Benjamin Franklin in Philadelphia. He suggested the topic of Franklin's visionary friends, because the other participants were concentrating on several of the great man's personal and professional associations throughout his long and distinguished life in science and industry, politics and diplomacy, and journalism and publishing. Surely the most inspirational moment at the symposium was to hear a lecture by one of the finest contemporary Franklin scholars, Claude-Anne Lopez, editor emerita of the Franklin Papers at Yale.

Several themes in this book have been presented at many conferences, chief among them the annual meetings of the East Central/American Society for Eighteenth-Century Studies, and I appreciate the questions raised and the criticisms directed at my work. I also presented some of the arguments in this book at a conference organized by J. G. A. Pocock at the University of California, Los Angeles, Center for Eighteenth-Century Studies at the William Andrews Clark Library in March 2002.

I would also like to thank former Provost Dan L. Jones of Towson University for the sabbatical leave he granted me in 2001–2002 to work on this book. In addition, I would like to thank Gabrielle Spiegel, former chair of the Department of History at the Johns Hopkins University, for appointing me to a visiting fellowship in the department for three years. The seminars at Johns Hopkins are among the most delightful and stimulating on any university campus.

I also want to thank the readers of all or parts of the manuscript. Michael T. Davis at the University of Queensland, H. George Hahn at Towson University, Nally Preseaux, and Emma Casale devoted considerable time to comment on an earlier and, undoubtedly to their dismay, much larger version of the manuscript. Their comments were most helpful in guiding me to its final shape. I especially thank George Hahn for his close reading and for suggesting the title. Vincent Carretta of the University of Maryland, historian of science Louis Rosenblatt, and Stephens Broening, visiting fellow in history at Johns Hopkins, gave thoughtful critiques of parts of the work. Any errors that remain are my own.

JoAnn Fruchtman commented on two versions of this book, saving me from making serious errors, and Liana Fruchtman-Colas provided me with an important critique of an early draft. Over the years, Shira and Hannah Fruchtman have offered sympathetic support as I regaled them with stories of Franklin's visionary friends.

Johnny Saunders has proved to be a superb editor and critic of my work, and I deeply appreciate the time and effort he devoted to the manuscript. Finally, John Oakes and Jofie Ferrari-Adler at Thunder's Mouth Press have long stood by this project, and I thank them for publishing it.